for Neil

Kananaskis Country Ski Trails

GILLEAN DAFFERN

Rocky Mountain Books

Front cover: *Mt. Sir Douglas from the ridge between South Burstall and Burstall passes. Photo, Alf Skrastins.*
Title page: *Canmore Nordic Centre. The Big Dipper on the Green Rsecreational 15.*

The Publisher wishes to acknowledge the assistance of Alberta Culture and Multiculturalism and The Alberta Foundation for the Arts in the publication of this book.

Published by Rocky Mountain Books
#4 Spruce Centre,
Calgary, Alberta T3C 3B3
Printed and bound in Canada by
Jasper Printing Group Ltd., Edmonton

Canadian Cataloguing in Publication Data
Daffern, Gillean, 1938-
Kananaskis Country ski trails

ISBN 0-921102-20-8

1. Cross-country skiing--Alberta--Kananaskis Country--Guide-books. 2. Kananaskis Country (Alta.) --Description and travel--Guide-books. 3. Trails--Alberta--Kananaskis Country--Guide-books. I. Title.
GV854.8.C3D33 1992 917.123'32 C92-091931-9

Introduction

Trails

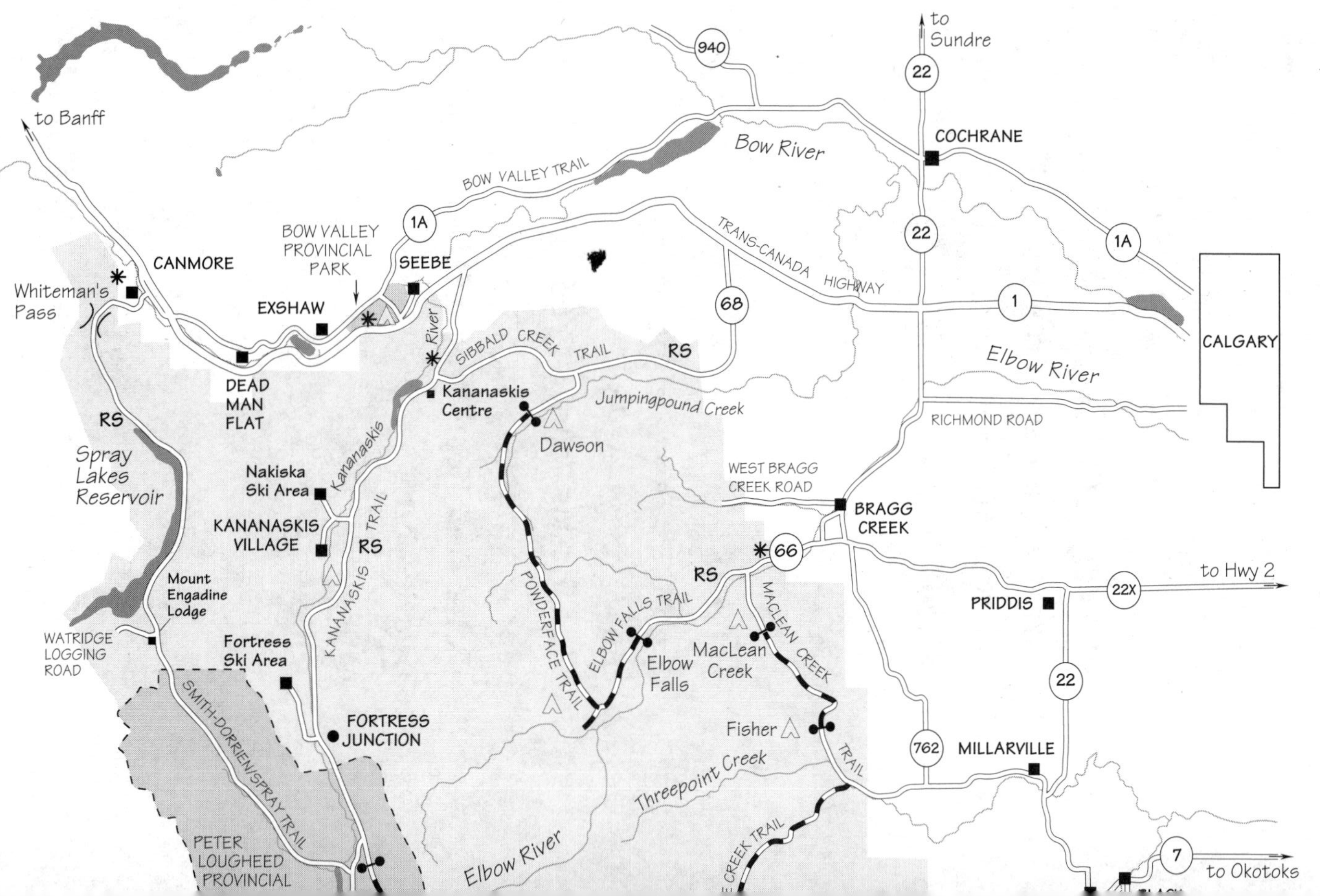
to Banff
to Sundre
940
22
COCHRANE
Bow River
BOW VALLEY TRAIL
1A
BOW VALLEY PROVINCIAL PARK
CANMORE
SEEBE
Whiteman's Pass
EXSHAW
TRANS-CANADA HIGHWAY
22
1A
68
1
CALGARY
River
SIBBALD CREEK TRAIL
RS
Elbow River
DEAD MAN FLAT
Kananaskis Centre
Jumpingpound Creek
RICHMOND ROAD
RS
Dawson
Spray Lakes Reservoir
Kananaskis
Nakiska Ski Area
WEST BRAGG CREEK ROAD
BRAGG CREEK
KANANASKIS VILLAGE
TRAIL
RS
66
to Hwy 2
KANANASKIS
Mount Engadine Lodge
RS
22X
POWDERFACE TRAIL
ELBOW FALLS TRAIL
MACLEAN CREEK
PRIDDIS
WATRIDGE LOGGING ROAD
Fortress Ski Area
Elbow Falls
MacLean Creek
22
SMITH-DORRIEN/SPRAY TRAIL
FORTRESS JUNCTION
Fisher
762
MILLARVILLE
TRAIL
Threepoint Creek
PETER LOUGHEED PROVINCIAL
CREEK TRAIL
Elbow River
7
to Okotoks

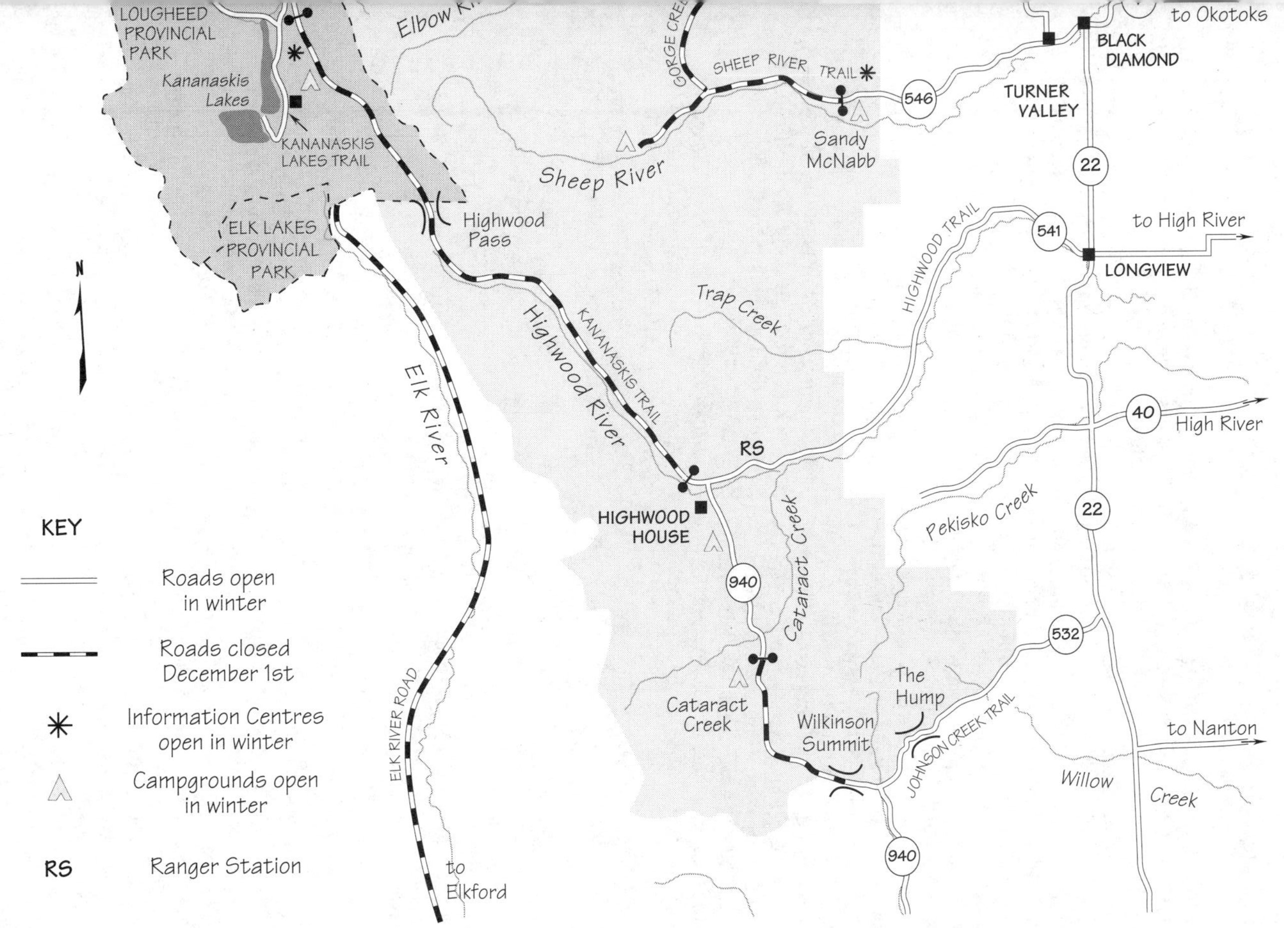
LOUGHEED PROVINCIAL PARK
Kananaskis Lakes
KANANASKIS LAKES TRAIL
ELK LAKES PROVINCIAL PARK
Highwood Pass
Sheep River
SHEEP RIVER TRAIL
Sandy McNabb
546
TURNER VALLEY
BLACK DIAMOND
to Okotoks
22
541
to High River
LONGVIEW
HIGHWOOD TRAIL
Trap Creek
40
High River
Highwood River
KANANASKIS TRAIL
RS
HIGHWOOD HOUSE
Elk River
940
Cataract Creek
Pekisko Creek
532
The Hump
Wilkinson Summit
JOHNSON CREEK TRAIL
to Nanton
Willow Creek
ELK RIVER ROAD
to Elkford
N
KEY
Roads open in winter
Roads closed December 1st
Information Centres open in winter
Campgrounds open in winter
RS Ranger Station

KANANASKIS COUNTRY

WHERE IS IT EXACTLY?

The 4,000 hectares of K-Country, as everybody calls it, is located on the eastern slopes of the Canadian Rockies west and south of the Winter Olympics city of Calgary, Alberta. The west boundary adjoins Banff National Park, Mount Assiniboine Provincial Park, Height of the Rockies Wilderness, Elk Lakes Provincial Park and B.C.'s Elk River, while the eastern boundary coincides neatly with the eastern boundary of the Bow/Crow Forest which is only about 20 minutes driving time away from the outskirts of Calgary. Highway 1A (Bow Valley Trail) and a string of communities — Canmore, Dead Man Flat, Exshaw and Seebe — mark the northern boundary, while Highway 532 (Johnson Creek Trail) delineates the southern end, beyond which is the fascinating country of the Oldman River.

GETTING THERE

Calgary is served by major airlines, several bus companies and by train from the east. Greyhound buses running between Calgary and Vancouver along the Trans-Canada Highway, will deposit you in Canmore at 10 am and pick you up at 5.30 pm (1992 schedule), but that's it as far as public transportation goes. You need a car. Unfortunately, the concept of ski trains to Banff and Canmore offering breakfast and apres ski hasn't caught on yet.

The main thing for motorists to know is that winter road closures ensure that 40% of K-Country is out of easy reach of skiers after November 30th. Although there may be times when I grumble, the fact that it's also out of reach of hunters makes me happy knowing that wildlife can get on with the already tough job of winter survival without being shot at. And of course the province saves money by not plowing the roads.

The largest bits in reach are all very accessible from Calgary, Banff and Canmore via the Trans-Canada Highway (Kananaskis Trail, Spray/Smith-Dorrien Trail). Smaller pieces in the Elbow, Sheep and Highwood regions can be reached from Bragg Creek, Turner Valley and Longview. Peruse the map.

The following roads are closed:

- Highway 40 (Kananaskis Trail) between Kananaskis Lakes Trail and Highwood House, December 1-June 15
- SR 66 (Elbow Falls Trail) west of Elbow Falls, December 1-May 15
- SR 546 (Sheep River Trail) west of Sandy McNabb Recreation Area, December 1-May 15
- Gorge Creek Trail, December 1-May 15
- McLean Creek Trail between McLean Creek campground and Fisher Creek snowmobiling staging area, December 1st-April 30th
- Forestry Trunk Road 940 between Cataract Creek campground and Wilkinson Summit, December 1-April 30
- Powderface Trail south of Dawson Day Use Area, December 1-May 15

WHAT IS K-COUNTRY LIKE?

The scenery in the west is much like that in Alberta's national parks: calendar mountains harbouring the odd glacier, icefield and lake and rising as high as 3449 m (that's 11,316 feet for those of you who haven't gone metric). Valley floors are generally flat and filled with old spruce. But rarely pristine. In K-Country left-over logging and exploration roads often wind their way through valleys, providing easy access to that gorgeous country above treeline where the weather can turn against you at the drop of a ski pole. Suddenly you're into the serious business of route-finding in a whiteout and battling against wind and blizzard. You'd better know how to assess avalanche hazard.

Conversely, the eastern boundary of K-Country, known as the foothills, is a downright friendly place of flat open valleys and rounded hills covered in fire-succession pine and aspen below the age of 80 years, dissected by exploration roads, seismic lines and logging roads.

Terrain-wise, the foothills are perfect for skiing. While avalanches appear to be non-starters (no need to worry much about them), cutlines can cause an enormous amount of confusion.

The in-between country of the Front Ranges has characteristics of both plus a propensity for deep canyons and rocky ridges. While it is my favourite area for summer hiking, I have to admit that in winter it has its drawbacks like the enormous one of being a snow shadow area. Anyway, most of it is out of reach because of road closures.

NO BEARS

If you're afraid of bears, winter is the season for you. Unfortunately, beavers and all the other interesting little critters like ground squirrels also retreat to underground dens. But there's still a long list of animals to watch for like feral horses in the foothills, moose, elk, deer (Mule and White Tail), sheep, coyotes, wolves, wolverines, martens, snowshoe hares, mice and voles. It appears to be the best season to spot cats like lynx and I once met someone who'd shared the Evan-Thomas Creek trail with three bobcats. (I was ten minutes behind him and saw nothing.) As for birds, your most likely bets are white-feathered ptarmigans, great horned owls, dippers, and above all whiskey jacks who compile lists of all the popular lunching spots and pass it around to their friends.

Two insects are particularly interesting: the spider-like snow cranefly and the snow flea which both have a horrible knack of settling in ski tracks and getting squished. I wish they wouldn't do that! Be very careful should you be kind-hearted enough to move a cranefly from the track — it has anti-freeze for body liquids which is why it can function at temperatures around -20°. It's called "living on the edge of death" so any sudden jolt like being dropped or whacked by a bit of snow falling from your glove can start off a chain reaction resulting in instant crystallization.

The snow flea, on the other hand, only emerges during Chinooks, looks like an inky blue pinhead and congregates in the thousands. Read Ribbon Creek Ski Trails for more information on the fascinating order of Collembola.

If you're going on a leisurely outing into the foothills it's a good idea to fling a book on animal tracks into the pack. Whereas in summer a valley seems empty of animals, in winter you know it's not. Tracks tell stories, often bloodthirsty ones of cats running after snowshoe hares with blood and scraps of fur strewn all along the trail. Other signs of winter survival are peeled aspen bark, snapped willow branches and big depression beds in the snow.

WHAT TO EXPECT OF THE WEATHER

In K-Country, temperatures are variable and unpredictable, much more so than in the National Parks, and can run the gamut from +15° to -40°. In November through to late January expect cold snowy spells with winds out of the north or east and temperatures plummeting to -25° to -40° or lower. After mid February you can enjoy an increasing number of days with clear skies and sunshine that actually feels warm.

And then there are the Chinook winds! The foothills are particularly prone to Chinooks which come roaring out of the west, raising temperatures by as much as 20° in a few hours; the nemesis of West Bragg Creek and Sandy McNabb ski trails. What was excellent on Friday, can be mush on Sunday. Thing is to hit the trails on the Saturday when conditions are still good and the temperatures a balmy +10° with sunshine. At times of Chinooks, the trails to the west of Highway 40 are likely to be socked in with a heavy snowfall. The very worst scenario is when the Chinook ends suddenly and the temperature plummets. There you are, with the aid of all-purpose klister, enjoying a day out under the Chinook arch, only to have the temperature drop 20° in the afternoon and a snowstorm blow in from the east. Suddenly, your skis are wearing 6 inch heels. You forgot your wax remover, you say?

SEASON AND CONDITIONS

Generally, the season kicks off in the west (Smith-Dorrien ski trails, Burstall Pass, Chester Lake) around the beginning of November and carries on until May, while in the east, late December through to the end of February is more realistic. Having said that, I have skied West Bragg in both October and late March and encountered powder on both occasions. Sometimes, a season opener blizzard blowing out of north and east will dump 30 cm of snow in the foothills and nothing in the mountains. In some locations the season is dependent not so much on precipitation but on temperature like at the Canmore Nordic Centre where the ability to make snow, using water from Rundle Reservoir, can advance the opening date and delay the closing date by several weeks. Usually the end of the season is not determined by lack of snow, certainly not in the west anyway, but by a hot sun bottoming out the snowpack and making skiing miserable.

From November through to February you have this wonderful powder thanks to cold temperatures and ineffectual sunlight. You wish you could ski all day; indeed, you may have to if it's too cold to stop and refuel. This is when Power Bars and Cold Buster Bars come in handy. Meanwhile, in the foothills you have to get used to a pattern of snow denudation and renewal. The Chinooks, remember?

By mid February, warmer temperatures and a hot sun bring changes. That powder slope you schussed in January is crud come March. South-facing slopes alternately glaze and freeze over. In treed valleys with dappled shade and sun, progress on alternating ice crust and soft mush is tricky. More skis are broken at this time of year than any other. After a snowfall things improve, but it's only temporary now. On groomed trails get out the klister or skate. At least stopping for lunch is a pleasure.

AVALANCHE DANGER

In the season of 1990/91, K-Country had more periods of high hazard than anywhere else in the Canadian Rockies. Unless staying on a safe trail, bring an avalanche transceiver, snow shovel, companions with transceivers and shovels and a strong dog which knows intuitively which way is up and out. Of course, having a transceiver doesn't give you license to head for the nearest avalanche slope at Highwood Pass, and it certainly doesn't guarantee that you'll be pulled out alive. Unless you know how to assess danger, don't go anywhere even remotely risky. But the sun is shining, the slope is beckoning and someone has broken trail ahead of you. What could possibly happen on such a gorgeous day? Read "Avalanche Safety for Skiers & Climbers" to find out.

Forecasts are readily available at all visitor centres and by phoning 1-800-772-2434.

REGISTRATION

Backcountry registration is voluntary, but it's a good idea if you're going far back into the backcountry. Registration boxes are available at all visitor information centres and at some trailheads.

ABOUT DOGS

Dogs are banned from the Canmore Nordic Centre and the Peter Lougheed Provincial Park trail system. Elsewhere, dogs must be kept on leads. The rationale behind leads is to stop mutts chasing after wildlife which is already stressed out by winter survival. Also, dog lovers, coyotes are very fond of dog meat — particularly Chihuahuas. When skiing up a hill, the dog should be on the same side of the trail as you. Skiers cartwheeling over a stretched lead are not amused and such incidents could lead to fisticuffs or banning of dogs altogether. Finally, K-Country requests owners to pop a poop pan and plastic bag into your pack for clean-up.

WHAT'S OPEN IN WINTER

Canmore and the Bow Valley
At the east end of the valley, you're either camping at Willow Rock campground in Bow Valley Provincial Park or, much more comfortable, treating yourself to a night at Rafter Six Guest Ranch on Highway 1 (restaurant and bar), or Kananaskis Guest Ranch at Seebe (bed & breakfast, restaurant). And then there's Nakoda Lodge on Highway 1A in the Stony Indian Reservation which offers accommodation, restaurant, and a superb Sunday brunch which makes me drool just thinking about it. The hamlets of Seebe and Exshaw have gas and limited groceries. Dead Man Flat at the "gap" has motels, bed & breakfasts, time-sharing chalets at Alpine Resort Haven, an RV site at Green Acres Motel, gas cum grocery stores, and one or two eating places. Monday to Friday, information is dispensed from Bow Valley Provincial Park Visitor Centre between the hours of 8 am and 4.30 pm.

Canmore is making the transition from mining town to tourist town in fine style. If winter camping is your thing, Restwell Trailer Park is your only choice, but who wants to camp when there's such a fine selection of motels and hotels to choose from, ranging price-wise from the Alpine Club of Canada's clubhouse above Indian Flat to the Hyatt Regency Hotel above the hoodoos which should be ready for banquets in 1995. Likewise, eating places run the gamut from burger joints to British-style pubs to high-class restaurants which require a change of clothes. Gas, groceries, film labs, confectioneries, gift shops, and book shops selling maps. Canmore has most everything you need including a ski shop – Altitude Sports. If you want to rent touring equipment try Spoke 'N Edge or Chain Reaction Sports at the Drake Inn. If looking for high performance skis, children's skis and pulks, you'll have to pop up to Trail Sports at the Canmore Nordic Centre. Finally, the Information Centre is located in the strip between the Trans-Canada Highway and Highway 1A.

Kananaskis Valley
Barrier Lake Visitor Information Centre (movies, fireplace) is open Wednesday to Sunday 9 am-4 pm. Kananaskis Village is of course fully operational, offering everything from overnight accommodation, restaurants, bars and gift shops in three hotels to information desk, grocery store, nordic ski rental shop (Peregrine Sports) and jacuzzi at the Village Centre. Ribbon Creek Youth Hostel offers more rustic lodgings at the bottom of the hill. Nearby Nakiska ski area has a cafeteria, lounge, baby-sitting, ski shop, and rental shop with a selection of touring skis, poles and boots. Overnight camping (some plug-ins) is available at Mount Kidd RV Park (snack bar, groceries, whirlpools). The new kid on the block — Sundance Lodges (unserviced sites, winterized teepees) — is considering opening on a limited basis with reduced winter rates and special monthly rates for RV's.

Farther south, Fortress Mountain Ski area has a cafeteria (includes set evening meal between 6 and 7 pm) and a licensed lounge open until the late hours which dishes up a variety of meals between 6 and 8 pm. Overnight accommodation is available by phoning months ahead to the Calgary office at 264-5825. Or you can park your RV in the parking lot (some electrical plug-ins available). At the junction of the ski area access road and Highway 40 is Fortress Junction which sells gas, guide books, groceries and hot snacks including my favourite hot apple cider.

Spray/Smith-Dorrien
While a tete a tete is unlikely with a ranger at Spray Lakes Ranger Station at Three Sisters Dam, you can check on current trail condition by perusing the notice board outside the information kiosk (telephone available). Mount Engadine Lodge at the junction of Watridge logging road offers overnight accommodation and meals. If camping is your thing, Spray Lakes day use area halfway down Spray Lakes Reservoir is the only place to park.

Peter Lougheed Provincial Park
The Visitor Centre is open 7 days a week 9 am to 5 pm all year round (excepting April) for information, entertainment (movies, displays) and for lounging in front of a fire. Pocaterra Ski Hut (tables, notice board, public telephone outside) opens the first week of December and is thereafter open 7 days a week, 9 am to 5 pm until the snow melts. Boulton Creek Trading Post (restaurant only) operates Boxing Day until January 1st, then weekends only until approximately late March. Boulton Campground loop 'B' is kept plowed for overnight camping. If you're a group, Lower Lake group campground is accessible by car, bus or ski. William Watson Lodge has RV sites and chalet accommodation 7 days a week all year round for handicapped persons, senior citizens and their families.

Highwood
Tough luck! Highwood House (gas, groceries, Laurie's home-made snacks) closes down in October while the information centre has no regular winter hours. If camping, drive to Etherington Creek campground overflow area (snowmobile staging area) or Cataract Creek campground snowmobile staging area with winterized shelter on the west side of Highway 940. The nearest town is Longview — motel, historic hotel, gas, groceries, and an amazing number of eating places for its size. Where's Longview? Well, it's located south of Black Diamond on Highway 22 and is famous from a TV commercial and for its beef jerky as taken on expeditions to the Himalaya and which apparently tastes fabulous even at 20,000 feet. When Longview Meats is closed try Chinook Gas and Grocery on the corner of Highway 22 and the Coal Trail.

Jumpingpound
The only facility open is Dawson day use area on Powderface Trail which is open to all for winter camping.

Sheep
Sheep River Visitor Information Centre opens on a casual basis on weekends whenever the skiing is good at Sandy McNabb. Winter camping is available at Sandy McNabb equestrian campground. Bluerock equestrian campground at the west end of Highway 546 stays open until the highway closes on December 1st. If you're really stuck, Fisher Creek snowmobile staging area on McLean Creek Trail is another possibility. The nearby oil and gas towns of Turner Valley and Black Diamond provide everything you need in the way of motels, bed & breakfasts, restaurants and bars, gas and groceries. There's even a movie theatre in Turner Valley which makes a change from watching TV in the motel room. Closer to McLean Creek Trail, Mesa Creek Guest Ranch off Highway 762 does Bed & Breakfast and has its own network of visitor ski trails.

Elbow
Elbow Valley Visitor Information Centre opens on weekends between the hours of 9 am to 4 pm. On weekdays head for the Elbow Ranger Station between the hours of 8.15 am and 4.30 pm. Little Elbow equestrian campground at the west end of Highway 66 is open until the highway closes on December 1st. After this date the nearest campground is McLean Creek campground (2 loops) on McLean Creek Trail where you can expect a rousing early awakening by snowmobiles. Just outside K-Country boundary is the town of Bragg Creek which offers limited motel accommodation, bed & breakfasts, gas, groceries, gift and antique shops and an eclectic assortment of restaurants and tea houses. Believe it or not, the Ice Cream shop is just as popular at minus 20.

Further afield, Homeplace Guest Ranch is located just off Highway 22 towards Priddis and has its own trail network. How many people know that Camp Gardner (operated by the Boy Scouts Association) is open to the public for winter camping.

ABOUT THE BOOK

TRAILS FOR EVERYONE

What is going on? It used to be that racers trained on groomed trails and tourers broke trail in the backcountry. Now, a whole generation of skiers are learning to ski on groomed trails and be quite content to go nowhere else. Racers are venturing into the backcountry on skinny skis and tourers are donning lycra to partake in loppets.

Groomed trails are packed, trackset, and signed at junctions. Some centres have warming huts, cafeteria, ski shop and other such luxuries.

Backcountry trails are skier-set. A fair number have parking lots, washrooms at air temperature and a picnic table or two at the trailhead. Occasionally you will be parking at the side of the highway. Trails following official hiking or equestrian trails have signposts at trailheads and junctions and possibly red markers on trees. Unofficial summer trails have no such aids and often require you to sort out your trail from a mishmash of logging roads and cutlines. All I can say is it must be heavenly to write a guidebook to the National Parks!

Routes require route-finding ability and avalanche hazard know-how. You're on your own here.

HOW CAN YOU GRADE SKI TRAILS?

Given reasonable snow conditions, grading is dependent on *technical* difficulty, like trail width, tightness of bends, steepness of hills, general awkwardness. Don't be surprised to find a few discrepancies between this book and area brochures.

Easy — flat, suitable for beginners

Easy intermediate — rolling

Intermediate — moderately steep hills, narrower trails

Hard Intermediate — steep hills, narrow twisting trails

Difficult — very steep hills, the reserve of competent skiers

BUT, after a metre of fresh snow, even the most difficult hill will be easy. Conversely, in spring crust and mush, even the easiest hill will upgrade to intermediate, and intermediate hills to difficult.

Grading doesn't take into account the length of a trip, remoteness from a trailhead, route-finding problems or avalanche hazard. Look for this information in the trail overview.

One last thing: don't compare the difficulty rating of groomed trails with backcountry trails which are potentially much more serious.

TIMES

I hope you're not expecting me to tell you how long it's going to take you to ski a trail. Time depends on too many variables like snow conditions, weather, type of gear, your technique, fitness and endurance, weight of your pack, how many people are breaking trail, what you had to eat for breakfast, how you feel after a night out in the Canmore bars and so on. Even an easy one-hour trip under reasonable conditions can take all day if you have to break trail through 30 cm of bottomless sugar and have a hangover.

MAPS

It was not an easy task to produce clear maps. Topo maps of the area are not metric, neither are they up to date in showing road realignments and new roads like the Watridge Logging Road for instance. Trails if shown at all are usually inaccurate. I'm sorry to say the resource maps on which I pinned great hopes have their fair share of inaccuracies and omissions as well. So please bear in mind that I am neither a surveyor nor a cartographer and haven't got all the time in the world to go tramping round logging roads making accurate maps. I'll be more than happy to hear from you if you find any discrepancies.

I'm sure you critics out there are saying, "why isn't north at the top of the page?" In case you haven't noticed, maps have been turned sideways and upside down both for the convenience of the skier and to fit them onto the page *at the largest scale possible.* Regardless of the scale which varies with each map (some maps have a lot going on in a small area), contour lines are at 100 m intervals throughout. A "T" by the side of a trail means a hill, the horizontal stroke indicating the direction of higher ground.

Below is a key to the types of lines:

———	trail as it follows established ski trails, hiking or equestrian trails or old roads
- - - - -	routes
- - - - -	trails or roads not in use
··········	powerline
— — —	cutline
··×···×···×	fence

DISCLAIMER

Although written in a light-hearted manner, it is not the intention of this book to make light of what is a potentially hazardous sport. Make no mistake, cross-country skiing in the backcountry can be dangerous for the unprepared. Cold, wind, blizzards, avalanches, terrain traps (rocks, deadfall), unsafe river and lake crossings, plus the possibility of debilitating injuries, equipment failure, and becoming lost or exhausted are just some of the hazards you may have to deal with. While I have done my best to provide accurate information and to point out potential problem areas, it's up to you to learn the necessary skills for mountain travel, not to venture on a trail beyond your ability, and to make intelligent decisions not only during the trip but *before* the trip as well. I don't care if you've set your heart on the Robertson Glacier. If it's snowing to beat hell and the cloud's down, why not have a terrific day in Peter's Park on the groomed trails instead? Finally, carry topo maps at all times; the maps in the book are not a substitute.

USEFUL PHONE NUMBERS

Public Avalanche Information Bulletin
1-800-667-1105

Snow Conditions and Information
Kananaskis Country

Calgary Office	297-3362
Canmore Office	678-5508
Canmore Nordic Centre	678-2400

Visitor Information Centres

Barrier Lake (Kan. Valley, Ribbon Ck.)	673-3985
Kananaskis Village Centre (Ribbon Ck.)	265-5120
Peter Lougheed Prov. Park (Kananaskis Lakes, Smith-Dorrien, Mount Shark)	591-6344
Highwood House	558-2151
Sheep Valley (Sandy McNabb)	933-7172
Elbow Ranger Station (West Bragg Ck. & Sandy McNabb)	949-3754
Elbow Valley (West Bragg Ck.)	949-4261

Other numbers

BC Parks, Wasa	(604) 422-3212
Camp Gardner	242-9267
Fortress Junction	591-7371
Fortress Mountain	591-7108
Homeplace Guest Ranch	931-3245
Kananaskis Guest Ranch	265-7094
Kananaskis Village Hotels	800-332-1013
Mount Engadine Lodge	678-2880
Mount Kidd RV Park	591-7700
(Ski) Nakiska	591-7777
snow phone	232-8477
Nakoda Lodge	264-4831
Rafter Six Guest Ranch	673-3622
Sundance Lodges	591-7122
Trail Sports	678-6764
William Watson Lodge	591-7227

In an Emergency call

Kananaskis Country Emergency Services or nearest RCMP	591-7767

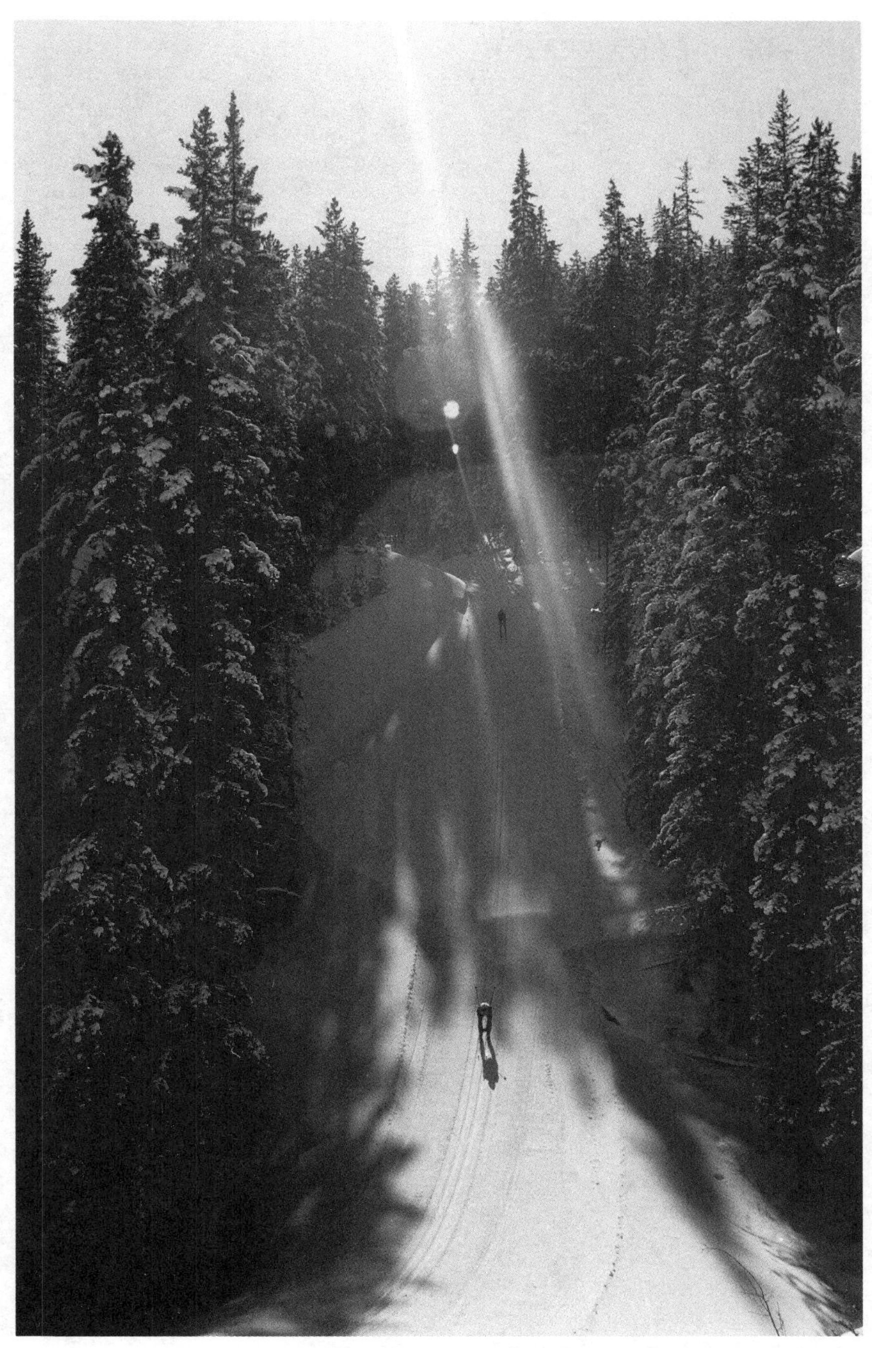

Into the Big Dipper. The Green Recreational 15 at the Canmore Nordic Centre

CANMORE NORDIC CENTRE **Groomed**

58 km of trails
Maximum elevation 1550 m
Map 82 O/3 Canmore

Access by Car The Nordic Centre is located on the western outskirts of Canmore. Follow the Smith-Dorrien/Spray Trail, also called the Spray Lakes Road, for approximately 1.8 km from the centre of Canmore (signs). At Rundle Reservoir turn right.

Access by trail from Canmore Not a ski trail exactly. Get to Rundle Power Plant on a channel of the Bow River by either walking along the west bank of the Bow River from the bridge, or by crossing the two old railway bridges from Fairholme Drive. Climb steps up the open bank. At the first terrace there is a choice of routes.

1. You can either carry on climbing steeply up the open bank above the underground pipeline to Smith-Dorrien/Spray Trail below Rundle Reservoir, picking up an access from Three Sisters Drive en route.
2. Or (if you want to get skiing sooner), turn right onto a trail running along the terrace above cliffs of glacial till. Turn first or second left and climb to the biathlon trails first met with near bridge #6 on the Rec 5. Or, go further along the terrace and take the next left turn onto the Georgetown interpretive trail which joins the trail system at #27 on the Rec 5.

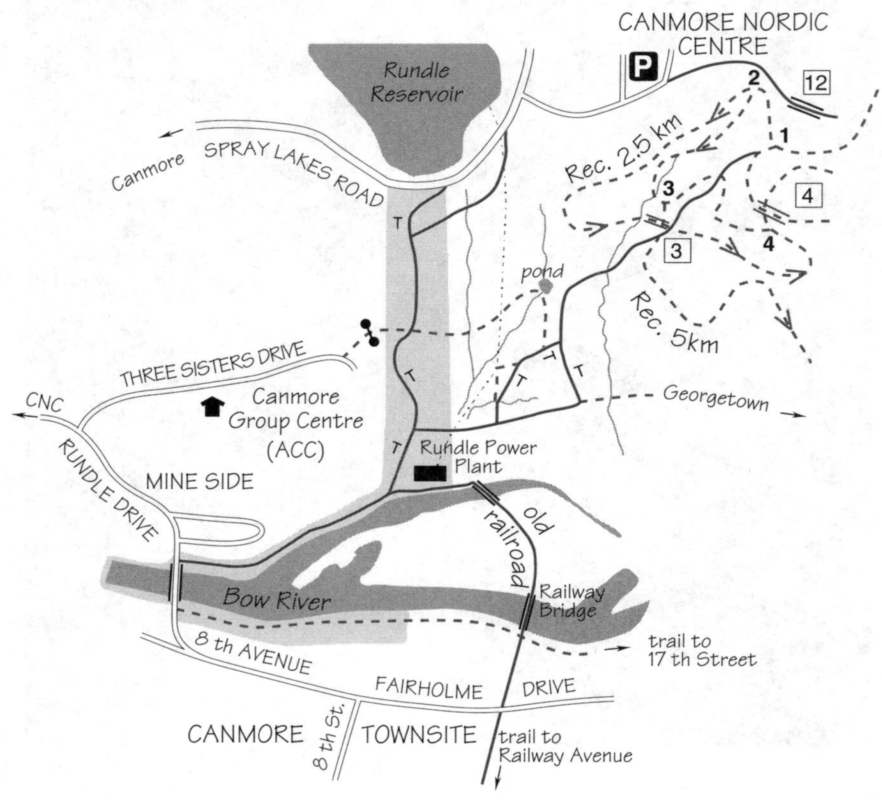

The stadium, backdropped by two of The Three Sisters. The photo was taken during the 15th Olympic Winter Games in 1988.

Facilities and Services It's pretty good knowing we have someone like Ron Henderson managing the Canmore Nordic centre. Friend to racer, race organizer and recreational skier alike, Ron and his staff run an efficient friendly operation which somehow manages to keep all the demanding factions happy — no mean feat I'd say.

The first building you come to when you drive up the access road is the Day Lodge (open 7 days a week from 9 am to 5 pm). Inside is an information counter, video display, Rundlestone fireplace, couches, tables, a first-rate cafeteria, washrooms with showers, meeting rooms, race offices, ski patrol headquarters and a decor of flags and photos by Mike Keller of the 15th Winter Olympic Games. It seems most people leave their packs lying around on the floor of the lodge when they go off skiing. Ron wants me to stress that lockers *are* available in the shower rooms because not too many people seem to know about it. The Lodge, by the way, is available for private functions like weddings and banquets. To arrange for catering write to Markus Aschauer, Canmore Nordic Centre, Box 1979, Canmore, Alberta TOL OMO.

Trail Sports, operated by ex-Aussie John Gallagher, is located opposite the day lodge and rents high performance equipment (including pulks, children's skis, boots, bindings, poles both standard and high performance) and sells all the things you left behind at home like waxes and wax remover. Trail Sports also offers lessons of all kinds, ski tours, race viewing tours with commentary, ski waxing, tuning and repair. It's open between 9 am and 5 pm, 7 days a week. Their telephone number is 678-6764.

Other facilities include a 32-point Biathlon firing range, Biathlon race offices, and separate waxing huts for cross country skiers and biathletes. Waxing huts can be reserved for groups by applying in writing 2 weeks in advance. One of three Canada-wide Training Centres is on the drawing board and will likely be built halfway down the access road between Trail Sports and the biathlon waxing huts. Look for it to be operating by about 1995.

Scattered along the trails are a few picnic tables and cozy two-man shelters.

The 2.5 km Blue Recreational trail is lit for night skiing. Twining about the Rec 2.5, as it's called, is the paved roller skiing track for summer training. Come summer the Nordic Centre becomes a mountain biking centre with all facilities open.

There's even a ski orienteering course. Orienteering maps are sold in the cafeteria. Finally, tours of all the above can be arranged by contacting the office staff.

Area Overview Sited on the north-east slopes of Mount Rundle, the network loops through pine forest with not much in the way of clearings, discounting the large unnatural one at the strip mine. Because of this, the area tends to be cool with winds generally blowing down valley and up the XC stadium into the faces of race officials. In mid-winter, the Rundle buttresses cast long shadows over everything north of the meadow which accounts for the better snow out there, while In the XC stadium, the sun goes behind Chinaman's Peak at 1 pm and out again at 2 pm before finally setting below Whiteman's Pass at 3 pm.

The 56 km of trails look like they were casually designed by dropping a plate of spaghetti onto the floor, but actually, they were very carefully arranged — they had to be, since this is the smallest Olympic site in the World — with innumerable crossovers, crossunders and junctions. I particularly appreciate Spaghetti Junction at 38, 86, 89, and 90. But there are others just as convoluted.

A one-way system is in effect with arrows at junctions pointing "home". The problem for the tired and confused tourer is that you may be standing only 100 metres away from "home" as the crow flies, but forced by the arrows to go all round the boonies for another 5 km. Personally, I'm not averse to a little bushwhacking (it pays to know the loops). One cutoff has become so well-established it's been trackset and given a name "The George Smith Cutoff" after master racer George Smith of Canmore. On Banff Trail there are maps with little arrows saying "you are here" which is ironical given that this is the only trail you can't get lost on in the company of hundreds. Only two trails are two-way: Banff Trail and part of the Upper Strip Mine Road below 61.

Trails are graded: green-easy, blue-intermediate, black-expert along each section between junctions. Bridges are numbered mostly for the benefit of Bill Brooks and the trail crew.

The most popular trails are packed, groomed and trackset for racers which means that on long downhills, gathering speed at an alarming rate, you have to fight down the urge to snowplow lest you catch your tips in the tracks and perform a spectacular cartwheel. The other problem for snowplowers is the wandering tracks syndrome on bends. Main loops like Banff Trail, the Rec 10, the Rec 15, are always packed and trackset, while obscure connectors and less used trails are packed if time permits and it's here where you might find a bit of powder. Normally, biathlon trails are only packed since biathletes only skate.

Trails divide naturally into two areas, cross-country trails situated mostly above Banff Trail and biathlon trails situated mostly below Banff Trail.

In case you haven't twigged, many of the trails at the Nordic Centre are *not* for novices or timid skiers who will be frightened out of their wits. Stay in the stadium, on Banff Trail and a few other little loops which I'll tell you about. The term "recreational" does not mean that the trail is easier; indeed, the Rec 10 incorporates all the worst hills! Because these trails were built to Olympic and world class racing standards it's difficult for non-racers to ski loops like the Rec 10 really well because you're either herringboning uphill (racers skate) or going downhill at speeds in excess of 60 km/hour. Right now, there is a push on to build some easier trails for recreationists starting with the connector between #125 and bridge # 22.

Snow is minimal compared to Mount Shark which is why snow making augments the natural stuff around the stadium end. Biathlon trails below the biathlon stadium get the least snow and are the first to feel the effect of warm weather.

Avalanches are not something you normally associate with the Nordic Centre. But on the 12th of February 1990, the same day as the monstrous slide in Healy Creek, a slide came down a gully off Rundle, broke over the retaining bank and washed down onto the end of the Rec 15, hurling broken trees and a 3-m high wall of debris onto the trail. Bob the lawyer tells me it wasn't there when he passed by at 12.30. Now the trees have been penetrated, this section of trail has been closed indefinitely.

While on the subject of closures, remember that the original purpose of the Nordic Centre is to host races in cross country, biathlon and nordic-combined. So don't get miffed if on race days some trails are closed to the public. Notices telling you which ones are pinned up on the outside wall of the Day Lodge next to the front door.

The Mad Trapper of Canmore!

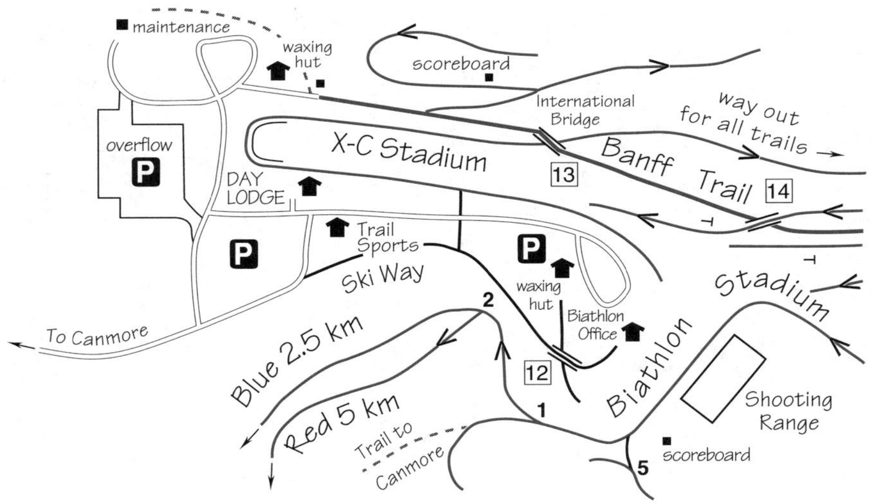

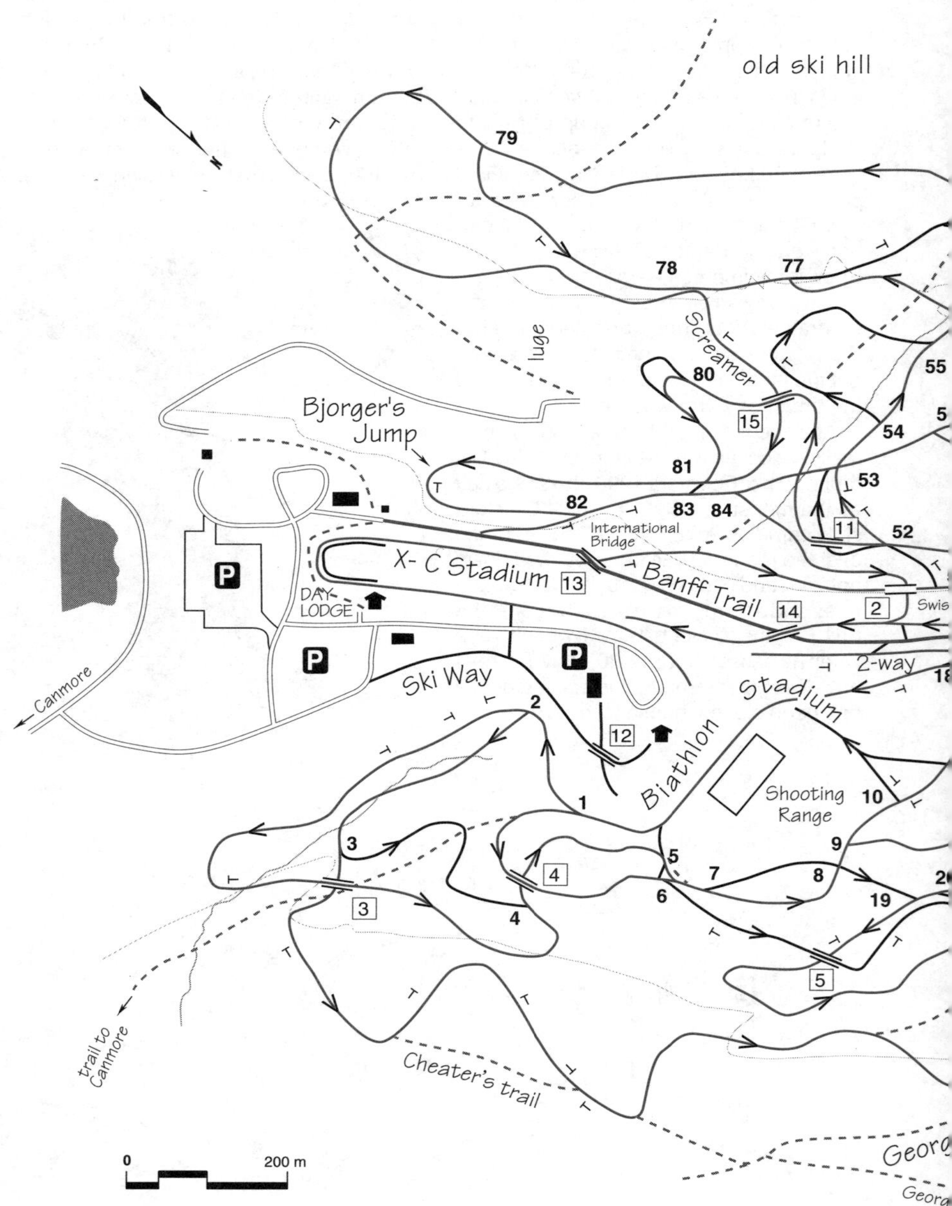
old ski hill
79
78
77
luge
Screamer
80
55
Bjorger's Jump
15
54
81
53
82
83
84
11
International Bridge
52
X- C Stadium
13
Banff Trail
DAY LODGE
14
2
P
P
P
2-way
Ski Way
Stadium
Canmore
2
12
Biathlon
Shooting Range
10
1
9
3
5
4
7
8
3
6
19
4
5
trail to Canmore
Cheater's trail
0
200 m

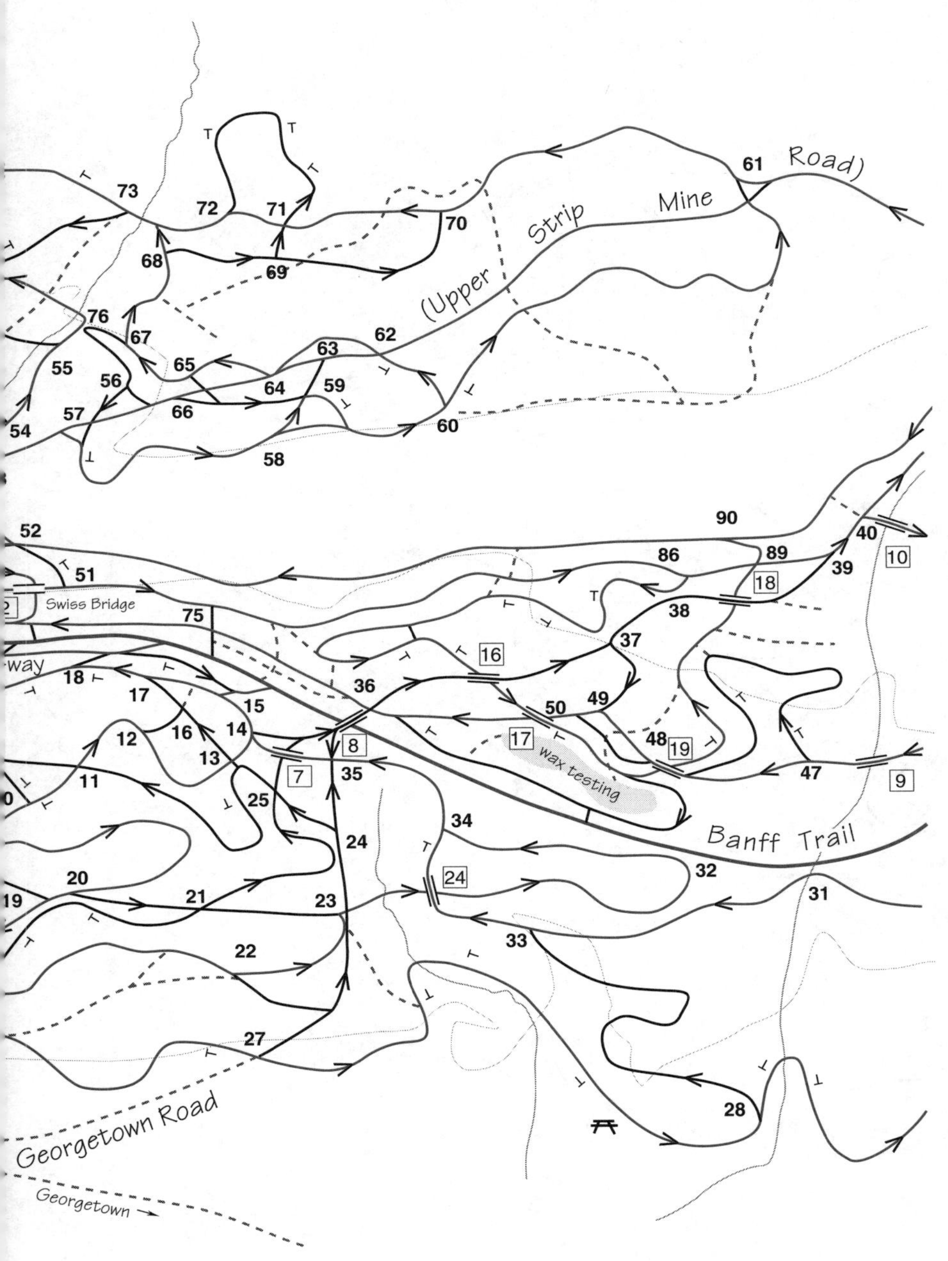
(Upper Strip Mine Road)
Swiss Bridge
Banff Trail
wax testing
Georgetown Road
Georgetown →

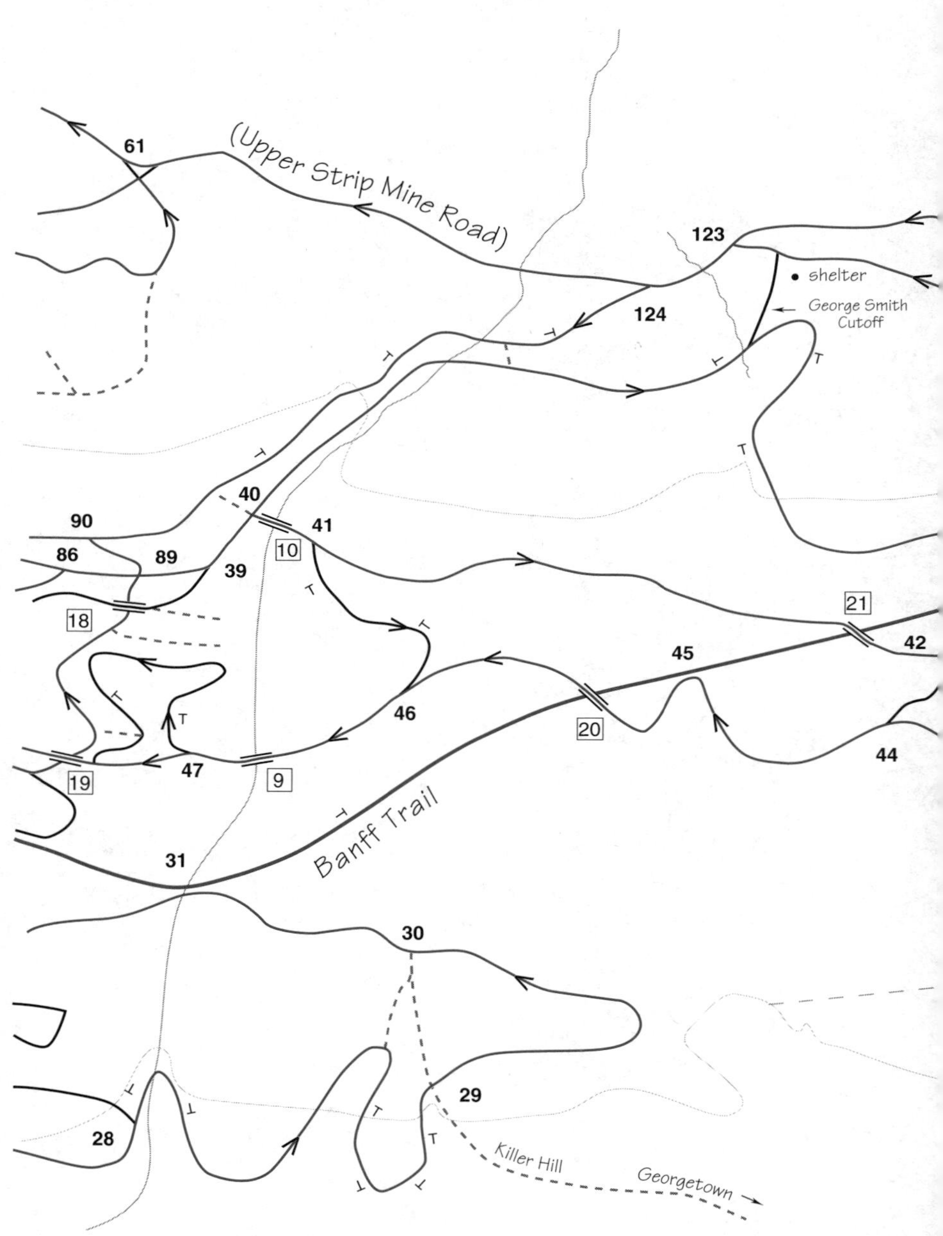

61
(Upper Strip Mine Road)
123
shelter
George Smith Cutoff
124
90
86
89
40
41
10
39
18
21
42
45
46
47
9
19
20
44
Banff Trail
31
30
29
28
Killer Hill
Georgetown

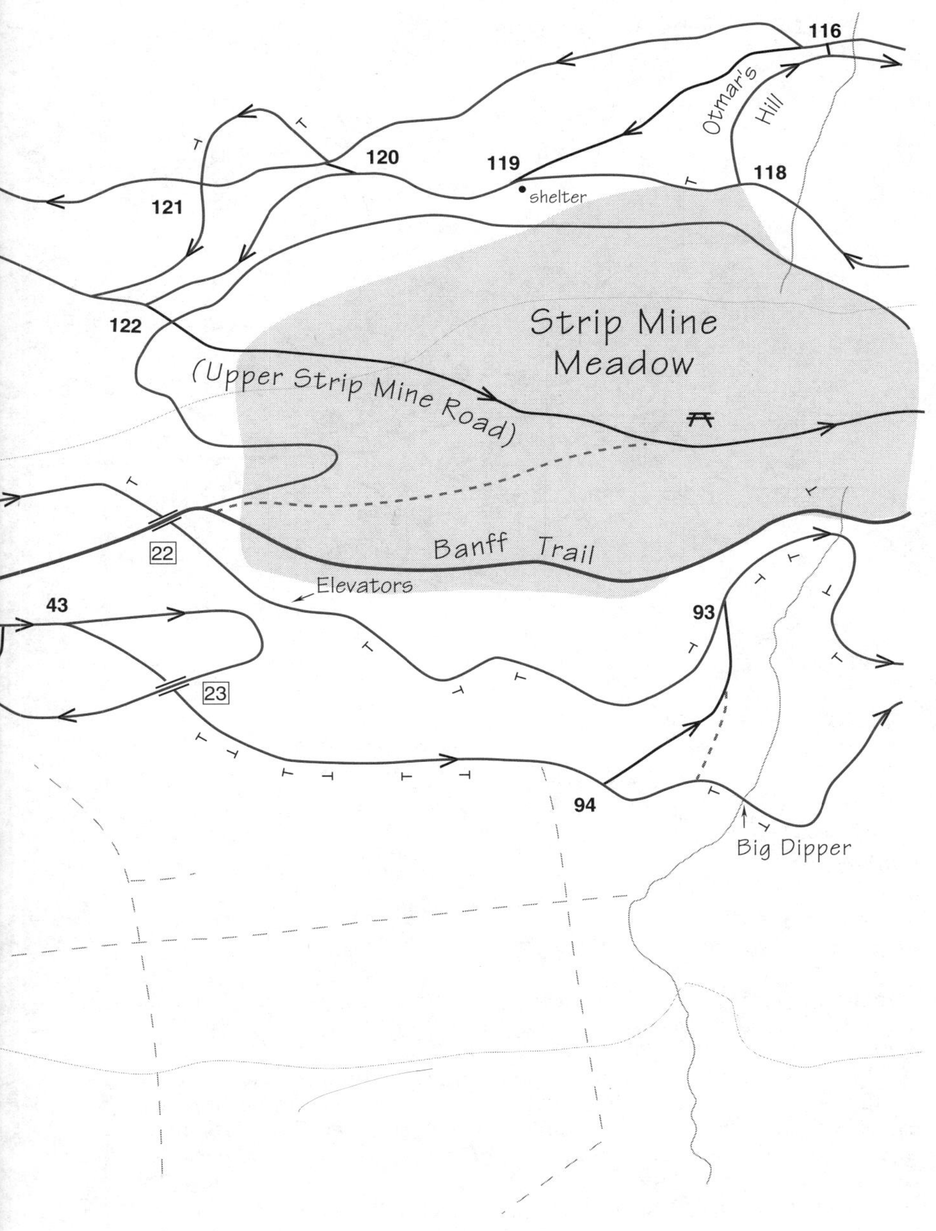
116
Otmar's Hill
120
119
shelter
118
121
122
Strip Mine Meadow
(Upper Strip Mine Road)
22
Banff Trail
Elevators
43
93
23
94
Big Dipper

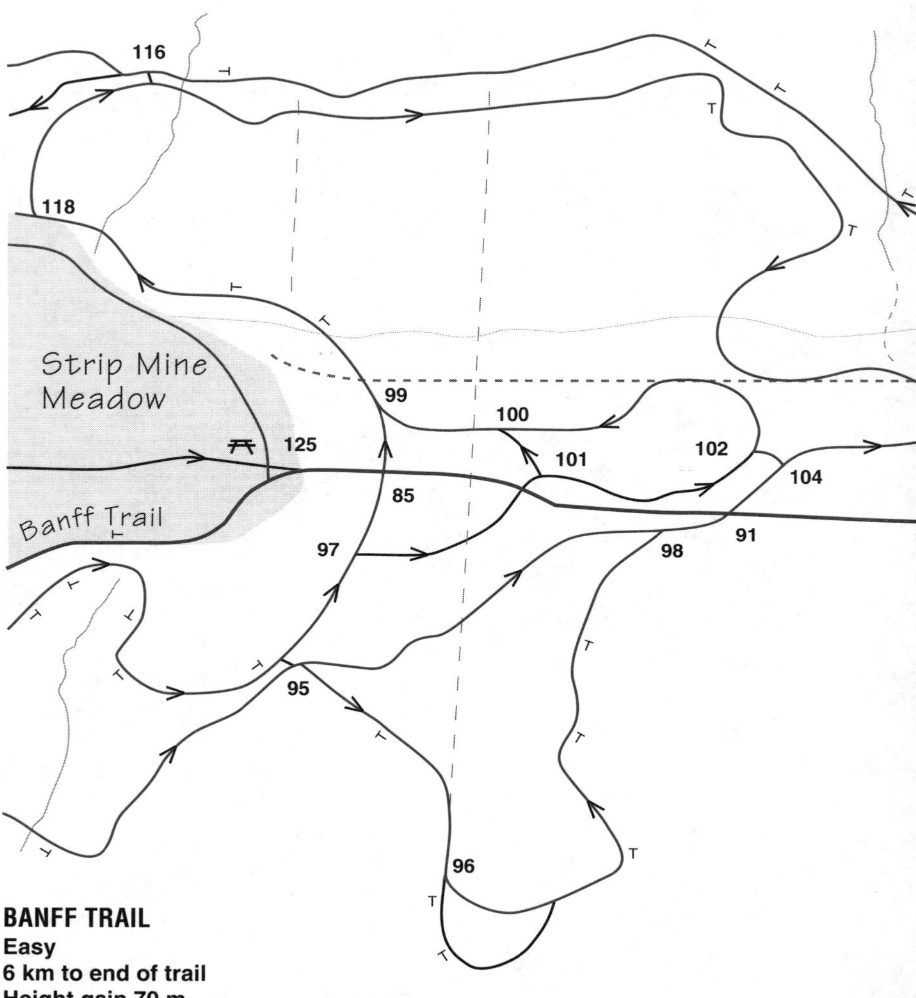

BANFF TRAIL

Easy
6 km to end of trail
Height gain 70 m

The easiest and most scenic trail of the lot follows the old access road to Strip Mine Meadow and beyond, to a point close to the boundary with Banff National Park. Contrary to what you might think, this road is not flat, but has long rolling hills very popular with families and beginners who also like it's two-way system. When you've had enough exercise for the day you can simply turn round and head back to your spot by the fireplace without consulting the map. Try one or two of the easy variations.

As you can see from the map there are two ways to start (or finish) this trail:

Start 1. The longer but easier start begins above the XC Stadium on the road proper which means skirting all round the outside of the Day Lodge, the stadium and waxing huts to get there. It's a dead flat road which crosses the International bridge — a great spot from which to watch a race.

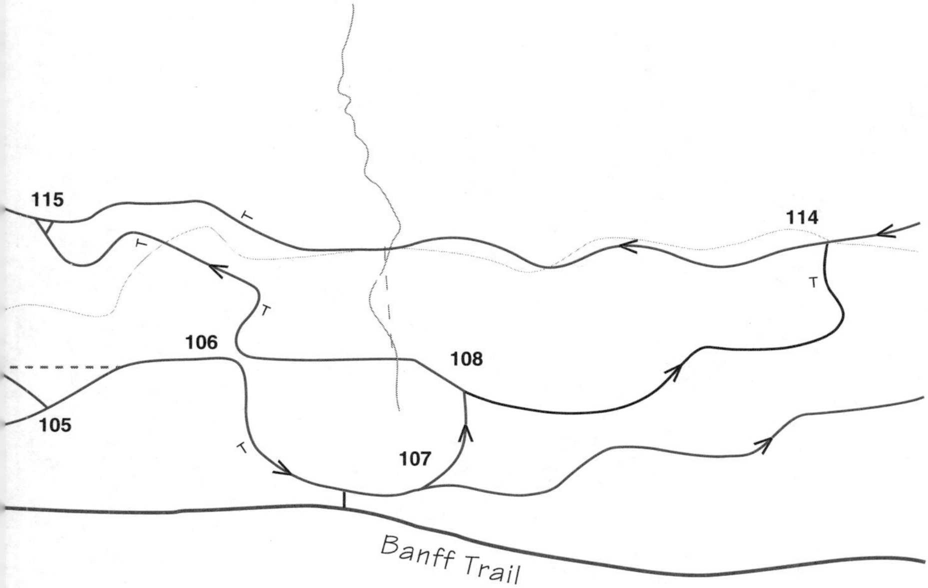

115
114
106
108
105
107
Banff Trail

Banff Trail at Strip Mine Meadow. Behind are the many buttresses of Mt. Rundle.

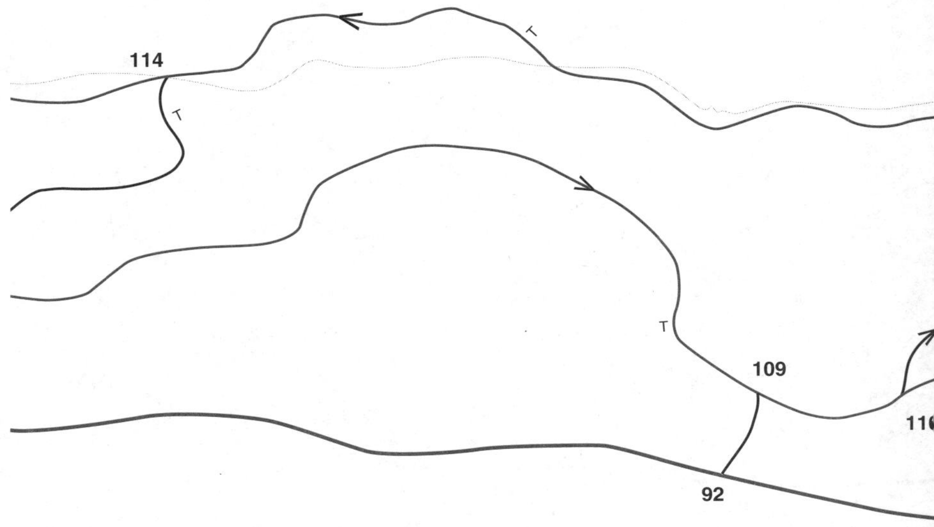

Start 2. From the XC Stadium ski down by the side of the fence towards the Biathlon Stadium, but before getting there, head a bit left and climb a hill with multiple tracks used for wax testing to a point past 18 where transferring to Banff Trail is easy.

Beyond the junction of starts expect some downhill, then a long seemingly endless uphill under three bridges and over bridge #22 to the first congregating spot with a fabulous view of Strip Mine Meadow and Mt. Rundle. The road used to head straight across the meadow, but now does some intense undulating near to the Rec 10 in an effort to escape the wind and arrives at the far end of the meadow at 125, another congregating spot. This is the half-way point where you have to decide if you want to go on. If it's sunny and warm and the picnic table's empty, the temptation to stay put is overwhelming because the last stretch is notably downhill (uphill coming back) into the dark deep forest where the trees are bigger and the temperature falls a degree with every one-step double pole. And there is absolutely nothing to see at road's end except another location map telling you "You are Here".

But the dead-end situation may be changed by the winter of 1993/4. Quite apart from the fact that septuagenarians need an easy 50 km course in time for the World Masters in 1995, the recreational skier undoubtedly needs a greater percentage of easy terrain. So to this end a brand new trail will double back to 31 on Banff Trail via an undulating traverse *below* all the deepest sorties of the Rec 15. Expect viewpoints and picnic tables.

Options

1. Easy intermediate loop at Strip Mine Meadow

Try out the Nordic Centre's latest trail built in the summer of 1992 which enables half-wayers to make a finishing loop around Strip Mine Meadow. No need to torture yourself with the rigours of the Rec 10. You leave Banff Trail at 125 and loop much lower down above the escarpment, crossing Upper Strip Mine Road in the process and winding down to bridge # 22 on the opposite side of the meadow.

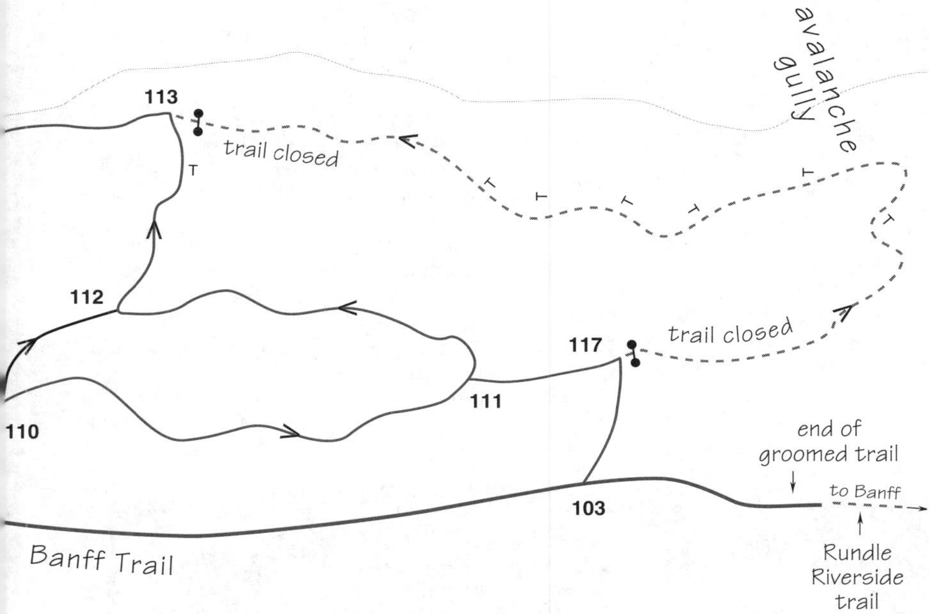

avalanche gully
113
trail closed
112
117
trail closed
110
111
end of groomed trail
to Banff
103
Banff Trail
Rundle Riverside trail

2. Easy alternative going out
At 91 which is a little way beyond Strip Mine Meadow turn left and follow though 104-105-106-107-109-110-111-117, then turn right and ski through to Banff Trail at 103. Undulating with a snowplow hill after 106.

3. Easy alternative coming back above Banff Trail
At 45 turn left and cross bridge #20 over Banff Trail. Follow through 46-bridge #9-47, by the low trail over bridge #19 to 48-49-50-under bridge #17-36. Get back onto Banff Trail by a cutoff a few metres right of bridge #8 or carry on to 75. A very gentle trail with nothing in the way of downhills until the little one between 50 and 36. Whatever you do, don't turn right at 47!

4. Easy alternative coming back below Banff Trail
Turn left onto 32 just before the wax testing area. Follow though 34-35-over bridge #7-14-15 where you can easily escape onto Banff Trail and so miss out a tiring uphill. Almost flat.

The 1990 avalanche across the Green Recreational 15.

BLUE RECREATIONAL 2.5

Intermediate
2.5 km loop
Height gain 70 m

Day Lodge-Biathlon Stadium via walkway-1-2-over bridge #3-4-under bridge #4-5-6-7-8-9-10-11-12-13-14-15-17-18-Biathlon Mass Start Area-XC Stadium.

This is the biathlon loop illuminated for night skiing which is probably the best time to ski it anyway since it pokes into some pretty dark places in the forest. Good fun downhills but nothing too steep.

After 2 you shoot off towards Canmore via a long sidehill by the side of a creek. A short steep uphill, bend and downhill deposit you even further down the creek. Surprisingly, the climb back up to the bank above the penalty loop and firing range is not too bad considering you're almost back where you started from. After 9 there's a straightforward downhill past junctions 10 and 11 and you turn right into Cottonwood Alley, another enormously complex area. At 14 you join the Rec 5 and after 15, foregoing the temptations of Banff Trail, join the crowd of herringboners to 18, just a few glides away from Banff Trail. Keep left, though, and in the spirit of the trail, finish with a good downhill run into the biathlon stadium area.

Blue Recreational 2.5. The downhill between 9 and 11. Note the light standards.

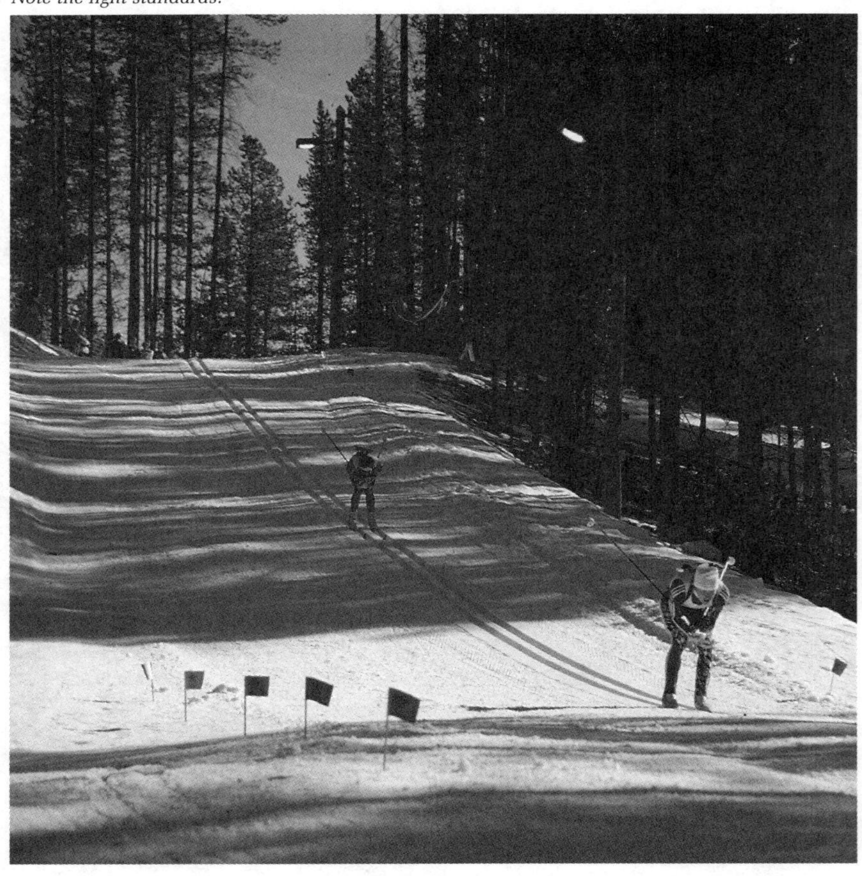

RED RECREATIONAL 5

Hard Intermediate
5 km loop
Height gain 150 m

Day Lodge -Biathlon Stadium-1-2-3-under bridge #3-27-28-29-long way to 30-31-33-over bridge #24-34-35-over bridge #7-14-15-17-18-Biathlon Mass Start area-Day Lodge.

A looping forest trail following for the most part the perimeter of the biathlon area. Tell the graduating skier trembling on the brink of the first big hill that this is the next easiest trail after Banff Trail — according to the area brochure!

Hard intermediate? Actually, this trail suffers from schizophrenia, having hills worthy of Calaway Park's roller coaster but also relatively flat stretches. The steepest downhill occurs right after bridge #3. Did you know that at the bottom of that first big hill there's a narrow forest trail which misses out the next horrific uphill downhill combination? Cheater's should also make a note of the unmarked junction after 27 where you can exit to 23. Then it's back for more fun as you shoot off down by the side of a creek. A short stubby step out of the valley floor brings you to a picnic table above a drop-off — a nice quiet spot with a bit of a view. After 28 the hills are much tamer and quite honestly if you want to ski the Rec 5 without the terrors of the beginning then join in along that unofficial trail from 23 via the Beginner's 3.5. Another escape route presents itself at the top of the hill after 28 and at 29 but there's not much point to it except for variation's sake. At 29, by the way, you cross the Georgetown summer interpretive trail which goes off down Killer Hill. (I can't believe we used to ski it!) The stretch between 31 and 15 is flat after which comes the herringbone hill to 17 and the compensatory run down to the Biathlon Stadium.

BEGINNER'S 3.5

Easy
3.5 km
Height gain 60 m

Day Lodge-Biathlon Stadium-1-over bridge #4-6-7-8-9-20-19-under bridge #5-22-23-under bridge #24-32-34-35-over bridge #7-14-15-Banff Trail-75-18-Biathlon Stadium area-XC Stadium (or, follow Banff Trail under bridge #14-over bridge #13-XC Stadium).

After seeing so many beginners scaring themselves silly on both the Blue Rec 2.5 and Red Rec 5, and what is more, sprawled all over the trail in front of me, I herewith present my own easy route which I think you'll enjoy a whole lot more. A mishmash of biathlon trails and connectors, the Beginner's 3.5 always takes the easiest option.

It certainly takes the easy way to 9, but instead of careering down the intermediate hill to 11, turns right and makes a leisurely descent past 20 and 19 and under bridge #5 — a little surprise acceleration there (crux) — and loops around to 22 between big spruce trees. At 22, keep left lest you stray onto the roller ski trail. Cross over the Georgetown Road at 23. After this it's easy pleasant going through to 34 where the Rec 5 joins in and on to 14 where you meet Rec 2.5 and a whole lot more people. Unlike the two rec trails, at 15 transfer onto Banff Trail and return past 18 into the Biathlon Stadium area. Or if you don't fancy the final run into the stadium area, keep right on Banff Trail proper which enters the XC stadium above the stands.

I told you it was easy!

YELLOW RECREATIONAL 10

Hard Intermediate
10 km
Height gain 275 m

XC Stadium-under bridge #13-over bridge #2-51-86-89-39-40-under bridge #22-93-95-97-85-99-118-119-120-122-123-124-61-70-71-72-73-79-78-under bridge #15-81-82-83-84-under bridge #2-over bridge #14-XC Stadium.

Kilometre for kilometre this is a demanding course with steep uphills and fast downhills including the once dreaded Elevator.

Shortly after crossing bridge #2 which would not be out of place in a Japanese Garden but is actually called the Swiss Bridge by the trail crew because of its height, comes a long undulating section with the climb up past Spaghetti Junction. At 40 keep left, climbing to a high point at an opening, where you can shorten the route by half and cut out most of the worst hills by turning left up George Smith's cutoff to the upper level of the Rec 10 just before 123.

Brave souls continuing on are faced with the dreaded black diamond, precursor of a steep curving downhill which spits you out under Banff Trail and into another downhill called, ominously, the Elevator. There's no need to worry now. It's been de-elevated ever since two mountain bikers locked handlebars in mid air. Below Strip Mine Meadow the trail weaves around the head of a creek and includes one horrid little uphill, the only hill at the CNC I've ever sidestepped My excuse is that it was icy at the time.

After 99 begins the biggest climb of the lot around the edge of Strip Mine Meadow to a small shelter at 119. Slumped on the two seater, you view Mt. Lady McDonald across the valley with weary eyes. Another steep little climb, then the angle eases off for a long way as you continue on to Upper Strip Mine Road, passing another shelter and a picnic table near George Smith's cutoff.

At 124 you leave Upper Strip Mine Road and continue easily all the way to 79. Between 73 and 79 is the high point where you cross the old ski hill. After 79 there is nowhere to go but down. Indeed, you're not allowed to go anywhere else but down The Screamer if you want to get home, short of sliding down the luge run of course. A little easing off at 81, then you're into Bjorger's Jump where test skiing indicated excessive banking was needed to stop skiers spinning off the bend and over the bank onto the roofs of the waxing huts.

So near and yet so far. Turning your back on the stadium you climb up Scoreboard Hill to 83 and make a half loop under bridge #2 and over bridge # 14 into the XC stadium. I'm developing an aversion to bridge #2, not because it harbours the steepest or longest hill, but because a sharp bend, a sudden drop in altitude and the bridge abutments all coincide at this one point. In Jackrabbit races a row of mothers are lined up against the wall to act as buffers, but they are, unfortunately, unavailable on a full-time basis.

78 to the XC Stadium is the usual finish for most loops. However, there's nothing to stop you from escaping down the access road from 82 to Banff Trail!

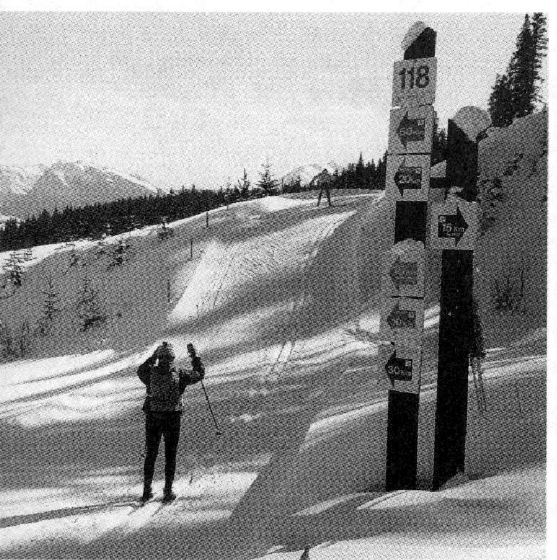

Yellow Recreational 10 at 118 at the top end of Strip Mine Meadow.

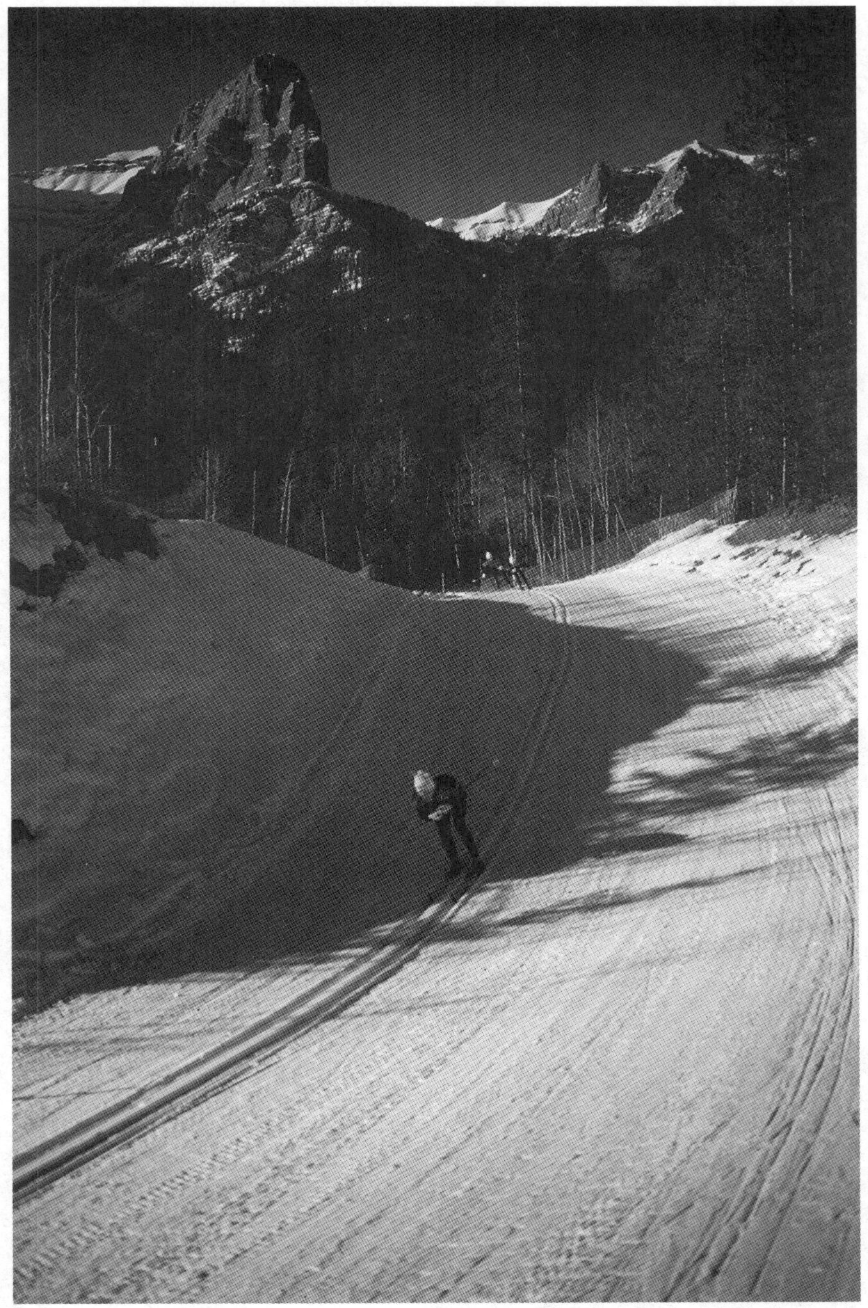

The bend below the Screamer; the usual way into the Stadium. Mt. Rundle behind.

GREEN RECREATIONAL 15

Hard intermediate
14.5 km
Height gain 370 m

XC Stadium-under bridge#13-over bridge #2-51-86-89-39-40-over bridge #10-41-over Banff Trail on bridge #21-42-43-under bridge #23-94-95-98-91-104-105-106-107-109-110-111-112-113-114-115-116-120-121-123-124-90-52-53-54-55-76-77- 78-under bridge #15-81-82-83-84-under bridge #2-over bridge #14-XC Stadium.

The Rec 15 gives you a grand tour of the remote north end of the Nordic Centre where the snow is natural and plentiful. Though not considered so challenging as the Rec 10, it nevertheless has some horrible hills of its own, notably the Big Dipper which is more of an emotional problem, and the spate of tiring uphills between 114 and 116. Who said the upper leg was flat?

Green Recreational 15 near 54. Photo taken during the World Cup in 1987.

On a cold day the beginning climb to 40 is a pleasant way to get warmed up. In fact, all the way to 42 the going is pleasant. After 43 the CNC syndrome manifests itself in not one but three roller coaster hills, culminating in the Big Daddy of them all — the Big Dipper or whatever you call it. Planners with a weird sense of humour put in link trail 94-93 for weak-kneed skiers who want to chicken out at the last moment onto the Rec 10 (Yellow) where you're not much better off, though I discovered you *can* escape onto Banff Trail even further to the left. If the downhill zoom at the speed of sound takes your breath away then the sudden stop *near the top* of the hill makes you feel as if you've just arrived on the top floor of Bankers Hall only to discover that the elevator has no floor. You scramble to get the legs working before the inevitable slide into the abyss. Backwards.

After all this excitement the long stretch to 117 is exceedingly mild though you can if you want take on Special Red's loop between 95 and 98 for a little downhill and uphill practise. Between 106 and 111 are four cutoffs to the upper leg, of which 107-108-114 is the easiest. Unfortunately, the trail between 117 and 113 is out of bounds ever since an avalanche cut across the north end in 1990. This is a great pity because between the avalanche track and 113 is a series of concave dips which are the Nordic Centre's speciality.

You're on your way home now. Uphills begin after 114 and culminate with an exhausting drag after 115 to the high point of the Rec 15. At 124 is a warning sign "Steep Hill". You laugh. After what has gone before this downhill looks so innocuous, but take it from me it's a long and quietly dangerous hill because of accumulating speed. Racers always have a good tumble or two around junction 90. At 52 (so close to home) the trail heads away up the hill one more time before joining the Rec 10 at 78.

MASTERS 5

Easy intermediate
5 km
Height gain 90 m

XC Stadium-under bridge #13-over bridge #2-51-86-89-39-40-over bridge #10-41-over Banff Trail on bridge #21-42-43-over bridge #23-44-45-over bridge #20-46-over bridge #9-47-over bridge #19-48-49-50-under bridge #17-36-75-over bridge #14-XC Stadium.

This loop was first used at the Canadian Masters Championships in February 1990 for everyone over the age of 30. Since it is also the blind skiers racing loop, there are obviously no horrid surprises in store. The loop to try after Banff Trail and Beginner's 3.5.

Follow Rec 10 and Rec 15 the usual way out of the XC Stadium to Spaghetti Junction at 86, and continue up to 40. Stay on the Rec 15 and get your reward for the uphill climb. Nothing steep. But as you schuss down from the bridge over Banff Trail put on the brakes; you are going to turn left at 43. The return leg is easy and pleasant; I especially like to linger between 67 and 47 where bridge #9 spans a mini-gorge. After 36 comes a long section parallel to Banff Trail which is only a few metres to your left and which brings you to the usual finish for Rec 15/Rec 10 *between* bridges #2 and #14. All that remains is the final downhill which spews you out into the far end of the XC Stadium.

Next time try it with your eyes shut.

LADIES 5

Difficult
5 km
Height gain 135 m

XC Stadium-under bridge #13-over bridge #2-51-86-38-under bridge #16-over bridge #17-under bridge #19-under bridge #18-89-90-52-over bridge #11-over bridge #15-80-81-82-83-84-under bridge #2-over bridge #14-XC Stadium.

The Olympic Ladies 5 km loop is no easy day for a lady. Short but sweet, it features some hills you wouldn't normally ski.

Take the normal route out of the stadium to 86 at Spaghetti Junction. Turn right here, gearing up for some terrific bends coupled with downhills. A left-hander, then a right-hander, followed by a straight hill of the concave variety. Curving close above Banff Trail you hear voices (easy escape available). Then it's away again, up then down a totally unnecessary hill, and under and over two bridges to the wax testing area. This signals yet another cutoff to Banff Trail and also the start of the steep winding climb back up to Spaghetti Junction.

At 89 cut across to Green Rec 15 at 90. At 52 the Rec 15 is left temporarily for a pleasant whirlabout past 80 to 81 where the routes reconverge. It's immensely heartening after having just skied the Ladies 5 to pause on bridge #15 and watch the beginners coming down the Screamer. Finish in the usual fashion, being careful not to deflate your ego on Bjorger's Jump just in case your friends are watching through the Day Lodge windows.

SPECIAL RED 15

Difficult
15 km
Height gain 505 m

XC Stadium-under bridge #13-over bridge #2-51-86-89-39-40-under bridge #22-93-95-96-98-91-104-102-100-99-118-116-105-106-107-108-106-115-116-120-121-122-123-124-90-52-53-57-58-59-60-62-64-65-67-68-73-79-the short way to 78-under bridge #15-81-82-83-84-under bridge #2-over bridge #14-XC Stadium.

The Ultimate. A combination of the Rec 10 and Rec 15 with some extra hills thrown in for good measure. Well, you don't have to race it like Pierre Harvey!

You follow the Rec 10 to 95, then deke off down to 96. This first aberration, and I use the word deliberately, would be totally enjoyable if you didn't have three herringbone hills back up to 98 where you join the Rec 15. I always think it would be great to reverse the direction — have a Reverse Day once a year or something.

At 118 at the top edge of Strip Mine Meadow, you take off up Otmar's Hill to 116. The hill down to 105 is my favourite. I just adore it, perhaps because I'm usually alone and it's hardly ever trackset which means you can snowplow the corners without feeling guilty about not keeping to the tracks. After 106, that is the *second* time you reach 106, is a really steep uphill to 115, followed by the uphill I hate on the Rec 15. Together they make up one colossal climb of about 90 metres. Image racing up *this* combination. And don't forget the loop between 120 and 121. If you haven't done this totally unnecessary loop, you haven't done the Special 15. The next detour occurs at 53 and takes you on a very pleasant tour of easy trails up to the Rec 10 on the ski hill slopes. The final deviation in the quest for steep hills is the cutoff between 79 and 78. Phew!

UPPER STRIP MINE ROAD

Easy Intermediate
3.5 km
Height gain 90 m

XC Stadium-under bridge #13-over bridge #2-51-52-over bridge #11-Upper Strip Mine Road-53-57-58-60-61-Upper Strip Mine Road-62-63-64-66-57-53-84-under bridge #2-over bridge #14-XC Stadium (or variation from 84).

The route down Upper Strip Mine Road (which I should hasten to add is two-way) is proving a very popular escape route from the Rec 10 at 61 and that includes the deviation at the bottom end to preclude the obligatory finish, Honest Ron, everybody does it, which just goes to show that people are desperate for another route into the stadium.

Start off in the usual way to 51. Here turn left and arrive at 52. There's a direct trail to 53 (steep) or much flatter trails either across bridge #11 or under bridge #11 which gain you Upper Strip Mine Road a little lower down. Climb past 53 to 57 where you turn right and after having gained the top of a ridge, follow it easily all the way along to 61 on the Rec 10.

Most of the descent is a simple downhill run along Upper Strip Mine Road past ten junctions to 84. You can if you want make it a little more interesting by taking off at 62 and re-emerging at 57 via 64-65-67-76-56. Below 57 the road steepens and in lieu of traffic lights you've got to watch for skiers zooming across the road from left to right. At 84 turn left and return the usual way. Or you can take the short-cut. Just past 84 head off right down an unofficial trail which deposits you on your outgoing trail. It will have occurred to you that the quickest way into the stadium is against the one-way system which wouldn't please Ron at all. Even if it is only a hundred metres. So what everyone does is cross the trail then ski the open slope between the trail and Banff Trail, gaining Banff Trail just to the left of the International Bridge.

The very first race at Canmore, February 4th 1979. Skiers are Ian and Neil Daffern.

More about the trails Everybody knows that Canmore (an amalgamation of Townside, Mineside and Prospect) grew up as a coal mining town. But just below the Rec 5, at the bottom of Killer Hill, was another community called Georgetown. As opposed to the Canadian Anthracite Coal Company (CACC) which had a monopoly with the CPR, Georgetown Collieries (1910-1916) had the steamship bunker trade and later changed the company name to the Canmore Navigation Coal Company. All the shareholders were British, so when World War 1 started, monies had to be directed towards the war effort which meant the company ran into financial difficulties and was forced to close the mine. Many of their abandoned roads and trails have since been incorporated into ski loops and a summer interpretive trail to view the site of the townsite which, I must confess, I find a rather boring meadow with not an artifact in sight. You can have a much more exciting time grubbing around outside the mine itself.

As expected, the coal lands were transferred to the CACC. Still, nothing much happened until 1967 when the CACC, now operating under the name Canmore Mines, experimented with a strip mine around which the ski trails now revolve — Strip Mine Meadow. They justified the eyesore by stating, "recreation facilities will be created", never for one moment envisaging the 15th Olympic Winter Games.

As coal mining phased out in the 1970's and before tourism became the number one industry, locals began using the roads for recreation. i.e. walking their dogs by car. An alpine ski hill was cut between the stadium and the high point of the Rec 10 and even higher up the gully, but, as far as I can ascertain, no T-bar was ever erected and skiers had to walk up a winding trail which is still discernable here and there between 73, 79 and 78 where it crosses the ski trails. Talk about bad timing. A decade of lean snow helped do it in and lots of mini pines grew up and were cut down as Christmas trees.

In 1977 cross country enthusiasts Otmar Setzer of Haus Alpenrose, Alex Graham, and other locals looked at roads, trails and cutlines to see if anything could be made of them. Otmar produced four Xerox sheets stapled together and

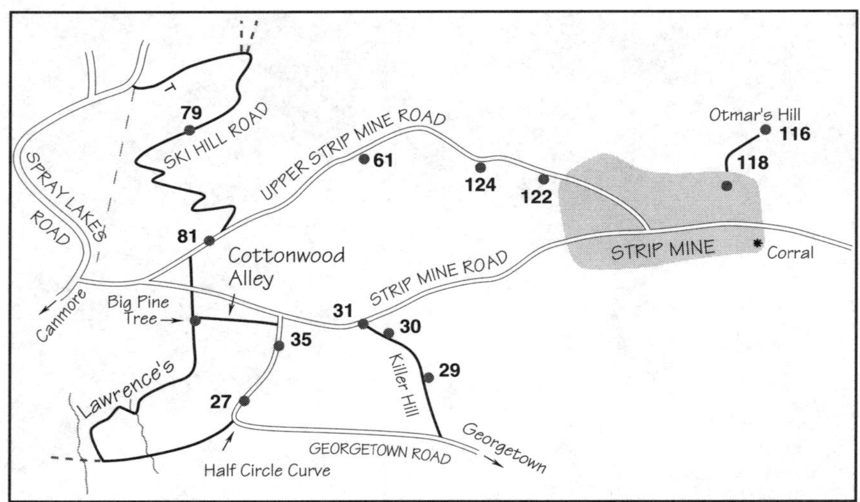

Otmar Setzer's map of 1977 ski trails. The numbers correlate to today's junctions.

handed them out to people he happened to bump into on weekends like Don Gardner, who was later to propose Canmore as an Olympic site and ourselves who were definitely not in training for races but were pottering around investigating cutlines and remarking on the remarkable way the snow quantity improved once you got beyond the strip mine and the corral. We were persuaded to both officiate and perform in the Nordic Centre's first and second race on February 4 and 11, 1979 which went down Lawrence's and up the Georgetown road. There were, I think, about a dozen of us. But for skiers there was continual frustration with dog poop and snowmobile tracks. It didn't seem the area could ever amount to anything.

But along came 1983. Having won the bid to host the cross-country portion of the 1988 Winter Olympics, UMA Engineering's bid for Bragg Creek was thrown out in favour of Canmore which had proximity to everything Including Rundle Reservoir for snow-making. Blame it all on Don Gardner who bent the ear of the King of K-Country, Ed Marshall, who advised Peter Lougheed who made the final decision. The right decision as it turned out, since Canmore is now the undisputed centre of nordic ski racing in Canada. It must be because ever since the Olympics, national team racers and coaches from eastern Canada have been flocking to the town in droves.

But back to the trails. After Gardner Associates had done the feasibility study, Don, Bjorger Pettersen, Bill Brooks (Biathlon), and Al Merrill (outside advisor) settled down to the nitty gritty of trail design. I'm told I mustn't forget Clarence and Irvine Servold who were also involved when ski jumps as well as bobsled and luge tracks were part and parcel of the plan. Garry Carson (landscape architect) was the man who pulled it all together and soon smoke from burning trees was drifting across the stadium site. By the spring of 1986 the bridges were up but not the approaches and, not to put too fine a point to it, let's just say a screw-up was made of bridge # 2. "Always a nightmare" says Don.

The opening ceremony of the Canmore Nordic Centre took place on December 6 1986 with the Mad Trapper presiding over alpenhorns, hot air balloons and politicians who spoke the word "legacy". A Jackrabbit race the following day preceded a World Cup Nordic-combined race by just one week. Talk about being shoved in the deep end!

After this came World Cups in all three

Howdy nabs a press photographer. Photo taken during the 15th Olympic Winer Games.

disciplines and the Olympic Games themselves, starting February 13 1988. Flags waved from flagpoles, up sprang souvenir stalls, tents for race officials, utility trailers for organisers, and luxury ATCO trailers with gold-plated bathroom fixtures for European royalty. There's many an interesting tale to be told of those two weeks, like the story of the lone racer from Mexico who always came in last, hours after anyone else, and together with the customary blanket and kleenex was handed a booby prize of his favourite Oreo Cookies which, like Red Rose Tea, is *apparently* only available in Canada. At every succeeding World Cup the Oreo tradition continues regardless of the fact that Roberto is moving up in the standings. "Jeff, nip down to Marra's and pick up a large bag of Oreos for Roberto". It's a wonder the manufacturers haven't cottoned on to this and done a bit of sponsoring.

One of the spin-offs from the Olympics has been Alberta's dominance in Junior National cross country and biathlon competition. So for me, the most exciting up-coming event is not some future World Cup but the opening of a National Training Centre under a National Team coach. Ten, 20 years down the road might we not see one of our own standing on the Olympic winner's podium?

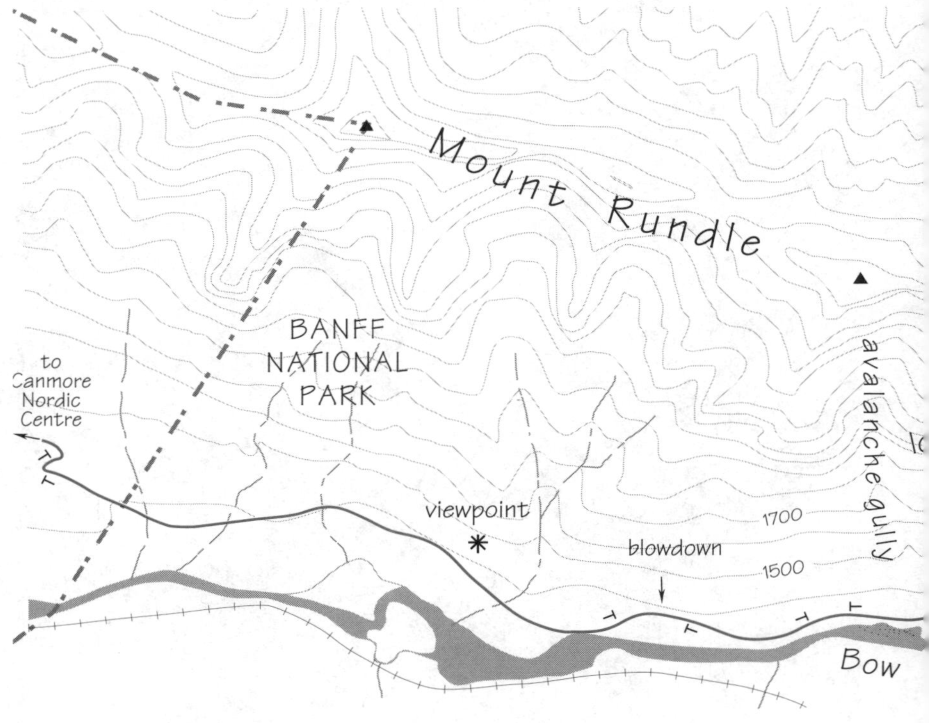

RUNDLE RIVERSIDE TRAIL

Backcountry

Intermediate
16.3 km between parking lots
Height gain S-N 83 m, N-S 190 m
Maximum elevation 1485 m
Map 82 O/3 Canmore,
82 O/4 Banff

Access

1. Canmore. Canmore Nordic Centre on Smith-Dorrien/Spray Trail (Spray Lakes Road).
2. Banff. Take the road to Bow Falls parking lot. Continue across the Spray River bridge into Banff Springs Golf Course, and follow the service road past the clubhouse to a fork where the plowed service road descends a hill. Park at the fork.

Facilities The Canmore Nordic Centre is open 7 days a week, 9 am to 5 pm. (See page 17 for full list of the facilities). More to the point, the cafeteria opens for breakfast at 10 am.

Overview I'm not saying this trail is for you because it might not be. You would have to be a little masochistic, though I hear it's improved a lot lately; been widened in one or two spots. Basically, it connects the Canmore Nordic Centre to Banff Springs Golf Course along the Bow River valley and if you start from the Canmore end there's much more downhill. Like Goat Creek, it requires a car at both ends. Also like Goat Creek you can make it a two-way trip, though most people don't bother now the golf course club-

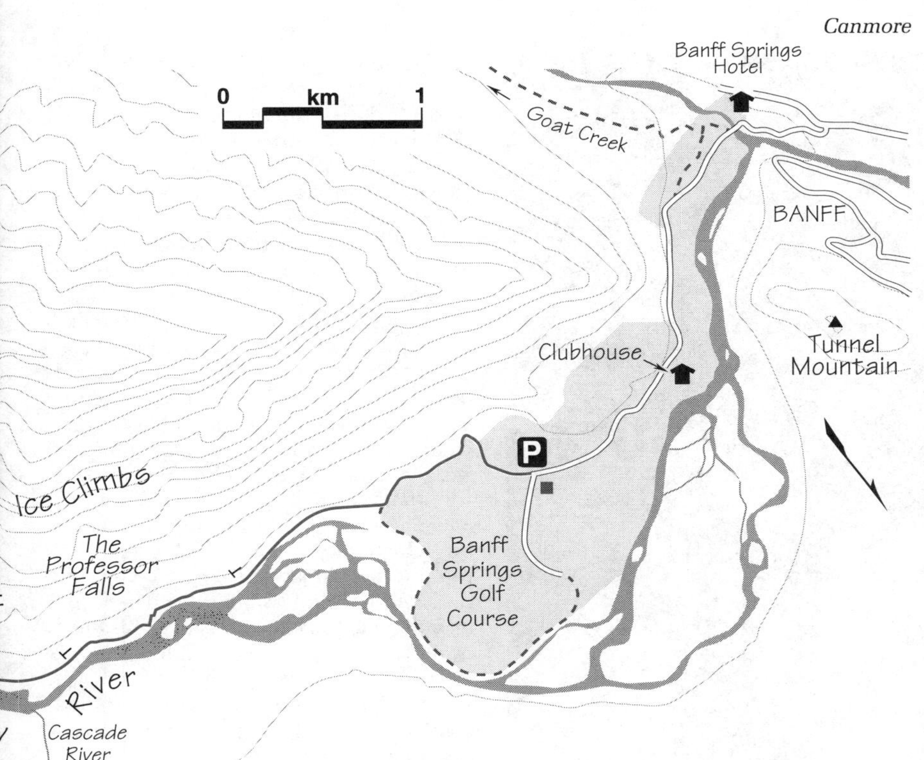

house has closed its winter doors and the incentive to make the last sitting for Sunday brunch has evaporated. Even if you have two cars, driving into Banff for eats is not quite the same thing as taking your skis off at the front door of a restaurant. With the car heater going all out and a comforting fug developing, you may even elect to carry on home to have a leisurely afternoon reading the Sunday newspapers. But if you do want to make the day longer, consider tacking on Goat Creek trail, only reverse the loop of course so as not to forfeit the downhill run. $45 will get you a guided trip around the loop courtesy of Trail Sports at the Nordic Centre, the price including transportation to the trailhead, guide and a packed lunch.

One last thing, the trail needs sufficient snow before you can even contemplate this trip. It's always deeper at the Canmore end.

Starting from the Canmore Nordic Centre, race along Banff Trail's easy trackset road to its end at kilometre 6. See pages 20 through 27 for a map of the trail and page 24 for a description.

After reading dire warnings about the trail not being trackset, you plunge into dark forest on a very narrow trail which winds down to a lower terrace, crossing the boundary into Banff National Park somewhere en route. The flat section along the aspen terrace becomes mildly rolling below a rock band, then climbs to an alluvial fan with a view of the east side of Mt. Rundle, a breathtaking vista of black buttresses and deep canyons slicing into the rock. You cross a strangely tiny creek issuing from a canyon and arrive at the Bow River in a flurry of enthusiasm. You look at your watch and think you're doing great; nearly two thirds of the trail is behind you. Little do you know.

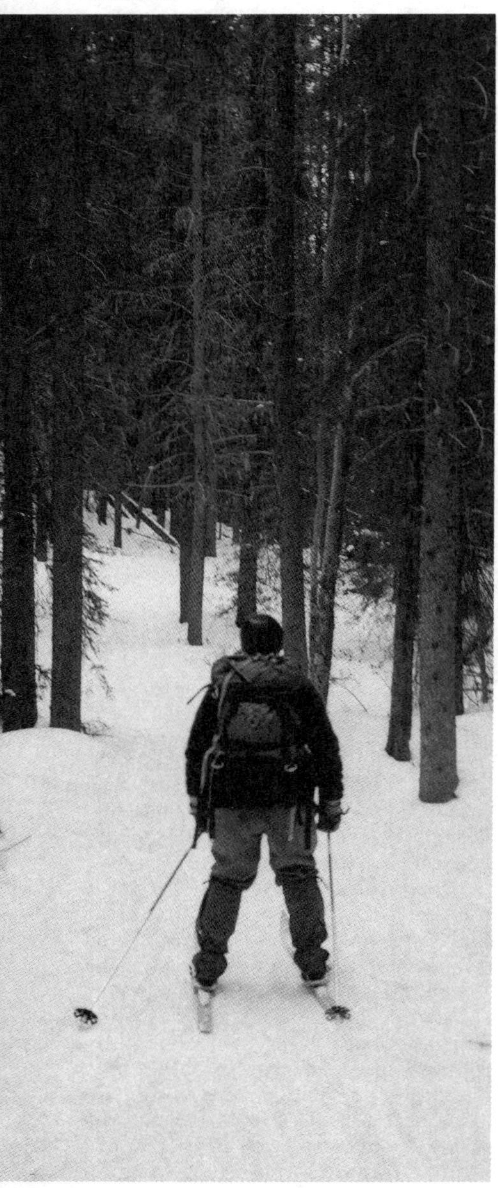

The trail down to the bench

From here on the trail is trying to get along the river bank and not succeeding very well (the river is usually still running). Straight off, there's a climb up the bank. The following descent requires care in the blowdown area where too many pointy logs are waiting like daggers to impale the careless cornerer. At the next up/down, the trail crosses a small cliff and is supported from underneath by logs. Right on the highest point the steepest downhill of the whole lot takes off. By the time you've ground to a halt half a kilometre away you won't know which is quivering more, your heart or your quad muscles.

Just beyond a bridge over a side creek is another alluvial fan viewpoint. In 1990 it was swept by an avalanche from top to bottom so it probably behoves you to stand somewhere more sensible if you want to view the spectacular cliffs of Rundle. And not only cliffs but frozen waterfalls with names like La Goute, Sacrebleu and The Terminator, a V6 horror which rarely forms completely. A little further on, after a short descent to the river, The Professor Falls can be seen up a draw to the left, and is recognisable by its five tiers of blue ice quite low down.

The trail becomes very unsatisfactory around this point. Quite apart from the heavy imprint of ice climbers' double boots, and the fact that the westerly wind is always having a go at snow removal, the trail itself is twisting and turning along the river bank which is OK if you're walking. The first time I skied it, I was schussing down a hill and suddenly realized I was about to run over a flock of goldeneyes — who happened to be on the water at the time. But as the trail moves away from the river, everything improves and you hardly have time to register the boulders when you arrive at an information kiosk and the golf course service road which is sometimes trackset.

Turn left and not right unless you want a tour of the remote south end of the Banff Springs Golf Course. After a straight, the road makes an uphill bend to the left, then heads right past a gazebo to the fork where your car is parked.

(It's quite OK from the moral point of view, to say to heck with the last hill and head off right across a green which is dead flat and half as short. This way you hit the plowed bit of service road and have to turn left up the hill to the fork.)

THREE SISTERS TRAILS

Backcountry

22 km of trails
Maximum elevation 1676 m
Map 82 O/3 Canmore

Access From Canmore, follow the Smith-Dorrien/Spray Trail (Spray Lakes Road) out towards the Canmore Nordic Centre. At the end of the hairpin bend, turn left into Three Sisters Golf Resorts access road and park near the gate without blocking it. If parking is a problem, drive a little further up the highway to Quarry Lake parking lot on the left-hand side.

At some time in the future, you're going to be able to drive up the access road and park much closer to your objective. But right now — winter 1992 — the access described is the most suitable one for the following two loops.

Area Overview Although Three Sisters Golf Resorts own a part of the land you are about to set skis on, they have no quarrel with walkers or skiers using the old roads. You don't need to keep looking over your shoulder waiting for someone to shout "Hey you!", or feel righteously indignant about access to your favourite valley being cut off. The "No Trespassing" signs are mainly there to discourage law suits should someone be silly enough to fall down a mine shaft.

Photo above:
Grotto Mtn. from the viewpoint at the end of Meadow loop.

The potential is enormous, given the existing roads both navigable and overgrowing. I mean, the area is about three times as big as the neighbouring Nordic Centre, and the terrain very similar with benches, maturing forest and the odd reclaimed meadow with rusting artifacts. For added spice are holes in the ground flagged with "Extremely Dangerous" signs. The long shadows flung from Mt. Lawrence Grassi, The Three Sisters and Wind Ridge ensure that what snow there is stays nice and cold. As you might expect, the higher you go the better the snow. In good years you can transfer from hiking to skiing boots in about the third week of November when the grizzlies are still going walkabout.

Assuming some development is going ahead, it's going to take some time before accesses are sorted out. So while the residential road system is being established, expect disappearing roads, new roads and roads which change without notice. The only points of reference which won't change are the powerlines.

The two loops are nothing more than suggestions in the small area between the entrance and Three Sisters Creek. It's quite likely, says Brooke Melchin, that the company will develop their own trail system which, given the vast number of existing roads, would be mainly a matter of putting up route markers. Keep tuned.

MEADOW LOOP

Easy
8 km loop
Height gain 83 m
Maximum elevation 1433 m

An easy introductory loop to a viewpoint in the environs of No. 5 Mine. A spate of "No Trespassing" signs marking Three Sisters Golf Resorts boundary are useful navigational aids.

Start off along the Three Sisters Golf Resorts Access Road. Shortly after passing the information trailer turn first right (berm), then transfer first left onto a lesser road, taking all the animal traffic, which climbs onto a bench and parallels the access road. At the T junction, dirt pushed into mounds are only a minor irritation and you can easily push through to the powerline on the right. You're going to be coming back this way so remember the thumbnail clearing opposite.

Turn left and ski under the double powerlines, watching for the first road sneaking into the trees on the right. An orange post gives forewarning. It's an easy climb up to a 4-way junction despite some wobbling around some reclaimed workings. Almost as soon as you cross the intersection, you're descending alongside another set of workings. On skis your best bet is the open draw right of the road where the snow lies deepest. Arriving on a major road which for clarity I'll call "Lower Bench Road", turn right.

The next bit along a bench fascinates with a view to one side of the reclaimed strip mine down below and on the other a rock cut with coal seams, and a bloody great hole in the ground surrounded by tottery rock. At a hollow overgrown with alders two side roads leave the left side of the road in a V. Go down either; the left-hand is the longer route since you have to ski back along the third side of what turns out to be a triangle. After they join, you ski below the filled-in entrance to No. 5 Mine to another road come up from across the meadow and follow it up to the meadow's highest corner. Last time I was here the graders were busy scraping up the grass lower down so I can't guarantee a quiet few moments, but there is a most amazing view of Grotto Mountain seen from end to end, blushing pinky yellow in the low winter sun.

Return The road from across the meadow turns into the forest and straightaway joins "Lower Bench Road" at a T-junction. Turn right and ski back past No. 5 Mine and the rock cut, only this time stay right of your approach road and treat yourself to an easy downhill. Just as Pigeon Mountain comes into sight above the aspens, step left onto another road which has the effrontery to end a few metres before the powerline right-of-way. However, I'm sure you can manage a few minutes of shuffling between trees. Arriving at the trail under the power poles turn left, pass two roads on the left and so arrive back at the thumbnail clearing where you can either follow your incoming tracks back to the Access Road, or, for a change, take the next road to the right off the right-of-way called option on the map opposite.

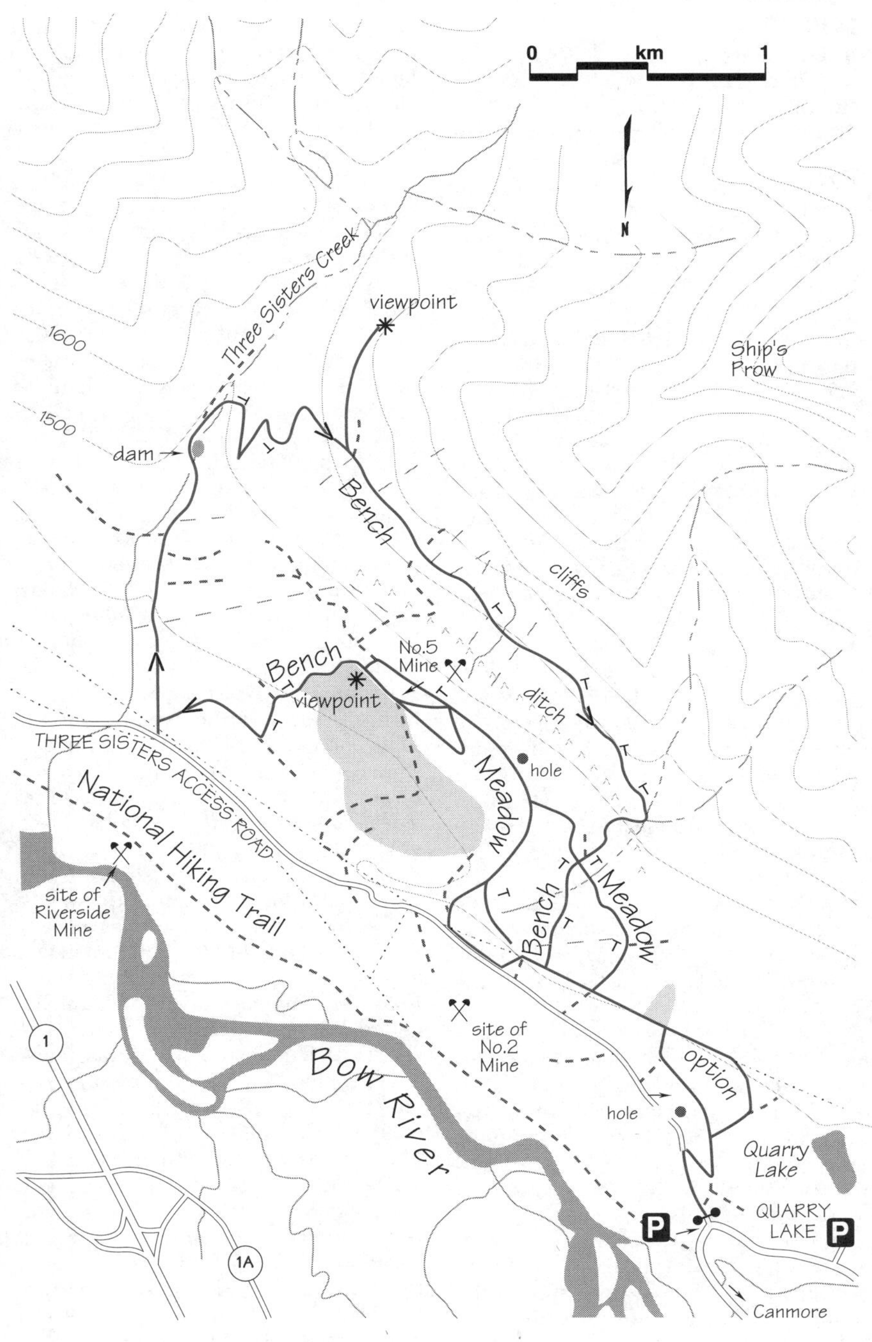
0 km 1
N
viewpoint
Three Sisters Creek
1600
1500
Ship's Prow
dam
Bench
cliffs
No.5 Mine
Bench
viewpoint
ditch
hole
Meadow
THREE SISTERS ACCESS ROAD
National Hiking Trail
site of Riverside Mine
Bench
Meadow
1
site of No.2 Mine
Bow River
option
hole
Quarry Lake
QUARRY LAKE
1A
Canmore

BENCH

Intermediate
14 km loop only
Height gain loop 327 m
Maximum elevation at viewpoint 1676 m

Even the most mundane road can be exciting under snow if it has a few hills and this one has some zingers and occasionally leads to viewpoints. Ski the loop in the clockwise direction and wait until Three Sisters Creek is frozen unless you think paddling in Solomons makes a pleasant change to skiing. I write from experience having skied the loop anti-clockwise and faced with two watery crossings of Three Sisters Creek decided the climb back up to the top of the hill was the greater of two evils. I was wrong and vowed to treat myself to some Gortex socks for my next birthday. Of course there is no reason why you can't just ski it anti-clockwise to the viewpoint and return the same way.

Follow the second paragraph directions for Meadow Loop to the powerline.

Head left and disregarding all roads to the right, (the second one is your return road), follow the trail under the power poles back to the Access Road. Here turn right and ski alongside the road for a very short distance to where "Lower Bench Road" (next road) turns off to the right. Simply follow it up the hill past the bench with the rock cut to its closest approach to the reclaimed strip mine which has risen up to meet it. Cut left into the meadow.

You're probably asking "why can't I continue along "Lower Bench Road"? It's obviously cutting across to Three Sisters Creek". That's what I thought from studying old air photos with a magnifying glass, so I tried it and was soon having a horrible time tangling with mini spruce trees and alder bushes needing three metres of snow — which they won't ever get. So step onto the meadow and follow a vague road heading right around the south-west corner and down the south edge to the south-east corner where a "No Trespassing" sign marks the roads's more obvious continuance in the trees. Keep left at a junction half-way down the hill. At the bottom turn right and emerge in another five minutes or so onto Three Sisters Creek road.

Turn right and start the slow climb up Three Sisters Creek, passing all manner of cutlines and overgrowing roads which presumably at one time connected with "Lower Bench Road". Suddenly, the valley narrows. Cross Three Sisters Creek below the rock and concrete dam, then fork right and re-cross the creek above the reservoir. This leaves you speculating at the bottom of a steep bank topped by vertical cliffs of yellow glacial till. Tread lightly up the middle of the slope (scree beneath the snow), then head diagonally right on a discernable trail into the forest where the road recommences and makes three zigzags with out-sized corners for viewstops of The Three Sisters. The last zig is a bit of a bummer but is followed by a much flatter section to the high point of the loop at a T-junction with wood pile.

If you feel like visiting the viewpoint, turn left and follow the slowly rising road to its end at an open slope (view of The Three Sisters) where a game trail carries on around a steep corner. It was here I got a nasty shock one early November. Fresh grizzly tracks. It's stupid I know, but somehow you never associate bears with skiing. The bear had climbed up from the creek and for all I knew was lurking around the corner of the trail looking for a den. I didn't fancy a wildlife drama unfolding with me as the star victim, but before leaving I hurriedly prepared to shoot off a half dozen shots of the view— after all, that is what I'd come up for — only to find I'd run out of film. Hoping the shutter clicks didn't sound too much like a tasty morsel, I fumble changed the film while keeping my eyes glued on the corner. No doubt if the bear had come snuffling into view I'd have got off a lovely close-up to be remarked upon later after the RCMP had developed the film to see what had caused the tragedy. Anyway, I got the required shots (all in focus), then

The view across Three Sisters Creek to First and Second Sister.

hastened back down the road to the wood pile for a viewless lunch without once looking back over my shoulder to see if the bear was tagging along behind. Hardly likely! On a Bow Waters Canoe Club outing with 10 people, such an incident would cause little comment other than "Oh look, there's some bear tracks, let's have lunch here and look at the view", but when you're by yourself you tend to get a little emotional.

Back to the loop. For the next couple of kilometres you are skiing along a bench between alder bushes which need clipping in places. A few thousand years ago you would have been skiing along the top of a lateral moraine and a peek over the edge would have disclosed a wall to wall glacier instead of the Trans-Canada Highway. As it is you can see nothing much except a vague glimmer between trees, numerous cutlines left and right and a big cliff on the left. Near the end of the traverse, sporadic downhills precede a fabulous downhill run all the way down to the powerline. Shoot straight at the 4-way junction.

All that remains is to head left under the powerline to the thumbnail clearing, then return the way you came up. Drivers excepted, stop off at the Rose & Crown for a pint; you've earned it after following this description.

More about the area From the moment the first train arrived at a divisional point named Canmore in 1884, free-lance coal prospectors were busy looking over the land west of the river, and by the next year Marsh Mine on the north-east slope of Wind Ridge and Cochrane Mine just north of the power plant were going full blast. Ultimately though, all individuals and small companies sold their leases to the mighty Canadian Anthracite Coal Company (CACC) whose American shareholders were also big wigs with Eau Claire Lumbering Company. Their first mine was No. 1 in Canmore Creek.

Starting in 1891 the CACC leased the Canmore property to H.W. McNeill who opened the hugely successful No. 2 Mine in 1903. In 1938 the CACC and McNeill's Canmore Coal Company consolidated under the name Canmore Mines. Without doubt, the best known miner during the optimum period of 1938-1960 was Lawrence Grassi who spent all his spare moments building trails in the Lake O'Hara area and up to Grassi Lakes and another one up Pigeon Mountain which was never finished. For his efforts he was rewarded, long after he was dead of course, by having the mountain overlooking the coal lands named after him.

By the mid 1960's, coal orders began falling off, and despite a lucrative contract with Japanese steel mills, the writing was on the wall. "That which was not is. That which is....will never be again.". Scrawled on the wall of a small building still standing at Number 2 Mine site this little gem no doubt refers to the environment *pace* peace symbol, but could apply equally well to the coal mines, inasmuch that Canmore Mines sold out to the U.S. based Dillingham Corporation in 1969. It was during this unsettled period in the early 1970's that a strip mine operated north of Three Sisters Creek (the meadow). In 1971 No. 5 Mine closed down after 30 years of operation. Actually, some of the roads you are skiing date back even earlier than the 1940's to the late 1920's when there had been some initial development of the nearby Musgrove Slope.

Around 1972, anticipating the final closure by seven years, the real estate arm of Dillingham Corporation had UMA Engineering develop a master plan for a winter resort area, but since no suitable ski slopes could be found, changed it to a summer resort plan with cottages and one golf course. When the land was sold to Patrician Land Corporation another concept plan was ordered in 1981 on "one of the largest undeveloped sections of prime tourist property in the province". At a cost of 875 million, "Echo Resort" (new resort would echo Vail) with mandatory golf course would extend into Wind Creek where Olympic ski trails would wind about the residential road system — a whimsical idea given that four years to a day before the Olympics there was absolutely no snow in Wind Valley. As it happened the idea fizzled on the drawing board when the parent company, Peter Pocklington's Fidelity Trust, went into receivership.

When the land was sold to Three Sisters Golf Resorts, yet another concept plan was drawn up in 1991, also by UMA Engineering, with proposals for several golf courses and accessories like condos, strip malls and wildlife viewing area — the whole bigger than the towns of Canmore and Banff put together. Without going into the machinations between the developers and the Economic Development and the Environmental departments of the Tory Government, let me just say that I personally am tiring of golf courses in mountains for a large number of reasons. Of course the fact that I was once turfed off Kananaskis Country Golf Course for wearing a Mo Zeegers T-shirt is probably something to do with it as well. With the way things are going in the Bow Valley — there were proposals for 8 golf courses at last count which seems a little excessive — tourists will soon be booking their two weeks vacation on the longest golf course in the World stretching from Banff to Seebe, and which, given the Tory government's call for accelerated development in K-Country, could ultimately extend all the way up the Kananaskis Valley and back down the Smith-Dorrien and Spray to Banff.

Skogan Pass from Dead Man Flat. From the traverse is a superb view of The Three Sisters.

SKOGAN PASS FROM DEAD MAN FLAT Backcountry

Intermediate
9.5 km
Height gain 670 m
Maximum elevation 2073 m
Map 82 O/3 Canmore,
82 J/14 Spray Lakes Reservoir

Access Trans-Canada Highway. At Dead Man Flat interchange, follow signs to Alpine Resort Haven. At the top of the winding hill, turn right, instead of left, into a parking area which is unlikely to be plowed.

Overview In lean snow years, the Skogan Pass trail from Dead Man Flat lost its popularity. And still people shun the trail in winter. Well OK, so it's a powerline right-of-way and access road combination. But with plentiful snow, it's a thousand times more enjoyable on skis than on foot, and you know you're going to get a good run down at the end of the day.

Depart the parking lot via an old road at the top right-hand corner, currently the start to the Mt. Allan Centennial trail. In a few minutes you intersect the powerline and turn left, still en route to Mt. Allan.

Ahead of you the right-of-way rises in many steps to the skyline, but the boredom of seeing where you're going to be toiling for next hour is relieved by two forays into the forest on the left side. The first one is quite long. After the Mt. Allan trail turns off to the right, the incline steepens for the final climb to the skyline — a false one as it turns out. The power poles plummet into a trough then rise again to the summit of the pass up a slope which would not disgrace the 90-m ski jump at Canada Olympic Park. You can if you want tag along this way. Better though to follow the sensible access road which waves good-bye to the powerlines and zigzags uphill, aiming to traverse below Little Pigeon Mountain on open slopes. Don't laugh too hard at the old sign tacked to a tree telling motorists the road ahead is closed to traffic, because it may just come true if the Canmore and Bow Valley Chamber of Commerce gets it wish to have a highway built over the pass to Ribbon Creek.

Around the next bend the road disappears temporarily and you have to navigate the rising traverse on trust with just a fringe of yellow grasses marking the outside edge. I've never skied here without the wind blasting away, swirling the loose snow about. But what an amazing view-point for the Three Sisters, Wind Ridge and the superb north ridge of Collembola!

Back into the forest, the road reasserts itself, dipping and rising around every fold of the hills on much-improved snow. It's maddening; at one point you're only metres away from the lowest gap in the watershed ridge. But no, the access road must draw close to the powerline it is accessing so this involves another 90 metres of totally unnecessary height gain and means crossing the ridge further to the south. Definitely keep left at one junction, unless you wish to access the ski jump.

Presently the ground flattens and no doubt you'll meet ski tracks come up from the other side of the pass from Ribbon Creek. At the height of land, double back right and climb up to the right-of-way where all winds meet and sing in the wires, and where every great view is spoilt by power poles.

Return Once past the open traverse, progress quickens up considerably down the switchbacks. Even the right-of-way is great fun.

More about the trail When Dominion geologist George Dawson and his party crossed the pass in the 1880's making for the coal basin around present-day Canmore, an old Indian trail was already available. By the 1920's, forest rangers riding between the cabin at Dead Man Flat and Boundary Cabin at Ribbon Creek were calling it the Canmore Boundary Trail over Dead Man Pass and stringing a telephone line along the route via trees or tripods. Up to about 10 years ago you could still gawk at tripods and insulators

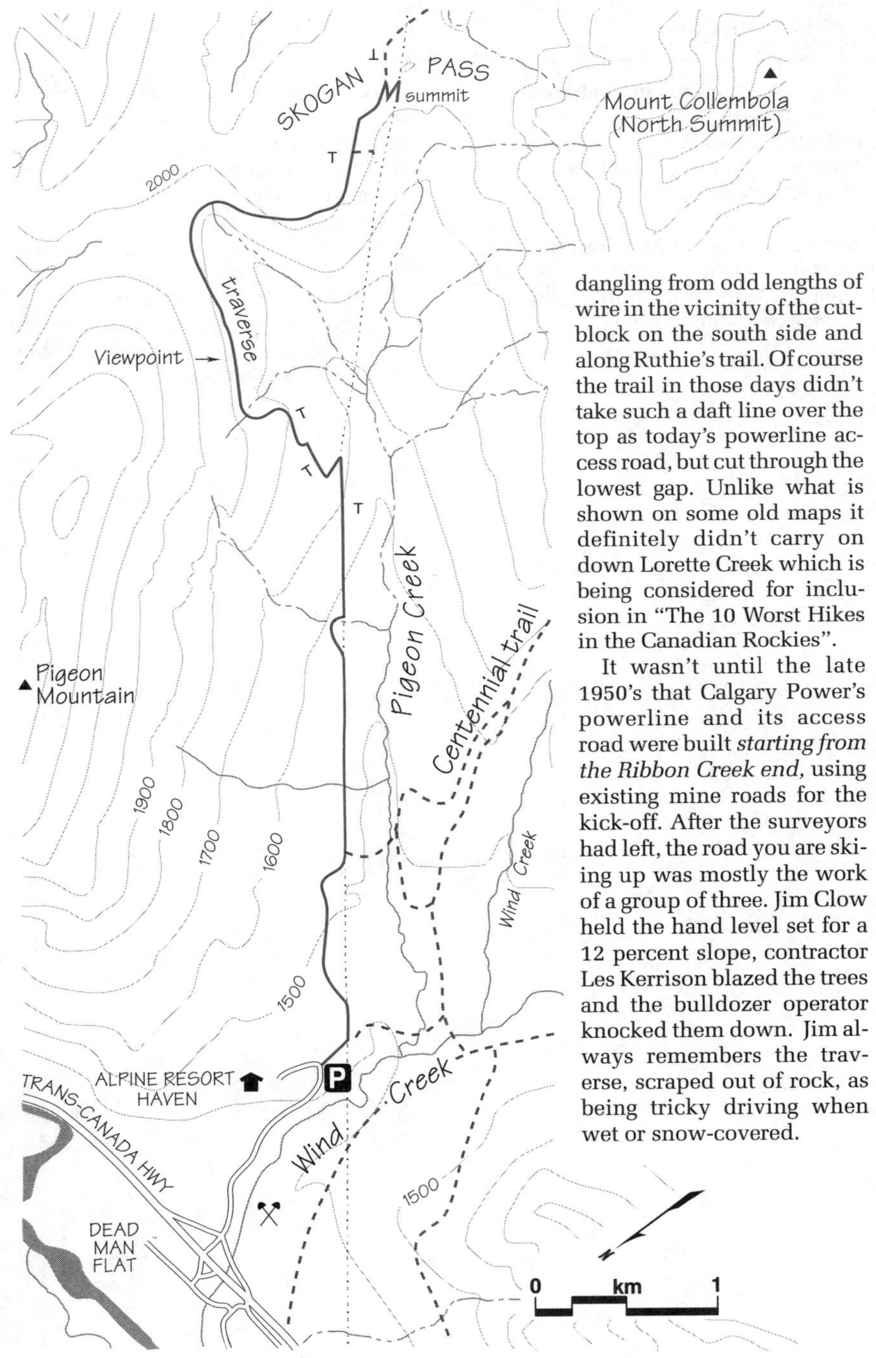

dangling from odd lengths of wire in the vicinity of the cut-block on the south side and along Ruthie's trail. Of course the trail in those days didn't take such a daft line over the top as today's powerline access road, but cut through the lowest gap. Unlike what is shown on some old maps it definitely didn't carry on down Lorette Creek which is being considered for inclusion in "The 10 Worst Hikes in the Canadian Rockies".

It wasn't until the late 1950's that Calgary Power's powerline and its access road were built *starting from the Ribbon Creek end,* using existing mine roads for the kick-off. After the surveyors had left, the road you are skiing up was mostly the work of a group of three. Jim Clow held the hand level set for a 12 percent slope, contractor Les Kerrison blazed the trees and the bulldozer operator knocked them down. Jim always remembers the traverse, scraped out of rock, as being tricky driving when wet or snow-covered.

HEART CREEK

Backcountry

Easy with one intermediate hill
4.6 km return
Height gain 40 m
Maximum elevation 1370 m
Map 82 O/3 Canmore

Access East-bound Trans-Canada Highway. At Lac des Arc interchange drive to Heart Creek parking lot on the south side of the highway.

Overview The summer interpretive trail which works equally as well as a winter interpretive trail, is short and awe-inspiring. The most exercise comes from stepping on and off bridges; the greatest danger is running into pedestrians with dogs. It's a great pity you have to start from the Heart Creek parking lot since it turns an easy ski into an intermediate one. If you're a beginner, try and persuade your driver to drop you off at the creek crossing on the Trans-Canada Highway.

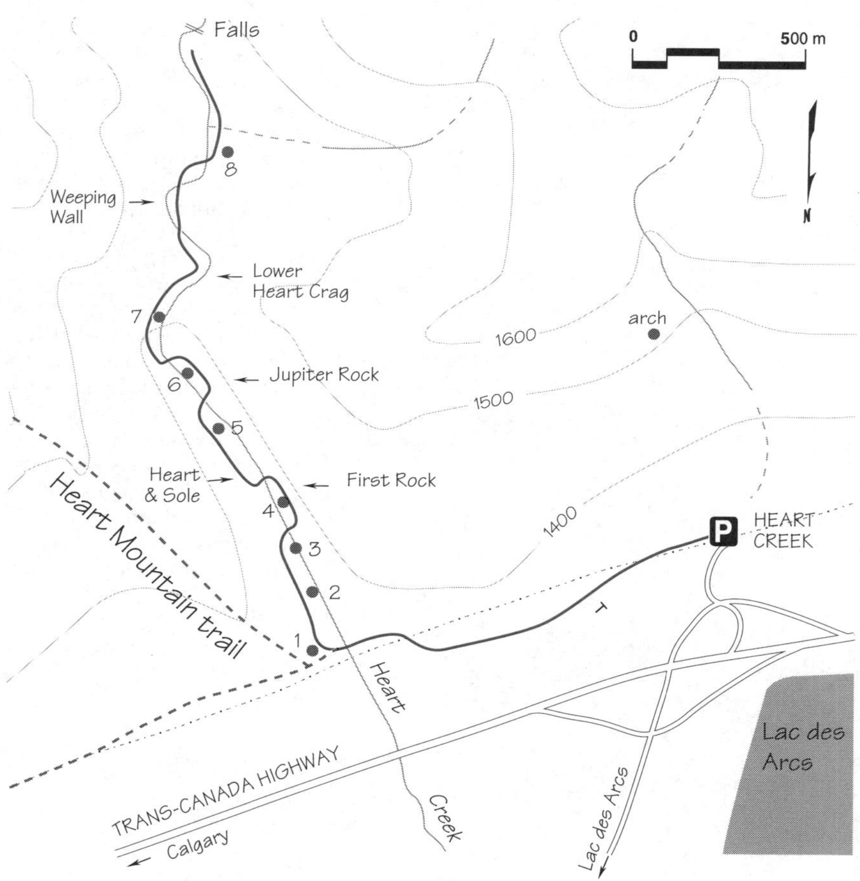

Lower Heart Crag from the 6th bridge

From the parking lot the trail rounding the ridge under the powerline into Heart Creek is desperately narrow and has this straight steep downhill. Make up your mind to go for it. Bailing out in full view of motorists zipping along the Trans-Canada Highway is very embarrassing because you never know who's watching. Once over with, the rest of route is a doddle.

Cross over bridge number one to the trail junction on the east bank of Heart Creek. Turn right and simply follow the trail up valley, crossing seven more bridges. The further in you get, the narrower the valley, and the higher the cliffs on either side. West-side cliffs have names: First Rock above sign # 4, Jupiter Rock with its Cyclops Eye above sign # 6, Spectacular Lower Heart Crag between signs #7 and 8. That's Heart and Sole above the third bridge. Between the sixth and seventh bridges ice smears on the weeping wall may be decorated with a few fledgling ice climbers.

Strange isn't it, you'd think it would be glacial in this sunless canyon, but it's not. In fact, it's unnaturally warm, a mini ecoclimate created by the unfrozen waters of the creek condensing into clouds of mist. It's a great place to watch dippers.

The trail ends below the high rock step. In summer, the much-touted waterfall which is heard and never seen lies hidden in a fold of the canyon walls, accessible only by a paddle and scramble. Ah! you think, now it is winter I will be able to admire this frozen confection of ice without getting my feet wet. It is, therefore, a horrid disappointment to see the river running as free and as deep as ever and to hear the waterfall falling as usual. Unlike normal creeks, 75% of Heart Creek arises from springs which burst out of the ground only a short distance beyond the rock step.

Return A nice glide.

JEWELL PASS VIA QUAITE CREEK

Backcountry

Intermediate
4.5 km to Pass
11 km circuit return
Height gain 290 m
Maximum elevation 1630 m
Map 82 O/3 Canmore

Access East-bound Trans-Canada Highway. Park on the shoulder at Quaite Creek logging road opposite the Loder Peak signpost. Note this is not the official summer start.

Facilities Backcountry group campground in Quaite Creek with picnic tables.

Overview Beloved by mountain bikers, the old logging road to Jewel Pass makes a short fun day for skiers with nothing too desperate. Don't be put off by lack of the white fluffy stuff at the highway. Sheltered from scouring winds, the valley holds the snow really well. In mid march of 1991, for instance, the trail sign at the pass was down by my knees and the snow perfect powder. This trail is official so look for signposts.

Head up the logging road into Quaite Creek, a narrow valley with a bend halfway; the road squashed between the river and rocky slopes with whiter-than-snow slabs of Palliser limestone. I hope you haven't chosen a day when 20 Boy Scouts are marching to the campground, or I should say *stumbling* to the campground, thinking of the whacking great holes in the trail I encountered the last time I skied the trail. Usually, such tracks end at the sawmill site where the valley opens up into a large sun-trap meadow. Though 2 km into the trip is a little too early for lunch, you'll find picnic tables for elevenses located across the meadow at the edge of the trees.

Just beyond the meadow, in a flurry of official signs, the way-in logging road divides and makes a loop with Jewell Pass. The official summer route follows the right-hand (west) road which is wider with more concentrated uphills, has better quality snow and above all, is shorter. A couple of signposts mark the pass.

Circuit If you do the circuit I like to keep the west road snow intact for the descent — one of K-Country's great downhills. Going clockwise then, keep left on the east leg, ignoring all kinds of overgrown roads turning right. This east road is a long-winded affair which takes twice as long as the official route, winding in and out of the contours of McConnell Ridge, climbing, descending, facing every mountain in turn, but never so narrow or overgrown that the way isn't obvious. Pass by occasional trees marked by an orange X which show you you're still on route. Moose tracks replace scout tracks and coyotes whelp in the boggy heartland of the valley. "Where on earth is the Pass?" is a thought which keeps surfacing.

High up, when heading straight for Barrier Lake Lookout at the time, stop and look back at Grotto Mountain since it's the best view you're ever going to get. Shortly after this, the road begins the sweep across to the pass. But what's this, the road ends? Don't panic. For a couple of minutes head in a 2 o'clock direction, following trees daubed with orange Xs to another road. Turn left and keep left (all right roads lead into the heartland and degenerate). Some last minute climbing which included in 1991 a grade 7 scramble over a large fallen tree brings you to the pass at a 4-way junction with signpost: left for Jewell Pass and Prairie View trails, right for Quaite Creek west leg, straight on for the option.

Jewell Pass is ho-hum as a viewpoint; too many tall trees in the way. McConnell Ridge and the east summit of Heart Mountain are your lot and both are tree-covered. A viewing platform might not be a bad idea.

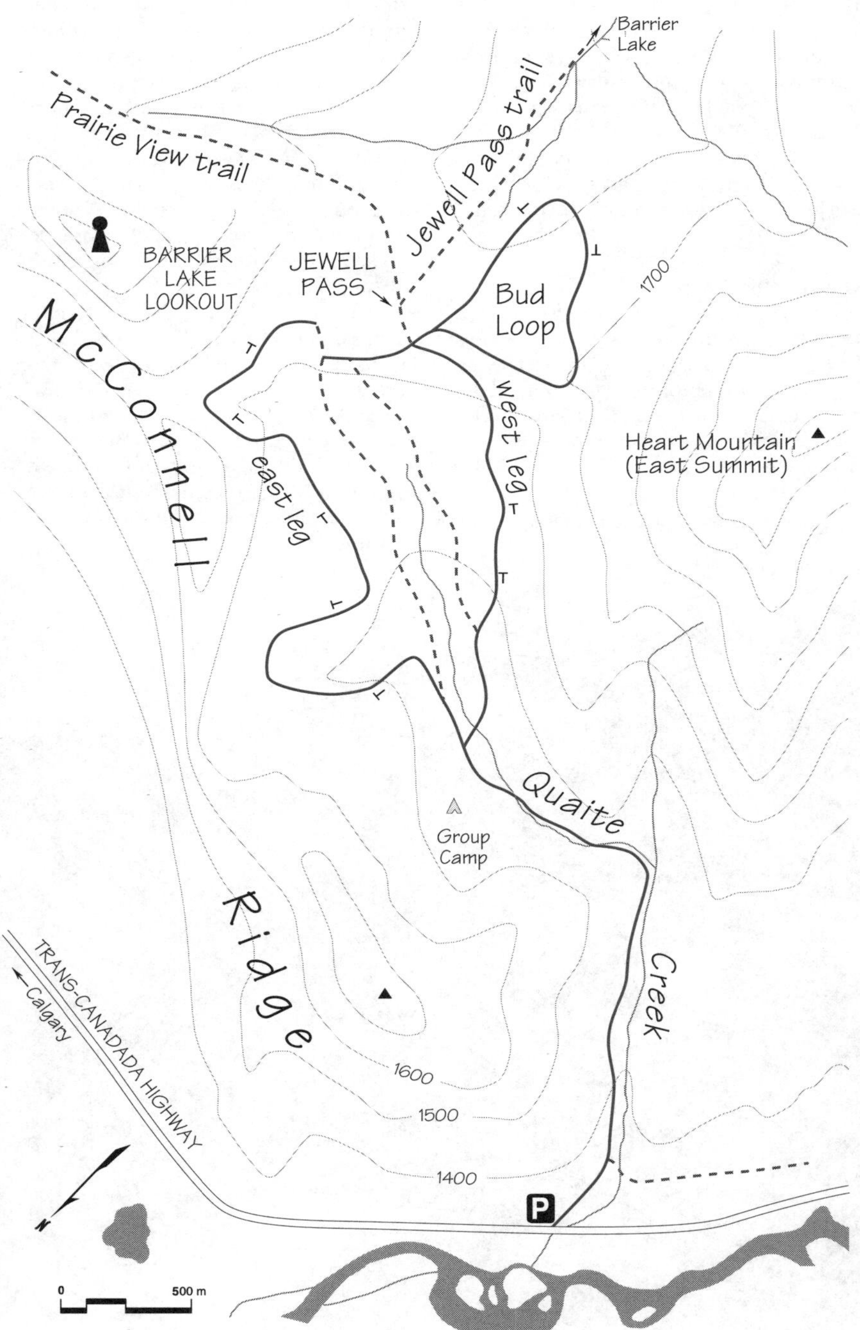
Barrier
Lake
Prairie View trail
Jewell Pass trail
BARRIER
LAKE
LOOKOUT
JEWELL
PASS
Bud
Loop
1700
McConnell
east leg
west leg
Heart Mountain
(East Summit)
Quaite
Group
Camp
Ridge
Creek
TRANS-CANADADA HIGHWAY
Calgary
1600
1500
1400
P
N
0
500 m

Descent Turn right onto the road with the signpost. The west leg is on my list of memorable downhills; views of Mts. Yamnuska, Fable and Grotto flash by unnoticed as you plow through the powder. Lower down, when the speed slows, you pass two overgrown roads to the right, then make a final rush across a bridge to the junction in the meadow. Turn left and glide for home.

Option: Bud Loop
If hungry for more light skiing, there's a little loop on the south side of the pass (2.5 km, 105 m height gain and loss). Before you go I should tell you that all the roads come courtesy of Bud Jewell who had a lease to log Douglas Firs still standing after a fire.

On descent, the west leg road gives a good view of the gable end of McConnell Ridge. Yamnuska peeps over the top.

From the 4-way junction I've just mentioned you climb straight up the hill and step over a fallen tree. Remember this. Carry on, climbing happily up the obvious road which edges along the north side of watershed ridge towards Heart Mountain, then crosses over to the south side and makes wavy downhills. This is so much fun while it lasts, but when it dumps you at a low point in an aspen grove, your spirits will be sagging. Here you are, somewhere in the depths of Jewell Creek, and you've got to get back to the pass. The return really isn't bad at all. The road turns sharp left and after a steep step peters out in an almost flat draw where the sun falls in and all winds are stilled. Ski a straight line up the draw to the watershed ridge and emerge on the outgoing road at the fallen tree. Here turn right and schuss down to the 4-way junction at the pass.

PRAIRIE VIEW — Backcountry

Intermediate
5 km to lookout site
Height gain 421 m
Maximum elevation 1798 m
Map 82 O/3 Canmore

Access Kananaskis Trail (Hwy. 40) at Barrier Dam parking lot.

Facilities Parking lot with washrooms

Overview The old fire road to the site of Pigeon Lookout makes a fine ski trail even if it is a trifle steep in one part. Well, beginners can always walk down that bit. Never go on a day when the mountains are socked in. What's needed is bright clear weather for the view plus sufficient snow which may be difficult to determine at the trailhead. Multiplying the amount at the parking lot by four gives a fairly good indication of what to expect.

Start off by walking across Barrier Lake dam. On with the skis and follow the road which winds round a meadow and up to a 4-way junction with signpost under the powerlines. Cross under the powerlines into the forest and climb one straight kilometre to a T-junction with Stoney trail (sign). Turn right, then almost immediately left onto the fire road.

The fire road kicks off with 11 easy zigzags through forest allowing absolutely no view. The 11th and final bend, a left-hander marked by a piece of yellow flagging tied around a tree (summer route to Yamnuska Centre), signals the start of more serious climbing up the east ridge. After the angle eases the road rehabilitates to a narrow trail traversing the south side of the ridge to a level opening where the lookout used to stand.

At one time the steps of Pigeon Lookout were available for collapse and coffee. In lieu of steps I recommend this spot for a standard K-Country bench or picnic table. Shuffling around, juggling poly bags, thermoses and gloves with fingers suffering from rigor mortis of the metacarpals, it's hard to give the stunning view to the south the attention it deserves. Still no prairie view note, but lots of mountains lining the Kananaskis Valley and when you tire of mountains you can play the game of counting ice fishermen on Barrier Lake.

Return A downhill nearly 5 km long! Bear in mind the large cairn located smack in the middle of the third and longest zig.

Option: McConnell Ridge
Half a kilometre away the main backbone of the ridge either beckons or repels above a line of cliffs. If you're in the former category, it's probably easier to ditch the skis not far beyond the trail sign and thrutch your way up 60 metres of steep ground to — a repeater station which comes as a bit of a shock. Finally, you get to see the prairies over the treetops of the east ridge.

I have never tried skiing along the rest of Prairie View trail to Jewell Pass, but once past the rocky ridge I should imagine if offers a good downhill run through open forest. If you try it you had better plan on having two cars and escaping down Quaite Creek to the Trans-Canada. Jewell Pass trail also lures with the promise of a loop, but with the usual minimal snow low down the idea soon palls *as a ski trip*. I once met a man sitting at the junction of Jewell Creek and Stoney trail pulling on his hiking boots to hike up to Jewell Pass. Apparently he had taken the short-cut by skating across the lake from the parking lot. "I always carry a long pole in front of me in case I break through the ice", he explained. I would like to ask that man what other skate & hike trips he recommends since this is obviously a new concept to be passed on to adventure tours racking their brains for new adventures for clients.

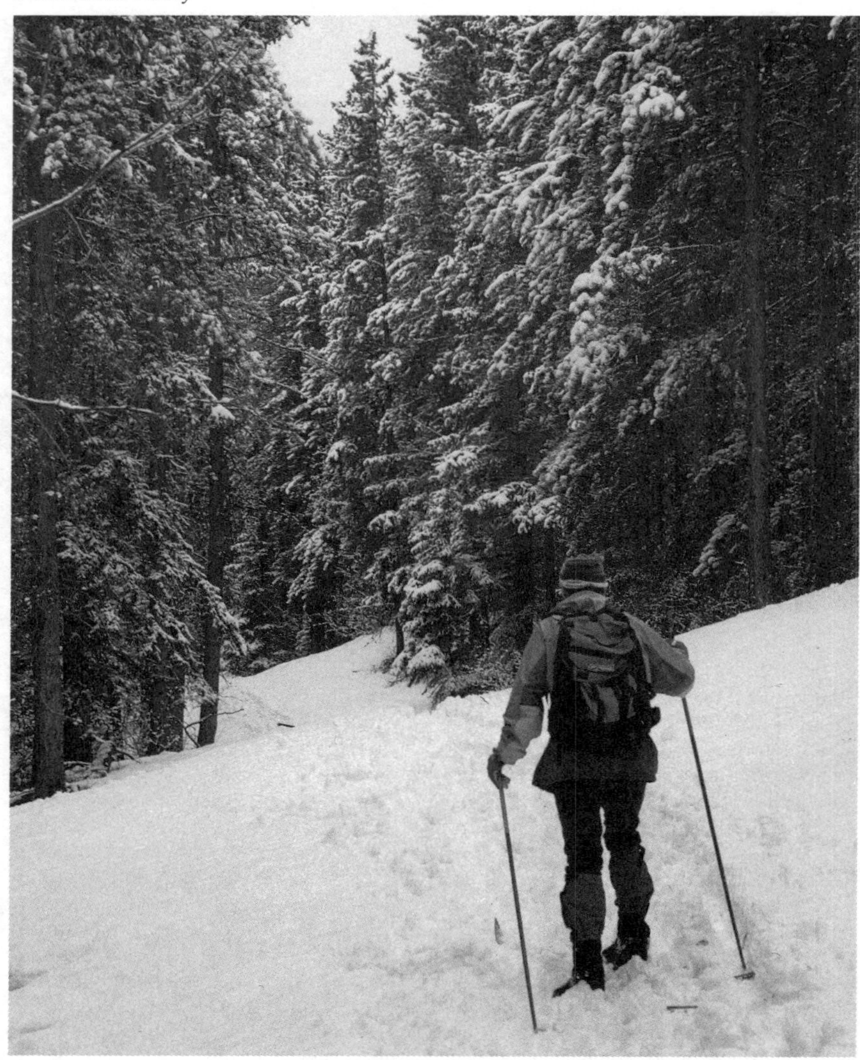

More about the trail For 24 years, the white lookout tower on the east ridge below McConnell Ridge proper was a landmark for people driving up Highway 40. When superseded by Barrier Lake Lookout on top of McConnell Ridge which had a 360 degree view as opposed to a 270 degree view, the old lookout was detached in 1984 and taken back home to the University of Calgary's Kananaskis Centre for Environmental Research which is where it had originated from in the first place. How many people know that the tower was built as a guard tower at POW camp #130. That's it, right next to the Colonel's Cabin, now painted a dull grey and housing artifacts relating to the Station's stint as a POW camp during World War 2.

Over the years the name Pigeon Lookout really confused hikers who thought it was located on Pigeon Mountain further to the west. Neither is it named after the birds. According to Ruthie Oltmann It was named after stool pigeons at the camp.

Photo opposite:
Just starting up the east ridge after the zigzags.

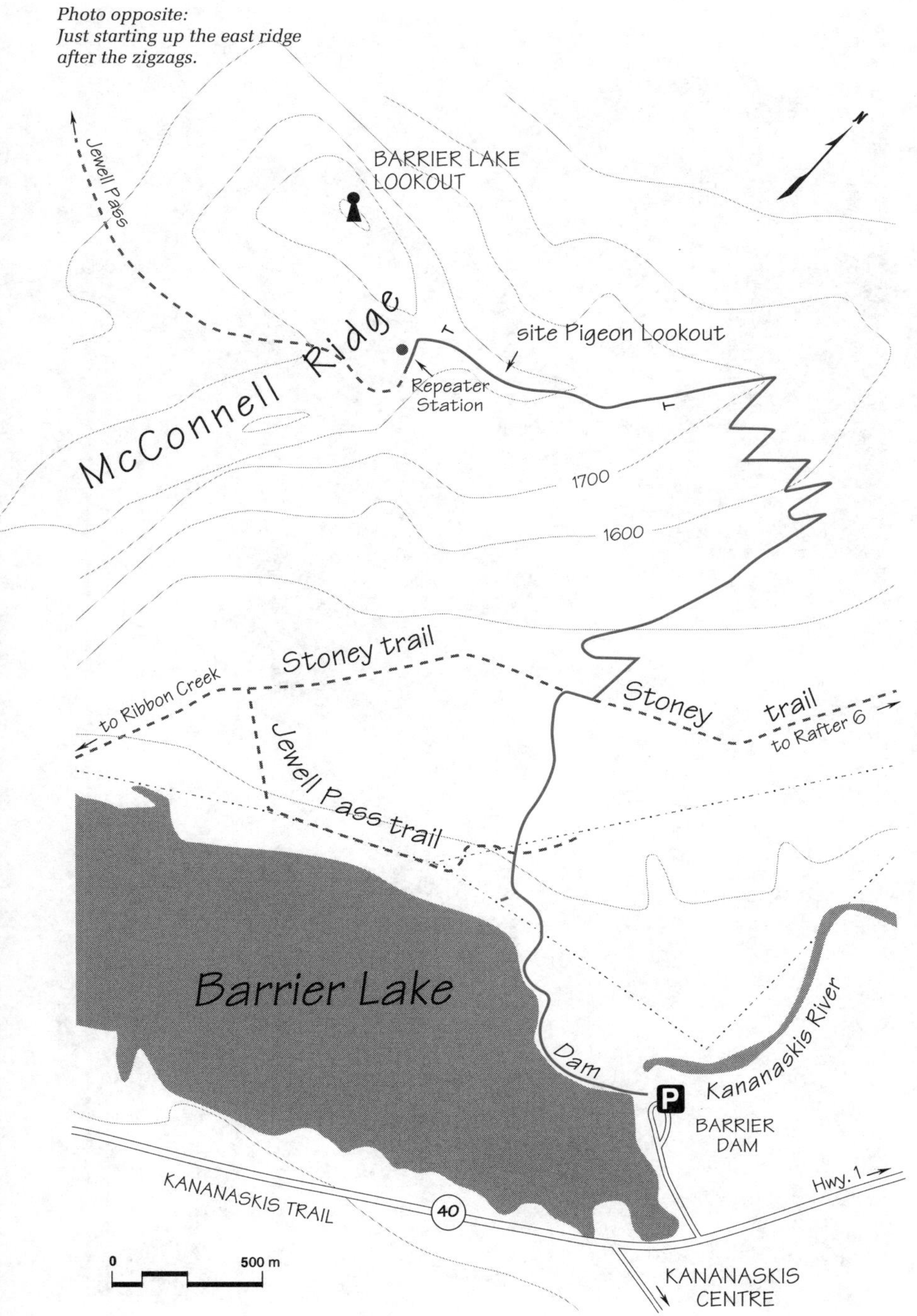

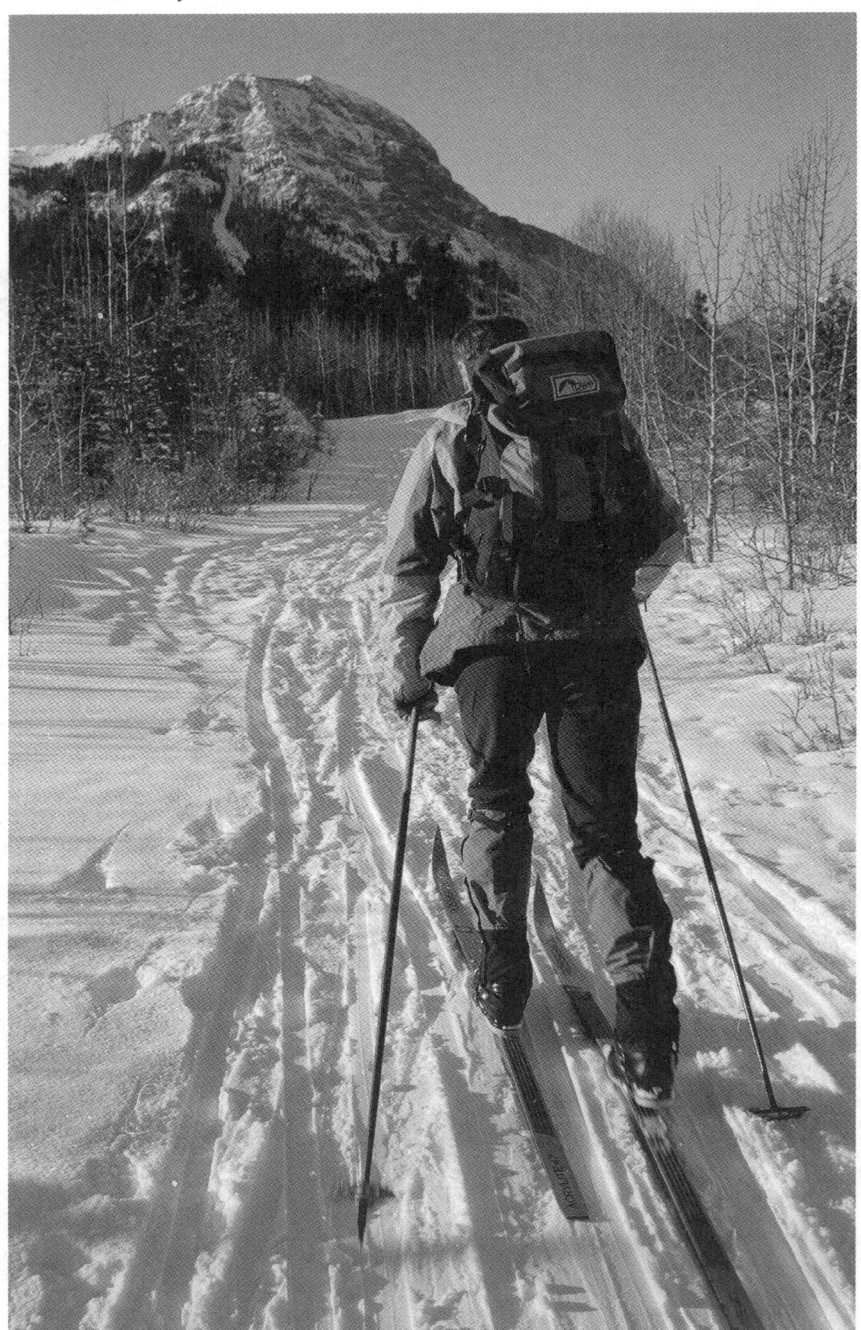

Heading towards Mt. Baldy at the start of the Old Mill Road.

LUSK CREEK TOUR

Backcountry

Intermediate
8 km loop via lower Cutoff
9.5 km loop via higher cutoff
Height gain 213 km
Maximum elevation 1578 m
Map 82 O/3 Canmore,
82 O/2 Jumpingpound Creek

Access Sibbald Creek Trail (SR 68) at Stony Creek day-use area.

Facilities Washroom, picnic tables at parking lot.

Overview In the shadow of Mt. Baldy is a network of old roads, a couple of which are used as official hiking-equestrian trails and duly signposted. A few years ago they were packed by residents of the Kananaskis Centre spearheaded by racers Mike and Judy (Buchanan) Mappin who occasionally ran a snowmobile over them after each fresh snowfall and used them for training and for coaching skiers from the Barrier Mountain Ski Club. Nowadays, perhaps because the Mappins have moved to Canmore and the ski club is defunct, you'll be lucky if someone has broken trail ahead of you, or if they have, it will be in the form of attractive diamond-shaped patterns courtesy of Kananaskis Centre snowshoers. The other thing to know about the trails is that the depth of snow increases dramatically the further you get from the highway, so don't be too put off by the skimpy amount at the parking lot. Finally, I recommend you ski this loop in an anti-clockwise direction. Novices who like all steep hills to be uphills should ski round in a clockwise direction.

From the trail sign you ski up a narrow trail to the Lusk Creek Road and turn right. At the top of the hill with one or two roofs of Kananaskis Centre showing, turn left at another trail sign onto the Old Mill Road. On your left is a very large sign, rapidly becoming historic, with a map of the Lusk Creek automobile tour of logging and reforestation dating back to the early 1970's. Spot the one glaring omission (no prizes).

The Old Mill Road might almost have been designed as a ski trail, so beautifully does it wind uphill through numbered cutblocks and forest patches of all ages to the lower cutoff. The trail surprises by its open aspect giving fabulous views of Mt. Baldy, McConnell Ridge, Yamnuska and that nameless group of hills between Lusk Pass and Sibbald Creek. Near the high point the lower cutoff to Lusk Creek Road turns off to the left at a signpost. In this direction expect one downhill.

Beyond the high point at the junction with the fire road, (easily missed), the pace quickens through a little hidden valley to the upper cutoff identified by a post in the angle of the two roads. If you keep right here, you'll be well on your way to Baldy Pass. The cutoff to left is disappointingly flat through aspens and you wonder why anyone would bother with it, apart from the obvious one of making more kilometrage, when all you get for your efforts is a nasty steep climb from the junction with Lusk Creek Road to the junction with the lower cutoff. Of course, some of you may think of this hill as a required element in what would otherwise be far too easy a day.

Any preconception of these roads being boring will be remedied by the Lusk Creek Road. Down slope of the lower cutoff are some amazing downhills: short steep ones, long gentle winding ones, and one which goes on and on and just when you think it's time to put on the breaks, the road straightens out into a long runout ending with a perfectly placed uphill. You'll know the one I mean.

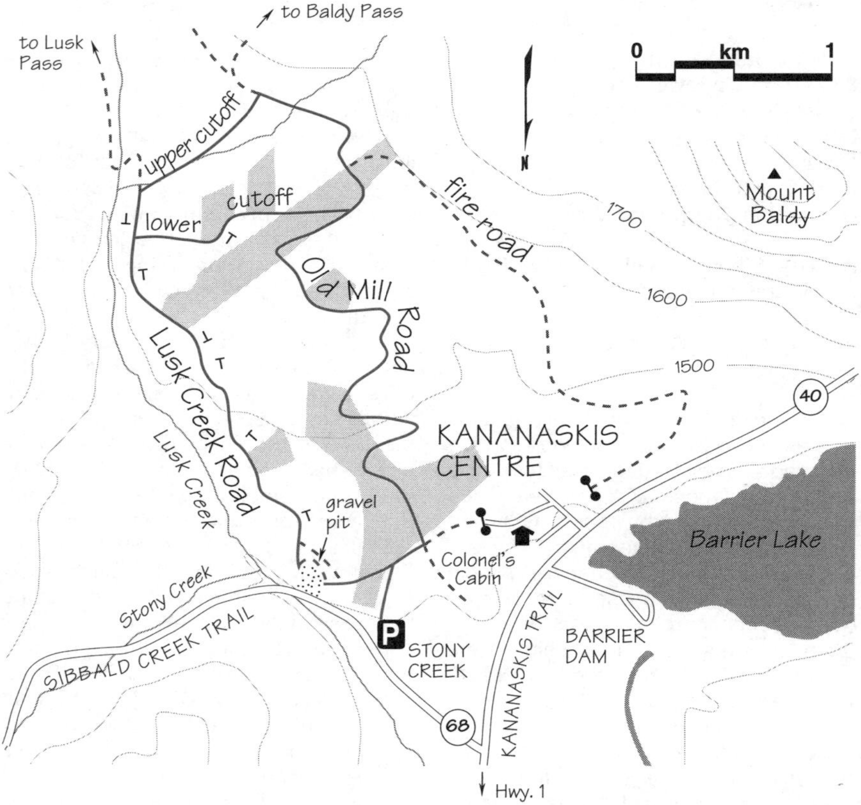

There is, unfortunately, a problem with the lowest point of Lusk Creek Road where a great chunk has been cut out by a gravel pit supplying Highway 68 with gravel. The summer connector is pretty nigh impossible to pick out unless imprinted by hoofs and in lieu of this I suggest you carry on to the pit and edge around the left side to where the road picks up. After this it's a simple ski up the road to the junction where you turn off right down the trail to the parking lot.

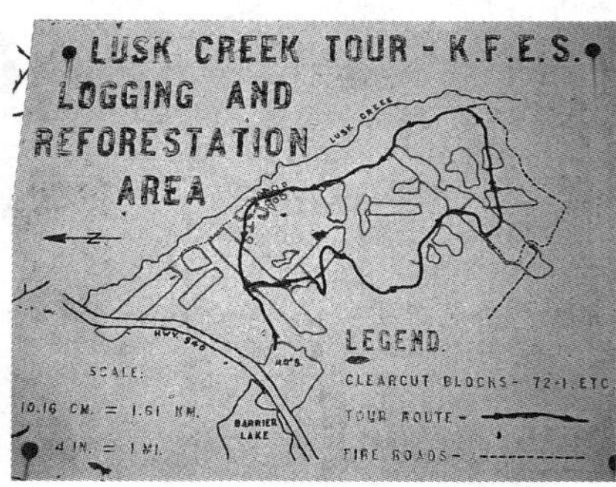

Historic map of the first automobile interpretive tour.

Options: Lusk Pass and Baldy Pass
See pages 62 and 64 for descriptions and maps.

More about the trails As you will see, the forest between Lusk Creek and Mt. Baldy has been considerably changed from what nature intended by experimental thinning, nursery beds, sample plots, transect plots, exotic species plots etc. It all started in 1932 when the Dominion Forest Service were looking for an experimental plot representative of the eastern slopes. Some plot. It extended south to Wasootch Creek, west to Marmot Basin, and north to Pigeon Lookout, a total of 62.60 square miles worked mainly by men from unemployed relief camps and by youths from youth training programmes intended to alleviate unemployment. The road built to the superintendent's cottage in 1934 was of course the fledging Highway 40, although it took a completely different tack to today's road by running along the *west* bank of the Kananaskis River.

At the outbreak of World War 2 the area where the buildings stand now was transformed into POW Camp #130. The POW's, when not tunnelling, climbing Mt. Baldy or turning out watercolours of Mt. Baldy, were set to work planting Scots pines, salvaging fire-killed wood at Ribbon Creek around Hummingbird Plume Lookout or clearing land for Barrier Lake Reservoir which MLA David Carter has suggested be renamed Prisoner or Prisoner of War Lake. The POW's built most of the barracks which were donated after the war ended to youth hostels up and down the Icefields Parkway, and if the bunk beds were thrown in for good measure it wouldn't surprise me in the least.

After the war ended the Forest Experiment Station became a Forestry School for field employees (replaced in 1960 by the Forest Technology School in Hinton). Most of the roads you are skiing on date from this period of the 1950's, 1960's, early 1970's. The Old Mill Road, for instance, was bulldozed in 1951 by the Olorenshaw Logging Company needing access to 300 acres of spruce at the head of the west fork of Lusk Creek. And come to think of it, the Lusk Creek Tour research project was the very first automobile interpretive tour, much like the newfangled tour in the Jumpingpound where you drive around comparing different aged cutblocks and sizes of treelings. Nowadays, the name "Forest Experiment Station" is passé and you (and by that I mean me) must learn to call the area by its proper name "Colonel's Cabin" which refers to the AFS's only on-going project: the Forest Management Trail. Since 1964 the University of Calgary has leased the POW camp site for the Environmental Studies Department which studies such things as dinosaur bones dug up in the meadows and packrats living in the cliffs behind the Emergency Services Centre.

If you want to nose around the foundations of the prisoner's skating rink, or inspect Colonel Hugh de Norban Watson's cabin, or compare soil samples and see how the Scots pines are doing by walking the interpretive trail, then you'll have to come back in the summer and use the entrance off Highway 40.

Highway 40 was also the access for the best ski trail of the lot: the fire road. So it's a great pity that since the second edition of the Kananaskis Country Trail Guide insufficient numbers of skiers have been out training the alder bush to keep to the sides of the road. Most of the other trails used for recreation now start from Stony Creek parking lot off Sibbald Creek Trail, so there's no need to go traipsing through the Kananaskis Centre. The only time you need to see residents other than on a school field trip is when you get back to your car at 9 o'clock at night and find you've left your lights on all day, need a boost and the car park is empty and all the downhill skiers have long since departed for Calgary. In this trying situation, Ed the maintenance man is very helpful but I wouldn't advocate you do this too often.

LUSK PASS

Backcountry

Intermediate
8.5 km to picnic area from parking lot
10.5 km to Powderface Trail from parking lot
Height gain to pass 366 m
Maximum elevation 1710 m
Map 82 O/3 Canmore,
82 O/2 Jumpingpound Creek

Access Sibbald Creek Trail (SR 68) at Stony Creek day-use area. Via Lusk Creek Tour (page 58).

Facilities Washroom, picnic tables at parking lot and on trail.

Overview This trail is relatively unknown to skiers, but I don't mind telling you about it because then, just maybe, the trail will be broken ahead of us for a change. Remarkably, in 1948 you could drive right through from the Forest Experiment Station to the Jumpingpound and in fact the red line was still showing on the 1975 edition of the topo maps though it had long since reverted to a trail. Now it's an official K-Country equestrian trail with markers and signposts and in winter a superb backcountry ski trail winding through a low pass in the Fisher Range to Powderface Trail the road.

Reverse the suggested direction of Lusk Creek Tour by heading out on the Lusk Creek Road. Shortly after passing the upper cutoff, the trail bends left and crosses Lusk Creek. The fact there is no bridge is not a problem.

Initially the trail travels along the flat east bank of the creek, soon turning away and developing a decided leftward bent as it climbs up a tributary to the pass. The further you go the steeper the angle and the deeper the snow. Seared in my mind is a trip in reverse direction undertaken in the pitch dark, *deliberately* I might add in case you feel like reporting us to the rangers for a ticking-off. The stupid thing was starting on this marathon trip in the dreariest days of the winter solstice when the sun barely staggers above the mountains so that when we ended up at the eastern trailhead for Lusk Pass at 7 pm the sun had already set three hours ago. But what I want to say is that rarely have I enjoyed such a thrilling ride down hills of exquisite light powder. Even in daylight there is very little to be seen except hillsides covered in lodgepole pines not yet at the cutting age of 80 years, so I can assure you that by skiing the pass in the dark we were not missing a thing. You don't come to Lusk Pass for the view.

But back to the trail description. Shortly after reaching the high point you slide down a gentle hill to a second reason for coming — picnic tables. This is Lusk Pass backcountry campground located in a sunny sheltered meadow which is clearly an obvious place for a turnaround.

If going through to Powderface Trail the road which is available in winter for snowmobilers and skiers, dig out the pile jacket ; the ongoing trail is gently downhill along the north bank of a cheerless V-shaped valley full of trapped cold air and, therefore, excellent snow. A short horror pitch to cross a tributary of Jumping Pound Creek indicates the end of the trail is at hand and all that's left is a brief trudge through meadows to the signpost on the road.

Jumping Pound Ridge trail starts a little higher up the road on the left side (signpost, bridge). Dawson trailhead and winter campground lies 10 km down the road to the left.

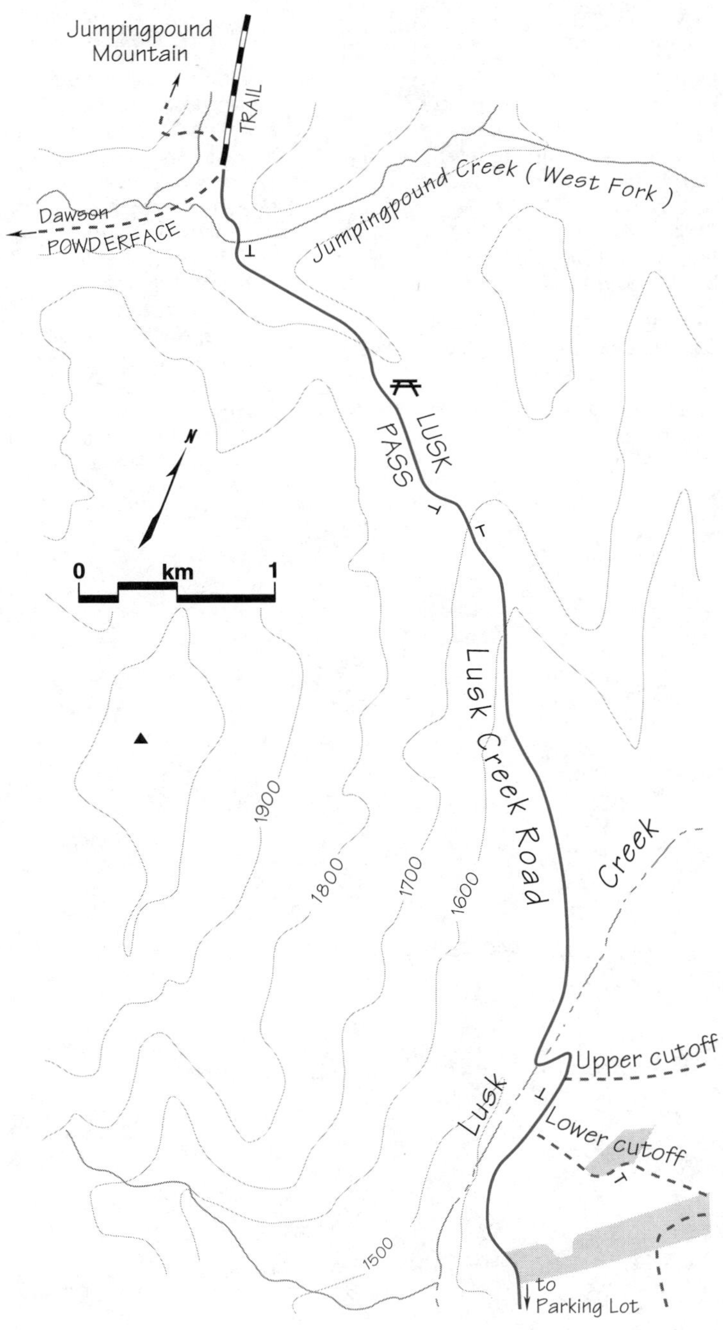

Jumpingpound
Mountain
TRAIL
Jumpingpound Creek (West Fork)
Dawson
POWDERFACE
LUSK
PASS
0
km
1
Lusk Creek Road
1900
1800
1700
1600
1500
Creek
Upper cutoff
Lusk
Lower cutoff
to
Parking Lot

BALDY PASS

Backcountry

Difficult to pass
Intermediate to sawmill site
10 km to pass from parking lot
7.7 km to sawmill site from parking lot
Height gain 564 m to pass,
360 m to sawmill site
Maximum elevation 1930 m at pass
Map 82 O/3 Canmore,
82 O/2 Jumpingpound Creek

Access Sibbald Creek Trail (SR 68) at Stony Creek day-use area. Via Lusk Creek Tour (see page 58).

Facilities Washroom, picnic tables at parking lot.

In winter this logging road is considered the safe route to Baldy Pass. Yes, I know people ski the pass from the south, but I honestly can't encourage every man and his dog to cross that steep avalanche slope just in case a slide thunders down the track at the very instant you're crossing. My other advice is to start early. Although this road is an official equestrian-hiking trail with no route finding problems, and you start off up the easy Old Mill Road, winds blasting over pass deposit unbelievable amounts of snow on the upper part of the route and you could be in for a tough time if no-one's gone before you.

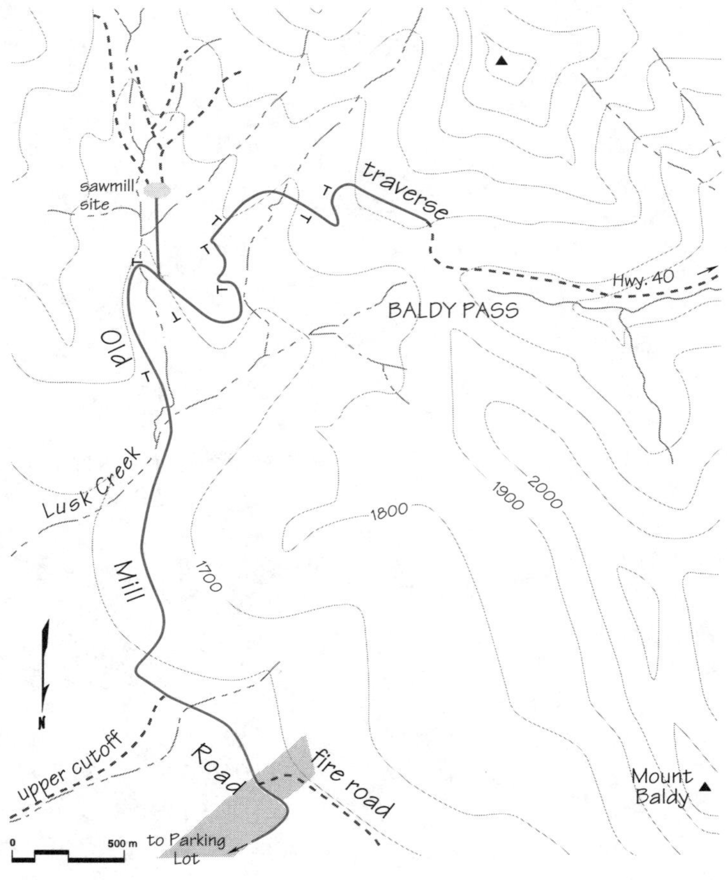

Start off up the old Mill Road. Keep right at the upper cutoff.

Still on the Old Mill Road, you're heading across to the west fork of Lusk Creek where the day's serious climbing kicks off after the creek crossing. An up-down combination leads to a re-crossing of the creek and a junction. If the appetizer hill has left you less than enthusiastic for much more of the same, there is an easy alternative by turning left onto the continuation of the Old Mill Road which ends in a meadow where the sawmill once operated. Unnamed ridges rear up on every side and you may have missed the sun. Should you feel restless, head for the uphill edge where logging roads take off for timberline skiing in the powder.

For Baldy Pass go straight up a berm where, a few years back, one of Canada's top nordic skiers performed a spectacular acrobatic stunt on a mountain bike, a cautionary tale to remember on the descent. This new road steepens, winding about in the deep shadow of Mt. Baldy. The sun is gilding the trees always higher up, you never seem able to catch up with it. And the wind is getting up, shaking the spruce trees which have suddenly replaced the ubiquitous pines. Unfortunately, the road stops at the end of a zig furthest away from the pass and a trail takes over for the last lap, making for an interesting traverse across steepening, ever-deepening slopes to a cairn on a rocky ridge blown clear of snow. Well, as you know, it's all been blown down the north slope. The pass proper is way down at the lowest point in the ridge, hardly worth stumbling down for since the view of Mt. Baldy and the peaks of the Kananaskis peeping through the V is definitely inferior.

Return The wild rush through deep powder is over far too soon and there is a terrible urge at the junction with the Old Mill Road to climb up and do it all over again. Lower down on the Old Mill Road the shadow of Mt. Baldy is always moving ahead, again thwarting skiers of afternoon sunshine.

Shady, rocky Baldy Pass looking towards the sunlit ridges of Mt. Baldy.

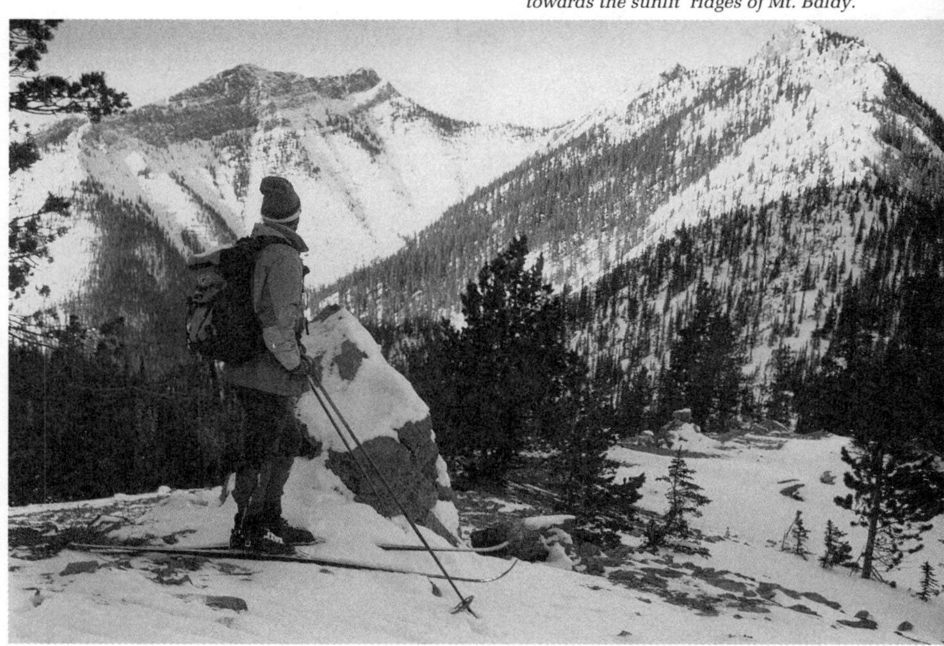

WASOOTCH CREEK

Backcountry

Easy
7.3 km to forks
Height gain 335 m
Maximum elevation 1737 m
Map 82 J/14 Spray Lakes Reservoir

Access Kananaskis Trail (Highway 40). About 10 km south of Sibbald Creek Trail (SR 68) park at the entrance to Wasootch Creek day-use area access road.

Facilities Picnic tables at the summer parking lot.

Overview For beginners wanting to sample the backcountry this is the ideal trip. You can't get lost no matter how hard you try, the views are spectacular and the terrain seemingly dead flat up a wide valley floor. Don't all rush off. If you wish to preserve the bases of your skis wait until the rounded rocks of the creek bed are covered by several snowfalls.

Start by skiing along the access road to the parking lot and picnic tables. From here a trail leads through a shallow draw into the valley proper.

As you ski along the flat valley floor bereft of trees apart from the solitary balsam poplar, there's plenty of time — like 90 minutes out and 90 minutes back — to look at the scenery. Coming up on your left is Wasootch Slabs, a beginner sports climber's playground with letters A through G daubed in white paint on every buttress for the benefit of mountain warfare trainees from the Canadian Army. Of course all this happened back in the 1950's in the days before guidebooks and topos. Also the target of climbers are the many spurs jutting out from the unnamed ridge on the opposite side of the valley, the greatest of which is Wasootch Tower, a sacred place if the origin of name Wasootch is to be believed. Further along, the ridge enclosing the valley to the north is assuming frightening proportions, the more frightening the bigger the boost to the morale of walkers like me who have scrambled along it in summer. Which brings me to the dilemma of what to call the thing in the next edition of the trail guide. I've decided I've got to make a stand against subdivision mentality, so both "Porcupine" and "Wasootch" are out. Let me know if you come up with something descriptive. Bristly perhaps?

So although the scenery is grand, the skiing is terribly tame apart from the odd scrape and when you get to the forks, identifiable by a definite narrowing and trees, it's time to turn around and ski back.

Wasootch Creek.
An unusual view of the east peak of Mt. Lorette.

More about the trail Some say the peculiar name "Wasootch" is derived from the Stoney word "wazi" meaning "one" and denoting uniqueness and solitariness in some way connected with Wasootch Tower. Aphrodite Karamitsanis assures us it's the Stoney word for "hail". Frank Powderface, on the other hand, says it's derived from the Stoney name Wasiju Waptan meaning White Man Creek after the murder of a white man, a name also attributed at one time to Evan-Thomas Creek further up the road. I'm confused.

But what *is* known is that Captain John Palliser named it in 1863 and that the valley has had a very long association with native people who used to camp down on the flats near the valley mouth. In fact, during clearing for the present highway, archeologists salvaged over 5,000 artifacts dating back to 4,500 B.C.

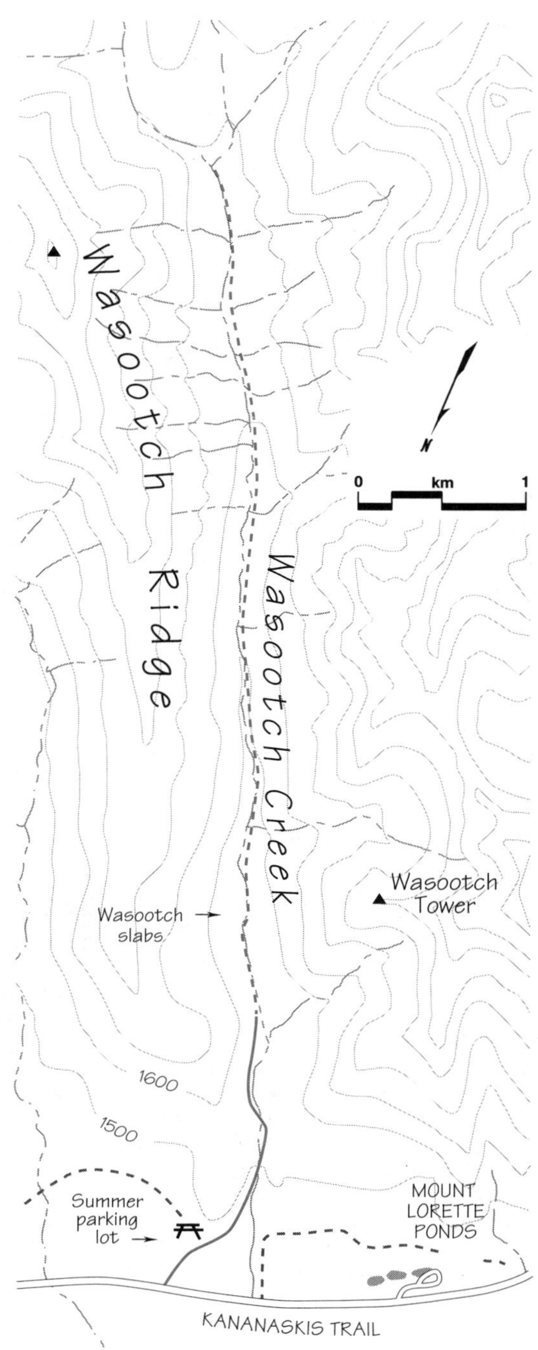

RIBBON CREEK SKI TRAILS

Groomed

48.8 km of trails
Maximum elevation 2073 m
Map 82 J/14 Spray Lakes Reservoir

Access Kananaskis Trail (Hwy. 40) at Ribbon Creek. Turn up the Nakiska Ski Area access Road. Where you go next depends on your starting point.

1. Keep right for Nakiska Ski Area .
2. For Kananaskis Village keep left across Ribbon Creek bridge.
3. For Ribbon Creek parking lot keep left initially, then turn first right before you cross Ribbon Creek bridge.

Facilities and Services

1. Nakiska Ski Area — Hobnob with alpine skiers in the Day Lodge with wraparound sun deck, snack bar, cafeteria and Finish Line Lounge. Satellite buildings house the ski shop and a rental/repair shop which rents nordic ski equipment. And why not take advantage of the babysitting service? That's not all. Up the hill at the end of Marmot Basin trail is Mid-Mountain Lodge with licensed cafeteria.

2. Kananaskis Village — three hotels: the Lodge (CP), the Hotel (CP), and the Inn, in order of de-escalating prices with dining facilities to match. For instance, you'll be welcomed at the Garden Cafe in Kananaskis Inn wearing gaiters and sporting mussed-up hair and red faces. The Samurai Sushi Bar, L'Escapade and Peaks Dining Room all require you to look a little more chic and have a hairbrush handy. For snacks and apres ski try the Bighorn Lounge in the Lodge and the Fireside Lobby Lounge in the Hotel, though again, if you're in nordic gear and not a paying guest it's probably best to head across the pond to Woody's Pub in the Inn. Sunday brunch at the Lodge is something worth planning for. All three hotels have swimming pools, hot tubs, steam rooms and exercise rooms in varying combinations for guests only. The Lodge is where you'll find 13 boutiques with opening hours posted on the door. Of more use to day visitors is the Village Centre and its lounge with fireplace, couches, lunch tables, and a grocery store next door where you can buy trail food and lunches ready to be nuked in the microwave. You may get lucky and have Ruthie Oltmann answering your every question at the information desk-post office (she travels around a lot and you could well bump into her at *any* information centre in K-Country). In the same building are meeting rooms, whirlpool, sauna, steam room, aerobics and fitness room, day-use lockers and last but not least Peregrine Sport and Rentals where you can rent nordic ski equipment, skates, hockey sticks and pucks, toboggans, snowshoes, and fishing tackle. As you may have gathered, completing the winter amenities is a skating pond and toboggan hill. (For ice fishing you'll have to go to Lower Kananaskis Lake, Barrier Lake and Spray Lakes Reservoir.) For information on sleigh rides, snow conditions etc, phone the information desk at 403-265-5120.

3. Ribbon Creek Parking Lot — We're down to the bare essentials here with washrooms at air temperature, picnic tables and a winterized picnic shelter. Ribbon Creek Hostel just down the road has room for 44 with five family rooms, kitchen and laundry.

Area Overview In good snow conditions these trails are incredibly enjoyable, ranging far and wide across the lower slopes of Mts. Collembola, Allan and Kidd with more viewpoints per kilometre than all the other networks put together. Most are the regulation 4-m width with bridges or culverts across streams and signs at all junctions.

Skiers have a choice. You can either go to great lengths to avoid the crass commercialism of the area like starting at Ribbon Creek parking lot for Skogan Pass, or you can put the cross country skier's natural distaste for development on the

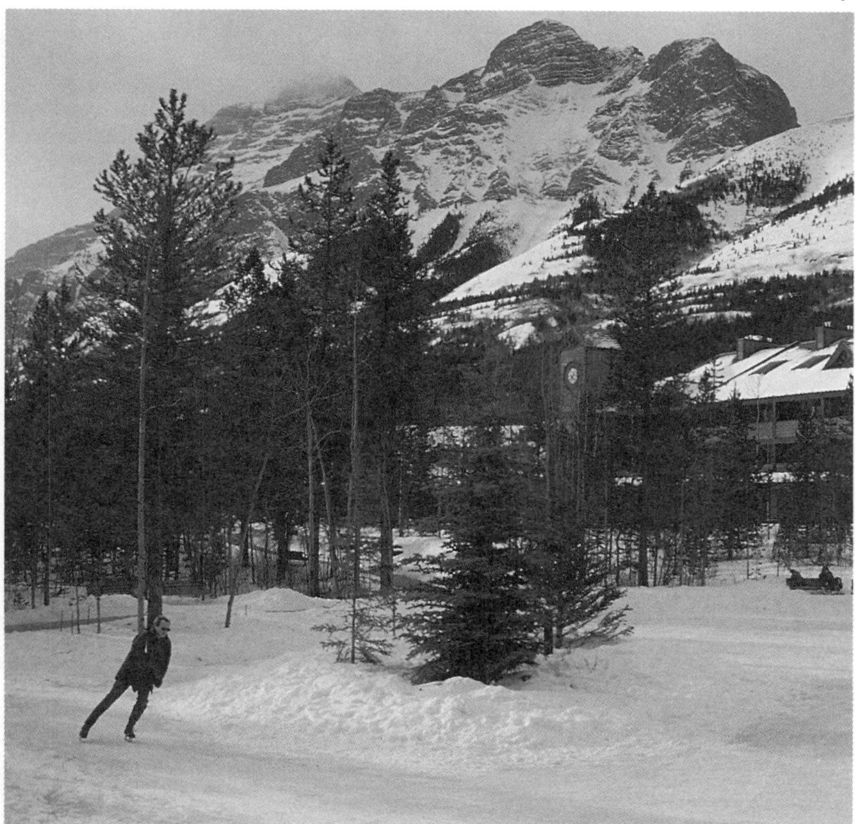

Kananaskis Village. The skating rink and Kananaskis Inn backdropped by Mt. Kidd.

back burner. In other words, unless you're off to Skogan Pass, why eat sandwiches standing up? For instance, if you're skiing the trails around Kananaskis Village why not plan the day around the Village Centre lounge for lunch. If you're flush there's three restaurants across the way and brunch on Sundays but then, I can't guarantee you'd ever get going again.

Other things to do in the middle of your crowded day include a spin around the skating rink, a tumble down the toboggan hill on a crazy carpet, and a ride on a horse-drawn sleigh where you can have fun frightening cross-country skiers. Likewise, at day's end why rush off home when there's plenty more to do like more eating (the Sushi bar may be open), pubbing at Woody's, soaking in the jacuzzi, and shopping for designer clothes and soapstone carvings.

HAY MEADOW

Easy
1.4 km

Used by logging ponies at the turn of the century for pasture, the flat meadows and aspen groves of Hay Meadow are ideal for beginners, Dipper watchers and lovers (still, Don — I saw a pair the other week). The place to stop is near the pumphouse, where the trail, meadow and Kananaskis River meet and you get this superb view of mountains in every direction.

But, beginners note, getting there requires descending the intermediate hill on the Troll Falls trail. If you want to avoid the hill, start from Stoney equestrian trail parking lot under the powerline just right (north) of the Nakiska Ski Area access road.

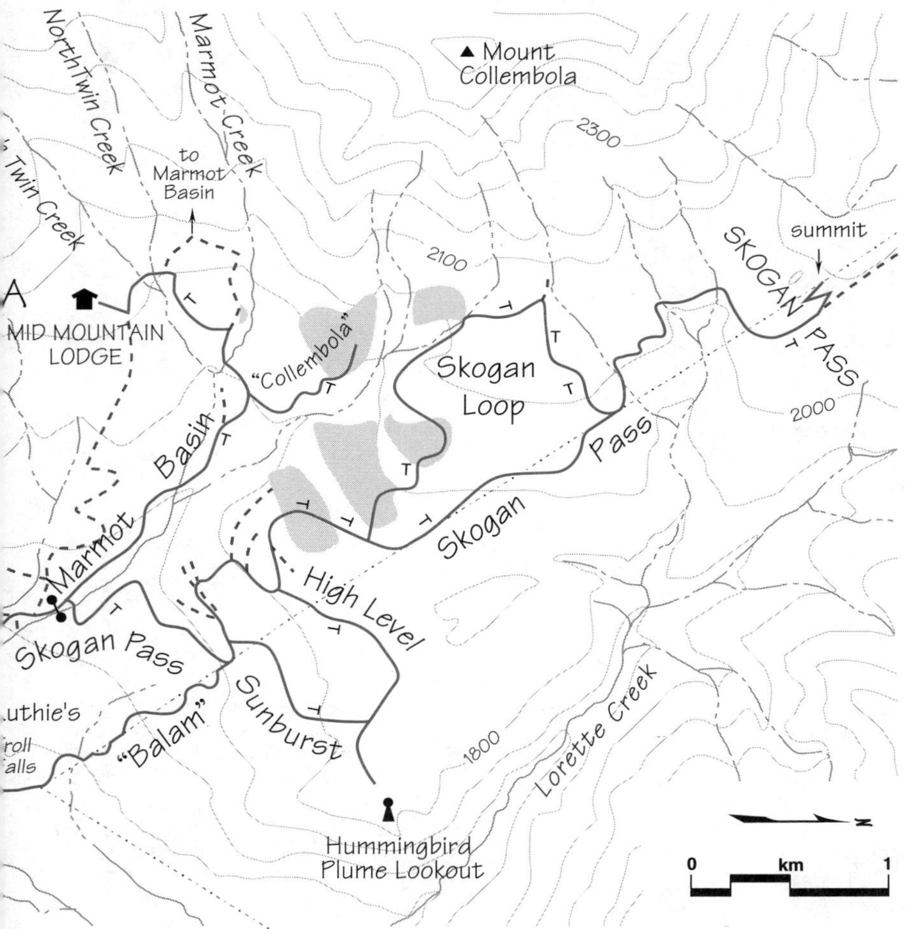

TROLL FALLS

Easy with one intermediate hill
1.5 km

Troll Falls was the very first trail built specifically for skiers at Ribbon Creek. Cut by Don Gardner in 1972 at the request of the Youth Hostel Association, it began life as a narrow winding trail very different in character to the present bulldozed swath cut by the Park's trail crews in 1982 and 1985.

Its rolling terrain makes it a little harder to ski than Hay Meadow with which it is often combined and in fact there's a good intermediate hill at the south end between the two trails. At the 4-way junction with Ruthie's and Hay Meadow, a narrower trail carries on to frozen Troll Falls which mustn't be missed.

Frozen Troll Falls, a great destination for novice skiers.

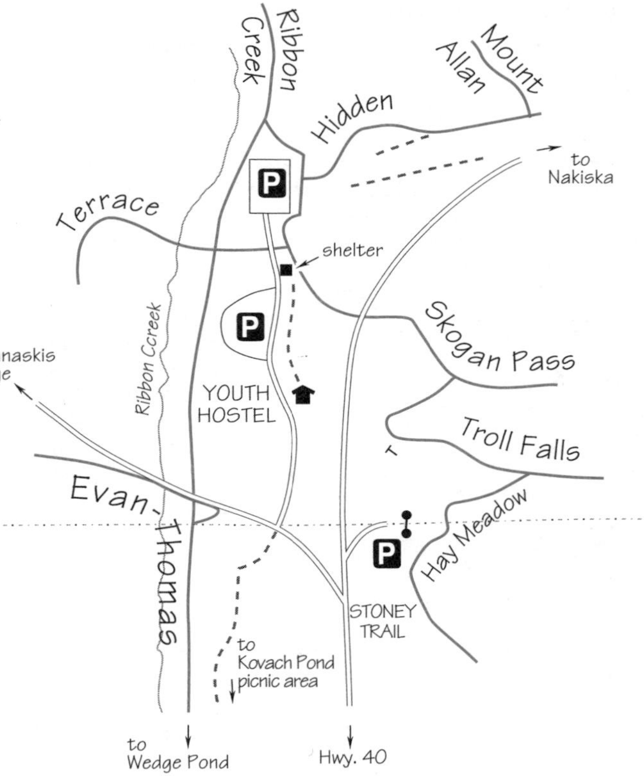

MOUNT ALLAN & COAL MINE

Intermediate
2.6 km
Height gain 170 m

Although you are not climbing to Mine Scar the direct way via the Mt. Allan Centennial Trail, this trail is quite steep enough thank you. The serious hills begin after the second bend and continue with no abatement past old Stump Meadow trail and the metal-clad cabin to a 4-way junction just below Coal Mine. On the other hand, Coal Mine was the main access road to the coal mines on Mt. Allan, and as such is wide, almost level and very often windswept. By the time you reach the reclaimed meadow at road's end any thoughts on lounging about in long yellow grasses watching bighorn sheep has long since gone. Of course you may be lucky with the wind, in which case it pays to wander further out onto the steep slope for the better view.

Return A small variation. Stay on Coal Mine until you come to the boundary sign with Nakiska Ski Area. Only then turn right and schuss down a narrower trail to the 4-way junction at the top of the winding downhill nominated for "Best Downhill" at Ribbon Creek.

Historic cabin on Mount Allan trail.

POWERLINE-NAKISKA CONNECTOR

Intermediate
1 km

This trail was built for those spectators at the 1988 Winter Olympics who were willing to walk from parking lots on the powerline to Nakiska Ski Area at the North Parking lot. It takes a somewhat zig-zag course, cutting across both Troll Falls and Skogan Pass trails and as such is a useful connector in more ways than one. Don't expect it to be machine packed.

RUTHIE'S

Intermediate
0.4 km

Ruthie's links Skogan Pass trail to Troll Falls trail at Hay Meadow junction. A casualty of Nakiska ski area, all that's left of Ruthie's is a fast fun downhill offering the quickest route to Troll Falls from the Day Lodge. When Ruthie Oltmann first skied this trail back in '72, the trees were strung with telephone line and insulators.

HIDDEN

Easy intermediate
1.5 km

About 15 years ago, this hidden trail was rarely used, the poor sister of the mighty Marmot Basin Road next door. Now it's the main connector between Ribbon Creek parking lot and Nakiska Ski Area, and has a brand new ending which winds all around the perimeter of the South Parking lot to the Day Lodge, then takes a kamikaze line down Sweetgrass, across Sun Dance, under the Bronze Chair and across Powderface ski runs to Skogan Pass trail. Hills are gentle except for the section around the parking lot which has a touch of the roller coasters.

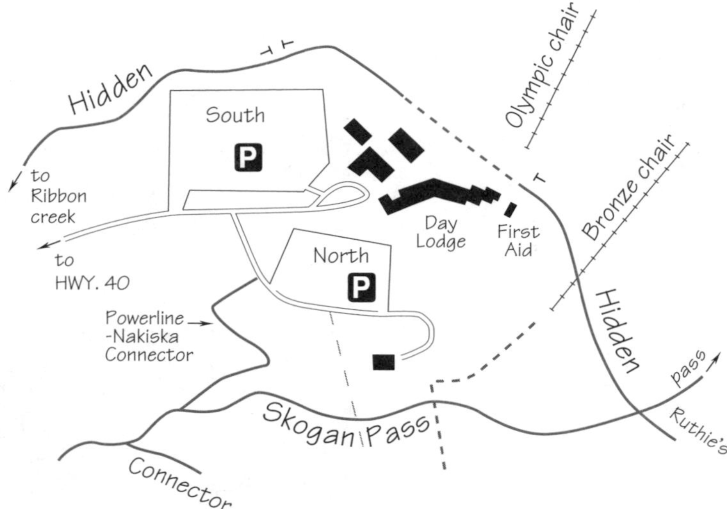

Opposite: Mt. Collembola looms over Skogan loop near the lower junction with Skogan Pass trail.

SKOGAN PASS TRAIL

Intermediate
8 km to upper Skogan Loop junction, 10.5 km to pass
Height gain 490 m to upper Skogan Loop junction, 625 m to pass
Maximum elevation at pass 2073 m

Skogan Pass trail is the main thoroughfare north of Ribbon Creek from which most other trails lead off. The trackset portion ends at upper Skogan Loop junction. To get to the pass is a much more serious proposition because you'll be pushing snow and there's the extra length and height gain to consider. Try and start before 11 am.

The trail starts from Ribbon Creek parking lot, crosses the Nakiska Ski Area access road, then skirts below the ski area where you get to refer to a number of signposts. After the 4-way junction with Ruthie's and Hidden where the short-cut from the Day Lodge comes in, you start a steeper climb up the side of an unnamed creek to Marmot Basin Road, now a snowmobile highway. Turn right. In about two minutes you pass a wide trail to the right which often gets mistaken for the ski trail on descent, but all you arrive at is a dam above Marmot Creek gorge. This is how most people discover Ribbon Creek's best kept secret which one fervently hopes will never become a tourist curiosity with fences and warning signs. A short distance from the false trail, the snowmobile road turns left and you carry on through a gate and so reach Marmot Creek where your trail turns right over Two Ton Culvert. So far it's not been exactly a quiet trip what with the cacophony of hissing snow guns, revving snowmobiles, squeaking chairlifts and screaming teenagers.

You breathe a sigh of relief as you start up the next section to upper Skogan Loop junction. Though it's only 3 km as the crow flies, the powerline access road exacts maximum winding to get up the steeper lower slopes of the long hill. En

Skogan Pass. The view through the power lines of Mt. McDougall in the Fisher Range. The left-hand wire pinpoints the summit of Old Baldy.

route there's a dozen old trails heading off in all directions, plus two official junctions with Sunburst and High Level near the powerline. All of this winding is followed by a straight in a cutblock. In lieu of historic tripods carrying the telephone line between ranger stations, the principal interest centres on the view behind your back of The Wedge, Mt. Kidd and the patterned slopes of Mt. Allan — a perfect excuse for stopping and taking a photo. After all, in another ten years you may see absolutely nothing. A final sprint along spruce avenue past lower Skogan Loop junction brings you to the powerline. Here turn left and resume slow climbing up the powerline access road to a three-pronged junction where all trackset trails end.

Return In fast conditions, the descent can be incredibly tiring, meaning that for a large proportion of time you're in a frozen snowplow position for which the experts have yet to come up with any adequate pre-season exercises. A reasonable time from upper Skogan Loop junction to Nakiska parking lot is 20 minutes.

Option: Skogan Pass (Backcountry)
In front, the powerline dives into a tributary of Lorette Creek. The obvious road to left is the wrong road. So many people used to go wrong here they made it into an official trail called Skogan Loop! Pass purists must pursue the narrower trail in the middle which descends slightly past the northern boundary gate of the Marmot Basin Project and contours round all the heads of Lorette Creek. The re-crossing of the powerline right-of-way is a good spot to look back one last time at Mt. Collembola — now showing the *mauvais pas* on the north ridge — before making the final push up to the pass, a level spot in the trees never properly determined. The idea, though, is to climb up to the powerline-right-of-way on your left for the "view". Most likely somebody's else's ski tracks will take you there.

SKOGAN LOOP

Intermediate
3.5 km
Maximum elevation 2057 m
Height gain clockwise 183 m, anti-clockwise 76 m

If you haven't skied the latest trail you have a treat in store. Clockwise seems better. This way you have a chance to soak in the vistas as you wind leisurely uphill through cutblocks. Between Mt. Lorette and Collembola, the 180 degree vista takes in an almost complete panorama of the Fisher Range, then further to the right, views of the Wedge, Mt. Kidd and surely that's the tip of Mt. Bogart poking up above Mt. Allan? The problems with south-facing cutblocks is that they let the sun and the wind have a go at the snow, a problem rectified by time as the seedlings grow taller. I only hope someone thinks to leave a few spaces for the views.

After a relief section in the forest, you arrive at yet another cutblock adjacent to the headwaters of Cabin Creek under the steep east face of Mt. Collembola which is so close it's a revelation and if you're anything like me you'll immediately start devising a summer route up the ridge while tackling the final and steepest uphill of the ski trail. Look back at the view one last time, then plunge into the trees on a ridge top.

Keep right at the meteorological instruments and claim your reward — a 76 m powder dash down the Marmot Cabin Meteorological Station access road to the powerline. Superb!

HIGH LEVEL

Easy intermediate
2.4 km
Maximum elevation 1874 m

Leaving from higher up the Skogan Pass trail, High Level offers by far the easier route to Hummingbird Plume Lookout. After crossing the powerline, you climb through spruce forest to what is possibly the trail's high point then descend to Sunburst junction where porcupines have eaten the relevant bit out of the map on the signpost. Turn left.

The trail ends in a hilltop meadow with a picnic table and a tiny wooden hut missing door and windows. It's rather interesting to search the inside walls for names of German POW's from camp #130 who wandered around the hillsides at Ribbon Creek salvaging burnt timber. It will have occurred to you that the lookout is a dead loss as a lookout. There *was* a view In the 1940's, but now the seedlings enclosing the meadow have grown much too high and you have to ski right to the edge of the eastern escarpment before you get that same view of the Kananaskis Valley.

SUNBURST

Difficult
1.6 km
Height gain 122 m

The direct way to Hummingbird Plume Lookout and still the steepest trail in the system, requiring constant herringboning should you be daft enough to climb up the hill. Use High Level for the ascent and reserve this trail for a fast fun descent.

"BALAM"

Backcountry
Difficult
2.5 km
Height loss 260 m

I thought I'd resurrect the old road twining about the powerline right-of-way below Sunburst cutoff which is used nowadays as an equestrian short-cut between Skogan Pass and Stoney trails. This is definitely a one-way rush in the downward direction which requires plentiful snow with a dollop of powder on top. It makes you drool just thinking about the Sunburst/Balam combo — a drop of nearly 400 vertical metres!

When you reach Stoney trail which is the powerline access road in the valley bottom, turn right. In about 500 m you should intersect Hay Meadow.

Hummingbird Plume Lookout at the end of High Level trail. Note the height of the trees.

MARMOT BASIN TRAIL

Intermediate
3 km
Maximum elevation 1935 m
Height gain 320 m

A trail with a destination fit for growing skiers: burger and chips at Mid Mountain Lodge.

After the original Marmot Basin trail was appropriated by the ski area as a snowmobile route to the lodge, the present trail was tacked on to another old road which runs up Marmot Creek, first on the south bank across from a line of picturesque sandstone cliffs and then on the north bank where the climbing takes your breath away. By now you're into the spruce zone, climbing on the new trail all around the head of Marmot Creek and Twin Creeks, squashing trillions of Collembolas on your way to the diesel fuel tank which is where you rejoin the snowmobile road. By heading right you reach Mid Mountain Lodge in about 5 minutes. It's been a hard climb and priorities shift from exclaiming over the great snow in the spruce forest to fantasizing about a deliciously cold Labatt's Blue in the cafe.

Return If you're an experienced telemarker why not return direct via the ski runs? Otherwise, I'd give Mapmaker and Homesteader a miss and return the same way which gives you plenty of chance to show off your prowess in snowplowing. It's a fantastic run down and when you get to the Day Lodge you'll need a cuppa hot chocolate to warm yourself up.

"COLLEMBOLA"

Backcountry
Easy intermediate
0.9 km to cutblock

On your way up Marmot Basin trail you've probably wondered like me where this road leads to. Would it, or would it not join up with Skogan Pass or Skogan Loop trails? So I followed it one day and had a marvellous time winding around the lower slopes of Mt. Collembola into a huge slanting cutblock above Cabin Creek. After much effort flogging around the most promising edges I sadly decided there was no connecting link to Skogan Loop and started back down. Just above the intermediate hill I was stopped dead in my tracks, "Hallo, that's strange!" On my way up the snow had been its usual pristine white self but now was black. And not from wispy bits of bryoria dislodged from the trees by the wind.

So you're about to find out why I call this unofficial trail "Collembola" and why the mountain above is also unofficially called Collembola. Pronounced Coll-*em*-bol-a, this strange Latin name was suggested by Don Gardner after Collembolas, or more specifically Hypogastrura (Achorutes) nivicola, a flea-like insect commonly called springtails or snow fleas which for years have been the object of study by visiting scientists from all over the world to the Kananaskis Centre for Environmental research. Only .08 inches long, you might be hard pressed to find one, but fortunately, after a Chinook thaw there are billions of the little inky-blue critters springing up all over the surface of the snow and through the snow pack in a kind of frenzied mating dance. Of course I'd seen them before in the Ribbon Creek area but never in such a multitude. I just wish they wouldn't congregate in ski tracks.

RIBBON CREEK

Easy
2.5 km to Link junction

A very popular trail. Starting from tastefully placed coal cars, you follow the combination logging road-trail through the gorge, overtaking family crocodiles and queuing up to cross two log bridges en route to Link junction where most beginners call it a day. It's only on the return run — one long glide — that you realize you've been gaining any height.

Option: Dipper Canyon (Backcountry)
It's worth carrying on in the same easy way for about another 3.5 km through "Toad Forest" (whimsical name bestowed by hostellers) to the forks and beyond that past ruins of log cabins built by the Eau Claire Logging Company to the start of Dipper Canyon. Going further means running risks below nasty avalanche slopes. In any case, the lure — Ribbon Creek Falls — is a huge disappointment in winter and low down on any ice climber's list.

KOVACH

Intermediate
5.4 km
Height gain 150 m
Maximum elevation 1710 m

South of Ribbon Creek, Kovach is a shoo-in for best snow, best viewpoint, best downhill run. The best downhill between the high point and Link can be schussed with intermittent checks, but slow down for the hairpin lest you scare the wits out of up-coming skiers. It's also a superb trail to ski in the opposite direction *once* you've climbed to the high point. You've still got downhills, but they're rather less steep and at the south end is a truly delightful series of easy S bends which wind you down to Terrace near Kananaskis Village. From the trail's high point, which coincides with the demarcation line of fire succession lodgepole pines and spruce untouched by the fire of 1936, you get this unique view of Olympic Summit's grassy south face. Actually, it isn't all smooth; there's a fine rocky ridge down the middle of it which we downclimbed one late November in the moonlight. Don't ask me what we were doing out so late!

Ribbon Creek trail near the quarry. Ribbon Peak in the background.

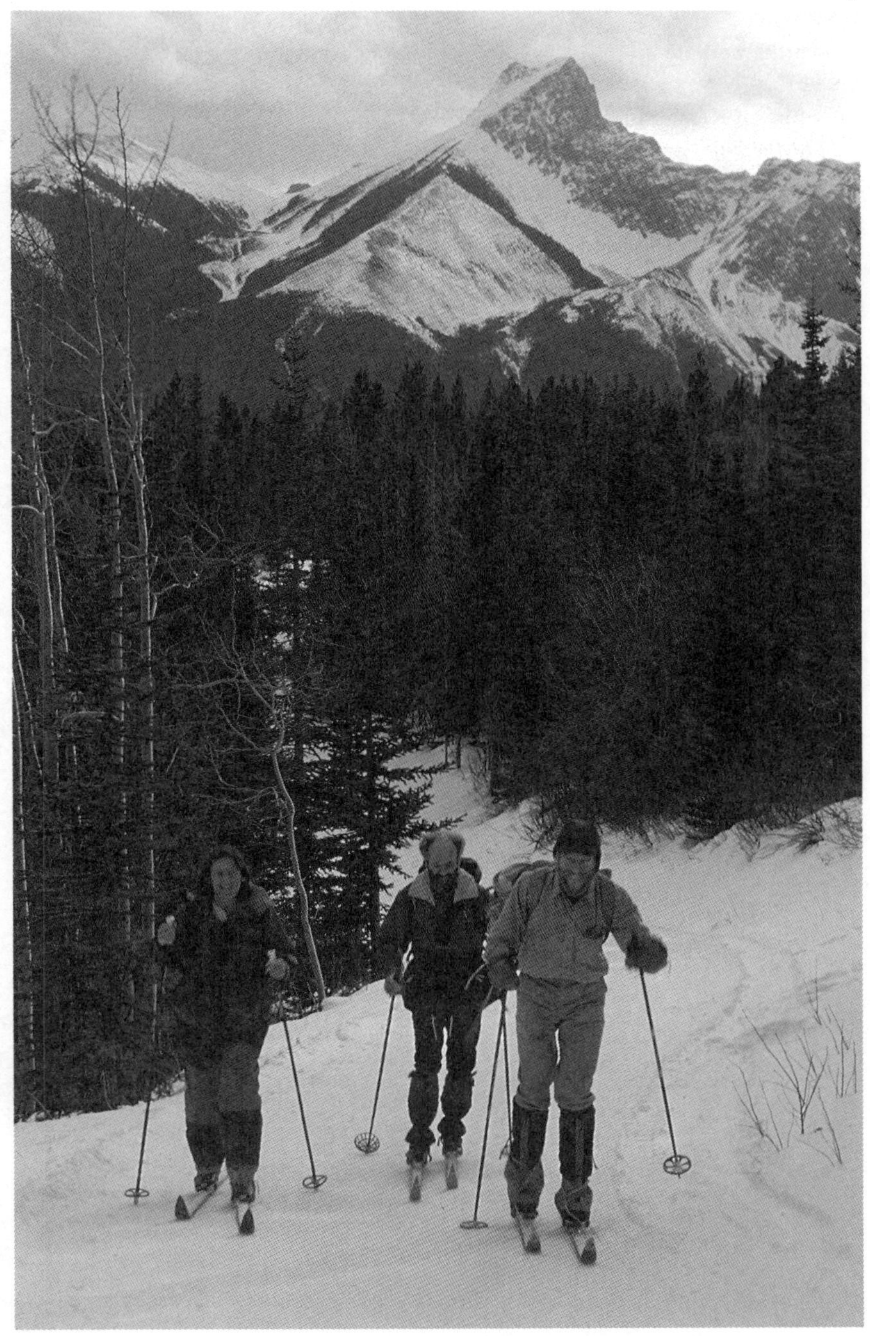

Kovach trail. Climbing the hill just north of Aspen/Kovach Link. The Wedge in the background.

LINK
Easy intermediate
0.8 km

Link links Kovach trail to Ribbon Creek trail. Considerably widened, it has lost its former terrors and is now a straightforward run to the bridge over Ribbon Creek through spruce forest draped with wispy black lichen. You can just about schuss the whole thing.

TERRACE
Easy intermediate
2.8 km

A useful trail connecting Ribbon Creek parking lot to Kananaskis Village and the south end of Kovach. The long hill out of Ribbon Creek gives it the intermediate rating. But with careful planning beginners can avoid it altogether by starting from the village end and making an almost totally flat loop with Terrace Link. Greatest hazard is horse-drawn sleighs full of Japanese tourists. Smile.

"KANANASKIS RIVER"
Backcountry
Intermediate
1.5 km to Kananaskis River
Height loss 96 m

If you carry on beyond the most southerly Terrace/Kovach junction you'll be speeding down Terrace hiking trail which is a road at this point and not groomed. At the bottom of the long hill, Terrace continues south via a narrow trail, but you go left, still following the old road winding down to the Kananaskis River. Or to be precise, at the very end you cross a stream from the beaver ponds, then skirt around a green to the bridge over the Kananaskis River put in at great expense to serve hole #15. It's a picturesque spot.

A couple of times I've cut across the Robert Trent Jones designed golf course to pick up Evan-Thomas trail north of the Clubhouse. I'm not saying that you should emulate me, but if you do, better use the golfer's access trails. See the map on page 90.

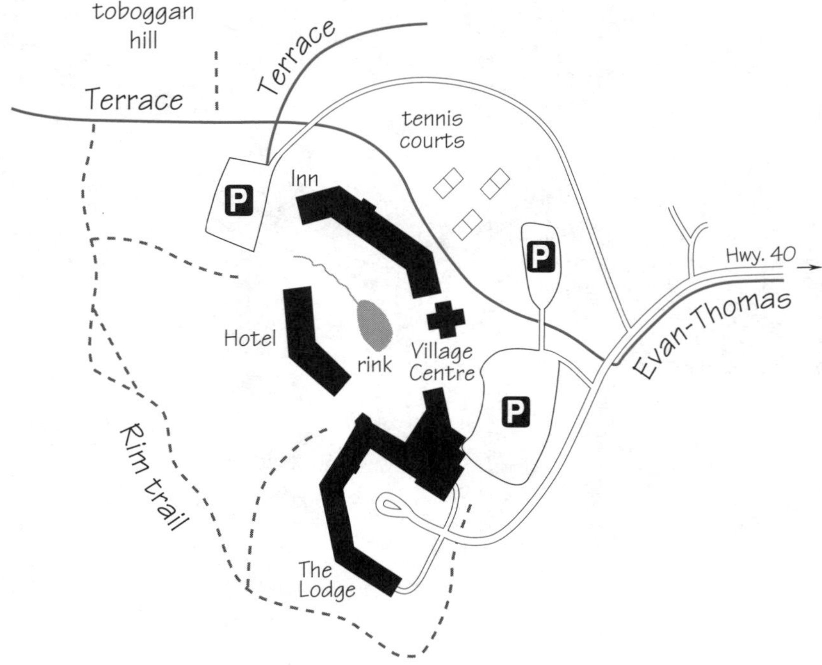

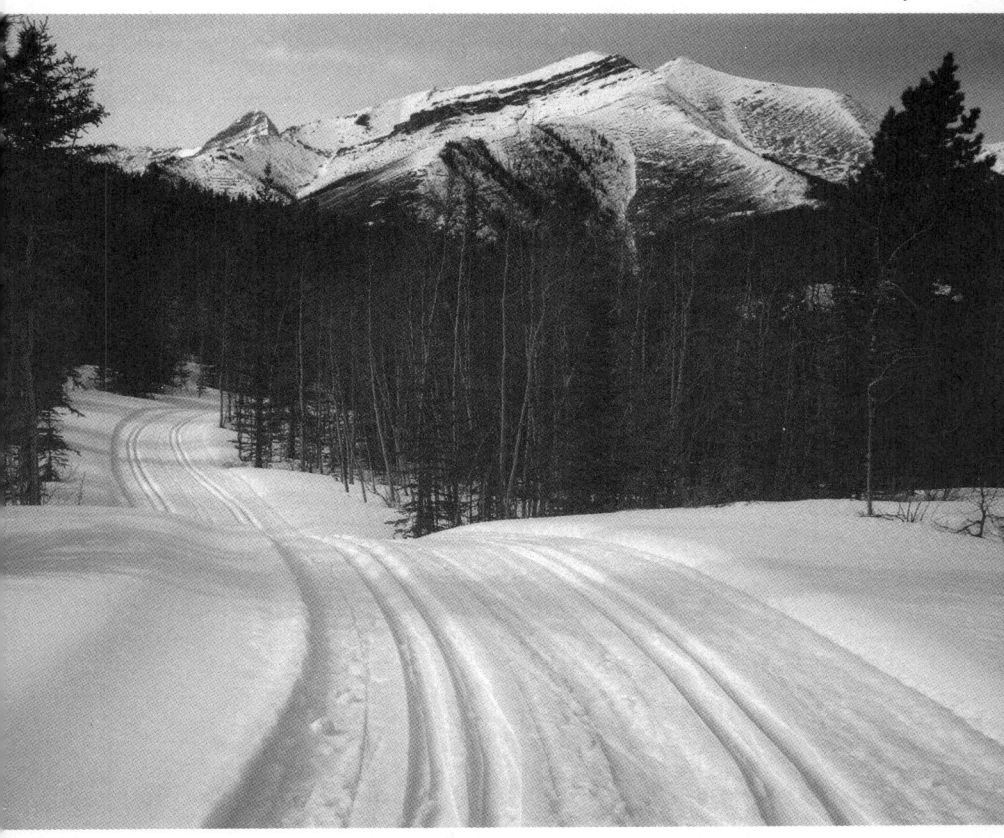

Terrace, looking towards the Olympic Summit of Mt. Allan.

TERRACE LINK

Easy
1 km

An easy trail most often skied in conjunction with Terrace to make a good beginner's loop. Listen for the jingle of horse-drawn sleighs coming your way.

ASPEN/KOVACH LINK

Easy Intermediate
0.2 km

Connects the mid portions of Kovach and Aspen and makes available shorter loops.

ASPEN

Easy intermediate
1.8 km

An easier alternative to the middle section of Kovach. Discounting the intermediate hill down to Kovach at the north end, most of the trail rolls along a bench with pretty good views over aspen treetops of the village and the valley.

More about the trails

I blame all that's happened at Ribbon Creek on Dominion Geologist George Dawson who in the mid 1880's crossed the height of land (Skogan Pass, alias Dean Man's Pass, Pigeon Pass, Canmore Gap) between the Kananaskis Valley and Dead Man Flat and wrote a report about it. By 1900 a bit of initial logging was going on down by Ribbon Creek near the parking lot. Strangely, another 40 years was to pass before Eau Claire & Bow River Lumber Company built a logging camp beyond the forks of Ribbon Creek, an action which galvanised a spate of other logging companies into salvaging burnt timber for mine props. On Hummingbird Plume Hill, conscripted POW's with a few moments to spare carved their names and camp number 130 inside the forest lookout.

But back to the year 1907. Following up an earlier report by geologist D. Bogart Dowling, coal prospector Martin Nordegg made his first trip into the area with Dowling and Tom Lusk to stake a claim. But again, presumably waiting for the horse and buggy era to pass, another 40 years went by with nothing much done. Then in 1947 another geological survey by M.B.B. Crockford and young assistant Gordon Scruggs (who named Marmot Basin after the large number of the little beasties around their campsite), led to a subsidiary of Nordegg's parent company called the Kananaskis Exploration Development Company making some drastic changes to the landscape. The next five years was a time of intense activity as trucks rumbled up and down the Marmot Basin Road and Coal Mine trail and every road in between to Mine Scar meadow where there was both a strip mine and an underground mine. I bet miners used the Mount Allan trail as a short-cut home; home being a collection of tar-paper shacks at the bottom of the hill. Called Ribbon Crick by residents, the village was later renamed Kovach after Joe Kovach who was district forestry ranger from 1940 to 1953. If you come back in summer and rummage around the Ribbon Creek parking lot area you can find a few foundations to exclaim over as well as an anomaly as perplexing as the Bermuda Triangle. Who was Moley 1900? Unfortunately, the market for coal was declining and in 1952 the mine closed and the village was abandoned. In 1960 the Youth Hostel Association succeeded in buying the old schoolhouse, a decision which had far-reaching effects for us cross country skiers.

At the same time as all the logging and mining was going on, the communication department was busy at Skogan Pass. First came the treeline telephone link between forestry stations at Canmore and Ribbon Creek via the Boundary trail which took in part of Skogan Pass and Ruthie's. The pack trail, by the way, was named after the old Boundary Cabin which is still standing in the grounds of the Emergency Services Centre on Boundary Flats (i.e golf course). A few decades later in the late 1950's it was the turn of Calgary Power to build a powerline and access road over the pass and it is this which doubles, *almost* in its entirety, as today's Skogan Pass trail. Starting at Ribbon Creek, the contractors naturally made use of the abandoned mine roads and bits of pack trail as long as the gradient was not more than 12 percent.

Theoretically, the Federal Government's Forest Experiment Station owned a large chunk of land around Ribbon Creek but it was 1962 before they entered the fray with the Marmot Basin Project which went on for 20 years and was the largest watershed research area ever in Canada. More new roads and trails were pushed through the bush to clusters of recording instruments. And the already beleaguered forest now sported a new patchwork pattern which still shows up clearly on air photos. Despite what you may think, the large cutblocks on Skogan Pass and Skogan Loop trails are not the result of tree harvesting but an experiment to see what effect clearcuts would have on stream flow.

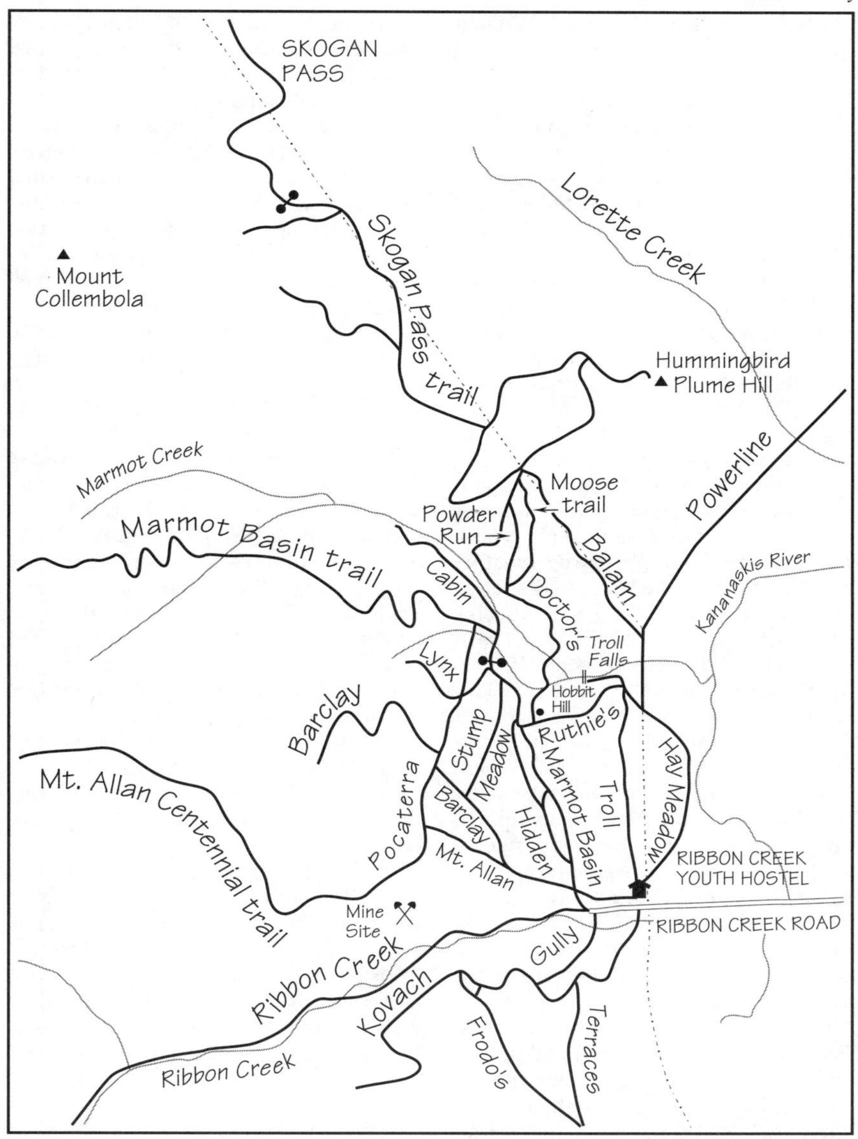

How the Ribbon Creek Ski Trails looked in the 1970's. "Don't get lost! Use your trail map" was the motto.

So you can see that by the 1970's Ribbon Creek was already an area of outstanding environmental interference.

What happened next was that Ruthie Oltmann, a keen skier, got the job as house mother at Ribbon Creek Youth Hostel. One of Ruthie's perceived jobs was to break trails for hostellers who wouldn't go anywhere unless the trail was broken. "Why did you only break trail to such and such a point?" they would ask her on their return. Ungrateful wretches! With Ruthie was climber/racer Don Gardner on his first job as a trail consultant via a STEP grant from the CYHA for improvements to the area. Between the two of them they explored all the old roads: clearing deadfall, giving roads and natural features names and mapping everything on a piece of paper pinned up on the hostel notice board. During this time (1972) a narrow twisting trail was cut to Troll Falls, deliberately made so narrow that snowmobiles couldn't get through. "If you haven't been to Troll Falls, you haven't been to Ribbon Creek" was the hosteller's motto. Would you believe that after traipsing around Ribbon Creek and doing a spot of ski mountaineering from Fryatt Creek Hut, Don went on to win a bronze medal at the Canadian National Championships in the 30 km event *with the same pair of skis*? I'm told the skis were on their last legs by this time and shredding splinters on the downhills! View the amazing multi-use Jarvinen skis with hickory bases at the youth hostel where they have been built into the fireplace for posterity.

For nearly a decade afterwards Ribbon Creek was a popular nordic skiing area when there was enough snow, though you could always find snow if you knew where to look. Do you remember Pocaterra (Coal Mine), Timber, Stump Meadow, Barclay (after Barclay Sisters Mary and Catherine who started the youth hostel movement in Canada), Lynx, Hobbit Hill, Doctor's (after Dr. Dave Gill —"You need a doctor if you ski it"), Moose, Powder Run, Balam (powerline), and Frodo's "which like Frodo's adventures was a little difficult to follow"? Everyone cottoned on to the new name Skogan Pass, though not many people made it that far. Boy, did this trail ever have a tough reputation in those days; you needed a fleet of trail breakers. Marmot Basin Road was the main thoroughfare to most of these trails. You can see the beginning of it at Ribbon Creek parking lot to the right of Hidden trail. If the Sunday morning rush hour up the Marmot Basin Road was something of a social event, the late afternoon rush hour down the road was definitely a race, with three or four people snowplowing madly abreast. "Bernie, remember to slow down for the icy patch near the parking lot".

Drastic changes came in the late 1970's and early 1980's when the area became part of Kananaskis Country. Ribbon Creek trail was rebuilt with bridges and —shamefully—the delightful Troll Falls trail was bulldozed to regulation 4 m-width in 1982 and again in 1985, causing Ruthie Oltmann, who didn't work for K-Country at the time, to write protest letters to the newspapers. But worst was to come in preparing Mount Allan for the 1988 Winter Olympics. Out went Marmot Basin Road and Marmot Basin trail, most of Coal Mine, all of Stump Meadow, most of Barclay, half of Ruthie's and the upper half of Hidden. It was like an era had ended.

But look at it this way. Although the area lost half of the trails north of Ribbon Creek, it gained a few substitutes and a whole new network designed by Don south of the creek when Kananaskis Village was built in the mid 1980's. Skiers have returned in greater numbers than ever before, even if half of them do speak Japanese.

MARMOT BASIN

Backcountry

Intermediate
7.5 km to Marmot Creek from Marmot Basin trail
12.5 km to Marmot Creek from Nakiska parking lot
2.5 km to Fisera Ridge from Marmot Creek
Height gain 640 m to Marmot Creek from Nakiska Parking lot
Height gain 730 m to Fisera Ridge from Nakiska parking lot
Maximum elevation 2300 m Fisera Ridge
Map 82 J/14 Spray Lakes Reservoir

Access via Marmot Basin trail. See Ribbon Creek Ski Trails on page 79.

Overview I hope the management at Nakiska won't start negotiating for a takeover if I tell you this is where the deep powder lives at Ribbon Creek.

A long time ago pre K-Country, lots of people skied the switchbacking trail into the Basin, some continuing on up Fisera Ridge where shiny metrological instruments shone brightly in the sun below the larches and were presumably attended to by Zedenek Fisera from the Forest Experiment Station. But have you ever tried to find the trail lately? With such a rag-bag of more recent roads overlying old tracks it's become extremely confusing. And what about the start? The original trail took off from the very end of the original Marmot Basin trail which has since been re-fashioned to link up with the new section of trail up Marmot Creek. So where *do* you go if you want to do a bit of telemarking? Read on and watch for red flagging.

Photo: Alf Skrastins

Powder on Fisera Ridge. You can glimpse a bit of the basin below Mt. Allan.

You've skied up the official Marmot Basin trail into the spruce trees.

Start 1. (shorter) From the top of the hill before the dip to North Twin Creek turn right up a road (flagging). At a junction your road turns right and appears blocked by a large fallen tree, thus losing brownie points because you have to climb over the spiky thing. Still, it's only a few minutes from here to where the original trail comes in from the left. Stay on the road.

Start 2. (original trail) Follow up the north bank of North Twin Creek. Shortly after passing an uphill road to the right, the trail itself bends to the right up a hill and intersects Start #1. Though the continuing trail can be traced with difficulty to the next zig, it's much better nowadays to turn left up the road.

You've hardly gone more than a half dozen glides before flagging indicates a left turn up a steep hill. This is followed by another left turn up an even steeper hill which brings you gasping to the road's high point on a bench. Turn left a third time onto an indeterminate road which zigs right, then left, then ends. The next rightward zig is the original trail (lots of flagging).

The old trail's gentle gradient is instantly recognisable to anyone who has been this way before and makes climbing through a mini patchwork of experimental cutblocks and spruce trees a real pleasure as long as you're not the one in front breaking trail. An extra long zig to the right ends at Marmot Creek now minus instruments measuring stream flow. This is the start of the meadows.

Option: Up the Creek

A kilometre of creek bashing between Mt. Collembola on the right and steep-sided Fisera Ridge on your left leads to widespread meadows under Mt. Allan. It's immensely satisfying to realize that while you're playing about in the powder, just around the corner on the next planet the alpine crowd are most likely skidding about on man-made snow. Of course you've paid your dues by merit of a horrendous 730 metre climb by your own efforts. Right? Snobbish thoughts like this have a way of back-firing and I now read that the management at Nakiska wants to double the size of the ski area by roping in the area around Twin Creeks. And that's just Phase One. I hope the name of the owners — Marmot Basin Ski-Lifts — isn't a portent for Phase Two.

Option: Fisera Ridge

From Marmot Creek continue along the trail which zigs back left past a metal sign reassuringly stamped "RIDGE". Ten minutes later your mouth is hanging open with wonder at the magnificent larch forest and the unfolding panorama of Mt. Collembola round past Mt. Allan to Olympic Summit. The meadow at the ridge's highest point gives you an unrestricted view in all directions and it's here where you decide what to do next. While a same-way descent is not to be sniffed at, consider plowing on to the saddle between the ridge and the east slopes of Allan then dropping into the head of Marmot Creek. From the ridge you can check for a ready-made track up the creek to make it worth your while.

Return — a genteel glide back down the trail followed by a fast finish down the roads. It's good to know that apart from the one fallen tree already mentioned, the roads are free of such pitfalls. There's good grass under the snow.

Return Direct Way Then there's the route straight down the hill following the short-cut summer trail. Problem here is you're so busy enjoying yourself you're liable to miss the peppermint stick flagging indicating a right turn. Still, you emerge on one road or the other and can then sort yourself out according to the map.

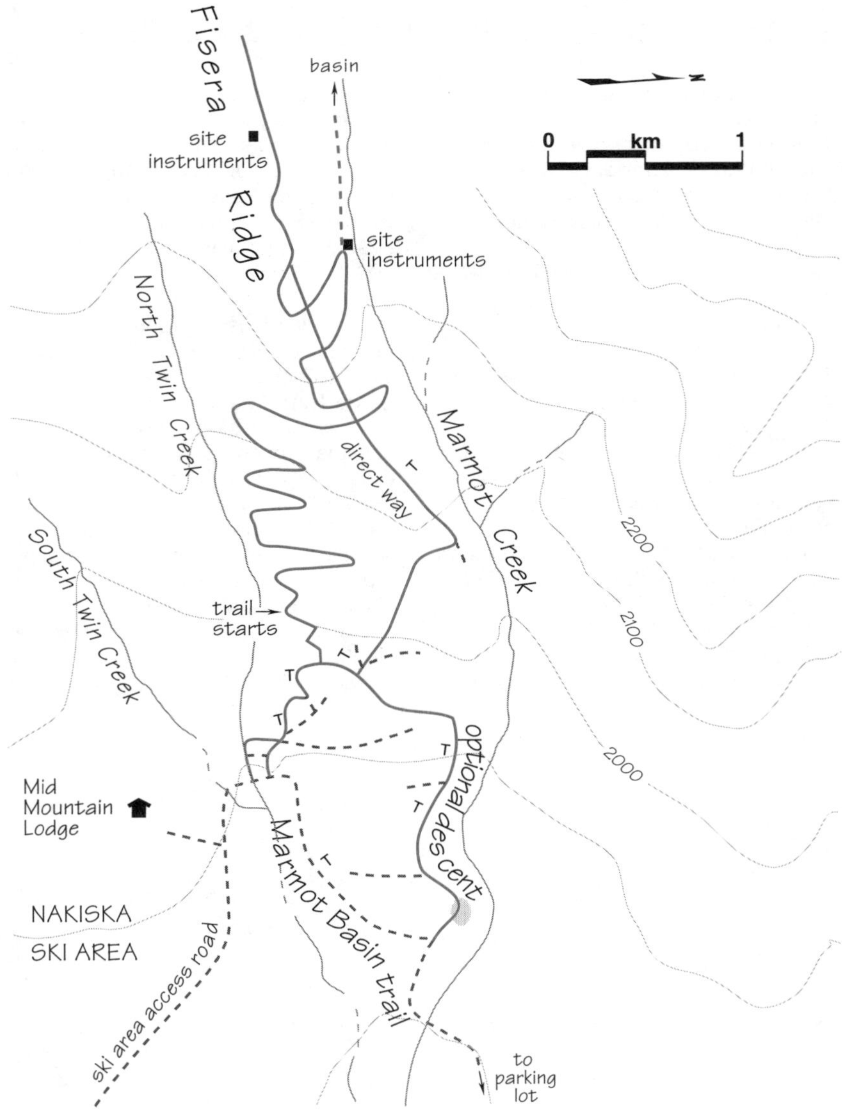

Optional Descent: This option opens up when you hit the top road on the bench and requires plentiful snow or a chain-saw job. Assuming you've standing on the road's high point, turn left down a short hill, gliding past roads belonging to the Direct Way and settle into a long traverse punctuated by stops to step over trees. Ultimately, the road turns right, amalgamating all the little downhills of the usual route into what would be one giant hill spoiled by a fallen tree at the half-way point. After this you keep left and ski through a clearing and on down to the official Marmot Basin trail.

EVAN-THOMAS TRAIL (BOUNDARY FLATS TRAIL) Groomed

Easy with easy intermediate hills at both ends
15 km between accesses 1 and 6
4.5 km Wedge Connector only
Maximum elevation 1554 m
Map 82 J/14 Spray Lakes Reservoir

Access Kananaskis Trail (Hwy. 40) at six locations:

1. Kananaskis Village
2. Ribbon Creek parking lot
3. K-Country Golf Course access road
4. Mount Kidd RV Park
5. Wedge Pond parking lot.
6. Evan-Thomas parking lot

.

Facilities Washrooms at 1,2,4,5,6 Picnic tables at 2,5

The many facilities at Kananaskis Village are already written about under Ribbon Creek Ski Trails on page 68.

Friendly Mount Kidd RV Park is owned and operated by brothers Philip and Barry James who are amenable to day skiers making tracks to the Campers' Centre which houses a snack bar, grocery store and whirlpools. The very large campground (hook-ups available) is open all year round. Reserve a spot by either writing Mount Kidd RV Park, Box 100, Exshaw, Alberta T0L 2C0 or by phoning 403-491-7700.

Overview Please, will somebody change the name of this trail? I get tired of explaining that, "despite its name this trail doesn't go up Evan-Thomas Creek. Okay, so it crosses the creek a couple of times and eventually ends up at the Evan-Thomas Creek parking lot. But it doesn't go up the creek. That's the Evan-Thomas *Creek* trail". To complicate matters further, the first section from Kananaskis Village to Ribbon Creek could be considered a part of the Ribbon Creek ski trails system.

Overall, the trail is the grand daddy of all access trails, accessing Kananaskis Village, Ribbon Creek parking lot, Nakiska

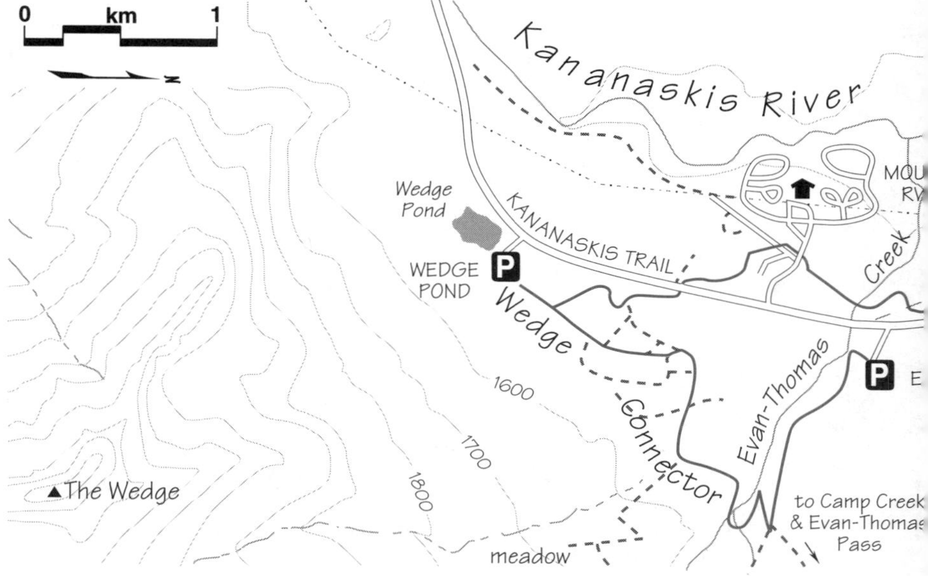

Ski Area access road, Highway 40 and Kananaskis Ranger Station, Boundary Stables, Kananaskis Country Golf course, Mount Kidd RV Park, Wedge Pond Recreation area and the Evan-Thomas parking lot. Personally, I find it hard to be serious about a trail which keeps crossing access roads.

A summer bike path, the trail is 4-m wide, packed and trackset and well-signed. While most of it is flat, hills at either end may cause a panic attack with beginners. Bear in mind that families with four year-olds on tricycles bike down the hills. Either return the same way, take two vehicles or wait for pick-up at one of the aforementioned accesses.

Technically, the trail starts from the 4-way junction on Terrace trail a few steps from the parking lot for Kananaskis Inn, and heads between the tennis courts and the Village Centre to the north side parking lots where a trail to the left of the parking lots access road leads to the main Kananaskis Village access road. A signpost on the far side of the road is the official start. You can also reach the signpost via Rim trail round the back of the hotels. See the map on page 82.

If route-finding is tricky around the village, the way down to Ribbon Creek is simple: a scenic glide along the bench top followed by easy swinging zigzags, liberally sprinkled with benches, down to the bridge. Cross Ribbon Creek, turn right at the sign and arrive at a T-Junction on the river bank. A right turn under the bridge leads to Ribbon Creek parking lot and all points west and north. Turn left (east) if going south. Squeezed between the creek and Kovach Pond access road, the trail ascends past bike racks to the Nakiska Ski Area access road. Cross the bridge over the Kananaskis River.

Turn right off the east end of the bridge and start heading south. The trail winds through the meadows of Boundary Flats that have somehow escaped being turned into golf course, crossing five bridges over creeklets (bench after the third bridge). The scenery is impressive in every direction: Old Baldy, Mt. Kidd, Mt. Collembola, Mt. Allan, and best of all, Mt. Lorette behind your back. The views, by

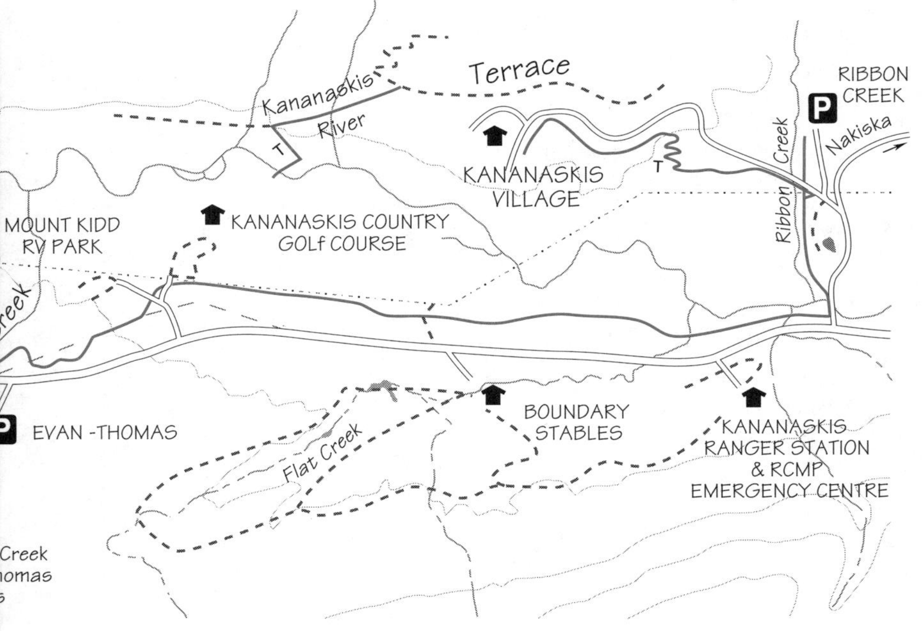

the way, come complete with a soundtrack of cars hurtling along Highway 40 which is just to your left. The attractive part ends when you cross a powerline access road (left to Highway 40 and Boundary Stables). Then the powerline itself comes in from the right and you ski along the east side of the right-of-way past maintenance buildings, switching over in a half kilometre to the west side between power poles and parking lots for Kananaskis Country Golf Course. Unfortunately, the golf course restaurant and bar is now closed in winter.

In the space of a few minutes you cross the golf course access road and two minor roads and turn onto a long straight, followed by a nice twisty section in the trees to your first encounter with Evan-Thomas Creek. Here the designers have thoughtfully incorporated seats into the attractive Rundlestone bridge, making it a natural gathering spot for Sunday-afternoon skiers from the RV Park who don't want to be out of earshot of civilisation (Highway 40 is only a few metres away). The bridge marks the halfway point and offers a superb view of Mt. Kidd and The Fortress.

What follows is another boring straight to the Mount Kidd RV Park access road. If you head down the road to the right you reach the Campers' Centre which is open and bursting at the seams with families rushing between the whirlpool, the snack bar and the video game room.

On your way again, you cross a minor access road, then it's once more into the pine forest for the brief stint to Highway 40 which for lazybugs like me is just too wide to shuffle across on skis without the possibility of being run over by a car at the centre line.

The section of trail east of Highway 40 is where you run into hills, most of them uphills in this direction. At the T-junction you join what's called the Wedge Connector, a piece of trail running between Wedge Pond day-use area parking lot and Evan-Thomas Creek parking lot.

THE WEDGE CONNECTOR

To Wedge Pond (0.5 km) Turn right, then right again into Wedge Pond Picnic area parking lot one minute off the highway. Interesting spot Wedge Pond. The original pond was drained, the rich soil of the lake bottom together with trillions of dead insect bodies carted away and used to top layer the Kananaskis Country Golf Course. The new deeper version is about as dull as the Western Irrigation Canal though I am willing to concede that in 50 years or so the vegetation will have grown back and if you part the sedges you'll find frog spawn once again and craneflies larvae crawling about the stones dressed up in pine needles. But wait! Wedge Pond may yet suffer the ultimate indignity of becoming a water hazard for the proposed extension to the golf course, and garden-variety sod will be rolled out to make a neat edge all around the shoreline.

To Evan-Thomas Creek Parking Lot and trail terminus (4 km) At the T-junction you turn left and ski along what could well be a future golf cart access road to a second bridge over Evan-Thomas Creek —pause to take in the view of Mt. Kidd— then continue uphill to a 4-way junction with Evan -Thomas Creek trail. Here you turn left and glide one last kilometre into the Evan-Thomas Creek parking lot.

A thought. If you've only got an hour or so to spare, the very pleasant undulating stretch between Wedge Pond and Evan-Thomas Creek parking lot is well worth skiing for its own sake. Forget the rest!

Opposite: the Wedge Connector between Wedge Pond and Evan-Thomas Creek. Through the trees is the south summit of Mt. Kidd.

Option: Backcountry explorations

Along the Wedge Connector between Wedge Pond and Evan-Thomas Creek are all kinds of old roads left over from Eau Claire logging days. Should the new Kan-Alta golf course meet final approval, chances seem excellent that the first road on the right — the one which parallels the Wedge Connector — will stage a takeover. Right now, its mid section is hopelessly eclipsed by willow bush. Only the fifth road on the right is worth following. It rises past log piles, dead-ending nearly 2 km later in two prongs going nowhere, though generations of topo maps still persist in showing the left-hand prong going all the way up Evan-Thomas Creek. Once a year on a rotten day in spring we have a go at finding the ongoing link and every year we go back to the car defeated. Too overgrown. There is, though, a passable trail for people with Gortex socks which starts from near the bridge over Evan-Thomas Creek and sports intermittent blazes and flagging, some of which is ours. Having followed it for only a few kilometres, I can't guarantee it goes all the way through. There is the little matter of the gorge under Mt. Mackay...

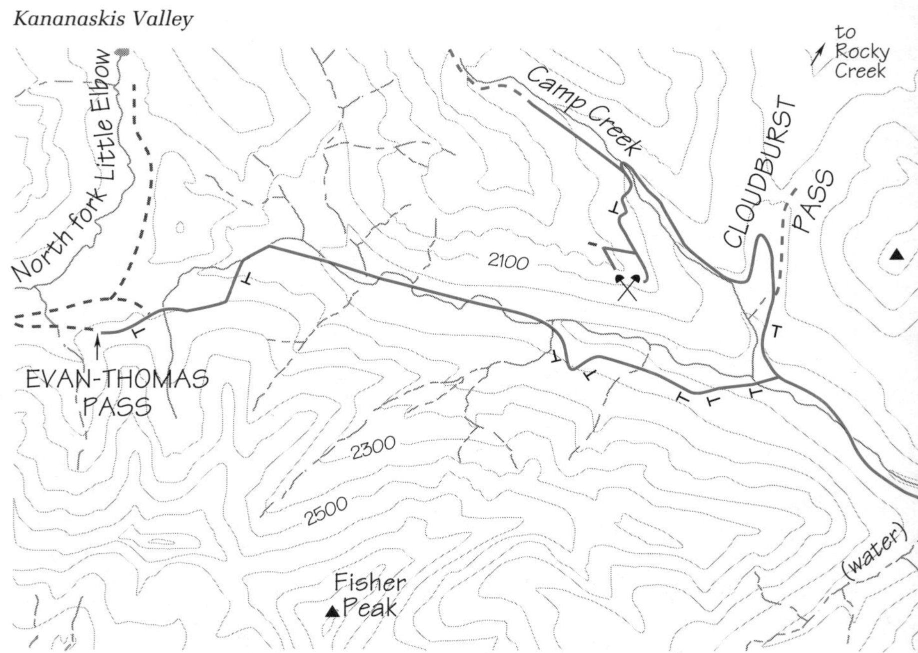

EVAN-THOMAS CREEK TO CAMP CREEK

Backcountry

Intermediate
11.5 km to Cloudburst Pass
13.5 km to Camp Creek junction
16 km to Evan-Thomas Pass, 6 km from Shatto road
Height gain to Cloudburst Pass 488 m, 717 m to ridge top
Height gain to Evan-Thomas Pass from parking lot 700 m
Maximum elevation at Cloudburst pass 1996 m, 2225 m at ridge top
Maximum elevation at Evan-Thomas Pass 2180 m
Map 82 J/14 Spray Lakes Reservoir

Access Kananaskis Trail (Hwy. 40) at Evan-Thomas Creek parking lot.

Facilities Washrooms at parking lot. Rustic furniture en route, hunter's camps in Camp Creek.

Overview The old coal exploration road up Evan-Thomas Creek to the Evan-Thomas-Rocky Creek watershed and Camp Creek makes a fabulous ski trip. Better surely than Evan-Thomas Pass as a destination and with more chance of getting there and back before dark. If determined to get to Evan-Thomas Pass then you'll have to step on the gas and make sure there's more than two trail breakers in the party for the final 6 km.

Don't expect signposts or bridges. This is one of K-Country's well-used unofficial trails, particularly popular with equestrians and by that I mean Guinn Outfitters of Boundary Stables who make it a part of their backcountry tour.

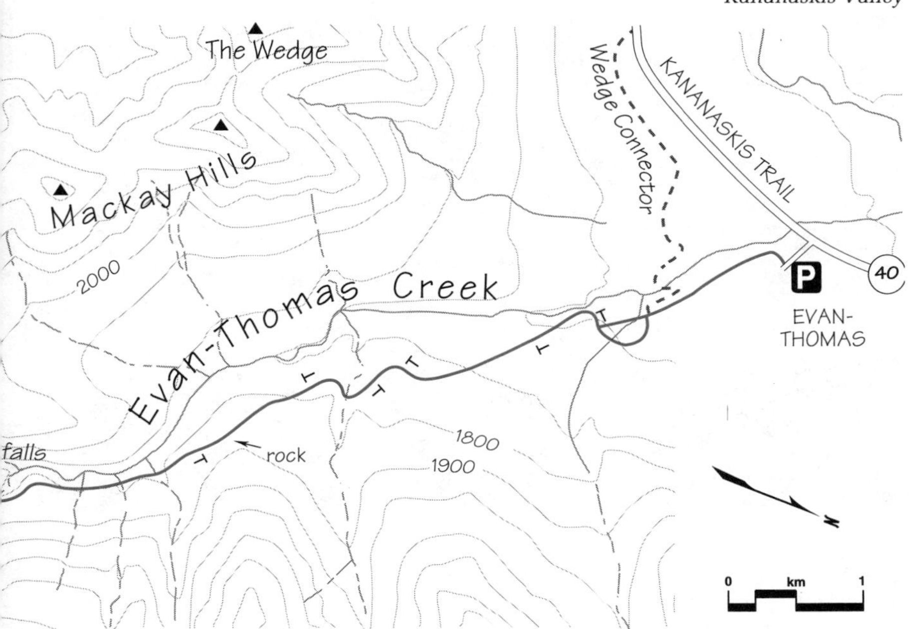

The first 1.7 km is packed and trackset, the southern terminus of Evan-Thomas trail which is not to be confused with this one. Just past the site of the proposed clubhouse for the proposed golf course is the 4-way junction where the groomed trail (Wedge Connector) turns right and you go left on the Shatto coal exploration road. Straight ahead is the short-cut, half as long but booby-trapped with ankle-grabbing willow bushes. Both variations joined, the road climbs and winds at a fairly constant gradient. The reason can only be guessed at. In this case, the creek is encased in steep cliffs with ice falls popular with ice climbers who walk up the creek bed from the bridge.

Thoroughly warmed up you arrive at the top of the first downhill where I swear whiskeyjacks perch in wait for skiers stripping off and having a bite to eat. The top of the slope faces south and has its own personal Chinook and, therefore, a few loose rocks. Another wave of uphills brings you to another high point with more waiting whiskeyjacks, another sunny bank and this time a much longer, steeper hill winding down to the valley bottom above the canyon. Go easy at the top, this time the rocks include a very large boulder courtesy of the 1990 spring runoff.

A little further on is a side stream crossing which would be unremarkable except that the water never freezes over. Although a fraction of its summer self, it still necessitates edging sideways across a log, being careful not to dip tips and tails in the water lest you set yourself up for a big scraping and re-waxing job. This is followed by a really delightful stretch along the east bank of Evan-Thomas Creek. You cross to the west bank and continue in the same easy way past a set of rustic lawn furniture to a junction. Straight down the hill is the cutline to Evan-Thomas Pass; right is the Shatto road to Cloudburst Pass and Camp Creek and the one most likely to have tracks.

The section to Cloudburst Pass is incredibly wide and so short a climb it always catches me off guard when it levels off in a meadow at the watershed. If pushed for time follow the longitudinal meadow through the gap to the true pass, a nice spot in the open offering views all round of the top halves of craggy moun-

From the hill out of Camp Creek is a glorious view of The Wedge (left) and the Mackay Hills (right).

tains. Fisher Peak is the only one with a name. Unfortunately the Wedge lies hidden behind the wind-scoured slopes of the Mackay Hills.

The longer alternative (about 2 hours return to pass) but one well worth the extra effort is to continue up the gently-inclined road into Camp Creek. Here the road splits, with one branch following the flat valley floor for a kilometre after which it's a simple matter of following the creek into the cirque. If you get that far. Rising up on both sides are designer slopes for telemarkers.

The left-hand road, more steeply inclined than anything previously encountered, winds uphill all the way to George Pocaterra's coal prospects in the larch zone on the ridge. What a spectacular location this is! Across the void of Evan-Thomas Creek is a top to bottom view of Fisher Peak, while in the opposite direction The Wedge is finally revealed in all its glory.

Return Would you believe less than an hour from Cloudburst Pass! Notwithstanding two uphills, this is just a fabulous ski out with much steeper downhills than expected.

Option : Evan-Thomas Pass
Reluctantly you abandon the well-travelled Shatto road and join the Evan-Thomas Pass exploration road-cutline which straightaway descends and crosses Evan-Thomas Creek. The upcoming climb is arduous, typical of cutlines. The worst part of it is that this hill and *the following three uphills* seem so unnecessary because the road then returns to the creek bed in one steep downhill swoop. On the map it makes sense to breeze along the creek bottom, but the reality is floundering through willow brush so that squashes that idea.

Now the flat middle section is a hiker's nightmare of mud and creek crossings, but under snow it's an easy plod with a terrific view ahead of my favourite unnamed mountain which fascinates with a left skyline ridge built like a rip saw. Hurry across the runout zone of a huge avalanche slope coming down from the right.

Where Evan-Thomas Creek bends to the right, the way on returns to the left bank of a tributary and is somewhat vague until it enters trees. Back in the open you probably noticed two breaks in the watershed ridge ahead. The road

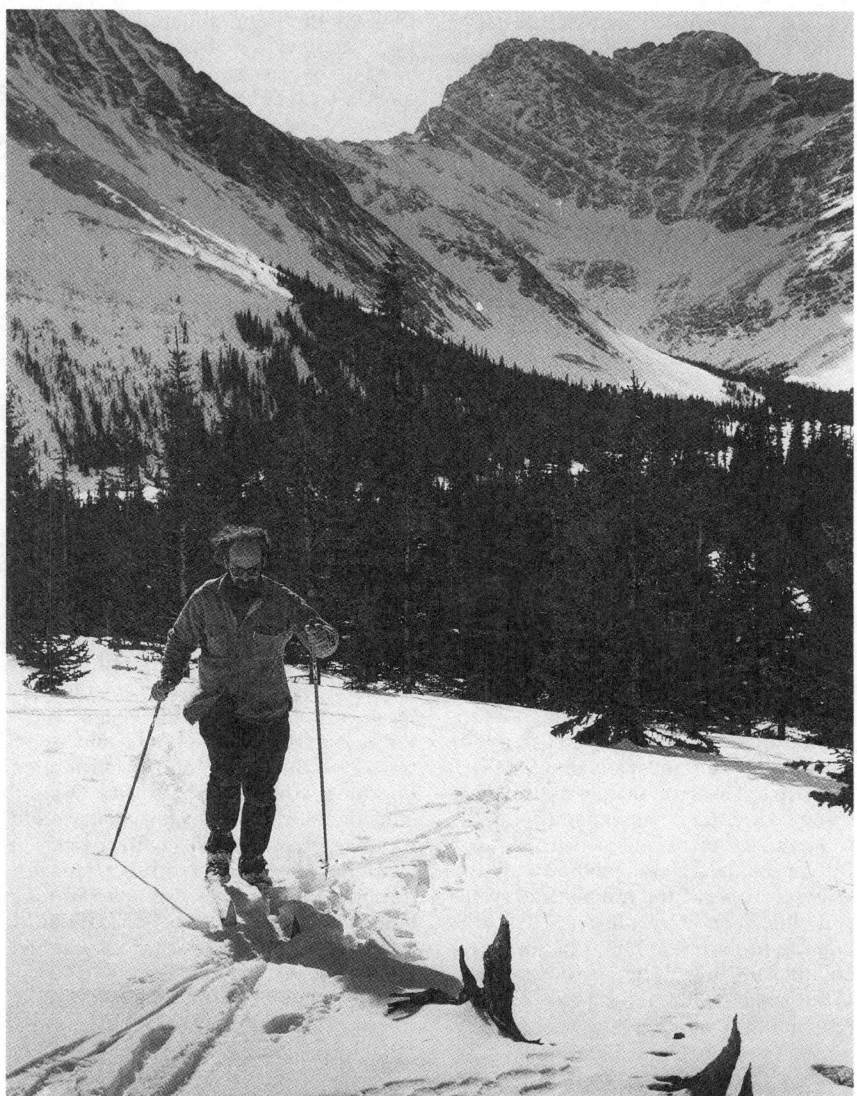

Evan-Thomas Pass and the headwaters of the Little Elbow's north fork below Mt. Evan-Thomas.

climbs towards the left-hand one, ultimately forsaking the true pass in favour of open spruce forest 50 m higher up and further to the east, thus offering a grand view of the Opal Range and the headwaters of the Little Elbow's north fork rimmed by Mts. Evan-Thomas, "Potts" and "Denny".

(At the base of the final uphill a trail turns off to the right and dekes through the true pass into the meadows of the Little Elbow. I thought you'd like to know.)

More about the trail This creek has had as many name changes as Elizabeth Taylor: Whiteman's Creek after the murder of a white man (possibly confused with Wasootch), Ithorhan Odabi Waptan "Many Porcupines", Cha se tida Wapta "Burnt Timber River", Kiska Tha Waptan "Mountain Goat Creek", Irhe Waptan "Rocky Creek" (the latter two applying more to Rocky Creek surely), Porcupine Creek, and finally Evan-Thomas Creek after Rear Admiral Hugh Evan-Thomas who I recall as making a couple of bad blunders during the Battle of Jutland in 1916.

When the creek was called Porcupine, Paul Amos's father Three Buffalo Bulls led George Pocaterra, in exchange for a favour, to the coal seams where pieces of coal were lying about the ground "as big as pianos". Pocaterra promptly staked a claim on June 30, 1910. He managed to interest the fur buyers Mackay & Dippie in the project and a syndicate was formed, marking the start of a life-long search for shareholders able to finance the project. Contrary to popular myth, George Pocaterra did not spend all his time wandering the Kananaskis as a romantic figure dressed in buckskins; he was first and foremost a businessman.

At first, it seemed that everything was going swimmingly: an expedition to the site with a group of engineers from a large British coal company and ten local miners who cross cut and trenched 27 seams and dug an adit resulted in the Brits offering to purchase the mine for an incredible million dollars! The talk was of building a railroad from Seebe up the Kananaskis Valley which was excellent for the purpose. Unfortunately, this was in 1914 shortly before World War 1 was declared on August 4th.

Fast forward to the 1920's. Favourable reports by consulting engineers, and negotiations with coal companies were again stymied by a second World War. In an emotional letter to Paul Amos, George wrote, "At the time it looked like something wonderful, but both myself and my partners have wished many times since that we had never, never seen that * coal in our lives. It has cost us around $70,000 (seventy thousand dollars) and that is a lot of money, over thirty years of worry and on my part also many years of work for ABSOLUTELY NOTHING".

But by 1944, Pocaterra ."whirled suddenly into an endeavour to give re-birth and active life to my old baby", was negotiating with new coal companies and drumming up new financial support. Rather than bore you with the specifics, let's just say that five years later Shatto Construction (brothers M.J. and W. R.) bulldozed a road over the top of Pocaterra's trail and assembled a new cabin in Camp Creek and that by 1951 the Cloudburst Coal Company was testing, reporting, exploring and excavating. Like nowadays, the road was susceptible to washouts, on one occasion forcing district ranger Joe Kovach, who was keeping an eye on things, to make the first ascent of Rocky Creek.

Although the new syndicate of Mineral Resources had enough money for development, it was all heavily invested in oil leases so when the syndicate was unable to pay off rental arrears, the land lease was abruptly terminated in 1959. Pocaterra promptly secured a new lease, re-staked the claim and incorporated Pocaterra Mines the same year. Despite considerable interest by the Japanese and promising negotiations with a German Coal company, the enterprise fell through, this time a victim of a waning market and the new Alberta Coal Policy released in 1976. In any case, George had passed across the Great Divide in 1972.

Call it fate that the beautiful grassy ridges of the Evan-Thomas were to remain unsullied.

GOAT CREEK TO BANFF

Backcountry & Groomed

Easy intermediate
18 km between parking lots
Height loss 300 m
Maximum elevation 1661 m
Map 82 O/4 Banff, 82 O/3 Canmore

Access
1. Smith-Dorrien/Spray Trail at Whiteman's Pass. Turn right into Goat Creek parking lot.
2. Banff at Bow Falls parking lot. Turn left off Spray Avenue towards Banff Springs Golf Course and park before the bridge over the Spray River.
3. Banff at Banff Springs Hotel. From the statue of Cornelius Van Horne, continue under the arch past the parking structure on the right to a small parking lot at the start of the Spray River fire road.

Facilities Washrooms at Goat Creek parking lot.

In Banff, restaurants to suit every taste, souvenir shops etc.

En route, picnic tables and rustic washrooms at Spray River Loop for the penniless who've brought sandwiches.

Overview Is it any wonder that this trail is so popular. Contrary to most other trails which climb uphill to a destination, this one goes downhill nearly all the way. And not only that, but downhill into Banff with innumerable eating and drinking places. To get maximum mileage out of this, you need a car at each end, or you could of course work off lunch by returning the same way — a 36 km return trip. But not many people do. Once settled in a warm fuggy restaurant sipping a carafe of vin rouge, it's extraordinarily difficult to get going again. The trail's signposted throughout and currently being packed and trackset by Parks Canada from the Banff end.

The first thing you do is cross the ditch and get onto the Goat Creek logging road. Keep right where other roads join in until you arrive at the Banff Park boundary at km 1.9. The next 7.2 km is the fun run down by the side of Goat Creek. In the days before guidebooks and before it became generally known there even *was* a road on the east bank, every pioneer of the trail suffered a slow bushwhack down the side of the creek bed. The joy on hitting the road at the bridge was tempered with sentences beginning with, "if only we had known about", but for some reason this information was kept a secret and never passed on to other "pioneers".

But back to today's lucky skiers. The road crosses the bridge to the west bank, and in another kilometre is winding down steeper downhills to the bridge over the Spray River. In store is a hard five minutes of uphill work to the all important junction with the Spray River fire road on the bank top. Unless you wish a lengthy detour to Spray Lakes Reservoir turn right.

A gentle uphill, then rolling downhills bring you to the turnaround point of the Spray River Loop at a picnic area. Go either way.

The road on the left — the continuation of the fire road — has downhills and *uphills* for heaven's sake, but has the advantage of leading straight to the Banff Springs Hotel. If you're parked at Bow Falls, cut off right about half a kilometre before the parking lot and descend to the Spray River via Golf Course ski trail #2. Across the foot bridge you make a left turn and follow the east bank across a fairway to the Spray River bridge. The parking lot is in sight across the bridge.

The road on the right, which straight-away crosses a bridge over the Spray River, is much flatter and ends with a nice downhill run onto the Banff Springs Golf Course. For some reason this final downhill terrifies beginners who have strayed onto the hill from the fairway, so be on full alert for bodies

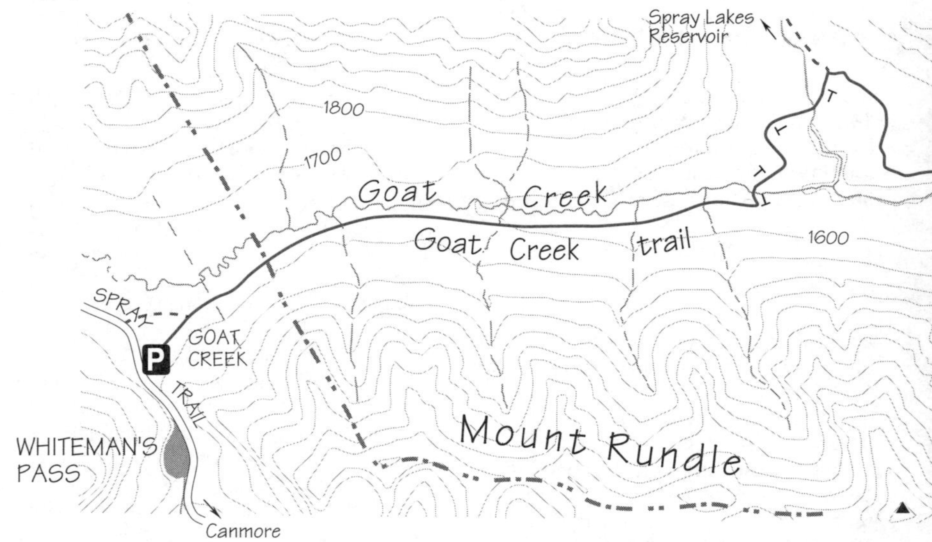

splattered all over the bends. Wend your way leftwards through the crowds to the large statue of a Bighorn sheep located on the clubhouse access road at Spray River bridge. Bow Falls parking lot is just the other side of the bridge.

More about the area I grieve for Goat Creek and the Spray River, both of them doomed by an unfortunate arrangement of topography. By the early 1950's the Spray Power Project was diverting all the water of the Spray and upper Goat into Spray Lakes Reservoir and man-made Goat Pond before sending it off to Canmore via canals and pressure tunnels. From Banff, the Spray River fire road followed the lower valley to the new reservoir which rose up 165 feet and covered two natural lakes, the forestry cabin and the fish hatchery cabin. Anticipating this project (Calgary Power had their eye on this valley since 1921), the Federal Minister of the Interior, under pressure from Calgary Power and the Alberta Government, had given the go-ahead to remove the upper Goat and the Spray Lakes from the national park as far back as 1930. Where were the environmentalists, you ask? Strangely enough, the Coal Operators Association of Alberta, alarmed that hydro-electric power would threaten their market, were instrumental in forming the National Parks Association of Canada and did some sterling work after the fact.

Prior to these bureaucratic manoeuvrings, the pack trail up the Spray River and Goat Creek was the popular way in to the fishing lakes, "the special territory of princes, presidents and millionaires". You could also join in from Canmore via Whiteman's Pass, but once you got to the pass the junction wasn't obvious, particularly if you were looking for the trail down Goat Creek. Just like 10 years ago. Mary Barclay, cofounder of the Canadian Youth Hostels Association, is fond of recalling the time a group of hostellers riding from Canmore to Banff via Goat Creek somehow missed the turning and ended up at first Spray Lake in the pitch dark. With only regulation sheet sleeping bags to keep out the cold, they were naturally ecstatic when the ranger showed up and invited them into his cabin.

Opposite: Not far from the trailhead and a view back to Chinaman's Peak.

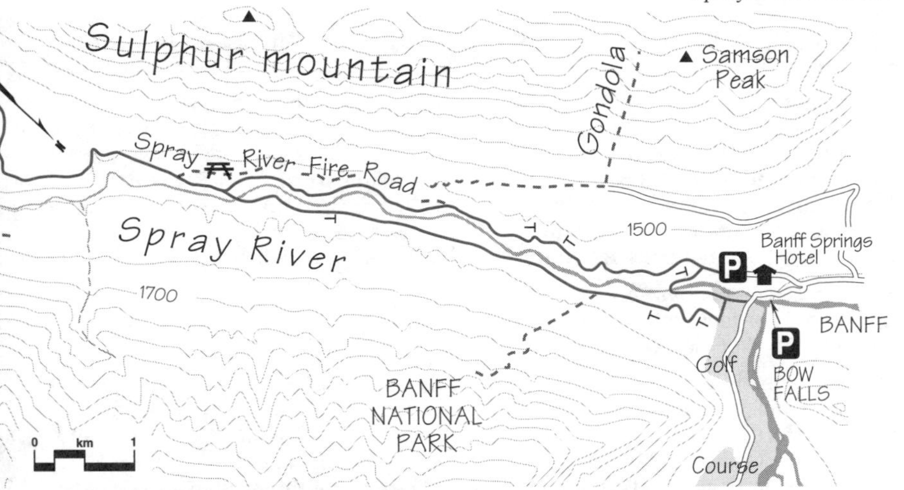

Photo: Alf Skrastins

RUMMEL LAKE

Backcountry & Route

Intermediate
5 km to lake, 8 km to pass
Height gain to lake 396 m
Height gain to pass 579 m
Maximum elevation lake 2246 m
Maximum elevation pass 2390 m
Map 82 J/14 Spray Lakes Reservoir

Access Smith-Dorrien/Spray Trail. Park on the road a few metres north of the junction with Watridge Logging Road.

Overview First timers to this gem of a lake should follow along in someone else's tracks since the narrow summer trail is not obvious. Neither is it official so don't expect help from signposts or red markers. From the lake you have the option of carrying on to windy Rummel Pass or doing a spot of telemarking, but be damn sure where you go. The tragic accident of 1991 is written up in the second edition of "Avalanche Safety for Skiers and Climbers" as a cautionary tale for all would-be telemarkers at Rummel Lake.

Starting above the bank, an easy stretch of logging road brings you to a very large cutblock at the Peter Lougheed Provincial Park boundary signpost. Take my word for it that the trail bends left here and climbs diagonally to the cutblock's top left-hand corner where you pass through an avenue into the upper cutblock. Here the trail wends right, then back left to the top left-hand corner where you should find some faded red flagging. Before plunging into the forest look back one last time at a grand view encompassing Mts. Birdwood, Fist, Smuts, Commonwealth, Cone Mountain and the reservoir.

The trail continues along a ridge paralelling Rummel Creek which is deep down in the valley to your left. Apart from the odd dip, the gradient is gentle and the trees spaced reasonably far apart. At an unspecified point (flagging on tree to right in 1991) you angle left and start the gradual descent into the creek bed, no doubt reached at half a dozen different

On the bench. Rummel Lake lies in the cirque below Mt. Galatea.

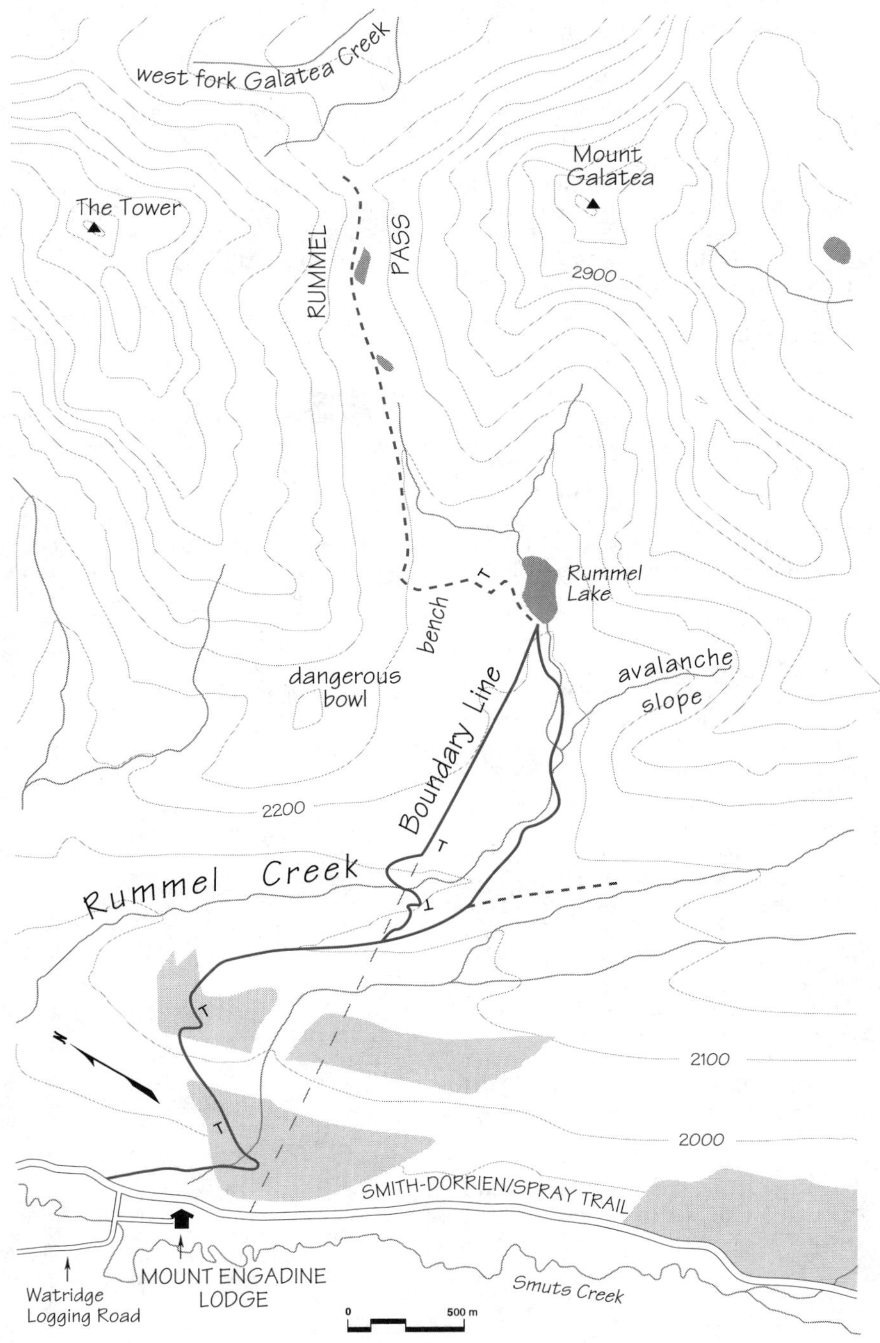
west fork Galatea Creek
Mount Galatea
The Tower
RUMMEL
PASS
2900
Rummel Lake
bench
avalanche slope
dangerous bowl
Boundary Line
2200
Rummel Creek
N
2100
2000
SMITH-DORRIEN/SPRAY TRAIL
MOUNT ENGADINE LODGE
Watridge Logging Road
Smuts Creek
0
500 m

points in half a dozen trips. It's an easy trudge up the creek bed, first on the right bank, then on the left to avoid the avalanche slope at the bend, then back right again through a meadow. Remember the tree? Rising up in the middle of the meadow like a homing beacon, was a quite magnificent tree in its time with an incredibly wide girth decorated in its last years by fluorescent yellow wolf lichen and which regrettably keeled over in 1990. So from Dead Tree Meadow, as I call it, you climb back into the trees, then at the flat move back left (or even further left to pick up the boundary line) for the final climb up to the lake.

In winter you miss the gorgeous green colour of the water, but never mind, the fishing registration box is almost the same shade. And before noting that Mt. Galatea makes a very impressive backdrop it is mandatory to read Duck Unlimited's sign about spawning beds. But it would be hard to ruin the magnificent scene completely.

Option: Rummel Pass
This is an easy trip.

First you climb easy-angled telemarking slopes under the larches to gain the bench north of the lake. Then you turn your back to the view and head into the flat upper valley past mangled krummholz and solitary boulders with ditches which make wonderful wind shelters. The further you go up this godforsaken valley the more concentrated the wind and the worse the snow, until finally you reach a winding rocky defile where you take your skis off and hike to the pass. While expressing amazement over grass, you become conscious of the constant banging of the wind against the cliffs of The Tower where the wind dragon lives. A quick downward glance into the dark forests of Galatea Creek's west fork and you're away from this eerie place to find a nice cozy ditch for lunch.

Return Don't hold your breath anticipating a carefree run down the cutblocks. You may be lucky, it may be snowing heavily and -20°, but most times the snow hereabouts is wind-crusted sugar mined with basket-eating tree stumps, and with the fear of running your tips under a log, falling on a dagger of dry wood and impaling your jugular, you tend to ski it cautiously. Next time you say it will be different but usually it is not.

Option return via the boundary line
A slightly more difficult option which is skiable either way is the recently cut provincial park boundary line between the lake and the trail on the ridge. Of course, being a straight cut through forest it's not exactly the scenic Icefields Parkway, but it's quite good fun to ski and not quite as straightforward as you might suppose. For instance, because Rummel Creek is so deeply incised at this point, zigs are necessary to get into and out of the valley, while open slopes on the west bank are an invitation to fool around.

Opposite top: the bleak environs of Rummel Pass.

Opposite bottom: The flats in front of Mount Engadine Lodge. Rudi's Piper PA20 marks the bend in Princess Anne loop.

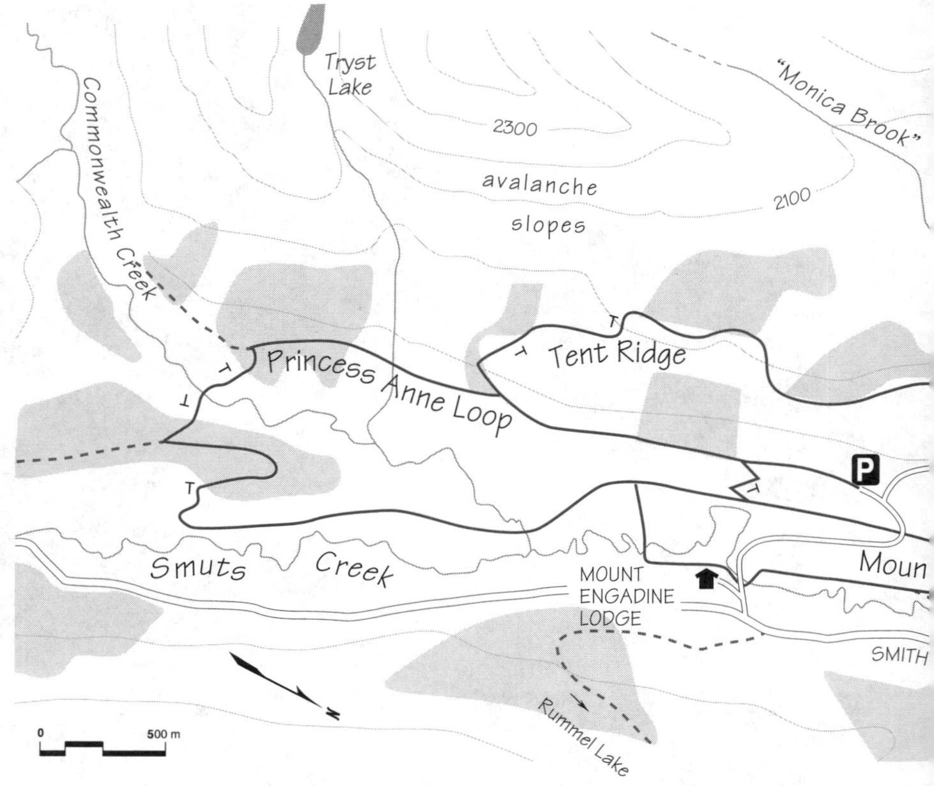

MOUNT ENGADINE LODGE SKI TRAILS

Sometimes groomed

21.6 km of trails
Maximum elevation 2027 m
Map 82 J/14 Spray Lakes Reservoir

Access Smith-Dorrien/Spray Trail. Turn west onto the Watridge Logging Road signed "Mount Engadine Lodge" and "Mount Shark". There are three accesses off the Watridge Logging Road:

1. 100 m from the road junction turn left into the Mount Engadine Lodge parking lots.
2. 0.9 km from the junction turn left up a secondary road and park at the end of the plowed section.
3. 1.8 km from the junction is a small parking area on the right-hand side of the road located almost precisely half-way between Tent Ridge trail and Shark Lake logging road.

Facilities That lonely outpost, Mount Engadine Lodge, offers accommodation and full board from Christmas through to mid April. Your hosts Rudi and Liesbeth Kranabitter also welcome drop-ins for breakfast, lunch and afternoon tea, but require reservations for evening meals in the Swiss style, so either register in the morning before taking to the trails or phone ahead to 678-2880. On request, Rudi (UIAGM, ACMG) will guide house guests into the powdery backcountry.

Overview These are perfect beginner trails, and offer a grand opportunity to combine exercise with three square meals a day if you're lucky enough to stay at the lodge. Most trails are based on the open flats of Smuts Creek and range south to north between Commonwealth Creek and Spray Lakes Reservoir with connections to Tent Ridge, Shark Lake, the Helipad and the Mount Shark parking lot. When he has time, Rudi does the tracksetting which means that sometimes the trails are back-country and it's up to you to navigate between orange markers on trees. Naturally, the pecking order always begins with Princess Anne Loop.

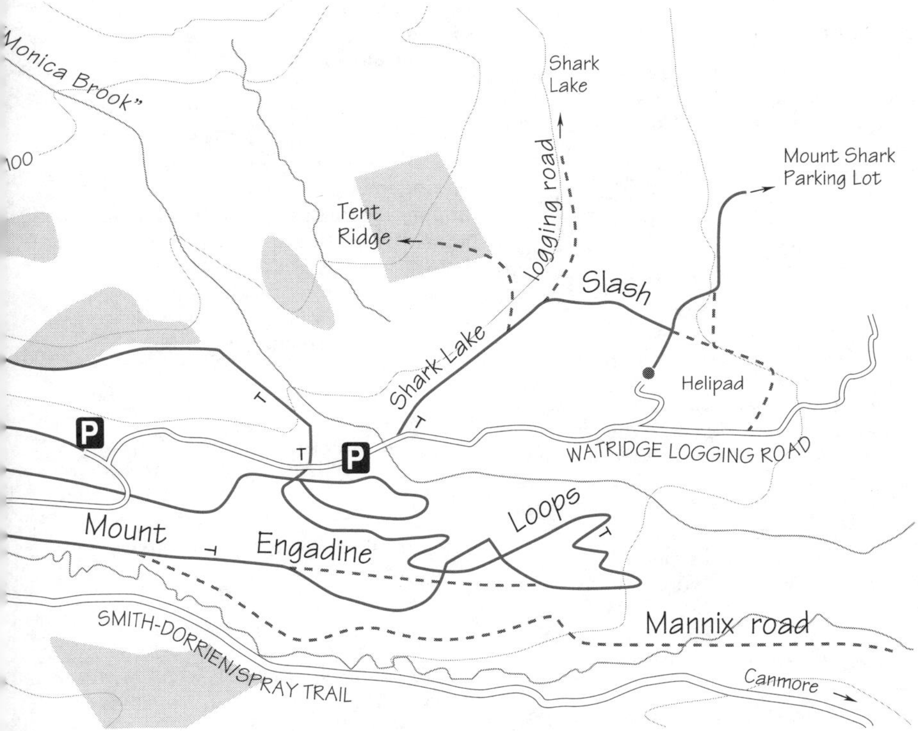

Admittedly there are grey days when the wind is howling up the flats throwing snow in your face, but fixed in my mind are spring days in April when a high-pressure system is stationary above the lodge, the sky a deep blue, the flats blindingly white like a TV commercial for washing powders. On such days the sun moves lazily around the heavens, illuminating the pointy Spray Mountains in the morning and gilding the Kananaskis Range at aperitif time, leaving you elated at the beauty of the place.

PRINCESS ANNE LOOP

Easy
8 km return

In front of the lodge this is a very busy trail with beginners making circles around Rudi's Piper PA20. But if Princess Anne on cross country skis for the first time in her life can get round the loop, or more to the point, if her less able-bodied bodyguard can get round the loop, then there's absolutely no excuse for you to keep hanging around in sight of the lodge. Ski further up the flats to just beyond Commonwealth Creek where you'll find the trail looping back via cutblocks and a logging road one terrace up to the west. This is where a few easy hills add spice to the trip.

Whichever way round you decide to ski the loop, Commonwealth Peak is the one mountain which demands to appear in every photograph. It was named after the Commonwealth Games in Edmonton and has more in common with the name "Smuts" than you might think, since it was Field Marshall Smuts who suggested the name "British Commonwealth of Nations" in 1917 to describe the autonomous nations of the British Empire. Personally, as a name for a mountain I find it entirely inappropriate.

TENT RIDGE TRAIL

Intermediate
3.5 km
Height gain 125 m

You should know that this trail is *not* the usual way to Tent Ridge. It doesn't even offer a good view of the ridge, just a passing glimpse from a cutblock. Although I have a definite problem with the name, I would have to agree with Rudi that this logging road makes a very fine ski trail with exceptional views (like all the trails). The south end is at threat from avalanches when hazard is high.

From access #3 along the Watridge Logging Road (or from Mount Engadine Loops) backtrack up the road a little way to the start of a logging road. After a steep beginning it gains height at a reasonable rate and carries you through cutblock # 27 with its passing view of Tent Ridge. A dip through a belt of trees and you're into cutblock # 31 which stretches far back and is suitable for all level 1 telemarkers like me. The view is certainly superb of the Smith-Dorrien valley, the high point both literally and scenically of the whole trail. Actually the route across the cutblock sticks closely to the cutblock's bottom edge (you probably missed the markers), but leave it for skiers coming in the opposite direction because the overpowering urge is to sweep across open slopes and make pretty tracks down to the bottom south-east corner where the road leaves the cutblock.

The final descent is a blinder: a short sharp hill followed by a longer stretch through trees into a third cutblock where all avalanche chutes meet and discharge their loads. At the bottom is a draw with speed bumps for avalanches which is all a bit alarming and a very good reason why this loop is better skied in an anti-clockwise direction so you can get through the danger zone in a matter of seconds. At the bumps the road turns sharp left and delivers you to Princess Anne Loop at the logging road on the bench (orange marker indicating the turn-off).

The west leg of Princess Anne loop. View from a cutblock of Commonwealth Peak.

MOUNT ENGADINE LOOPS

Easy anti-clockwise
Easy Intermediate clockwise
8.5 km of trails

On the north side of the Watridge Logging Road are fun figures of eight with connections to Princess Anne Loop, Tent Ridge trail and the trail to Mount Shark parking lot and the helipad. The trails descend half-way to Spray Lakes Reservoir where you'll discover a maze of old logging roads and with a bit of searching near Monica Brook, another of Johnny's Musko's poaching cabins. From an anorexic spruce forest are a new lot of views presided over by Mts. Engadine and Fortune. Expect three nice downhills if skiing clockwise, and a surprise view of your old friend Commonwealth Peak from a meadow if skiing anti-clockwise as recommended by Rudi.

Incidentally, the straight north of the bridge was the original Smith-Dorrien/ Spray Trail built by Mannix and Poole Construction to get at French Creek during the diversions.

TO HELIPAD AND MOUNT SHARK PARKING LOT

Intermediate
2.5 km to Mount Shark
2 km to Helipad from #3 access
Height loss to Mount Shark 97 m
Height gain to Helipad 30 m

Start either from access #3 or side step down the bank from Mount Engadine Loops onto the Watridge Logging Road. About 100 m down the road beyond "Monica Brook" turn left up the Shark Lake logging road. It soon levels and in about a kilometre just past the access road to Tent Ridge you turn off right down Slash as I call it, because you would be incredulous if you saw what you are skiing over. But covered by two or three metres of snow it's just another gently-inclined downhill of unblemished white which leads past umpteen slip roads, all on the left, to Helipad trail (signpost). Go left downhill for Mount Shark parking lot, right uphill for the helipad.

Mount Engadine loops offer new views of Mt. Engadine (left) and The Tower (right).

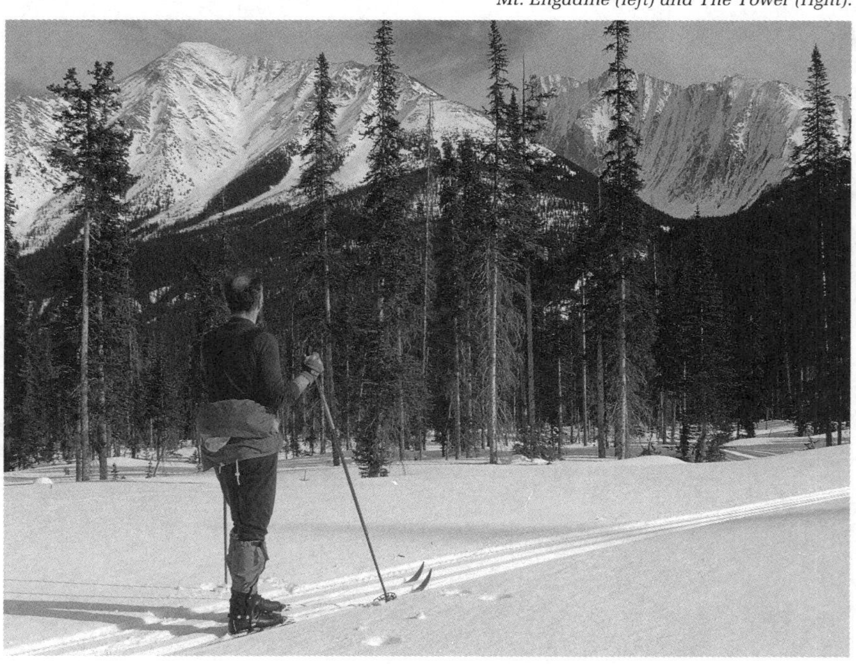

TENT RIDGE VIA GAWBY GULCH

Backcountry & route

Intermediate
3.5 km to base of ridge
Height gain 240 m to base of ridge
Maximum elevation 2134 m base of ridge, 2515 m ridge top
Map 82 J/14 Spray Lakes Reservoir

Access Smith-Dorrien/Spray Trail. Turn west onto the Watridge Logging Road and in 1.8 km park in a small parking area on the right-hand side of the road.

Overview This is the quickest access onto Tent Ridge for telemarkers that I know of. Obviously with greater effort you can reach the same spot from Mount Shark parking lot via Helipad trail.

About 100 m further down the Watridge Logging Road beyond "Monica Brook" turn left up the Shark Lake logging road which soon levels. A kilometre of easy going and you fork left up a secondary road into cutblock # 23. Now there is nothing to stop you from wandering up to the top edge of the cutblock and going in through the trees that way, but why not leave the snow clean for the descent? A better access route follows the logging road into a draw called Gawby Gulch, then climbs up the gulch all the way into the larch zone below the open slopes.

More about the area I remember coming up this way with Harry Connolly back in the early 1970's to check snow stakes for the upcoming ski area "Assiniboia". The amount of snow was truly impressive.

The saga of Tent Ridge began at Fortress Mountain Ski Resort. Wolfgang Eaman's father who was the maintenance manager at Snow Ridge, as it was then called, was chatting to his mechanical engineer Albert Allart and saying something like. "You know, I reckon Snow Ridge has been built in the wrong place, should have been built one ridge over". So in the season of 1967/8 Albert along with Harry Connolly from UMA Engineering revved up the snowmobile and came up the road from Canmore looking for this mythical ski area in the valley one over and lo and behold they found this mountain shaped like a ridge tent. At the time Spray Lakes Sawmills hadn't started logging in the immediate area, but had

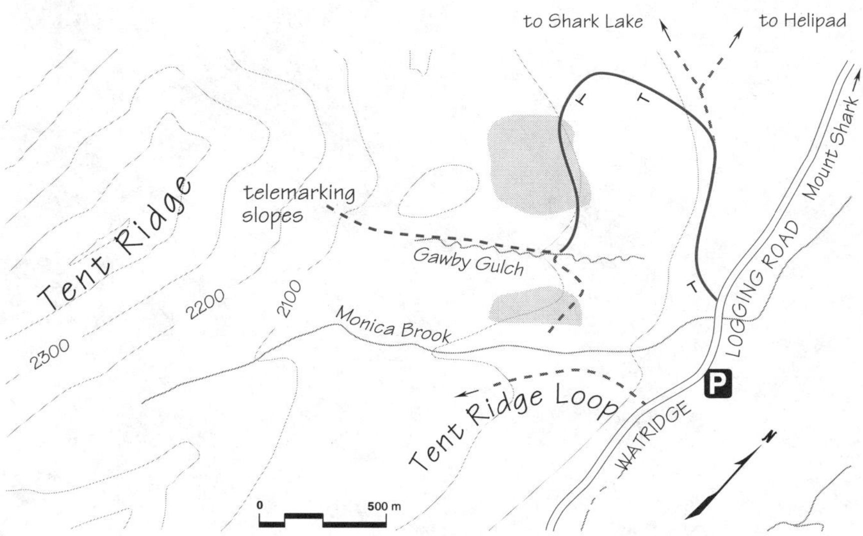

pushed in a few roads like the upper and lower Watridge logging roads. Setting up a shack at the 900 m junction of the lower road, Harry settled down to spending over 15 years of his life's weekends and holidays monitoring snow stakes and instruments to measure relative humidity, temperature, wind and precipitation. Although the cutblocks were not cut until 1971, the point is that when Harry's Spray Lakes Corporation, a subsidiary of UMA Engineering got serious about the Assiniboia project in the mid 1970's, the area was pretty well logged out by Spray Lakes Sawmills with ready-made ski runs in the offing.

The Alberta Government was not impressed. Not only was the scheme too far ahead of the Provincial budget, it was too far ahead in concept, especially the accommodation-on-site bit. This was pretty controversial stuff! "Not totally clear there is a need for such a development at this time" said the then Assistant Deputy Minister of Renewable Resources.

Ten years on, "hoaxed into a proposal no one had any intention of keeping", Spray Lakes Corporation's revamped plan for Tent Ridge and Mt. Sparrowhawk, was used, and I use that term deliberately, to secure Calgary the 1988 Winter Olympics, then, despite being loudly praised only the month before, was promptly discarded on decision day, citing lack of hotels in the vicinity and the cost of rebuilding the road up from Canmore despite a six million dollar budget for this very purpose. Into favour came a hill nobody wanted with trees intact, little snow and over-wintering sheep, but, more importantly it had three hotels at the bottom which badly needed some winter activity to keep the bogey man from the door.

Growing philosophical in his middle age and muttering phrases into his beard like "C'est la vie", Harry tells me the government encourages him to work on new schemes, to date a winter heliski operation on Mt. Sparrowhawk combined with a summer tour boat operation on Spray Lake Reservoir using a surplus steamer from Waterton Lake. Rather interestingly, the Minister of Tourism, Don Sparrow, is now urging Harry to keep the ski area on the front burner, so we may yet see a new Assiniboia rising out of the ashes.

Gawby Gulch is a lot of fun!

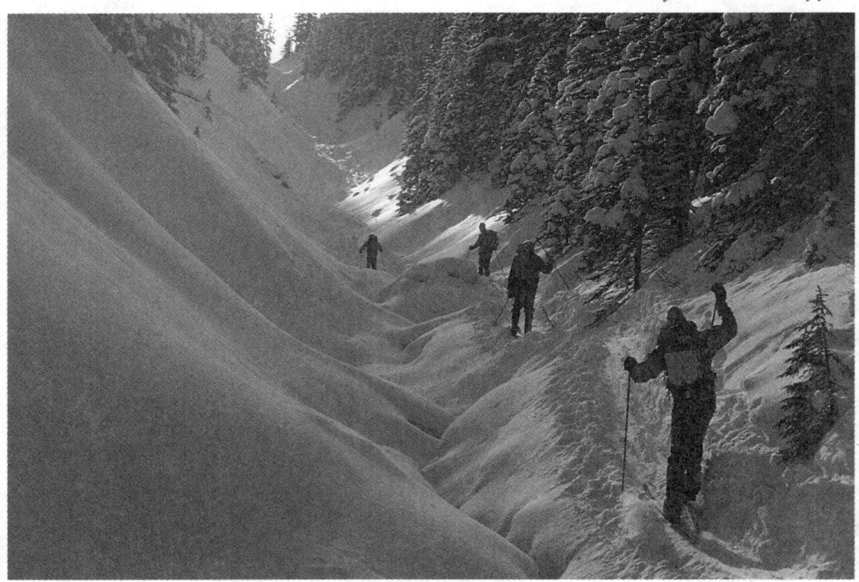

Photo: Bruce Jamieson

MOUNT SHARK SKI TRAILS — Groomed

18 km of trails
Maximum elevation 1814 m at helipad
Map 82 J/14 Spray Lakes Reservoir

Access Smith-Dorrien/Spray Trail. 11.4 km south of Spray Ranger Station or 6.2 km north of Mud lake, turn west onto the Watridge Logging Road signed "Mount Engadine Lodge" and "Mount Shark". Follow the road to its end at the Mount Shark parking lot in 5.3 km, (passing en route Mount Engadine Lodge to left at 0.1 km, a plowed logging road to left at 0.9 km and the helipad access road to left at 3.3 km).

Facilities Washrooms and picnic tables at parking lot. Rudi Setz Memorial Biathlon Range, two tiny huts for use by race officials in the Start/Finish Area.

En route is Mount Engadine Lodge described in detail on page 106.

Overview Everybody likes to ski at Shark, alias Spray Lake Ski Trails and Watridge Ski Trails. But before people got used to the trails at the Canmore Nordic Centre which require a Silva compass and orienteering map, the racing loops at Shark were actually bewildering to tourers and thus largely avoided. There is the story of tourers returning from a one day marathon around Marvel Pass. Arriving still reasonably fresh on the Watridge Lake trail in the dark, they got suckered into following all the convolutions of the racing trails and arrived at the parking lot knackered. At least they were spared the shame of a bivy on the 2.5 km!

There are no hills as scary as those at the Canmore Nordic Centre and the snow is a great deal better, falling early November and leaving late May. Due to cutbacks in funding, trails are packed and only occasionally trackset so it's a good place to practise your skating technique. Packing , by the way, is usually done on a Wednesday. Though you're travelling mainly through spruce forest, cutblocks and natural clearings at intervals offer astonishing views of Spray Lakes Reservoir, Tent Ridge, Mt. Shark, Cone Mountain, Mt. Engadine and even the tip of Mt. Assiniboine — all thoroughly snow plastered. Obviously it snows here a lot, but hardly ever on weekends and never on race days. When I think of Mount Shark, hot spring sunshine comes to mind; the mountains dazzling against a deep blue sky, and skiers skating leisurely around the trails in shorts and T-shirts.

You need to know a one-way system is in effect, that loops are colour-coded, junctions numbered, and trails 4-m wide. Recent additions include a trail from the parking lot to the helipad and the brand new Rudi Setz Memorial Biathlon Range and penalty loop located in beautiful parkland close to the Start/Finish area. In the winter of 1992/93 Brown, Orange, Pink, Grey and the old Yellow loops were dropped from the official brochure though I have retained the latter two, renamed Atom and Peewee, because of their use in Jackrabbit races. Long-time skiers of Mount Shark will also notice that major colour-coded loops have been switched around and very often have new configurations just to confuse you. For instance, the infamous Blue is now Red, the 5 km Men's A Loop. By way of explanation the instigator, Clarke Smith, tells me that people found the old system too confusing! Incidentally, the "P" in the trail descriptions refers to the perimeter trail.

On occasion you'll be sharing the loops with racing boy scouts and racers performing time trials. And there's a chance some loops may be closed during the Annual Spring Fling for instance. As you will have gathered, Shark's no longer a venue for high profile competition. But when there's a World Cup down the road don't be surprised to find Olympic gold medallists Vegard Ulvang and Bjorn Daehlie double poling around the trails, acclimatising.

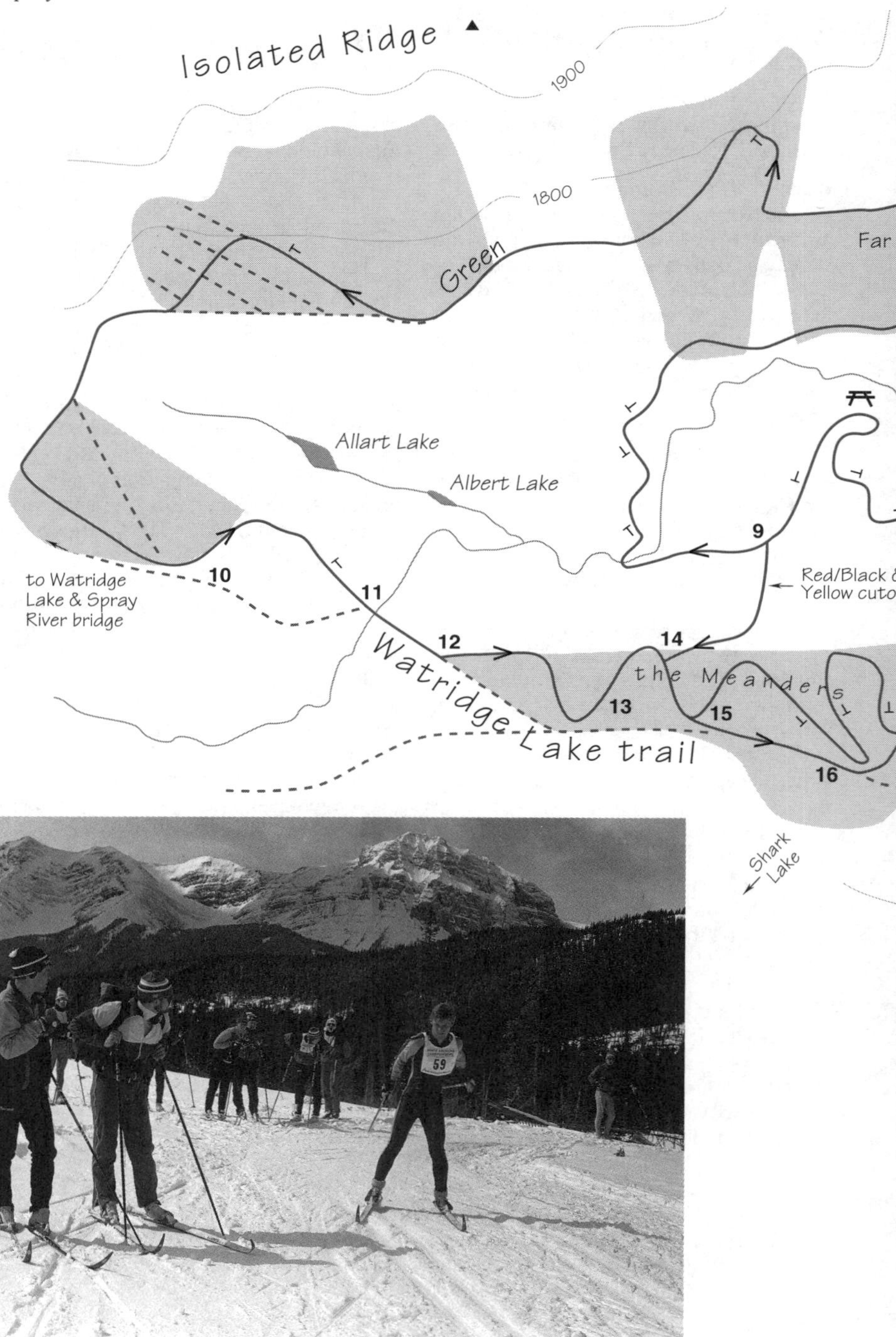
Isolated Ridge
1900
1800
Green
Allart Lake
Albert Lake
9
10
11
12
13
14
15
16
to Watridge Lake & Spray River bridge
Red/Black & Yellow cutof
the Meanders
Watridge Lake trail
Shark Lake

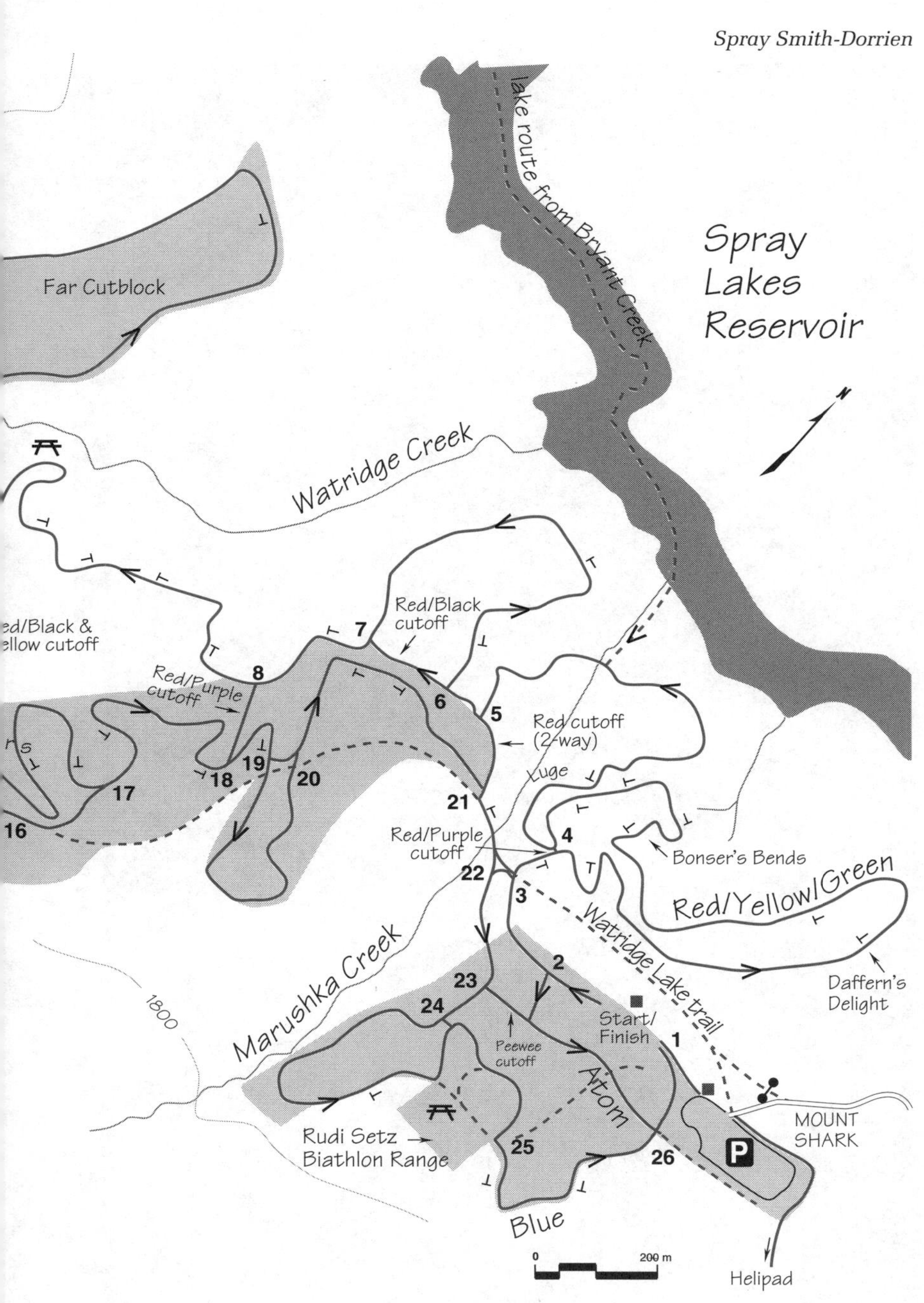

Photo opposite: the perimeter trail near 21 (Mt. Turner in the background). Photo taken during the North American Championships in 1986.

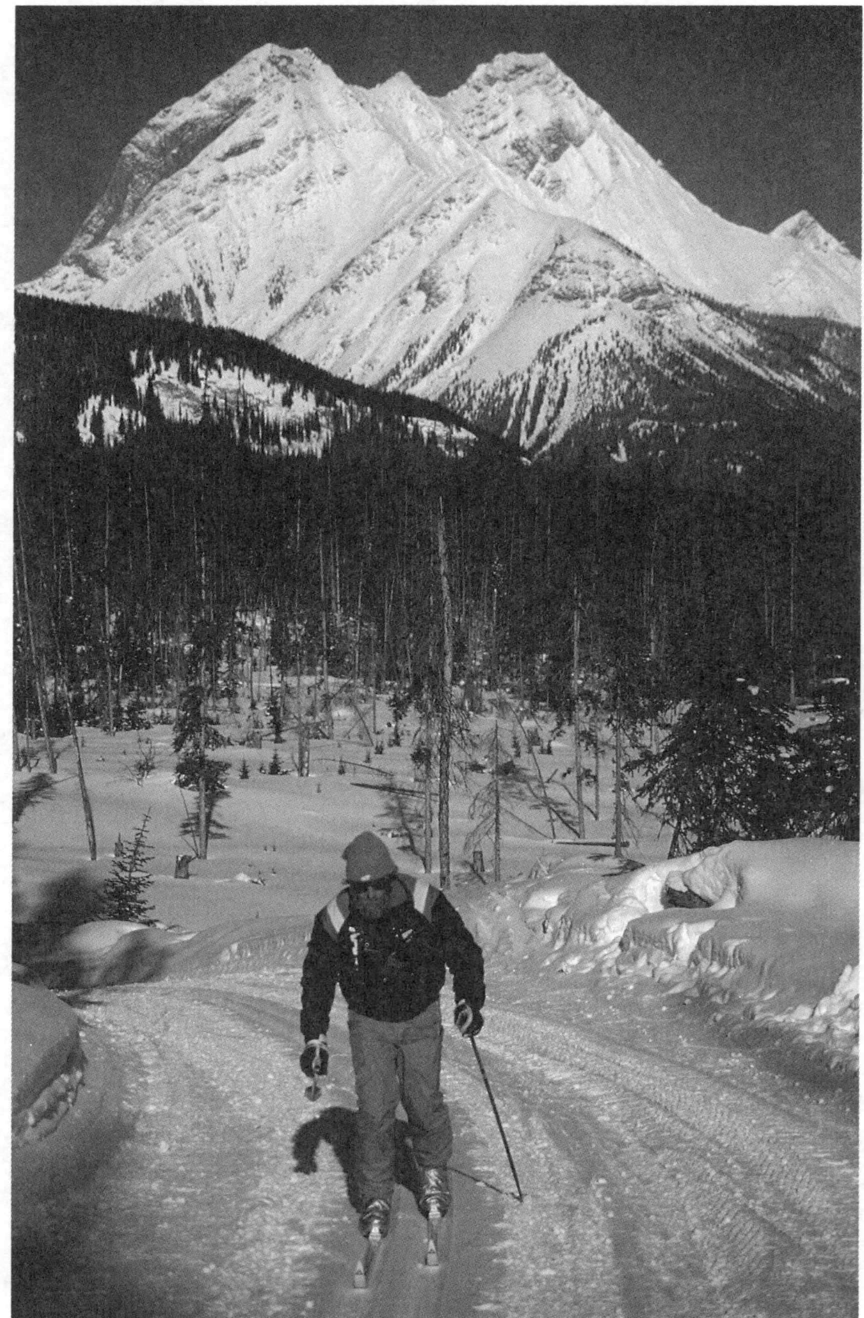

Skiing Blue (the perimeter trail) just beyond the biathlon range. The beautiful peak is Cone Mountain.

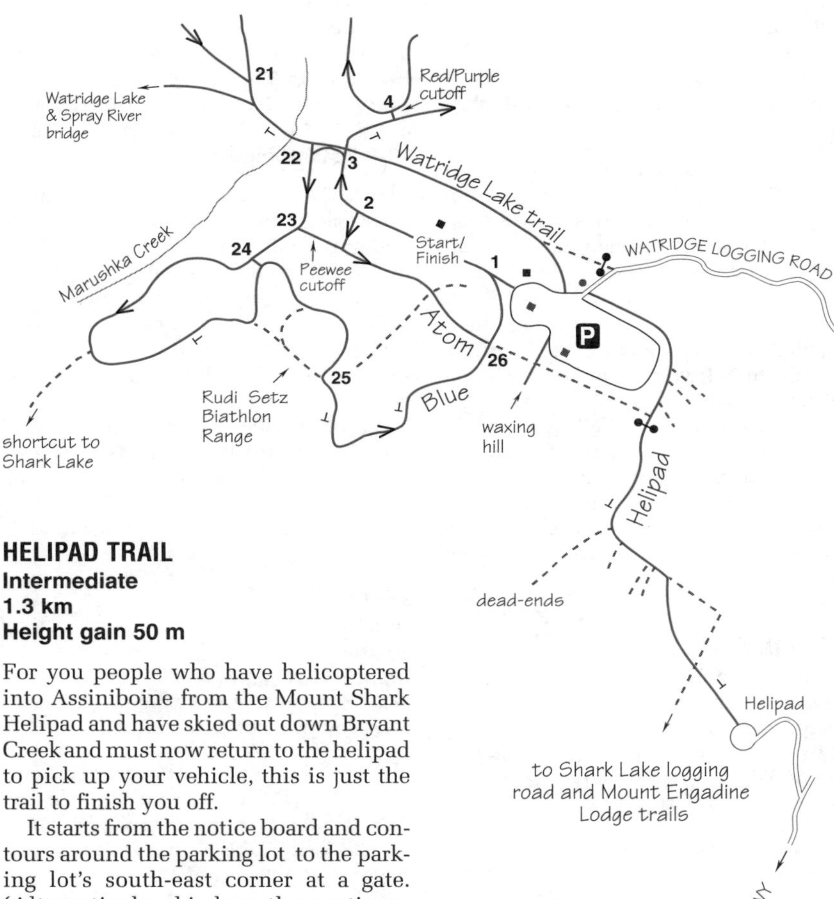

HELIPAD TRAIL

Intermediate
1.3 km
Height gain 50 m

For you people who have helicoptered into Assiniboine from the Mount Shark Helipad and have skied out down Bryant Creek and must now return to the helipad to pick up your vehicle, this is just the trail to finish you off.

It starts from the notice board and contours around the parking lot to the parking lot's south-east corner at a gate. (Alternatively, ski along the continuation of Atom at 26 to the same place.) The ongoing logging road offers you nothing but toil and sweat up two steep hills with a relatively flat stretch in the middle where Slash comes in from the right at a signpost.

ATOM

Easy
0.5 km
Start-1-2-26-P-Finish

An nearly flat loop close to the Start/ Finish area suitable for beginners and small children.

PEEWEE

Easy intermediate
1.5 km
Start-1-2-23-P-Finish

Just a little more challenging than Atom with a few rolling hills on either side of the biathlon range.

BLUE

Easy intermediate
2 km
Height gain 15 m
Start-1-2-3-22-P-Finish

Same as Peewee but with an additional 500 m tacked on in the middle.

RED

Difficult
5 km Men's A Loop
Height gain 94 m
Start-1-P-5-Red cutoff to 21-22-P-Finish

The glorious first 2.5 km takes in all the best hills including Bonser's Bends and Daffern's Delight which has had its top lopped off and no longer skis like a ski jump. Expect a gruelling climb back up to 4, then follow Red/Purple, Yellow and Green down the Luge and up into cutblocks at 5. "Enough" screams your lungs, strained to bursting point. So at 5 shortcut through to 21 (two-way, note), and finish in the usual way around the perimeter trail shared with Blue/Yellow/Green.

A Finnish coach in a burst of enthusiasm once called the initial 2.5 km the best in the world and certainly until the Canmore Nordic Centre came on the scene it set a new standard for racing trails in this area.

RED/PURPLE

Intermediate
5 km Women's B Loop
Height gain 85 m
Start-1-P-4-Red/Purple cutoff-P-8-Red/Purple cutoff to 18-19-shortcut to 20-P-24-25-P-Finish

Unlike Red, Red/Purple misses out the difficult 2.5 km of perimeter trail by turning left at the top of the first hill at 4 and straightway plunging down the Luge to a bridge over Marushka Creek. Since what goes down must come up, expect a tough climb up to 5. At 6 head back into the trees (another good downhill) for a second go-around above the reservoir. At 8 take the cutoff to 18, then at 19 on the Watridge Lake trail nip across to 20 the *short* way. One last thing to know about: at 24 Red/Purple deviates from the norm by slipping below the biathlon range to 25.

Note for history buffs: the photo on page 120 shows the downhill after 6 being christened by Canmore's Albert Mazzucchi one late November afternoon in 1984. Lots of snow, eh?

RED/BLACK

Intermediate
5 km C Loop
Height gain 52 m
Start-1-P-3-22-21-5-6-7-P-9-Red/Black cutoff to 14-15-P-17-P-19-shortcut to 20-P-23-26-P-Finish

The next easiest loop after Blue, Red/Black omits the most difficult hills on Red and Red/Purple by sneaking along the Watridge Lake trail, then edging along the top of the cutblocks to 7. But lest you think this loop is for chickens, coming up is a lengthy uphill followed by a superb series of downhills between 8 and 9 which leave you intoxicated on the misty banks of Watridge Creek (picnic table).

On the return leg the loop reverts to avoiding all difficulties. You've only half the Meanders to cope with and are surprised by the easy cop-out to the parking lot.

YELLOW

Difficult
10 km
Height gain 183 m
Start-1-P-9-14-15-the Meanders through 16 to 17-P-Finish

My favourite loop takes in all the difficult hills of Red/Purple/Black plus the Meanders and the loop south of the Watridge Lake trail. You'll be giddy by the time you stagger up to 21. Enough said!

GREEN

Difficult
15 km perimeter trail
Height gain 240 m
Start-1-P-15-the Meanders through 16 to 17-P-Finish

Green is the perimeter trail, a strenuous loop which takes in absolutely everything plus a spin around the far cutblock.

It's at 9 where you keep right and ski down to Watridge Creek where you won't want to miss the bridge. Did I mention the river never freezes over? A short herringbone step with following downhill leads into Far Cutblock where you make a

Canada's National Team member, Jean McAllister, having fun on Red.

steady climb to the far end (downhill). Double back under Isolated Ridge where the going is easy apart from two abberations devised by myself and the Trail Designer. Both offer 5 minutes of sheer uphill hell. (I often give them a miss by shortcutting across the level.) Thereafter the trail is quite enjoyable with some relaxing downhills past 10 and 11 to the Watridge Lake trail joined at the Watridge Creek bridge. Resisting the temptations of the old road, turn next left and take in all the convolutions of the Meanders, plus the loop south of the road and all of Blue Loop as it winds around the biathlon range. No cheating, mind!

More about the trails It was March 25 1984. While other officials from the Foothills Nordic Ski Club were dismantling all the paraphernalia of another race from the Smith-Dorrien Ski Trails, myself, a friend Fran Dymond and the future secretary of Nordic ski events at the 1988 Winter Olympics were labouring mightily over fallen trees at the south end of Spray Lakes Reservoir. On skis. What were we doing there?

We told ourselves that while the Smith-Dorrien logging roads would make fine trails someday for tourers, they were far too high in altitude to ever pass national and international racing regulations. Racers from PEI would surely pass out from lack of breath. Now the land at the south end of Spray Lakes Reservoir was within limits, but still high enough to get good snow from November through to May. We conceived it as an early and late season training and racing area and as a grand opportunity to design trails from scratch.

November 1984.
Trying out the hill after 6.

The Watridge Logging Road was under six feet of snow at the time so we started near Buller Pond by skiing down to the reservoir, then up into the trees where the Red 5 km loop goes now. My chief memory is of dead pink trees of enormous diameter, though why bark turns pink no one seems able to explain. We came away impressed and exhausted.

Early summer recces followed when all the melted snow had pooled into depressions as bogs. Sloshing about, we were joined by my younger son Ian and coach Rowan Bonser and had wonderful times wrapping ourselves up in top-o-fil (oversized ball of thread used for measuring distances) and naming fun features after ourselves, like "Daffern's Delight" which went over the edge of a steep hill like a ski jump, and "Bonser's Bends", suggested with alacrity as an alternative by Rowan after Tony was leaning towards another Daffern's Delight. Then we devised a long teasing uphill, but before it reached the Watridge Logging Road, we sent it back down the hill via "The Luge" which was a lot more luge-like when it was narrower. Then we drove and hiked down the Watridge Logging Road to the far end cutblock, now the site of the Green 15 km, where overgrown logging roads around the perimeter were obvious candidates to be roped in. Picking our way back through slash, I detected a serpentine logging road called the Meanders where you cover 2 km in 400 m as the crow flies, with uphill, bend, downhill, bend, uphill following each other in regular monotony. (Honestly, I shan't be offended if you get fed up and cop out on to the Watridge Lake trail.)

By September, with superb backing from Kananaskis Country's Bob Wood and with help from Provincial and Federal Job Creation Programmes, i.e. inmates from the Correctional Institute, the bare bones of the trails were cut and cleared to a width of four metres and the balancing beam over Watridge Creek replaced with a real bridge. The first time we tested the trails the snow was knee deep on November the 4th.

The Canada Cup introduced several young Scandinavians, including Vegard Ulvang and Marianne Dahlmo, to North America. Ulvang went on to win 5 gold medals at the 1992 Olympic Winter Games.

That winter much effort was spent making colour-coded signs with arrows pointing, we hoped, in all the right directions and in packing them around the loops and fixing them onto trees at junctions, an incredibly onerous task undertaken by Geoff, Robyn, Norm, Fran, Mike, Sylvia, Terry and Len from the F.N.S.C. There was a real sense of urgency since the Alberta Championships were only weeks away. But it wasn't until April 5th of the following season that Shark came of age so to speak. As the prestigious North American Championships got under way, the theme music for Mount Shark blasted forth from the loudspeakers for the very first time. What else but the theme from the movie "Jaws". It was an emotional moment.

Improvements and adjustments were ongoing the next summer and included some totally unnecessary uphills and downhills on the far 15 km and coming into the Start/Finish area to bring the courses up to the standard required by FIS. We were mystified by missing signs until detecting in proper Sherlock Holmes manner a few flakes of paint lying on the ground which pointed the finger at porcupines. It was obvious that inedible signs were a must. The season of 85/86 was Shark's heyday with Alberta Cup Races, a Canada /Scandinavia Cup (which introduced an immature Ulvang and Daehlie to the unsuspecting North Americans), the National Championships and the first annual Boy Scout Race. The Start/ Finish area became Tent City.

But never again was it to attain the same glory, for a mega-competitor was stirring down the road, namely the Canmore Nordic Centre. Looking back, it seems hilarious that Alberta flatlanders thought the controversial 2.5 km too difficult for competition (little did they know about the upcoming CNC trails). You can say it set a new *temporary* standard for racing trails in Alberta.

SHARK (MARUSHKA) LAKE VIA LOGGING ROAD — Backcountry

Easy intermediate
4.5 km
Height gain 36 m
Height loss 68 m
Maximum elevation 1920 m
Map 82 J/14 Spray Lakes Reservoir

Access Smith-Dorrien/Spray Trail. Turn west onto the Watridge Logging Road (signed "Mount Engadine Lodge" and "Mount Shark"). In 1.8 km park in a small parking area (usually plowed) on the right-hand side of the road.

Facilities Igloos usually, Tony's Place.

Overview On the next page I'll be telling you of another way into Shark Lake from the Mount Shark parking lot which is a lot shorter. This is the long way in. So why bother with it you're asking? Well, for one thing you're on the main logging road to cutblock #9 which ends adjacent to the lake and is therefore foolproof for people who can't navigate, and second, the road is clear of slash and mini lodgepoles which means you can ski this trail with very little snow. And you definitely can't say that about the other route.

About 100 m down the Watridge Logging Road the Shark Lake logging road (formerly the Upper Watridge logging road) turns off to the left. After a steep few metres it flattens and you ski past Tent Ridge access on the left, then Slash on the right at the bend. You turn the corner and after another flat stretch make a little climb to the road's high point where a circular clearing allows a splendid view of the reservoir. From here the road rushes off downhill with logging roads and skid trails forking off to left and right (the stuff of further explorations) into huge cutblock #9 where the fun runs out in an uphill. Make for the far end of the cutblock where a fringe of trees hides Marushka Creek and at a suitable place — there is no *one* place — slither down the bank to the creek. Simply follow it up to the lake.

There are an amazing number of accommodations and eating places at the lake shore, including a dozen or so igloos built by survival groups over the winter and Johnny Musko's poaching cabin in the woods which has been revitalised and is currently a cross between Little Red Riding Hood's cottage and the Little Mermaid's underwater palace tied down with fish nets. The lake scenery is grand but shady; the stop on your camera shows f3.5. It's just a little depressing while munching lunch to realize that all day long the sun circles the sky *below* the three peaks of Mts. Smuts and Shark and Tent Ridge.

Return the same way. Mostly uphill!

More about the trail I have to tell you that the official name of this lake is "Shark" as of September 4th 1991 which instantly conjures up images of monsters lurking below the ice ready to break through and nab a skier the moment they hear the swish swish of skis on the surface. Long ago the lake was called Cutthroat (OK, I could go along with that), and then Marushka for about 20 years, a gorgeous name dreamed up by Harry Connolly while promoting "Assiniboia". It isn't clear whether he was imbibing a bottle of vodka at the time.

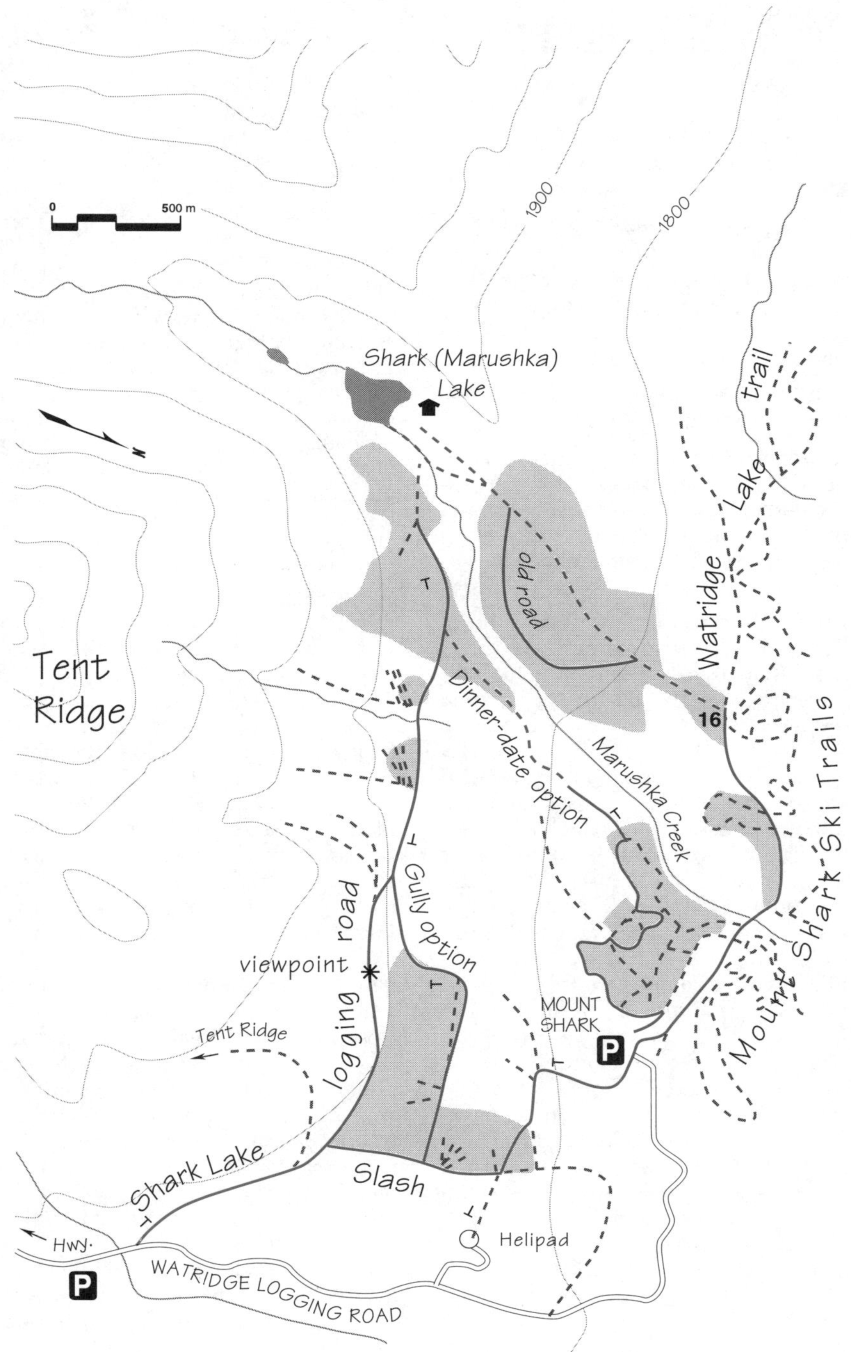
0
500 m
1900
1800
Shark (Marushka) Lake
Watridge Lake trail
old road
Tent Ridge
Dinner-date option
16
Marushka Creek
Mount Shark Ski Trails
Gully option
logging road
viewpoint
MOUNT SHARK
P
Tent Ridge
Shark Lake
Slash
Hwy.
P
Helipad
WATRIDGE LOGGING ROAD

SHARK (MARUSHKA) LAKE LOOP — Backcountry

Intermediate
9 km loop
Height gain 167 m
Maximum elevation 1920 m
Map 82 J/14 Spray Lakes Reservoir

Access Smith-Dorrien/Spray Trail. Turn west onto the Watridge Logging Road (signed "Mount Engadine Lodge" and "Mount Shark") and follow for 5.3 km to the end of the road at the Mount Shark parking lot.

Facilities Washrooms in parking lot, Tony's Place, igloos etc.

Overview For skiers like me who are backcountry skiers at heart, the loop centring around Shark Lake is a change of pace from charging all over the racing trails. Works well in either direction.

From the parking lot, start out on Watridge Lake trail towards Watridge Lake (see page 126). At junction #17 where one of the meandering racing loops comes close to the road is a clearing which used to be a parking lot when you could drive this far up the Watridge Logging Road. On your left is a cutblock, more of an alley really, which takes you through to huge cutblock # 8. Ski easily up the middle of # 8, weaving slightly right to hit the top edge of the cutblock just right of Marushka Creek which can be identified by its fringe of full grown trees. At last count, you cross 16 skid trails. Lest you think this is an easy way into the lake in summer, I can assure you it is not, for under the snow are millions of two metre-high conifers. (Pushing through this rotting mess of stumps, fallen trees, alders, and mini conifers, counting off ski trails, was one of my more horrid summer experiences, more so because I was suffering from stomach flu at the time.) Should snow be minimal, about a third of the way up the cutblock you can head diagonally left up a road strewn with logs only one metre high which ultimately follows the edge of Marushka Creek and ends up at the same place as the direct route.

At the high point right of Marushka Creek then, plunge into dark spruce forest. Again, the going is considerably easier under snow and you can expect to reach the lake in about 8 minutes. After 3 minutes, some folks slither down the bank to the creek and follow it up to the outlet. I don't know why. It's much easier to stay high — the ground is flat, the trees wide apart and you ski right past the door of Tony's place. Let no one enter who smokes either cigarettes or marijuana, or is humping around a crate of Labatt's Blue, but I'm sure none of this applies to you. A thermos of hot coffee is more likely.

Leave the lake by the outlet and in about 250 metres climb easily up the right bank into another huge cutblock, # 9, and there pick up the Shark Lake logging road as described on the previous page. A short downhill run precedes a long uphill to the high point of the day offering a view of the reservoir. In another kilometre, just before the right-hand bend, turn left down Slash, double poling past umpteen skid trails on the left until you hit Helipad trail at the signpost. Make a left turn. With a packed and trackset trail, the pace accelerates alarmingly, giving you your fastest run of day back to the car park.

Option return: Dinner Date Short-cut
(deduct 2 km)
Leave Shark Lake logging road near the east end of cutblock # 9 and head for the bottom corner of the cutblock where you turn right into the open forest. Traverse a bit, aim downhill a little and hope to emerge on a logging road which deposits you — on your backside usually — on the perimeter racing loop near the Start/Finish area. (Turn right for home.) Chances are excellent that you miss the first logging road and hit the next one to the east which terminates behind the biathlon range. Not so good.

Option return: Gully
For a faster descent turn left just before the high point on the Shark Lake logging road. The gully of choice is easily identified by a very tall dead tree standing, swaying, in the middle of it. Keep to the road in the gully bed which spits you out onto a level area. With enough snow and gumption, it's possible to continue straight on down the hillside to Helipad trail above the first steep hill. Otherwise, follow the gently-inclined road around to the right past a small clearing to a major logging road called Slash. Turn left and continue as for the longer route.

More about the area Since this is basically a tour of slash-strewn cutblocks, logging roads and skid trails, this is a good place to touch on the delicate subject of cleanup after logging. Ever since getting out of the area, Spray Lakes Sawmills have received an earful from the public about the mess left behind. Unfairly as it turns out. To set the record straight, co-founder Chester Mjolness tells me that the company was given a choice: to either clean up or have the government levy a charge for every board foot of reforestation and do the job themselves. Money changed hands but before the cleanup was anywhere near finished the area became Kananaskis Country. So the AFS didn't finish the cleanup to anything like the public's expectations, and K-Country cleaned up only the trails which were to become official which is why you shouldn't even attempt to hike this route in summer.

Historic Johnny Musko's poaching cabin rebuilt. A useful emergency shelter.

WATRIDGE LAKE TRAIL TO SPRAY RIVER Groomed & Backcountry

Easy to Watridge Lake turn-off
Intermediate to Karst Spring or walk
Intermediate to Spray River Bridge
5.5 km to Watridge Lake
6.5 km to Karst Spring
8 km to Spray River
Height gain to Karst Spring 107 m
Height loss to Spray River 122 m
Maximum elevation Karst Spring 1859 m
Map 82 J/14 Spray Lakes Reservoir

Access Smith-Dorrien/Spray Trail. Turn west onto the Watridge Logging Road (signed "Mount Engadine Lodge" and "Mount Shark") and follow for 5.3 km to the end of the road at the Mount Shark parking lot.

Overview A popular trail which uses the closed portion of the Watridge Logging Road, then continues past Watridge Lake and on down the hill to the Spray River bridge, the departure point for Bryant Creek and the Upper Spray River valley. The trail, signed "Watridge Lake" at confusing junctions, is packed and occasionally trackset to the watershed, after which you're on your own with a dozen other masochists. Most beginners turn around somewhere in the first few kilometres, loathe to leave the sunny cutblocks, but if you can hack the distance, why not try the optional trip to Watridge Lake and Karst Spring?

Start from the information board in the parking lot where 100 m of narrow trail leads back to the closed portion of the Watridge Logging Road beyond the locked gate. Turn left and simply follow the very obvious road, keeping alert for skiers zipping across at numerous junctions with the Mount Shark racing trails. There are three dips. The first crosses Marushka Creek immediately after junction #24, the second is hidden in a straight concealing a water jump in November, and the third is the long gentle runout to Watridge Creek which, you'll be amazed to discover, flows at an unflagging rate all year round. Throughout this section are delicious views of Tent Ridge, Mt. Shark, Cone Mountain, Mt. Nestor, the reservoir and a large number of peaks in the Kananaskis Range. You can even see the tip of Mt. Assiniboine.

After Watridge Creek crossing, the road turns along the left edge of a large cutblock under Isolated Ridge, but instead of fading away in overgrown obscurity as previously, now dekes into spruce forest as an undulating two-lane highway with a junction en route with the trail to Watridge Lake and Karst Spring (sign).

Although the trackset tracks end at the watershed, the new 4-m wide trail continues down the hill, zigging about a lot and ending with a super-fast runout to the flat before the bridge. Coming back up doesn't bear thinking about, yet racers sprint down *and up* again in less than eight minutes! Lolling against the rails of the Spray River bridge, quads quivering, you decide on your next move. Back up the hill (penalty for the downhill), or further up the Spray River Valley or Bryant Creek, thereby postponing the inevitable.

Option: Watridge Lake and Karst Spring
From the junction descend a short intermediate hill to the old narrow trail at the outlet to Watridge Lake, seen gleaming brightly behind a few scraggly spruce trees.

In winter it is even more obvious that cartographers have made an error as Dean Marshall discovered on a day in 1967. The lake is not the source of Watridge Creek, that strongly flowing stream you crossed earlier. The source is Karst Spring accessed by an official summer trail which crosses the outlet. A little narrow certainly, but skiable, though beginners may opt to walk the last two zigs.

At last the mystery is revealed: a dark rocky grotto and water gliding out under a slit in the cliff to thunder down the rocky creek bed as "Elizabeth Falls". Winter's lower water levels disclose boulders padded in bright green moss, a welcome change to technicolour for skiers suffering from White Eye.

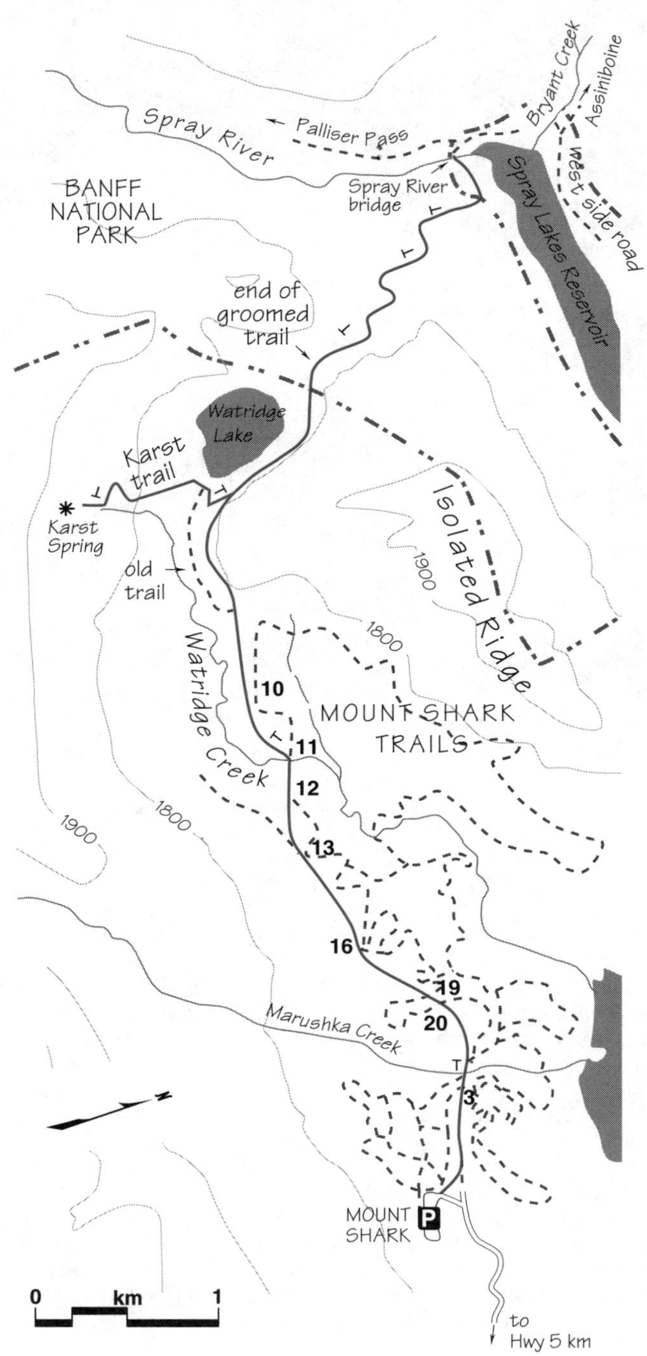
Bryant Creek
Assiniboine
Spray River
Palliser Pass
West side road
Spray River bridge
BANFF NATIONAL PARK
Spray Lakes Reservoir
end of groomed trail
Watridge Lake
Karst trail
Karst Spring
old trail
Isolated Ridge
1900
1800
Watridge Creek
MOUNT SHARK TRAILS
10
11
12
13
16
19
20
3
Marushka Creek
MOUNT SHARK
0
km
1
to Hwy 5 km

Karst Spring at its emergence. A summer shot when there is a little more water.

In case you think you are treading in the footsteps of its discoverer, you are not. After running into the "unique" creek one or two days previously, Dean Marshall, then foreman at Spray Lakes Sawmills, was actually making a preliminary survey much higher up the slope of Mt. Shark nearer to Shark Lake when he heard the sound of waterfalls. Lured by the extraordinary roar — yes, this is what it sounds like in summer — he pushed through the bush to discover what's been called the largest karst spring in North America.

More about the trail Formerly, the Watridge Logging Road ended in the large cutblock below Isolated Ridge and a narrow muddy trail carried on past Watridge Lake's grungy north shore down to the Spray River bridge. This last bit was nearly impossible to detect under snow. So it was rather a shock when, in the season of 1988/89, a 4 m-wide ski road suddenly appeared between the cutblock and the Spray River, doing away with all conjecture.

Regarding the name "Watridge", I would like to inform Aphrodite Karamitsanis that the origin of the name may never be found, because there's a possibility someone in the mapping department made a blunder, misreading an "r" for a "t" and transposing WARRIDGE, which appeared on all the early maps used by Spray Lakes Sawmills, into present-day WATRIDGE. Of course, by the same token someone previously could have changed the t into an r since the Dominion Survey out of Ottawa who were kicking around the area in the late 1950's called the lake WATRIDGE apparently. Still, the same premise holds. Who or what Watridge or Warridge was remains a mystery second only to the origin of Karst Spring, but I'm working on it.

BRYANT CREEK SHELTER

Groomed & Backcountry

Intermediate
18 km from parking lot
Height gain 168 m
Height loss 122 m
Maximum elevation 1844 m
Map 82 J/14 Spray Lakes Reservoir

Access Smith-Dorrien/Spray Trail. Turn west onto the Watridge Logging Road (signed "Mount Engadine Lodge" and "Mount Shark") and follow for 5.3 km to the end of the road at the Mount Shark parking lot.

Facilities Washrooms, picnic tables at parking lot. The sparsely furnished Bryant Creek Shelter is always open (wood stove, wood pile, wood bunks). If staying overnight you need a permit. For reservations call 403-762-4256.

Overview Ever since tourers got to know about the Mount Shark trailhead, a day trip up Bryant Creek to the shelter for lunch has become exceedingly popular. Bring your own pots, mugs and utensils. If, on the return, the uphill from the Spray River bridge proves too irksome I can offer an alternative route....

Ski the 8 km to Spray River bridge via Watridge Lake trail described on page 126.

At the junction beyond keep right and ski around to Bryant Creek bridge and up to where Spray Lakes Reservoir west side road turns into Bryant Creek trail at the Trail Centre. The words "Trail Centre" conjure up a heated building with washrooms equipped with showers and hand dryers and smiling rangers standing behind counter tops handing out pamphlets and advice. So it's a bit of a letdown to discover the same old notice board with maps and bear warnings. Not even a bench.

You turn left here onto the Bryant Creek trail proper and settle in for a nice bit of level skiing alongside Bryant Creek, keeping right lest you wish to visit a locked warden cabin. About 2 km after crossing a bridge over an unnamed side creek, the trail starts rising and (for you) ends with a steepish hill, and slight descent into a meadow about one hour from the Trail Centre. Across the meadow to the left is the shelter. If you reach the warden cabin which is on your right and decorated with antlers you've gone too far and need to backtrack for 700 m.

The shelter Photo: Alf Skrastins

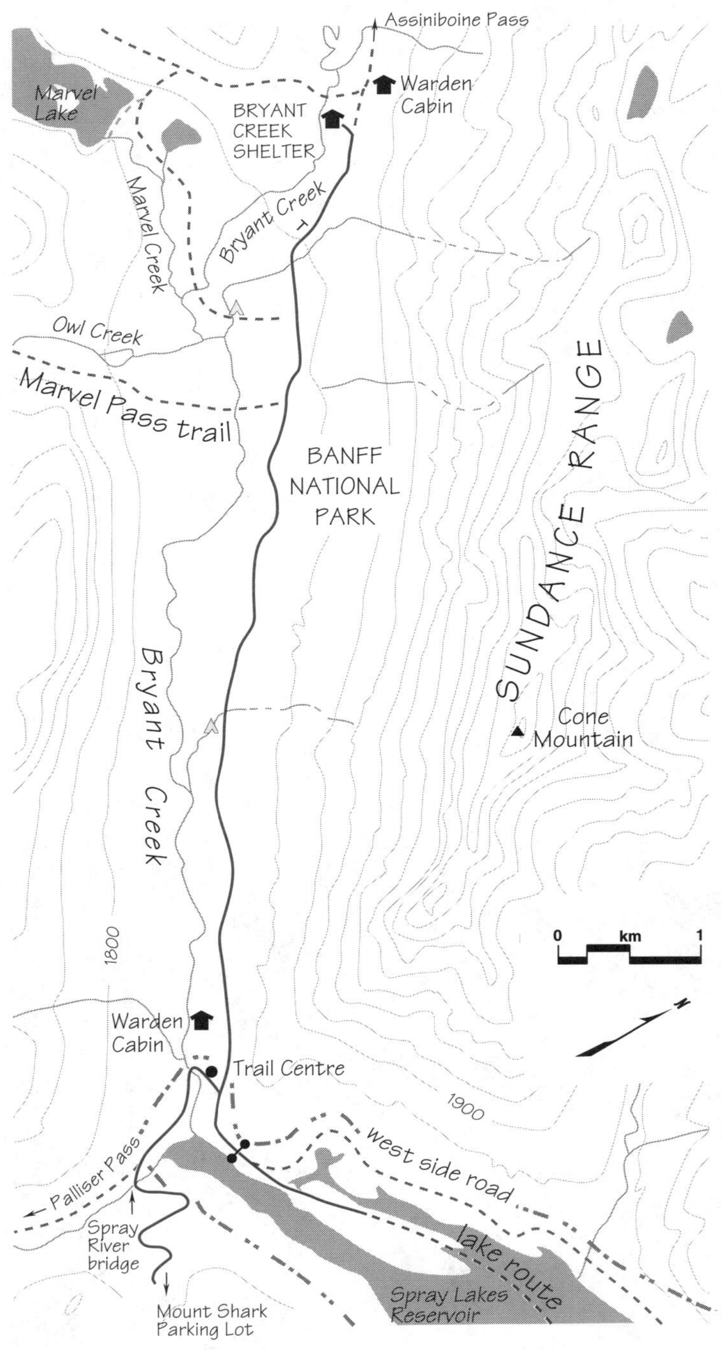
Assiniboine Pass
Warden Cabin
Marvel Lake
BRYANT CREEK SHELTER
Marvel Creek
Bryant Creek
Owl Creek
Marvel Pass trail
BANFF NATIONAL PARK
SUNDANCE RANGE
Cone Mountain
Bryant Creek
1800
0 km 1
N
Warden Cabin
Trail Centre
1900
west side road
Palliser Pass
Spray River bridge
lake route
Spray Lakes Reservoir
Mount Shark Parking Lot

With luck or good management — "I'm feeling a little slow today, you'd better overtake me" — someone will be there before you. Aha! Smoke is rising from the chimney. You open the door and grope through a fug thick enough to give you a headache and collapse gratefully on a hard wooden bunk. I forgot to mention in the overview that you'll need a foamy for overnighting.

Return A half hour to the Trail Centre.

Optional Return: Via the Lake for those of you who can't abide the climb from Spray River bridge. If you should fall through the ice, don't sue. Read the disclaimer.

Keep left at the Trail Centre on the west side road. After it turns north-east and just after a gate you turn right onto a side road and when this peters out, continue down the isthmus to its very end. There, take a deep breath of wind and cross the lake on black see-through ice, contouring around the big promontory of Isolated Ridge as you aim for Marushka Creek outlet (flagging can be seen with binoculars.) If you suffer from vertigo resist looking down or you'll freak out. Actually, once you get used to it, it's an amazingly interesting environment out there on the ice with coyotes trotting off in the distance between winter islands.

Nearing land, you can try skirting along banks of snow and buckled boilerplates for variety. But after arriving at Marushka Creek one way or the other, you must push through a few trees on the *far* side of the outlet (flagging) to gain the bottom of the 5 km loop. Turn right, cross the creek and climb to the cutblock adjoining the Watridge Logging Road. Follow Blue cutoff between 4 and 23 to the Watridge Lake trail, then return the quickest way to the parking lot. See also the map on page 115.

More about the trail If you're lucky enough to have a set of Boundary Survey maps you'll notice that the Bryant Creek trail was well-established by the time the Boundary Survey was delineating the Alberta-BC boundary in 1916. It had even existed in 1899 when well-known explorer/photographer Walter Wilcox passed this way with companions Louis Steele and Henry Bryant. By the 1920's it was very well trodden indeed by parties from the Alpine Club of Canada, who for $35 per person could walk or ride from Banff up the Spray River, Goat Creek and Bryant Creek into the Mt. Assiniboine area, then return via Sunshine Meadows to Banff, a trip people still do today though the bit en foot has been whittled down to half, and half of that can be done by mountain bike with bike racks at the Allenby cut-off.

After 1950 when the lower part of the trail was under water you drove from Three Sisters Dam down the west side of the reservoir to the cabin at Canyon Dam, and from there to another cabin near the gate where you left your car before turning the corner into Bryant Creek. It is interesting to learn that before Spray Lakes Sawmills had a go at building a proper road down the east side of the reservoir, getting to Mud Lake routinely involved a row across the lake from this point. Anyway, over the years the road beyond Canyon Dam deteriorated and added to the Assininboine walk-in was a brand new walk-in of 7 km to the bottom of Bryant Creek — all of which did you in before you ever got started, unless of course you happen to own a new-fangled mountain bike. Then in the mid 1980's a new access started gaining favour when people discovered you could drive down the Watridge Logging Road and walk in for one kilometre less.

Whatever your preference, 7 km with no hills, or 6 km with hills, the Watridge way is the only way in on skis since the west side road is impassable in winter. Nowadays most people fly in to Assiniboine and ski out which accounts for all the extra bodies on the trail in the afternoon initiating friendly conversations with day skiers. Arriving at the parking lot together you'll be asked to give the driver a lift to the helipad and I'm sure you won't mind.

PALLISER TRAIL

Backcountry

Intermediate
11.5 km to Palliser warden cabin from Spray River bridge
Height gain 162 m from Spray River bridge
Maximum elevation 1853 m
Topo map 82 J/14 Spray Lakes Reservoir

Access Smith-Dorrien/Spray Trail. Turn west onto the Watridge Logging Road (signed "Mount Engadine Lodge" and "Mount Shark") and follow for 5.3 km to the end of the road at the Mount Shark parking lot.

Facilities Backcountry campground at Birdwood Creek. Water in the Spray River near the warden cabin.

Overview Skiers are discovering that Mount Shark trailhead is the gateway to greater things than the racing trails and Bryant Creek. Namely, the splendid Upper Spray River Valley. There appears to be more advantages to skiing this valley than hiking it: no grizzlies to worry about, no river crossings to puzzle over, just the same wonderful scenery made even more spectacular by snow which is always plentiful and of good quality. The Palliser Warden Cabin (formerly Grizzly Cabin) makes a logical turnaround point.

For sorties up Currie Creek, White Man Pass, Spray Pass or Palliser Pass, bring a tent, an army of trail breakers and the Canadian Rockies Trail Guide. And then there's always the circuit described on page 150.

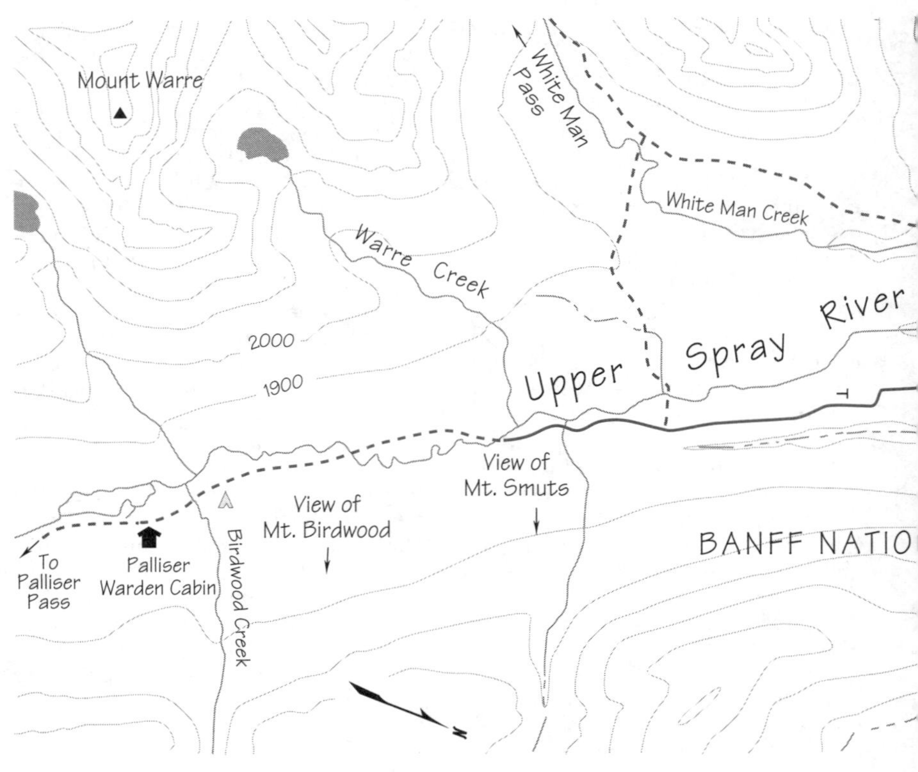

Follow Watridge Lake trail for 8 km down to the Spray River bridge (see page 126).

At the junction a few minutes beyond, turn left on to a wide historic track which climbs gradually along the west bank with the odd downhill to cross two flat meadows. At the third meadow, 3.2 km from the bridge, Currie Creek comes in from around the corner, the confluence an obvious snacking-camping spot equipped with grizzly escape ladder up the tree. Cross Currie Creek by the bridge and unless you're hot to explore White Man Pass, cross the bridge over the Spray a few minutes later.

Now on the east bank, you start the major climb of the day up a broad forested ridge to a fascinating labyrinth of knolls and depressions which are always fun to ski, although I must admit to finding one hill irritating in both directions in view of its extra slim width and face-slapping branches. Please, will someone bring an machete! But after this the trees thin out, the ground flattens and with luck you should arrive at a signpost around your ankles where the south cutoff to White Man Pass takes off across the valley. From here, a half hour should see you to the warden cabin.

An initial stint by the Spray River leads into the north end of the great longitudinal meadow reaching more or less all the way to the base of Palliser Pass. This is a new landscape with a brighter, windier look. Mountains on either side stand well back: Mts. Warre and Vavasour on the right, Mts. Shark, Smuts and Birdwood on the left playing peek-a boo-behind their outliers. Without doubt this is the fine open plain described by Lt. Warre in his journals, where streams are full of trout and the meadows teeming with porcupines, partridge, ducks, moose and grizzlies. He forgot to mention the willows, thankfully submerged under snow.

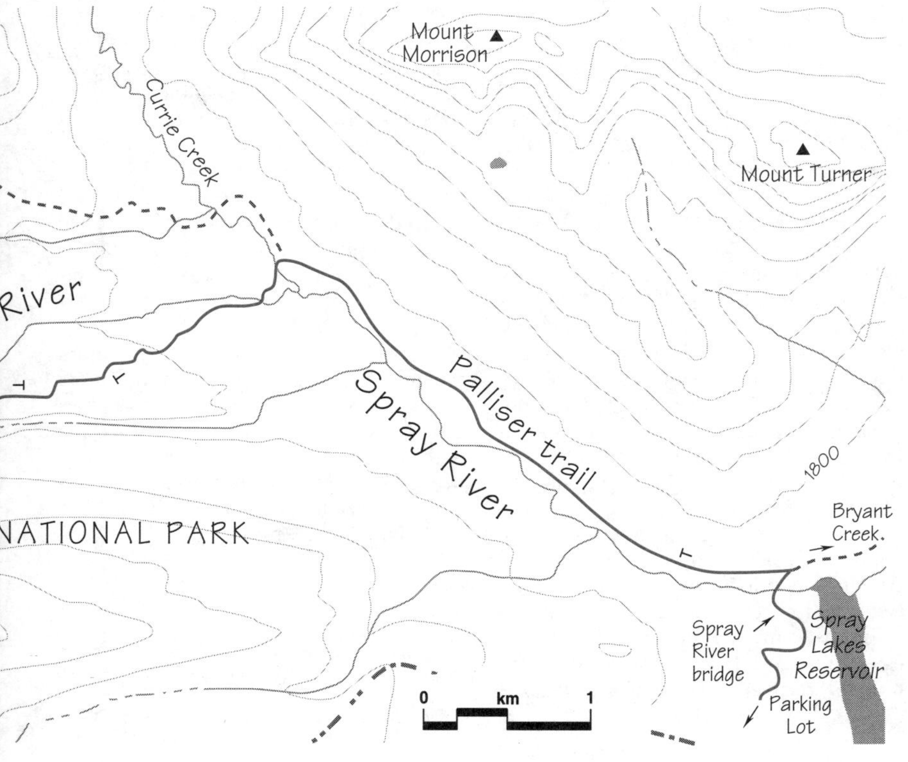

The Spray River, however, still flows freely at the bottom of a ditch four metres deep with snow bridges few and far between, a point to remember if you're skiing up the west bank aiming for the backcountry campground on the east bank. Five minutes from the campground *beyond* Birdwood Creek is Palliser Warden Cabin where a flag on a flagpole stiffens in the winter wind, a lonely sentinel back-dropped by magnificent Mt. Sir Douglas.

A mystery to end with! Is Mt. Birdwood, a perfect triangular piece of rock from this direction, "the remarkable pyramidal peak" noticed by George Dawson on his way over White Man Pass in 1885 and described as "four miles up to south from north end of the Spray Mountains"? Regrettably, he also called it the culminating point of the Spray Mountains which is Mt. Sir Douglas, though its trapezium shape and location another 4 miles up the valley would seem to preclude it. It was on the same trip that he noticed another shapely mountain to the north which he called Assiniboine.

Return A mix of flats and good powdery downhills. When conditions are iffy in the spring the section from Currie Creek to Spray River bridge can be quite technical. Allow about 2-2.5 hours to the bridge.

More about the trail It gives you a funny feeling to be following a part of the historic trail to White Man Pass, named after 121 white men, women and children who left Red River Settlement (Winnipeg) in 1841 and crossed the Rockies into Oregon Territory which at that time belonged to neither the US nor to Canada though the Hudson's Bay Company appeared to control the trade. The group was led by James Sinclair, guided by Cree chief Muskepetoon of North Kananaskis Pass infamy, and blessed by HBC chief Sir George Simpson who naturally wanted to put as many British subjects into Oregon as he could. Three years later lieutenants Warre and Vavasour, disguised as wealthy sportsmen dressed in beaver hats, silk shirts and frock coats, were sent out by the British Government as spies to look over Oregon Territory with a view to smuggling troops and supplies over the mountains. They reported back the infeasibility of White Man Pass as a route and to accentuate the point, returned via Boat Encampment and Athabasca Pass. Since it was obviously so much easier for US citizens to wander into Oregon territory than British subjects over White Man Pass or any other pass for that matter, the sheer number of US immigrants eventually settled the "Oregon Question" once and for all.

On their return, Warre and Vavasour bumped into Father de Smet, a priest from Oregon Territory who had travelled White Man Pass trail in reverse direction en route to Edmonton where he wanted to chat to the Blackfoot about their raids. Apparently, his relief was so great on reaching the pass he persuaded his Metis guides to erect a cross, and ever since the river to the west has been called the Cross River. Other interesting people using the pass include Dominion geologist George Dawson who you already know about and members of the 1916 Boundary Survey team who also investigated Palliser Pass and discovered an old Indian trail down the Upper Spray Valley with tepee poles at camping spots.

Since then, apart from solitary wanderings by forestry ranger Joe Kovach looking around in 1948 for a feasible route over the ridge into Burstall Creek and more recent visits by park wardens, outfitters and the odd trekker following Canada's hypothetical Great Divide Trail, the trails of the Upper Spray have remained largely unvisited. After all, there's no great urgency to hike through White Man Pass to get to Oregon any more.

Opposite top: Palliser Trail. Palliser warden cabin and the first view of Mt. Sir Douglas.

Opposite bottom: Commonwealth Creek. The entertaining traverse along the bank.

COMMONWEALTH CREEK & SMUTS PASS **Backcountry & Route**

Intermediate to valley head
Difficult to pass
5.8 km to valley head
7 km to Pass
Height gain to pass 512 m
Maximum elevation at pass 2341 m, high col 2393 m
Map 82 J/14 Spray Lakes Reservoir

Access
1. Usual approach. Smith-Dorrien/Spray Trail about 4 km north of Chester Lake parking lot, or about 2 km south of Watridge Logging Road park by the roadside. In other words, park opposite Commonwealth Creek. Now you know where the ski trail leads.
2. Longer approach. Watridge Logging Road at Mount Engadine Lodge. Follow Princess Anne Loop south along the flats to join up with access #1. Add on 2.6 km.
3. Longest approach. Watridge Logging Road. 0.9 km from the Smith-Dorrien/Spray Trail turn left onto a logging road which is plowed for about 150 m. Continue skiing along the road (it becomes the west leg of Princess Anne Loop) until you reach the cutblock on the *south* side of Commonwealth Creek. Add on 3 km.

Overview Commonwealth gives you two trips in one for A and B parties of a club trip. One is a short fun trip to the valley head, the other a more serious climb to Smuts Pass for which I recommend you use equipment more robust than racing boots since you may have some kick-stepping to do.

In the valley bottom, avalanche danger is almost nil unless hazard is rated extreme or the finger of fate is pointed in your direction and you just happen to get clobbered by a monster 50-year cycle avalanche. As is what happened in Healy Creek. Going to the pass is a different matter entirely; this is entirely under your control so someone in your party should be able to assess avalanche conditions and do some sensible route finding.

From the usual access (#1) drop down the bank and cross Smuts Creek valley. It's heavenly not to have to worry about bogs and river crossings. On the far side pick up Princess Anne Loop if trackset (access # 2), or otherwise follow orange markers into the trees and up a bank into a large cutblock where it pays to cut left up the hill to intersect a major logging road where access #3 joins in from the right.

If you've emerged at the right place you should be able to nip across the road onto a narrower logging road running above the south bank of Commonwealth Creek. At a round clearing prepare to take to the bank by pulling on a pair of waterproof overpants. For the next kilometre you're engrossed in a sometimes aggravating but always highly entertaining traverse through the narrows. Across the creek are some crags laced with lovely yellow ice formations which is why you're not following the summer trail. (I though you'd never ask.) The trouble spot on this side is an awkward corner where the creek from Commonwealth Lake serves up running water, green spongy moss and ice.

You emerge, I suspect considerably damper, from the narrows onto a wide valley floor which is flat and open. Hanging over its length are tremendous avalanche slopes falling from the ridge between The First and Mt. Smuts. Particularly dangerous is the last slope below Smuts so hurry into the narrow draw beyond which is safe (the open slope on the right has been logged). The valley opens out again into a cirque below the vertical north-east face of Mt. Birdwood to which clings a diminutive glacier, now indistinguishable under the mass of snow plastered to face. If you're going to stop for lunch, retreat to the protection of the forest.

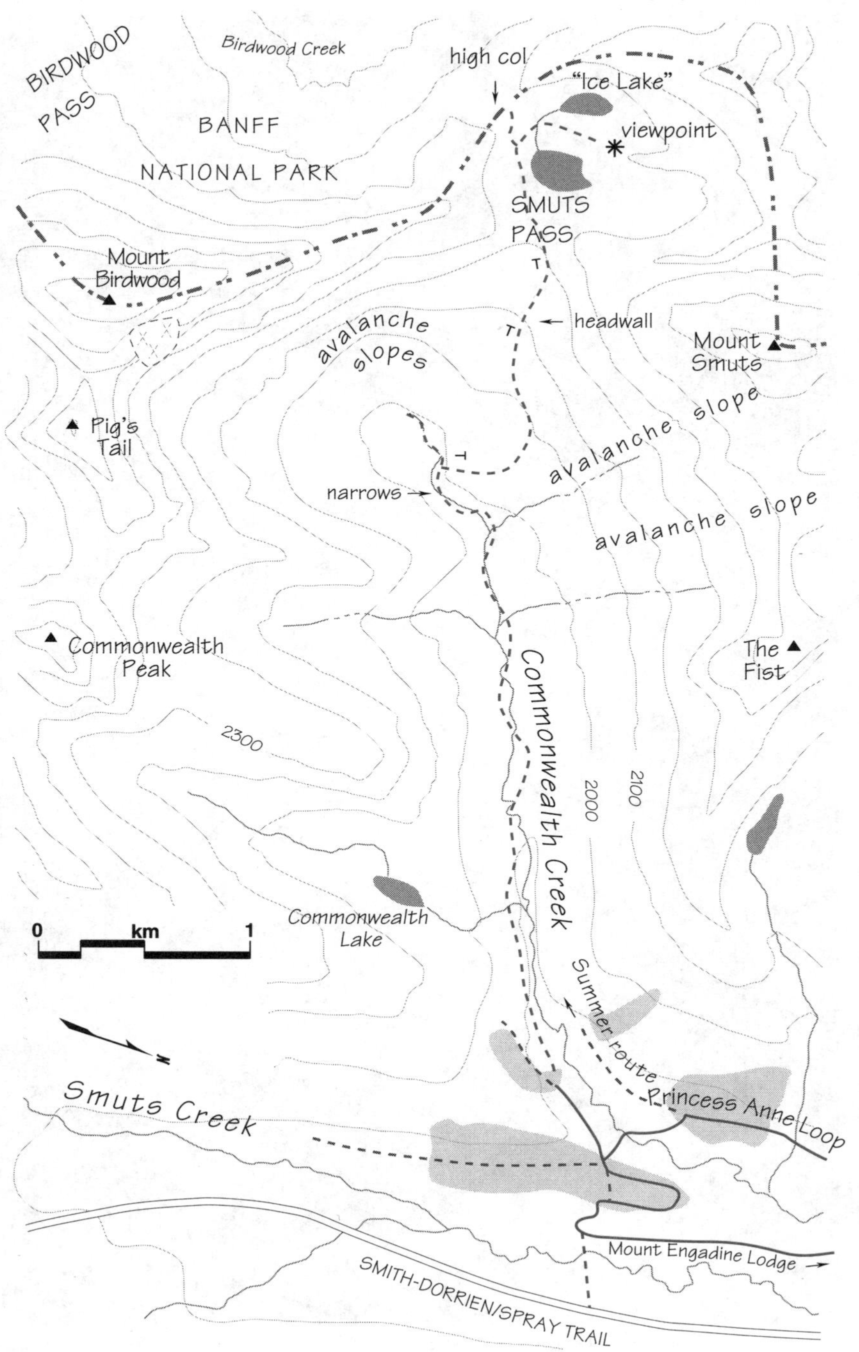
BIRDWOOD PASS
Birdwood Creek
high col
"Ice Lake"
viewpoint
BANFF NATIONAL PARK
SMUTS PASS
Mount Birdwood
headwall
Mount Smuts
avalanche slopes
avalanche slope
Pig's Tail
narrows
avalanche slope
Commonwealth Peak
The Fist
2300
Commonwealth Creek
2000
2100
Commonwealth Lake
0 km 1
Summer route
Smuts Creek
Princess Anne Loop
Mount Engadine Lodge
SMITH-DORRIEN/SPRAY TRAIL

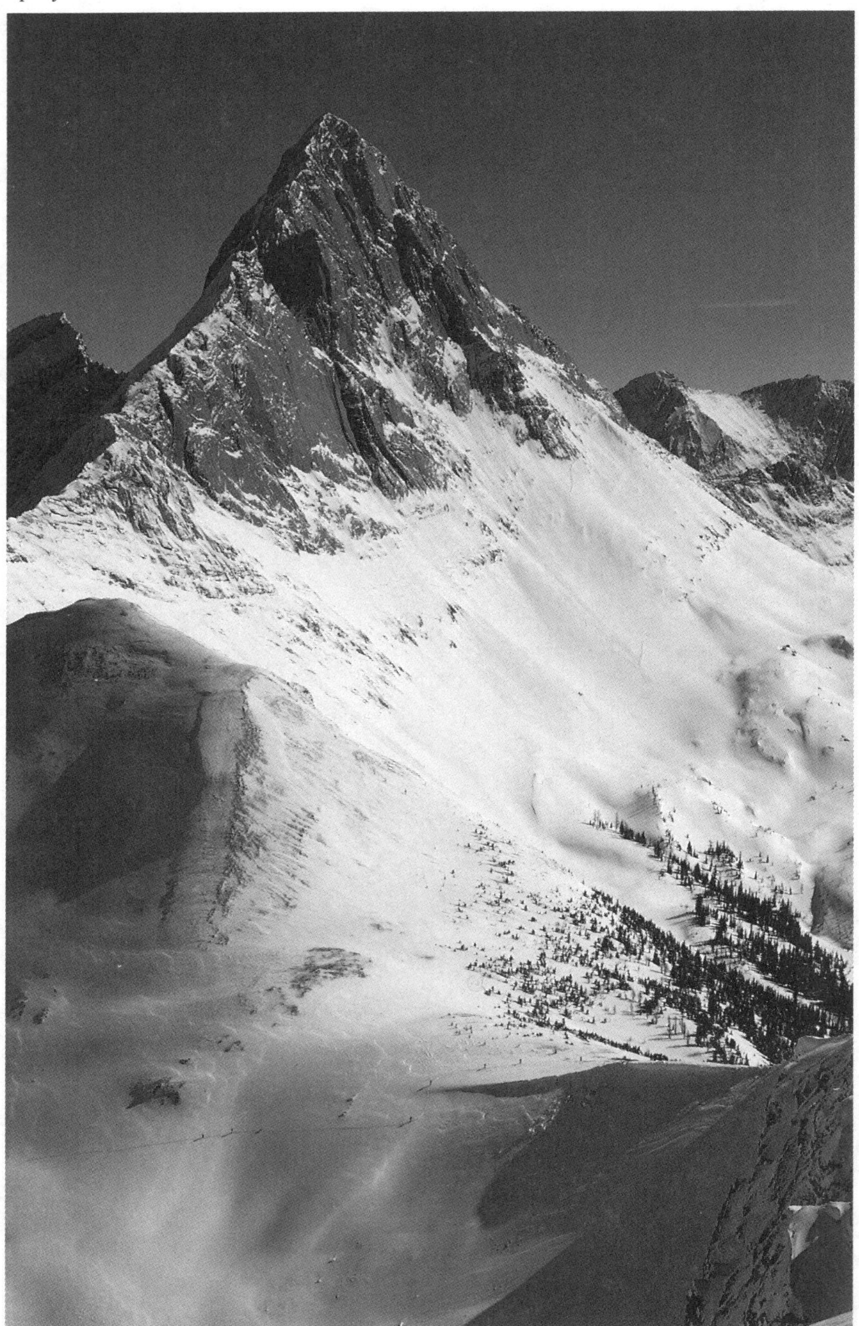

Photo: Alan Kane

Looking down on high col. The skiers have skied across from Smuts Pass, out of sight to the left. Below Mt. Birdwood, the dangerous slopes to Birdwood Col (right) are hidden from view.

Smuts Pass
The slope above the cirque rises in three steps. Getting to the pass depends on the avalanche condition of the second step.

First Step Starting from the head of the cirque, some skiers zig-zag up the steep slope of diminutive trees to the left of the forest. The slope is probably perfectly safe under some conditions, but I always ask myself why the trees are never destined to become adults and retreat from the cirque back to the demarcation line of forest and the logged area just before the narrows where there is a perfectly safe route. Start by climbing diagonally right along the demarcation line, turning left into the forest at any place which appeals (the shallow gully is good), then head diagonally left up easy to moderate inclines, aiming to come out at the bench below the second step. Of course this doesn't always happen since you can't see where you're going and sometimes you hit the bottom of avalanche slopes falling from Mt. Smuts on the right first, but that's OK. All you have to do is ski along the bottom of the open slopes.

Second Step Peruse the headwall which is bounded by a gully on the right. I don't know about you, but both summer and winter we climb up the gully a short way then traverse left onto a shallow rib sporting a few tattered larches which appears to offer safety from avalanches. Who knows what the snow will be like. You could be up to your knees in powder. But sometimes the wind blows down slope with such ferocity it turns the surface to concrete and higher up where the slope steepens you're reduced to a quiver, tiptoeing up with no means of support — I mean, ski poles are useless as ice axes aren't they? The other option on such occasions is to chicken out and kick steps, jamming your skis in as anchors which works well and is an excellent method of delamination. Fortunately, the steep rocky bit at the top can be omitted by a traverse right to a low point above the gully. In this way you arrive on the second bench which is immensely broad and flat.

The final step is very short and not very steep. You can generally make out a skiable trail rising from right to left.

What an inhospitable place Smuts Pass is in winter with no boulders to shelter behind; just a ridge of frozen scree and knife-edge ridges winging up on either side. If the day is fine, I urge you to move on into the sunken valley beyond, either traversing left-hand slopes to a higher col, or better still, stopping off at "Ice Lake" and enduring another half kilometre of trail breaking along its terrace in a northerly direction until you're about 50 m above lake level. Now look back for a rare and astounding view of Mt. Birdwood.

Descent From the bench below the second step I'm sure that some of you are going to take the direct line into the cirque via the avalanche tracks because you've always gone that way. Good luck! Cautious sliders like myself should more or less retrace the forest route which is almost as much fun, the trees being relatively wide apart, and when you get to the logged area make a beeline for the narrows by some good safe powder.

Option: Birdwood Pass
I know of the odd frazzled party which has traversed from the high col to Birdwood Pass via the steep avalanche gullies of the summer route, then run the gamut of more avalanche slopes in reaching Burstall Pass trail. If you're going to risk it, and this is not a recommendation, then at least miss out the first lot of gullies by dropping straight down a forested rib into Birdwood Creek and following the creek up to the pass. You want the left-hand notch which is marginally safer on the other side.

HOGARTH LAKES TRAILS

Backcountry

17 km of skiable trails
Map 82 J/14 Spray Lakes Reservoir
Maximum elevation 1990 m

Access Smith-Dorrien-Spray Trail at Burstall Pass parking lot.

Facilities Washrooms in parking lot.

Overview Adjoining Mud Lake is a labyrinth of logging roads and skid trails offering an afternoon's diversion within sound of doors slamming in the parking lot. I've suggested a couple of loops but there's umpteen variations to be made, particularly on the flat ground between the lakes and Mud Lake where you could map out a mini Canmore Nordic Centre. I hope you're not the first person to break trail.

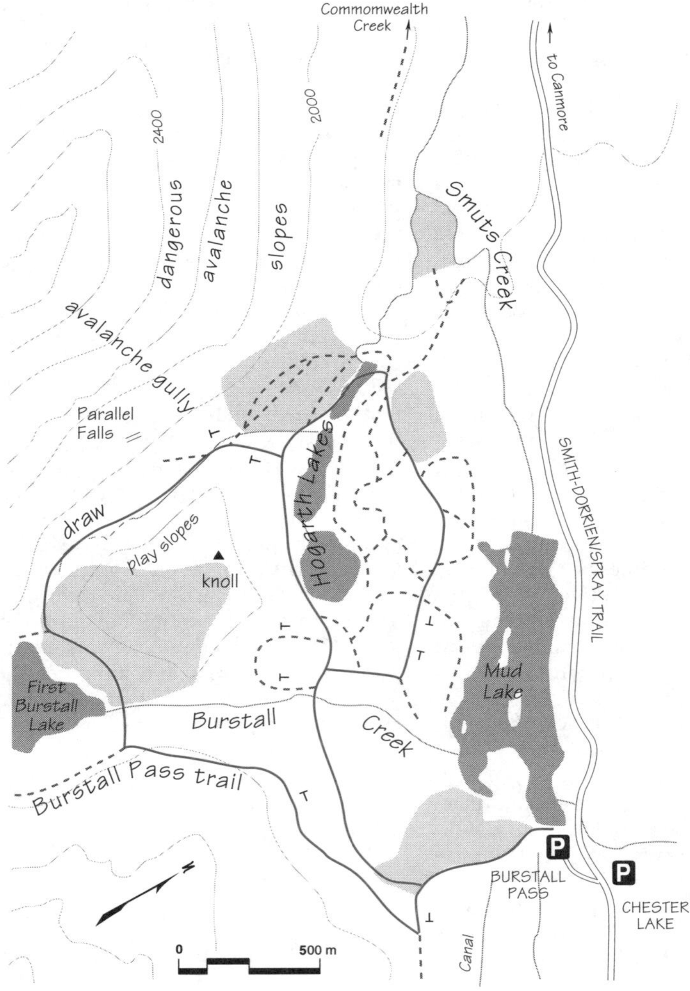

HOGARTH LAKES LOOP
Easy
7 km

The circuit of the three lakes is a delightful tour through spruce forest tagged with yellow discs. The views aren't bad either.

Start off by following Burstall Pass trail across the dam, then turn right *before* you start up the hill to the junction with French Creek trail. All is straightforward to Burstall Creek crossing. On the far side keep right, left (return leg), right, left, and in the shadow of a cliff speed past First and Second Hogarth Lakes to a junction with an uphill road to the left (First Burstall Lake loop).

Mindful that you're passing your first avalanche warning sign, you follow the road down to Third Lake, receptacle for avalanche debris from the unnamed ridge to the west, taking particular note of where the yellow disc trail leaves the road along the lake's west shore and heads across to the east bank, there rejoining the road in a position of perfect safety in a cutblock. Turn right.

The return leg undulates half-way between Mud Lake and the three Hogarth Lakes and as you can see from the map, there are dozens of possible variations using minor roads and skid trails, including my own favourite sortie down to the north shore of Mud Lake. And there's another which follows the rim of First and Second Hogarth Lakes. But nowhere does the road or indeed *any* of the roads cross Burstall Creek. So from a T-junction (yellow disc) you have to turn right and join your outgoing road near the creek crossing.

Hogarth Lakes loop. View from Third Hogarth Lake of Mt. Chester.

First Burstall Lake loop. Looking through the draw towards Mt. Burstall.

FIRST BURSTALL LAKE LOOP

Intermediate
7 km
Height gain 75 m

Cool forest, sunny cutblocks, great views, telemarking slopes: this little loop has it all. But when avalanche hazard is high or extreme, go somewhere else.

From the parking lot you follow Hogarth Lakes Loop past Second Hogarth Lake to the road junction near the first avalanche warning sign. Yes, I'm afraid you're going to have to climb the hill on the left past a junction on the fringe of the avalanche slope and further up yet to the lip of a draw. Abandoning the road (which continues up the hillside to the bottom of two grade 4 frozen waterfalls called Parallel Falls), enter the draw and be quick about it. Don't do daft things like stand and look at the wondrous view opened up behind you or take off your pack to pull on your jacket. In case you haven't noticed, you're a standing like a sitting duck at the bottom of an avalanche chute.

The draw is safe apart from one other hazardous spot two thirds the way along, but rather than hurry through to the end, treat yourselves to a dollop of superb powder blanketing the knoll on the left which is the north-westerly aspect of the cliff above Hogarth Lakes. From its slopes is a wonderful view of Parallel Falls and maybe the odd climber or two for entertainment. But back to the draw. When it ends, another road joins in from the right and you go left into a huge south-facing cutblock with another wonderful view across First Burstall Lake to Mt. Burstall, Whistling Rock Ridge and Burstall Pass headwall. Since the knoll's south slopes are one vast snowfield it's virtually impossible to detect the line of the road which heads ever so slightly downhill to cross Burstall Creek, then, clearly visible, rises to join the Burstall Pass trail.

Turn left. You may have been the first around the loop, but here a trail is a certainty and all you have to do now is get into a tuck and freewheel back to the parking lot.

To Mount Engadine Lodge

For some time now the idea of a long distance loppet (as distinct from the Great Cookie Race) has been stirring in the mind of the Events Chairman for Cross-Country Canada, aided and abetted by assorted race officials and his wife. One idea is to start from Sawmill parking lot at the Smith-Dorrien Ski Trails and connect the Chester Lake trails, Hogarth Lakes trails, Mount Engadine Lodge trails, Mount Shark trails, the Watridge Lake trail to Spray River bridge, the west-side road of Spray Lakes Reservoir and the Spray River trail in its entirety to a likely hotel in Banff for collapse and wine. Another idea is to cut out the Spray River bit and return to Sawmill via completely different trails. All trails exist apart from the stretch between Hogarth Lakes and Mount Engadine Lodge which presents a problem of astounding complexity considering it's only one kilometre long.

The missing link would appear to start from the turnaround point of Hogarth Lakes Loop just east of Third Lake. You head out confidently along a logging road going in the right direction but all it does is deliver you to a picturesque promontory where you're well and truly trapped between deeply incised Hogarth Creek on your left and deeply incised Smuts Creek on your right. Off to the north you can spot your objective — a new road — starting up in a belt of trees on the west side of Smuts Creek and in between a whole hillside of nasty avalanche slopes which slop snow up the far side of the creek beds. So you can see that to get from A to B requires either a wide circumnavigation to the east with one or two bridges costing in the region of 12,000 dollars apiece to carry the weight of a piston bully, or a completely new trail several kilometres long between the end of Mud Lake and the turnaround point of Princess Anne Loop. As I write this, K-Country is considering Rudi Kranabitter's proposal to run a snowmobile and tracksetter along the east bank route, so keep tuned for further developments.

Don't even think of a short-cut from the west side of Third Hogarth Lake along the bottom of the avalanche slopes.

One of many avalanche slopes falling to Smuts Creek.

BURSTALL PASS

Backcountry & Route

Intermediate
8.6 km to Burstall Pass
10 km to South Burstall Pass
Height gain Burstall Pass 497 m, South Burstall Pass 585 m
Maximum elevation 2377 m, South Burstall Pass 2460 m
Map 82 J/14 Spray Lakes Reservoir, 82 J/11 Kananaskis Lakes

Access Smith-Dorrien-Spray Trail at the Burstall Pass parking lot.

Facilities Washrooms at parking lot.

Overview A signed logging road and trail take you quickly into alpine country straddling the boundary with Banff National Park where fatigue is replaced by wonder at the fantastic snow and scenery. Looking for telemarking slopes? It's no contest, Burstall Pass is *far* superior to the ever popular Robertson Glacier. Be aware of avalanche danger along the route in times of high or extreme hazard.

From behind the washroom in the parking lot (trails always start from behind washrooms), you follow a well-beaten track across Mud Lake dam. Had you been here in the Spring of 1990 you would have passed a cabin on the left built for the French film "Jesuit Joe". Beyond Mud Lake keep left and climb a hill to French Creek junction, where, obeying a signpost down by your feet, you turn right onto the main Burstall Creek logging road. Most of height gain occurs in the first kilometre where minor side roads and skid trails forking left and right can be safely ignored unless you're actively seeking out variations. This brings you above the level of a small canyon holding Burstall Creek where First Burstall Lake Loop turns off to the right. Ahead, the rocky peaks of Mt. Birdwood and Commonwealth Peak are flushed from the early morning sun.

The remainder of the road undulates between avalanche slopes sweeping down to the road and the three Burstall Lakes of which you catch only glimpses between trees. Mind the boulder. A narrowing road with a surprise dip which catches some folks I know off guard every time precedes the start of the awkward trail down to the dryas flats beyond the lakes. Awkward because the trees are too close, therefore too little snow reaches the ground which is rooty. Early and late in the season an easy alternative is to glide one or two steps down to Third Burstall Lake and turn left. Whichever way you do it, cross the flats kitty corner to a point left of West Burstall Creek and two avalanches gullies (sign).

It's not a hard pull up the timbered headwall though herringboning and sidestepping must still be resorted to in one or two places. At the top you traverse the wide mouth of a gully (West Burstall Creek) which should be remembered for the return trip.

Aiming for South Burstall Pass (and Mt. Sir Douglas) from Burstall Pass. Photo: Alf Skrastins

The beautiful and sometimes treacherous powder slopes at Burstall Pass. Looking west across the sinkhole towards Mt. Assiniboine.

After this comes a long flat meadow below Birdwood Pass with its threatening avalanche slopes. It's sobering to think that in February of 1990 an avalanche swept right across the valley floor. Beyond the meadow the summer trail climbs the side slope but in winter you enter the narrow draw and when it creases into mini draws and a little bowl, herringbone left, then traverse right across a side slope to flatter terrain above, the sub-alpine proper with scattered spruce islands.

Right now you are heading for South Burstall Pass, so at the obvious place start climbing up a wide rib to your right, aiming for a bench higher up. Here, the up trail often divides and you can either traverse right across steeper telemarking slopes (better saved for the descent surely), or go left on the summer trail to gain Burstall Pass in a more roundabout way from the south.

The wide ridge of the pass has a complicated topography with bumps and dips further complicated by a deep sink hole to the west where the snow lies thick like a mantle of heavy silk. Not a place to wander about willy-nilly when the cloud's down. In fact, careless wandering off the ridge to the west is not too healthy at best of times and I have a photo of a slab avalanche to prove it. Though the view to the east is all encompassing, it's the view to the west which draws all eyes. "I say Norm, isn't that Assiniboine you can see over there?" Have you noticed how all views are judged by whether or not Mt. Assiniboine is in the picture.

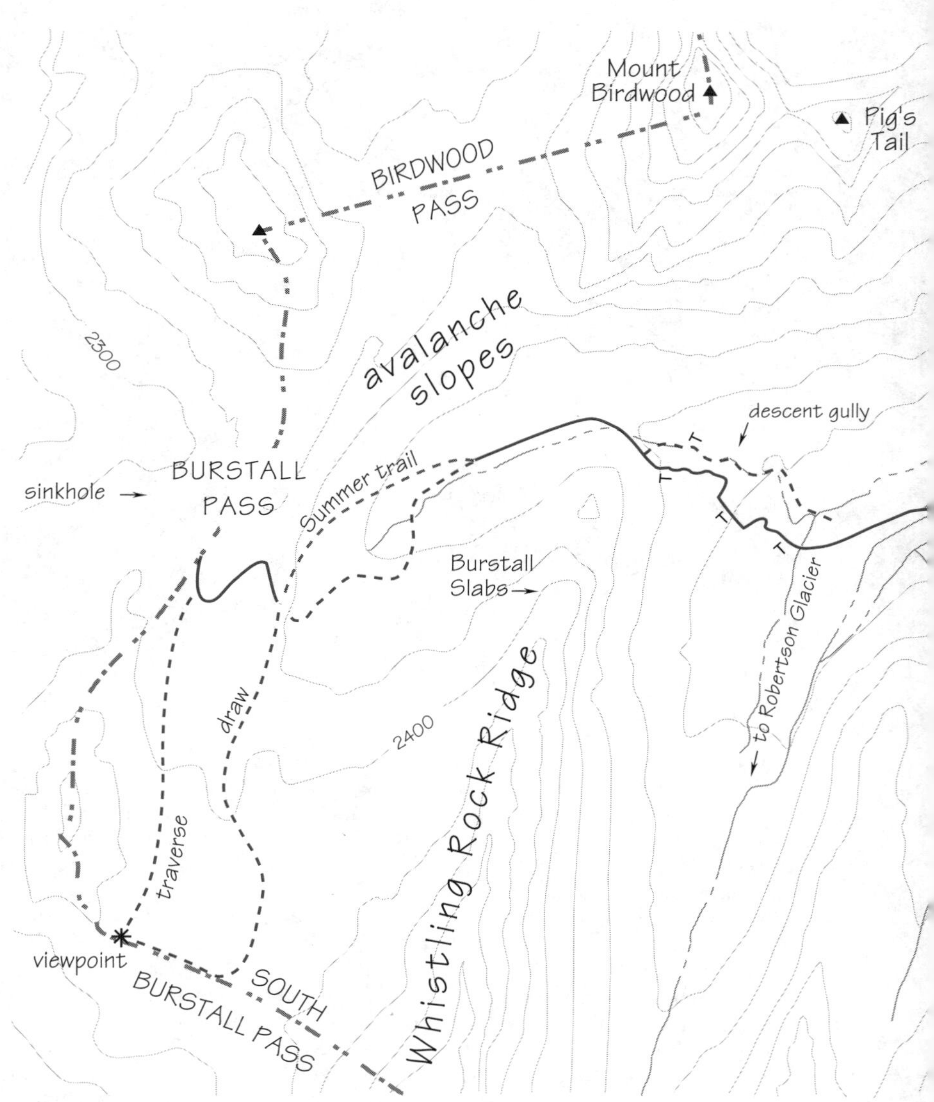

Return The hiss of powder, the whoops of joy, the profanities as someone takes a nose-dive are all part and parcel of the descent through the meadows. What I like about it is that we all get to choose our own way down.

From the top of the timbered headwall, most people descend the gully of West Burstall Creek which has one or two icy steps after a crowd of skiers has passed by. Lower down it flattens out and merges with an avalanche slope. Waste no time in getting down to the dryas flat.

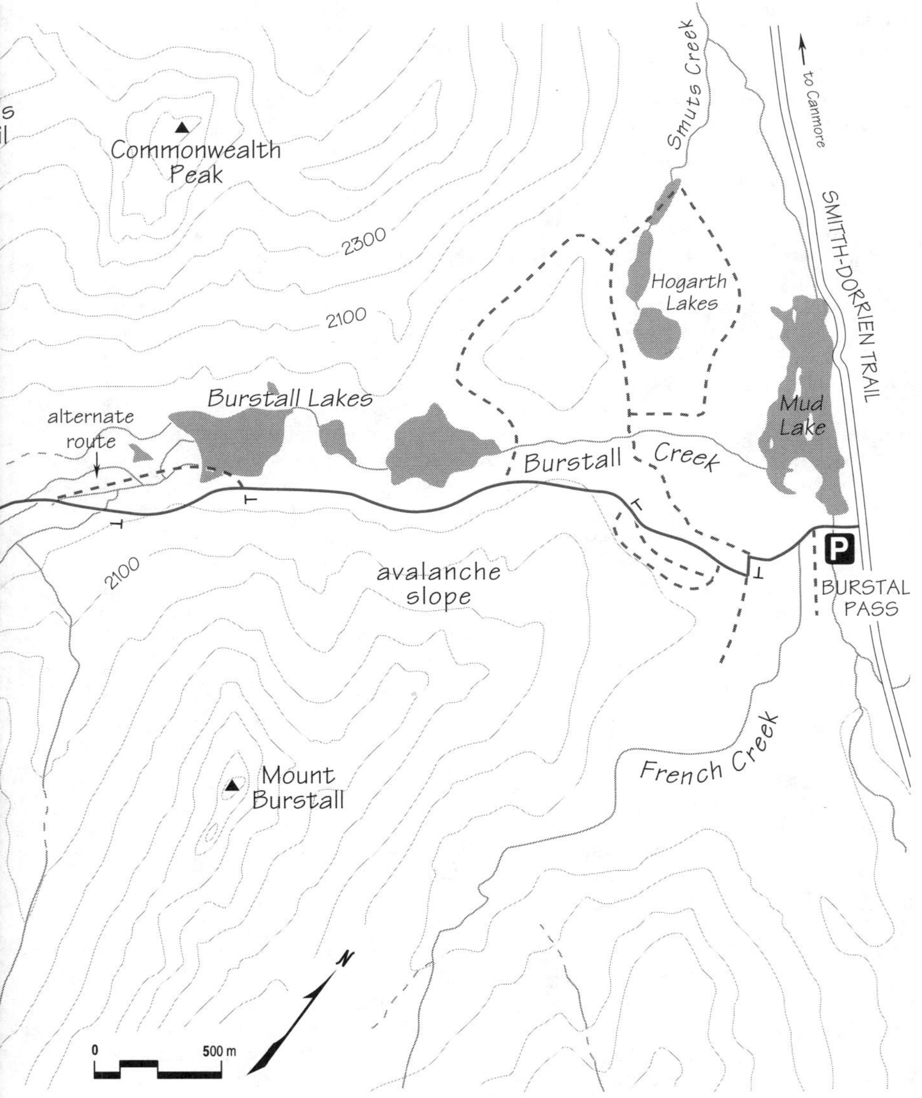

Option: South Burstall Pass
South Burstall Pass is an easy ski from the sub-alpine meadows. Simply continue up the centre of the valley which is so incredibly rocky you would never dream of coming up this way in summer. A knoll appears to block the way, but trust the draw winding sinuously to the right, then back left where it unfolds ever so gently onto the summit of the pass. A line of small cairns and one large cairn on top of a rock band mark the K-Country/Banff National Park boundary.

Despite lacking Mt. Assiniboine, this is just a stupendous viewpoint. The glaciated north face of Sir Douglas always reduces me to goose-bumps, while behind your back, the dogtooth mountains of Mts. Smuts, Birdwood, "Pig's Tail" and Commonwealth Peak are lined up four abreast.

Don't stop here. With minimum effort you can reach the end of the ridge to the west (one bench up) and look down over Palliser Pass and the Upper Spray River Valley towards the lesser peaks of the Royal Group. I recommend climbing up two benches (steeper) or onto the ridge top itself for the very best view incorporating both Palliser Pass *and* Mt. Assiniboine. As you can see from the front cover and the photo opposite, this unnamed ridge between the two passes is an unparalleled viewpoint for Mt. Sir Douglas.

Option: South Burstall Pass to Burstall Pass via the bench

Or, how to incorporate the two passes in one day. It's incredibly easy: the two being connected by an oblique bench (the one bench up) where you can make a few turns.

More about the trail In the early morning of October 6, 1948 district ranger Joe Kovach and Bill Balmer were at Mud Lake, trying to find a route over to the Spray River valley. They followed a good game trail along the south side of Burstall Lakes, then crossed over at the end of the last lake to the west and "climbed up to a summit that can be crossed very easily on to the Spray River". So any blazes you find are Kovach's. The main object of the trip, though, was to look over the timber and unfortunately they noted a very good stand of spruce on the south side of Burstall Lakes, another reason why Spray Lakes Sawmills came to the area on a subcontract for the Eau Claire Logging Company.

Getting in meant building their own road from Three Sisters Dam, the 1953 version of the Smith-Dorrien/Spray Trail which took a much higher line than the Mannix trail, the two merging at Mount Engadine Lodge at the junction of the Watridge Logging Road. Mud Lake was chosen as the location for No. 1 Sawmill and a string of bunkhouses down the east side of the road. Of course the new road opened the door for crazy tourists like ourselves who before K-Country closed everything off drove as far up the logging roads as we could get before pulling on our hiking boots. Having been spoilt, I still find walking up the Burstall Creek logging road awfully hard to take.

In winter it was different. The reputed powder meadows of Burstall Pass were as remote as the North Pole. You could only attempt to get up the Spray Lakes Road from the Canmore end which was navigable until about the end of December to a point near the end of the reservoir under Mt. Buller where the snow started getting really deep. You took along chains and tow ropes and expected to pull other people out of the ditch. If you were lucky like we were and had the right connections you got to stay in one of the bunkhouses. But even then, most times you had to ski another 10 km along the road to even get to today's parking lot so the trip took a lot longer and you rarely made the pass.

Who can forget that night between Christmas and New Year. There we were at Mud Lake, with two small kids in tow and defeated as usual (we had got to the meadow above the headwall). Under a full moon the bunkhouses were silent, empty, locked. The temperature was -30°, the time 7 o'clock and we were two hours from the car. Yes, I know how irresponsible this seems – there were no rangers in those days to tick us off – but call it fate because after we had reached the car, had realized we didn't need to fish out the overnight survival gear, and were slowly limping along the road on square tires, we came on two motorists casually dressed for the heated car interior dancing round a fire. One had lost his leather driving glove in the flames. Given their car was dead, it would have been hard to find two more ecstatic people when we rolled down a window and offered them a lift into Canmore. I often wonder what would have happened to them had we not happened along so late at night.

Photo: Clive Cordery

The ridge between Burstall and South Burstall Passes is one stupendous viewpoint. The glaciated north face of Mt. Sir Douglas rises above a sea of clouds spilling over Palliser Pass from BC.

PALLISER LOOP

Backcountry, Route & Groomed

Intermediate
Total distance about 40 km
Total height gain 807 m clockwise
Total height loss 931 m clockwise
Maximum elevation 2460 m
Map 82 J/14 Spray Lakes Reservoir, 82 J/11 Kananaskis Lakes

Access
1. Smith-Dorrien/Spray Trail at Burstall Pass parking lot.
2. Smith-Dorrien /Spray Trail. Watridge Logging Road at Mount Shark Ski Trails parking lot (see page 113 for directions).

Facilities Washrooms at both parking lots. Mount Engadine Lodge is not too far distant (see page 106). Backcountry campground at Birdwood Creek. Water in the Spray River near the warden cabin.

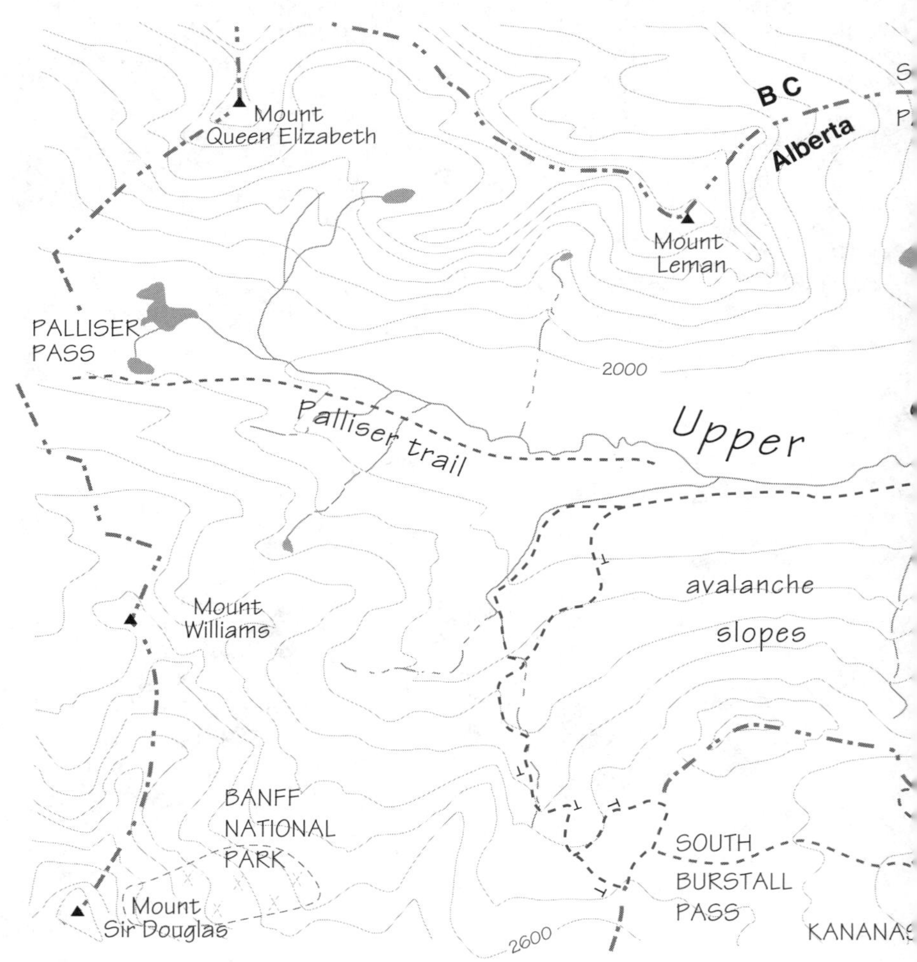

Overview Sub-title: Mud Lake to Mount Shark via South Burstall Pass and the Upper Spray River Valley. Attempted by a few and completed by even less, this circuit is one long strenuous day. It requires two cars, though this is not strictly necessary, bearing in mind that the chances of getting a lift from the Mount Shark parking lot is not great after dark. It also requires X number of daylight hours or moonlight or headlamps, stable avalanche conditions, no recent snowfall, a free Sunday (and probably Monday), thus allowing other people on Saturday to break trail both to South Burstall Pass and to Palliser Warden Cabin. This theoretically will leave you with just the middle section to break trail. As you will have gathered, the possibility of being caught out in the dark is good. In our case it occurred at the Spray River bridge. Of course the trip can be broken into two days with side trips to Palliser Pass and Spray Pass which is probably the sensible way of doing things. Although there is nothing very steep or exposed on this route and you don't need to be a fantastic skier you do need to be an accomplished plodder and route finder. When avalanche danger is high or extreme I would avoid it. Finally, you would be a dingbat to even think of skiing this loop in the opposite direction.

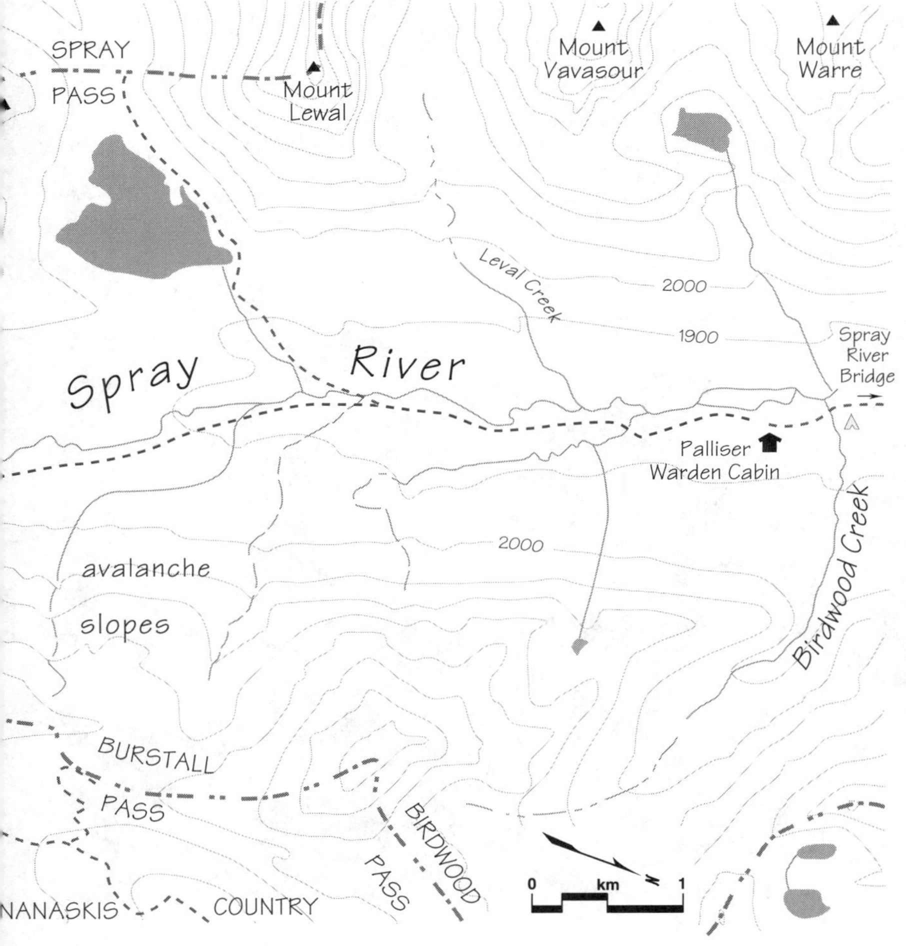

Be away nice and early to South Burstall Pass (see page 144).

From the pass, the route down the other side is via wide sloping terraces interspersed by rock bands arranged like hedges in a maze. To make the game more sporting, the rock bands can't be seen from above. Now experts can probably keep to the right on the steep stuff. The rest of us can either start from the left side or the right side of the pass. If the latter, start by skiing down a shallow draw to the first drop-off and at a solitary tree marking the spot slither down between cliffs to the broad terrace below which can also be reached from the left start. Contour left to centre cirque, then ski easily down a snow tongue with small trees towards drop-off number two where it becomes obvious you have to head right to round the end of the cliff where it peters out against a scree slope. This manoeuvre lands you on a narrower terrace which slopes down left into the head of the valley, at this point a V-shaped receptacle for avalanches thundering down the scree slope opposite. Hurry, weaving between boulders to a flat area on a lip of a small drop-off, a good spot for a breather with a close-up view of Palliser Pass and Mt. Queen Elizabeth.

Below is a hanging valley filled with trees and enclosed by ridges turned in like pincers out of which the creek escapes down steep slopes to the flat floor of the Spray River valley. What you do next is swoop below the left-hand ridge to the narrows where you have a choice of routes. You can either descend the steep creek bed, or cross the creek and ski along the top of the right bank for a way to billowy slopes of few trees slowly glazing in the hot sun of early spring, and only then ski down to the flats. There are an infinite number of places for the final drop; just bear in mind that the further right you go the steeper it gets and the more avalanche prone. This final drop can be glorious powder I'm told, but when we did it, it was not. Not after a week of glorious sunshine. Progress deteriorated to out of control lurches across

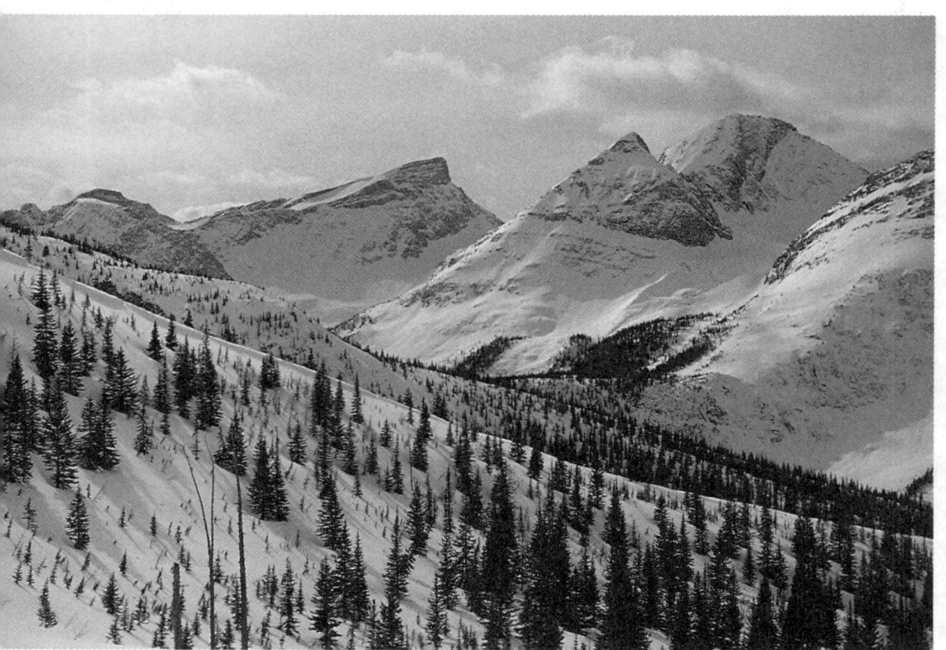

The Royal Group from the lip of the hanging valley. Route traverses left-hand ridge low down.

The flats of the Upper Spray River valley. Palliser Pass above skier, Mt. Leman to right.

a polished mirror 2 km across and 200 m high and was interspersed with innumerable kick-turns, preferably on the upside security of a tree (I'm still waiting for ski manufacturers to address the problem of retractable crampons). On this occasion I think we should probably have opted for the creek bed.

So there you are on the flats having a quick snack. The technical stuff may be behind you but don't get carried away. Coming up is at least 6 km of serious trail-breaking to the Palliser Warden Cabin, first along the flats of your little creek, then along the wider flats of the Upper Spray which seem endless, and indeed *are* endless. Scenery on the grand scale passes by slowly. Mt. Leman on the left followed by the gap of Spray Pass (so close, it seems a shame not to nip up to Leman Lake), then the triad of Mts. Leval, Vavasour and Warre. That the cabin is opposite the last one is a tad discouraging, but finally you get there and collapse under the flagpole, watching the sun sinking behind the mountains.

Read "Palliser Trail" on page 132 and "Watridge Lake Trail to Spray River" on page 126 for information on how to get to Mount Shark parking lot. One good thing: you almost certainly will encounter tracks from the Spray River bridge on and can look forward to a straightforward finish on groomed trails. Reserve some energy for that wretched climb up from the bridge.

If new to the area, have a flashlight handy for reading signposts.

FRENCH CREEK TO THE HAIG ICEFIELD **Backcountry & Route**

Intermediate
Traverse difficult
11 km to Icefield, 26 km circuit
Height gain 863 m, 1066 m circuit
Maximum elevation 2768 m, 2896 m circuit
Map 82 J/14 Spray Lakes Reservoir, 82 J/11 Kananaskis lakes

Access Smith-Dorrien-Spray Trail at Burstall Pass parking lot.

Facilities Washrooms at parking lot.

Overview This is one of those trails which is easier to ski than hike. Every weekend now sees parties of strong tourers starting out for, but not always reaching the icefield, so reserve this trip for the longer daylight hours of April or May. Of course, the snow low down in the trees may be the pits by then, but you can't have everything.

Yes, there is avalanche danger if you stray off the recommended route. Crevasse-wise, the French in winter is relatively safe unlike its summer self when it's been known to snare rangers.

From the parking lot follow Burstall Pass trail out across the dam at the south end of Mud Lake and up the hill to the junction where the Burstall Pass trail turns right.

You, however, go straight along the French Creek logging road, courtesy of Spray Lakes Sawmills, which climbs over a low ridge and down to French Creek. Keep left before the top of the hill and left after the initial downhill; the major road is pretty obvious and you won't even think twice about skid trails which are filling in nicely. Cross French Creek and continue along the road as it climbs along the east bank to the narrows above a really neat two-tiered waterfall in a gorge. Here the road ends.

The creek bed is the most efficient way in except when it comes to the steps. At the first step with waterfall number two, turn it on the left by sidestepping up a short steep gully of a tributary, then return to the main creek. Another easy stretch follows. The third waterfall is the most spectacular of the lot (in summer anyway) and requires a very much wider detour to the left.

It's important when nearing the big bend where the valley turns south-east *not* to follow the creek bed *or* to venture across the creek unless you want to play Russian Roulette with avalanche slopes below Piggy Plus. What you must do is cut the corner by climbing diagonally up the left bank into good safe forest, an effective move in more ways than one since it leads you naturally onto the moraines at treeline.

The creek is now below you to your right. There's nothing to stop you skiing down to it and starting up the toe of the glacier, but my own preference is for the draw to the left of the lateral moraine because the snow is always marvellous, and from the top it's just a simple slightly descending traverse onto the ice.

The French, really a little bit of the Haig Icefield spilled over into the trough between Mts. Robertson and French, is very easy-angled but hardly a five minute doddle. The col is a lot further away than it looks (those dots are people), and has the annoying knack of appearing the same distance away the higher you climb. You can measure your progress by looking behind you now and then; the scene is growing in magnificence and soon you are actually looking over the tops of Mt. Burstall and Piggy Plus to Commonwealth Peak and Mt. Birdwood which resembles a monstrous black beak. Just after passing the French pinnacle, keep left to avoid the deep moat around Robertson. Suddenly, mountains begin to stick up above the horizon. You have arrived on the Haig Icefield.

Return Though easy-angled, the French Glacier gives you a good run for your money, particularly if you take to the moraines! The rest is easy going punctuated by episodes of sidestepping down the two waterfall steps.

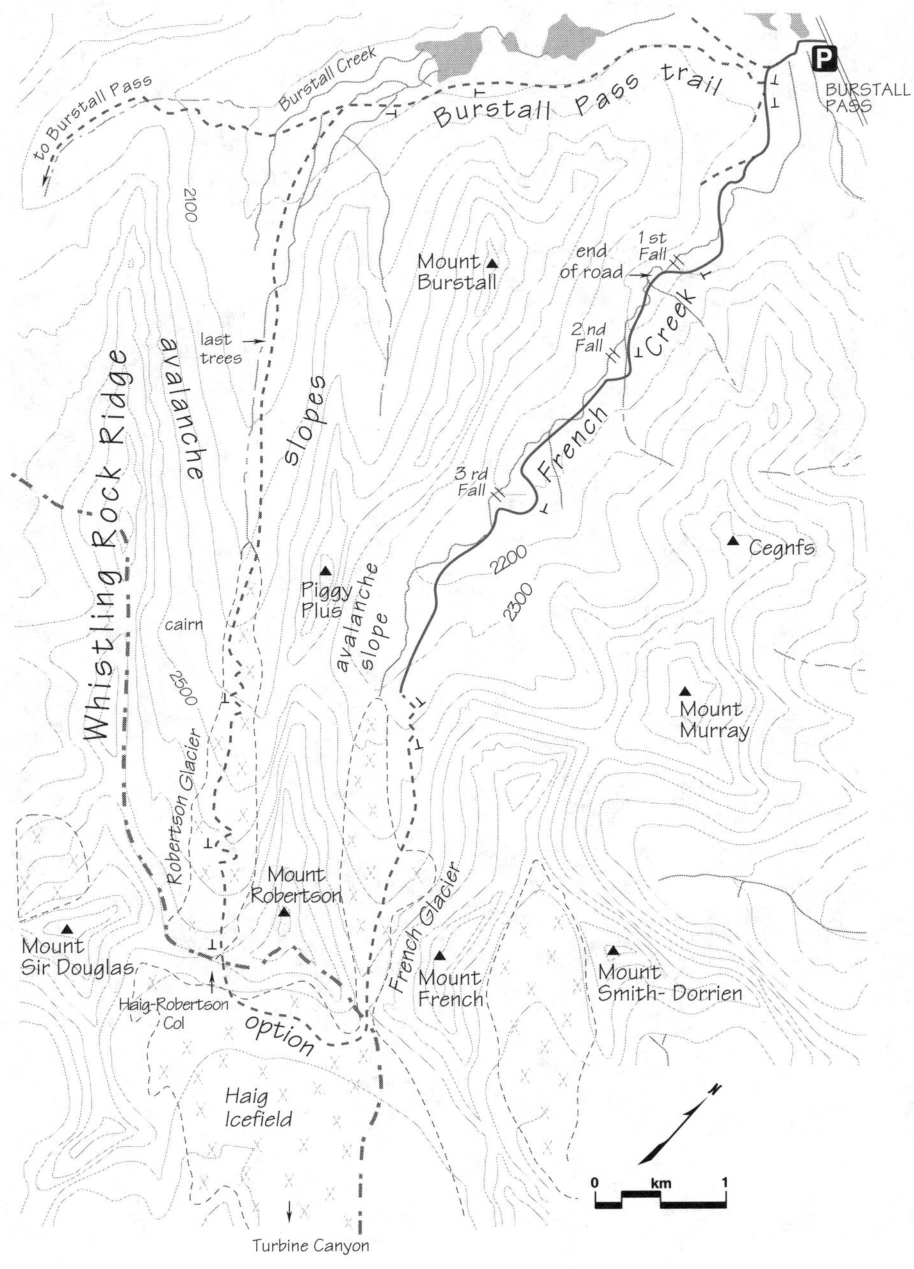

BURSTALL PASS
Burstall Pass trail
to Burstall Pass
Burstall Creek
2100
Mount Burstall
end of road
1st Fall
2nd Fall
3rd Fall
French Creek
last trees
avalanche
slopes
Whistling Rock Ridge
2200
2300
Cegnfs
Piggy Plus
avalanche slope
cairn
2500
Mount Murray
Robertson Glacier
Mount Robertson
French Glacier
Mount Sir Douglas
Mount French
Mount Smith- Dorrien
Haig-Robertson Col
option
Haig Icefield
Turbine Canyon
0
km
1

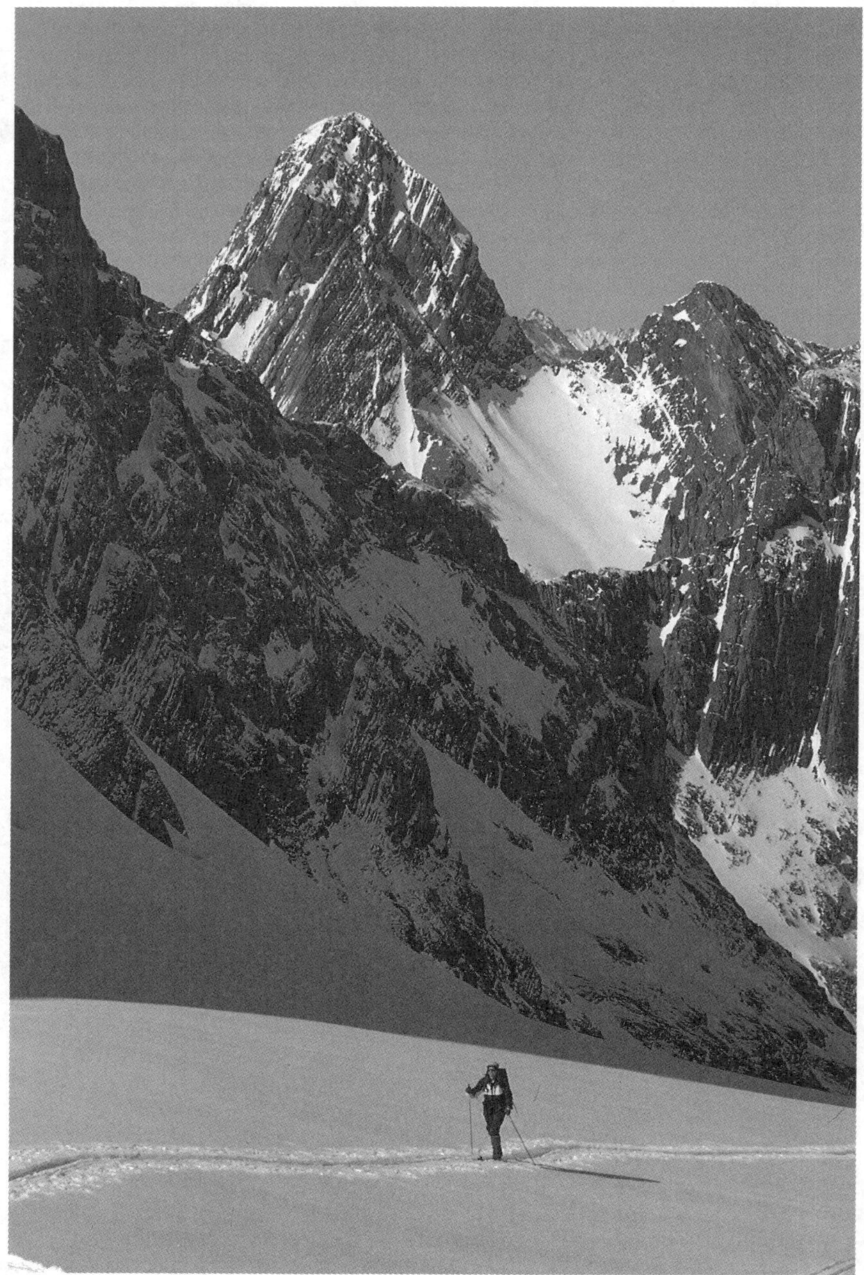

The French Glacier. Looking over Piggy Plus to Mt. Birdwood and Pig's Tail. Photo: Peter Haase

Option: French-Robertson Traverse
You don't have to return the same way. However, the option — up to the Haig-Robertson Col and down the Robertson Glacier — is not for anyone who gets wobbly on steep slopes. Nor is it a good idea if avalanche hazard is high or it's 3 o'clock in the afternoon.

One thing you have to remember is that the top of the Robertson is 137 m *higher* than the Haig Icefield and not go blithely off down Leroy Creek into British Columbia like one skier. Fortunately he was equipped with the kitchen sink and when found by search helicopter the next day had spent a comfortable night out in his sleeping bag which leads to the inescapable conclusion that with all the gear he was carrying he was expecting to bivy. Mind you, if his skis had been in working order, he could have skied back up to the Haig and no-one would have been any the wiser. As it was the RCMP found the incriminating guidebook in his car with a matchstick marking the appropriate page. Therefore readers, read the disclaimer at the beginning of this book, be able to read a topo map and mark the page in the guidebook — just in case.

OK. You've skied up French Creek and are now standing on the Haig Icefield, looking around in wonder at the towering grey cliffs of Mts. Robertson, French, Jellicoe and Sir Douglas. Turn right into BC and when past Mt. Robertson and its moat, climb the slope to the col, making a diagonal traverse from right to left so as to end up just right of the low point. Conditions can run the gamut from a terrifying row of avalanche runnels all the way across to a simple slope of snow and black shale early and late in the season. Most people ski part-way up the slope then kick steps the rest of the way.

More about the trail After Spray Lakes and Kananaskis Lakes were tossed out of the National Park in 1930, the country was laid wide open to logging and hydro-electric schemes. Not content with harnessing all the creeks running into the Spray River, Calgary Power under the guise of its chief engineer and the general manager from Mannix together with district forest ranger Joe Kovach spent September of 1953 looking over French Creek with a view to diverting it away from Smith-Dorrien Creek into Mud Lake. If you ever follow French Creek upstream from Mud Lake dam you will see that this is what has actually happened. Of course, most skiers haven't a clue about this since the logging road you follow deposits you in the creek above all the diversionary canals.

When skiers first started venturing into the valley to look for a glacier that was reputed to be up there somewhere, this valley had a reputation for difficulty, notwithstanding the logging road start. Admittedly, flogging through summer's tangle of willow brush with skis tied to the pack can be irritating. But gradually as more people tried to reach the French a rough trail appeared aided by flagging at strategic points. Honest K-Country, it was nothing to do with me! Then in the late 1980's large parties of provincial nordic racers (the National Team flew in) were moving up and down the trail heading to the icefield for summer training. A large campsite grew up at the toe of the glacier. "Enough" said the Powers That Are, "every alternate valley down the Smith-Dorrien is supposed to remain pristine". Kicked out of the valley, provincial skiers and the media are now forced to walk in the long way round via the trail to North Kananaskis Pass (National team skiers and CODA directors fly in) to — a hut which has started off a new wave of protests by conservation groups who are remiss in excluding the ranger's exclusive log establishment lower down the hill. Lest you've started packing your sleeping bag (we're a two-faced lot, I've decided), the hut on the Haig is a summer temporary and located miles away at the southern end of the icefield above Turbine Canyon.

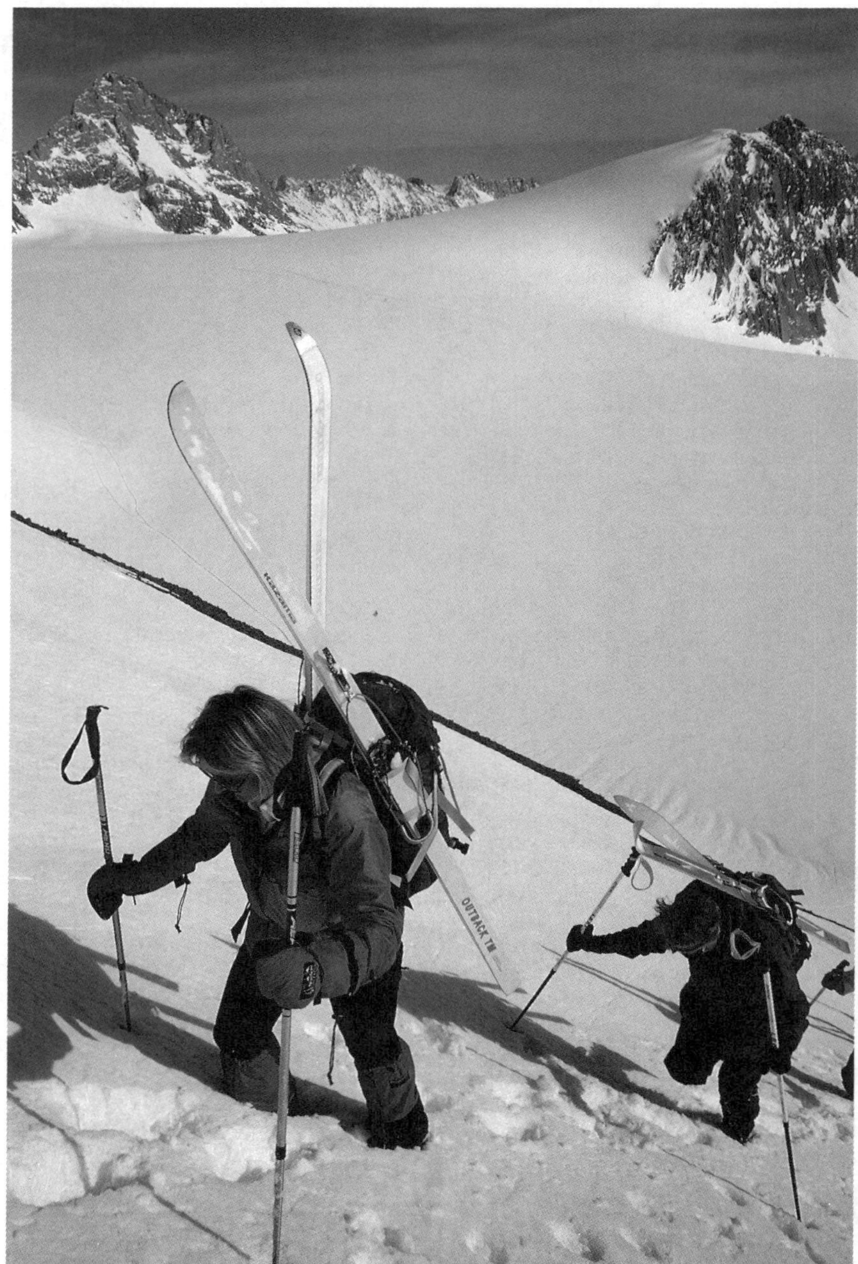

The French-Robertson Traverse. Climbing to the Haig-Robertson Col from the Haig Icefield. Mt. Jellicoe at left. Photo: Alf Skrastins

ROBERTSON GLACIER

Backcountry & Route

Easy to last trees
Intermediate/difficult to col
7 km to last trees
13 km to col
Height gain to col 1021 m
Maximum elevation at col 2896 m
Map 82 J/14 Spray Lakes Reservoir, 82 J/11 Kananaskis Lakes

Access Smith-Dorrien/Spray Trail at Burstall Pass parking lot. Via Burstall Pass trail as described on page 144.

Facilities Washrooms at the parking lot.

Overview How many times have you left Calgary saying with assurance while gathering the camera, "this is the day for Robertson Glacier". The sky is blue with not a cloud to the west. Arriving at the parking lot one and a half hours later, you notice clouds gathering about the summit of Mt. Birdwood and by the time you've skied the regulation 4 km into the valley, Sir Douglas has disappeared and mist is touching down on the Haig-Robertson Col. As you leave last trees the mist is rolling down the glacial trough and only the black-pinnacled ridge of Mt. Robertson pushes through the murk. Soon this too disappears and by the time you actually set foot on the glacier, the wind is howling, whipping up loose snow into your face and elsewhere polishing the boiler plates. The mist thins now and then disclosing crevasses high up on the right or a clump of rocks low down on the left, impossible to tell how far off they are or how big. You sigh, resigning yourself to yet another typical day on the Robertson.

Summer brings another scenario of skimpily-dressed snow fanatics, the kind that have "Down with Summer" car stickers, biking along the logging road with skis and snowboards strapped to the frame. This day's views are perfect, albeit sunglass yellow-coloured, and the weather a non-factor apart from the constant need to replenish suncream and Lypsol. Is the Robertson ever popular! It is, after all, the most accessible glacier in the eastern Rockies with slopes fit for telemarkers.

But when all is said and done, most skiers prefer the winter version even if 80% end the trip at last trees (easy with one fairly fast hill on the return). Some carry on to the toe of glacier (easy with avalanche danger), and a very few reach the Haig-Robertson Col (intermediate/difficult). If going beyond treeline, you must be very certain of avalanche conditions and tell your alter ego "No I'm not going" if hazard is high or extreme. Two tips: when Chinook winds are blowing, the area socks in badly so give it a miss. For conditions on the glacier I recommend heavier touring equipment or telemarking skis.

To Last Trees

From the parking lot follow Burstall Pass trail to the dryas flats where the routes diverge. By keeping left you turn south into the long thin valley between Piggy Plus and Whistling Rock Ridge. Winds funnelling down from Burstall Pass and the Robertson clash at this very spot, picking up all the loose snow and shifting it about dead skeletal trees, a surreal landscape best captured on video. Another kilometre of flat skiing through open forest brings you to the last clump of spruce. Lunchtime.

To Toe of Glacier

Easy and as scary as hell, this V-shaped passage is K-Country's answer to an Iraqi scud missile attack, with particularly heavy bombardment coming from Whistling Rock Ridge which is scarred with old avalanche tracks. Not a nice place though I believe climbers have found a nice little slab on the other side. Strangely enough, even if hazard is low, you still endure 20 minutes of the most incredible unease before arriving at a small knoll with cairn, gathering point for the next stage.

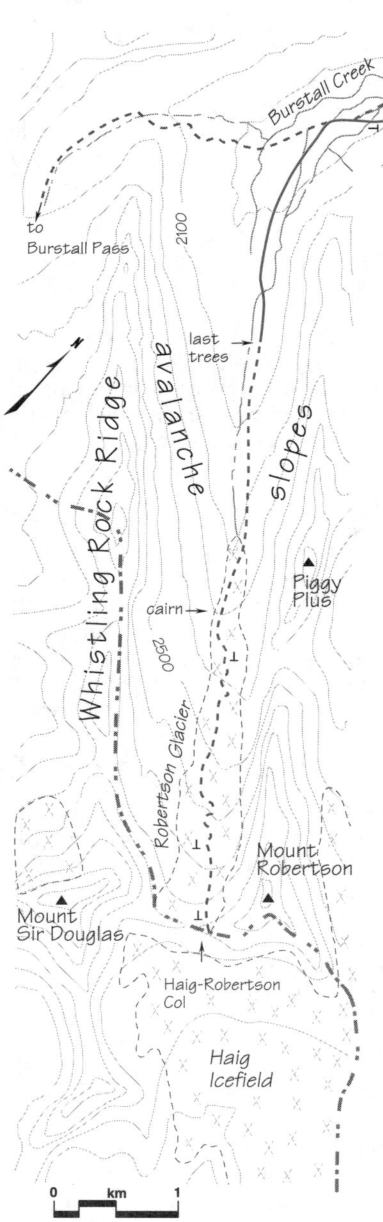

Haig-Robertson Col

There can be very few glaciers with such impressive surroundings as the Robertson. Confined between cathedral-like walls, it rises in three white waves, each one a little steeper than the last to the Haig-Robertson Col which is a lot higher and a lot further away than you think. The mountain responsible for summoning mist is Mt. Sir Douglas on the right which at 3406 m is the second highest mountain in K-Country.

The first step is easy and divided from the second by a gentle incline with built-in boilerplates. The second step rises like a concrete dam right across the trough and requires switchbacks. Another flat and then comes the final ridiculously small step onto the col which on occasion can be a giant headache — more trouble than everything else put together. Apart from the wind scoop below the col's low point, everything else changes without notice year by year. Sometimes all that's involved is simple sidestepping up the steep little ridge to the left of the scoop. But if a cornice rims the col and the steep ridge is wind slab (the scoop suddenly assumes disquieting well-like characteristics), then you've got to climb much higher to the left which means a wallow up a steep corner with bits of glacier ice showing through and a burrow through the cornice to finish off with. This brings you onto the col some 50 feet above the low point. Look down on the Haig Icefield, also named after Sir Douglas Haig. In summer the place will be buzzing with National and Provincial team racers doing their on-snow training.

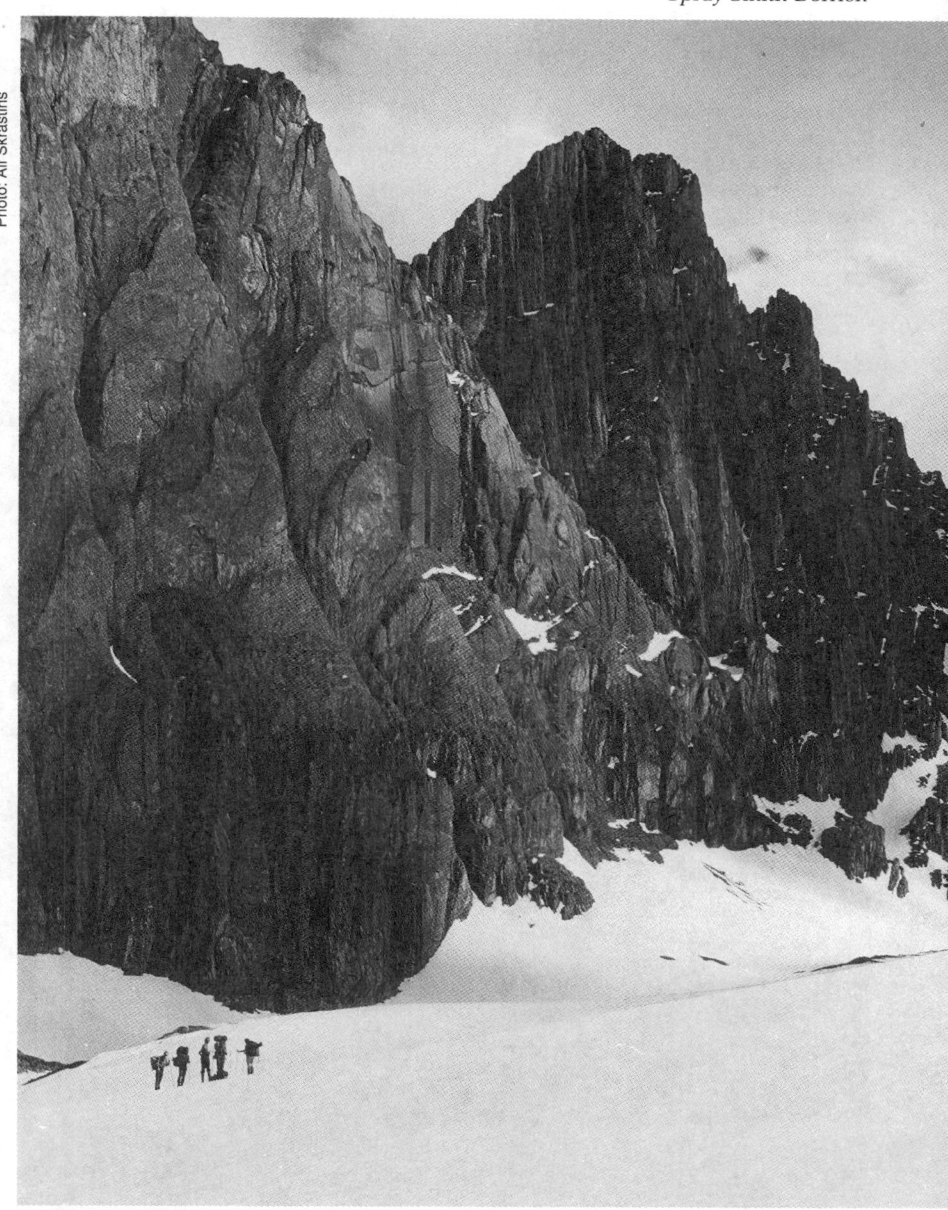
Photo: Alf Skrastins

Below the spectacular cliffs of Mt. Robertson. This is the gentle slope between first and second steps.

Return Everything depends on snow conditions. Usually you can expect reasonably good powder on the steps punctuated by windcrust on the two flatter sections. At first trees you're about 40 minutes away from the car.

CHESTER LAKE

Groomed & Backcountry

Intermediate
7.5 km return
Height gain 311 m
Maximum elevation 2216 m
Map 82 J/14 Spray Lakes Reservoir

Access Smith-Dorrien/Spray Trail at the Chester Lake parking lot.

Facilities Washrooms at parking lot.

Overview It would appear that the incredibly popular Chester Lake trail has replaced the Cascade Fire Road in Banff National Park as the traditional early season opener for Calgarians. It's an official K-Country trail, well-signed, just the right length and, most important, the snow comes early in November. But for some strange reason everyone thinks of this trail as easy. It's not. Not unless you're alone and it's just snowed 30 centimetres. While there's no avalanche danger on the trail, be vigilant if going further afield. Remember the story of the dog who took two days to dig himself out from under the snow.

Start from the top left-hand corner of the parking lot. The road keeps left of Blue trail, crosses Chester Creek and rises slowly to a junction where the one-way system goes into effect.

Turn right, following a tortuous uphill logging road with steep dished corners. Keep left, right and right past skid trails. When you join a level road go left, then first right, resuming the uphill plod. Keep left. Cross another level road, climb another steep uphill and arrive at the 5-way junction. Why bother with all this description since there will undoubtedly be tracks?

The summer trail turns right here, but in winter you take the second road from the left, the middle fork in a prong of three. At the end of a straight is a most important junction marking the end of the groomed logging road section. You'll know when you've got there by the people hanging about looking like a queue for tickets to Les Miserables, either waiting for downers to hurtle past so they can start up the trail, or solitious friends waiting for beginner downers who have probably said some way back, "Sod this! I'm taking my skis off and walking".

Flat meadows not far from Chester Lake. Mountains from left to right are The Tower, Gusty Peak and The Fortress.

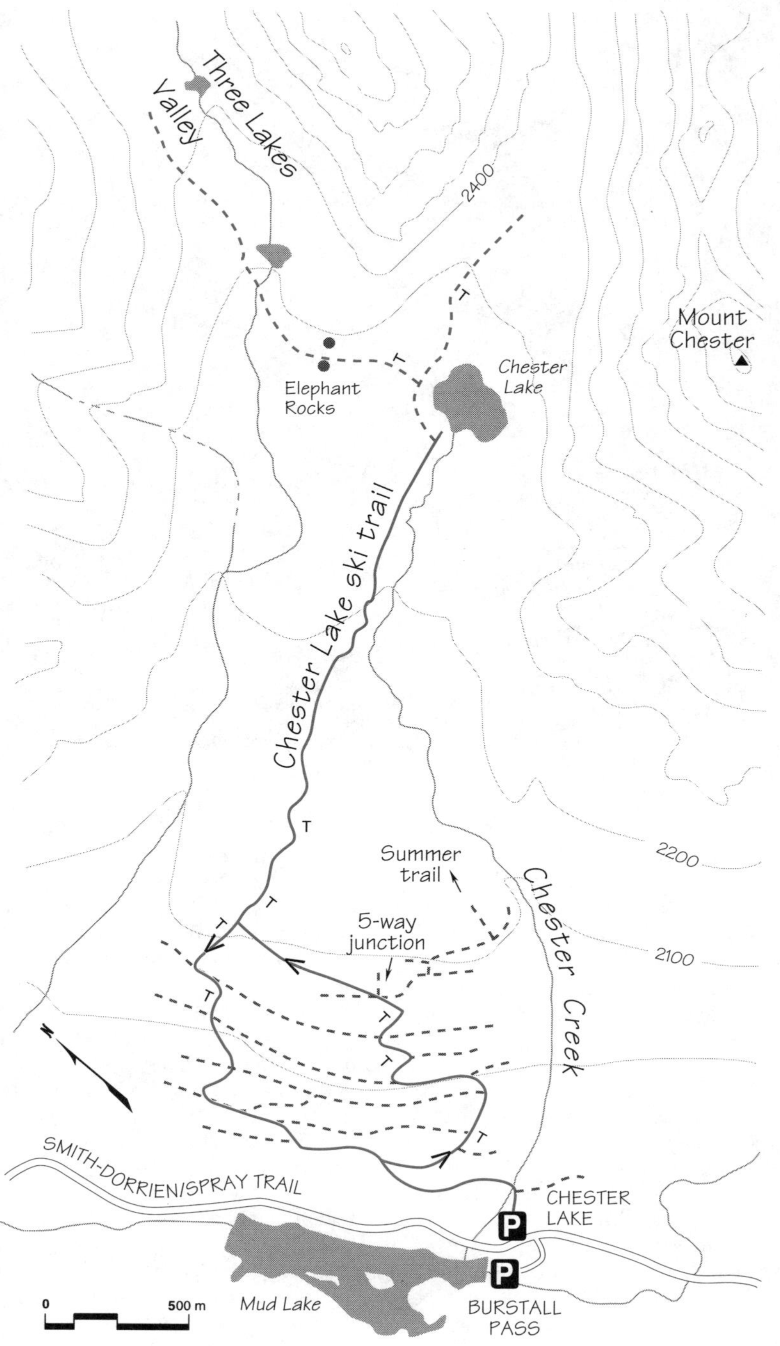
Three Lakes Valley
2400
Mount Chester
Chester Lake
Elephant Rocks
Chester Lake ski trail
Summer trail
2200
Chester Creek
5-way junction
2100
SMITH-DORRIEN/SPRAY TRAIL
CHESTER LAKE
P
P
0
500 m
Mud Lake
BURSTALL PASS

Exploring Elephant Rocks.

Yes, this is where you take to the narrow forest trail. My experience is that as soon as you start up the hill a downer will scream past yelling "track" or words to that effect. You flatten yourself against a tree, wishing that this were the section next due for twinning. This kind of nervy progress ends half a kilometre before the lake at flat meadows which make for a very pleasant finish.

Option: Elephant Rocks
Further exploration means either the upper valley beyond the lake, or Three Lakes Valley, one valley to the north or most often Elephant Rocks half-way towards the latter. You can spend all your spare time safely cutting up the powder between the rocks and the lake. To latecomers it looks like herd of Hannibal's elephants just passed through.

Return A tricky combination of narrow trail and twisting hills alternates with relief sections. Add to this hoards of skiers coming up and going down and beat-up snow and it's obvious you need to be at your nimble best.

At the junction with the logging roads the one-way descent route goes straight down the hill. The way is fast with five steep bends snowplowed into hard-dished shapes. Eyes watering, you are hardly likely to notice junctions, but for the benefit of skiers moving in slow motion in a snowstorm when every road and skid trail looks identical here are directions. At the first bend keep left, at the second bend keep right. Cross over a level road. Cross over another level road at a right-hand bend. Keep left, right, right, and left. This brings you to the end of the two-way system at the signed junction. Keep right all the way back to the parking lot.

SMITH-DORRIEN SKI TRAILS

Initially packed & Backcountry

29 km of trails
Maximum elevation 2112 m
Map 82 J/14 Spray Lakes Reservoir, 82 J/11 Kananaskis Lakes

Access Smith-Dorrien/Spray Trail. Two accesses:
1. At south end, Sawmill parking lot.
2. At north end, Chester Lake parking lot.

Facilities Washrooms at both parking lots. Picnic tables at Sawmill.

Overview I hope you're not a beginner. Most trails at Smith-Dorrien are for seasoned intermediates, on occasion demanding strong quads for long, desperate downhills.

None of the trails were built from scratch. All are logging roads traversing open spruce forest and cutblocks on the east side of the Smith-Dorrien valley roughly between James Walker Creek and Chester Creek. Such is the multitude of roads and skid trails, if you could cut them out and lay them end to end the "Smith-Dorrien trail" would stretch from one side of Alberta to the other. Marking them on the map was an impossible task, though if you volunteer for the next edition I shan't say no. Fortunately, the suggested loops are all colour coded and marked with little arrows.

But wherever you go, on the suggested loops or off on your own explorations, the views across the Smith-Dorrien to the Spray Mountains are spectacular so when you're exhausted, muscles quivering, view stops are admissible.

At the beginning of the season trails are packed to make a good firm base for rescue toboggans. Ever since the Heritage Savings Fund started drying up, the Smith-Dorrien Ski Trails network has been one of the casualties and unless Ribbon Creek is a complete washout, as is what happened in 1992, it's now up to skiers to make their own tracks in successive snowfalls. This could be considerable since snowfall is on a par with Elk Pass and comes in early November.

RED

Intermediate
6.8 km loop
Height gain 220 m
Maximum elevation 2090 m

Starts from Sawmill. My own preference is for skiing the trail in anti-clockwise direction, so keep right at the first junction. The flat bottom leg is probably the only stretch suitable for rank beginners in the whole network, and after turning the corner you're back in intermediate land with a vengeance because just past the Red Connector is the crux, a really steep dip into and out of Sawmill Creek. After this the going is reasonable up to the high point in the spruce. The final descent starts here and ends in the parking lot. First the drop to James Walker logging road, then the descent of the road itself which is consistently steep and sports a huge boulder near the bottom which doesn't come wrapped in a mattress.

RED CONNECTOR

Easy intermediate
0.1 km

The connector enables a small 3.1 km loop to be made at south end of Red — a favourite first ski of the season.

BLUE

Easy intermediate
4.1 km loop

Starting from Chester Lake parking lot, this is a very pleasant undulating loop with no horrid surprises but enough hills to keep the interest up. I'm especially fond of the lower leg which winds through shallow gullies deep in the spruce forest. Often used by Alberta's Provincial ski team for early season training so it's quite likely to be the one trail which is trackset.

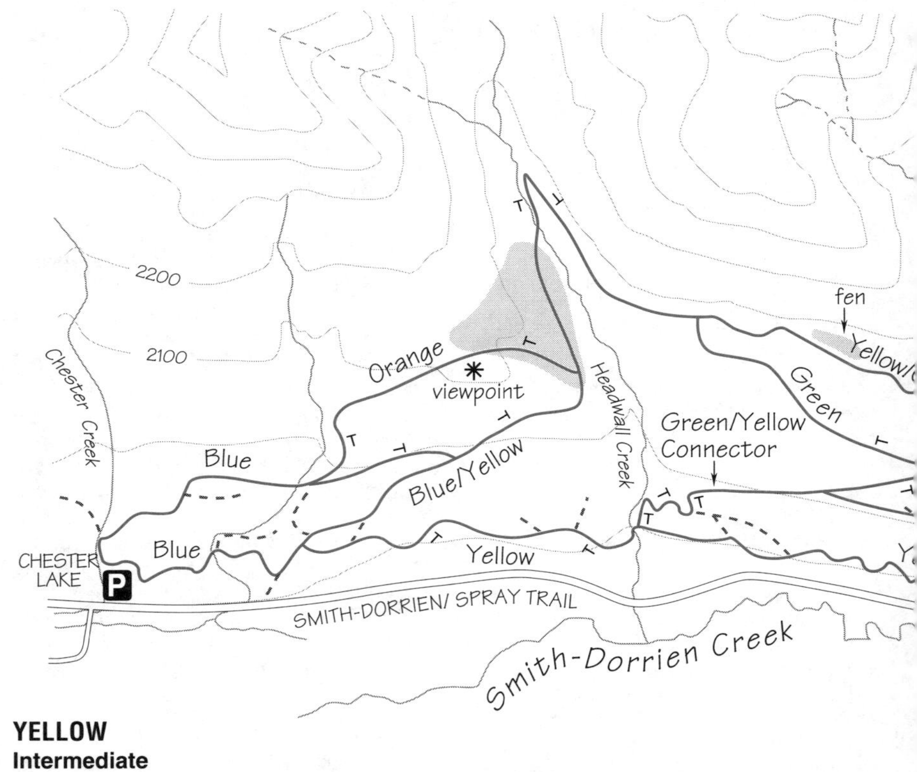

opposite: Yellow/Green descending to James Walker Creek from the fen.

YELLOW

Intermediate
14.5 km loop
Height gain 330 m
Maximum elevation 2088 m

Starts from Sawmill. The longest loop of one colour crosses James Walker and Headwall Creeks at both low and high levels and is generally skied in the clockwise direction for more terrifying downhills. The lower leg is such fun the way it skips along just above the highway on a miniature roller coaster track you may be tempted to return the same way, possibly utilising Green-Yellow Connector and a tad of Green for variety. So when you meet Blue it's decision time. Do you really want to climb up the long hill to Orange? Actually, it's not too onerous and when you reach the cutblock there's a long flat section to Headwall Creek. A short climb, an exceedingly sharp turn to the right and you're into the traverse leading to the high point near the fen where three uphills converge and everyone stops for a chat.

Coming up is the big downhill of the day. You start off gathering speed rather slowly down a winding draw, accelerate across a cutblock and are finally sent hurtling out across James Walker Creek courtesy of a hill which would not be out of place at the Canmore Nordic Centre. When we first looked at this final hill, we decided that the route at this point should make two zigs to the left. (It hasn't.) After this comes a relief section with some uphill even, then another incredible downhill shared with Red and Green.

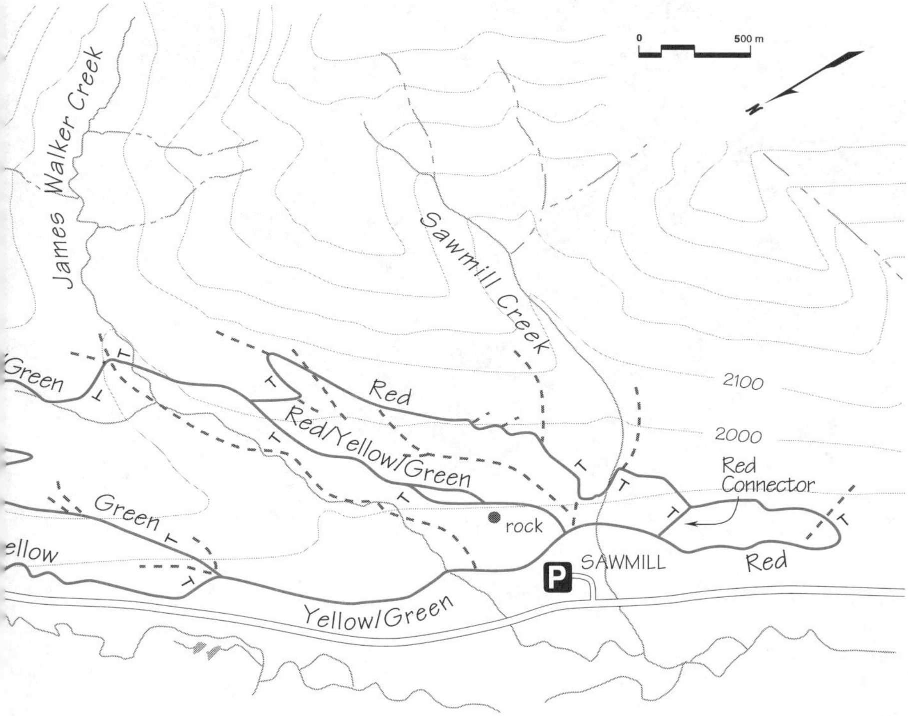

0 500 m
James Walker Creek
Sawmill Creek
Green
Red
Red/Yellow/Green
2100
2000
Red Connector
rock
Green
ellow
SAWMILL
Red
Yellow/Green

GREEN

Intermediate
9.6 km loop
Height gain 260 m
Maximum elevation 2090 m

Starts from Sawmill. It appears to ski more naturally in a clockwise direction. This way you can enjoy looking out over the valley to shapely mountains like Mt. Murray and Cegnfs while crawling up the incredible zigzags of the front face past a multitude of skid trails. You're definitely in need of a collapse by the time you join Yellow on the bench near the fen. If you're still struggling with the pronunciation of Cegnfs I'll let you off the hook by telling you the name derives from the initials of the first ascent party and is entirely unofficial.

Then comes the long hill described under Yellow. Did you know that for the first few years Green missed out the final drop and went careering off to the right along the north side of James Walker Creek, a reasonable road apart from the ice flows. As it is now, you cross James Walker Creek and share another long downhill with Yellow and Red back to the parking lot.

GREEN-YELLOW CONNECTOR

Intermediate
1.1 km

Steep and twisty describes the trail which enables you to make an interesting loop using Yellow and Green without climbing too high.

ORANGE

Difficult
1.8 km
Height loss 138 m
Maximum elevation 2112 m

There is only one logical way round to ski this trail — anti-clockwise. You climb from Yellow through open cutblocks to a viewpoint for Mt. Birdwood on a bench (telemarking area above) where you prepare yourself for the downhill to Blue. It all seems quite manageable at first. You are congratulating yourself when the trail turns a left-hander and suddenly it's desperation snowplow. You're fighting a trail which is getting steeper and steeper yet, sweeping you over a bank and along a runout too short to Blue where you crash in a heap of skis, poles and bodies. Unless you're proficient, ski this trail immediately after a snowfall.

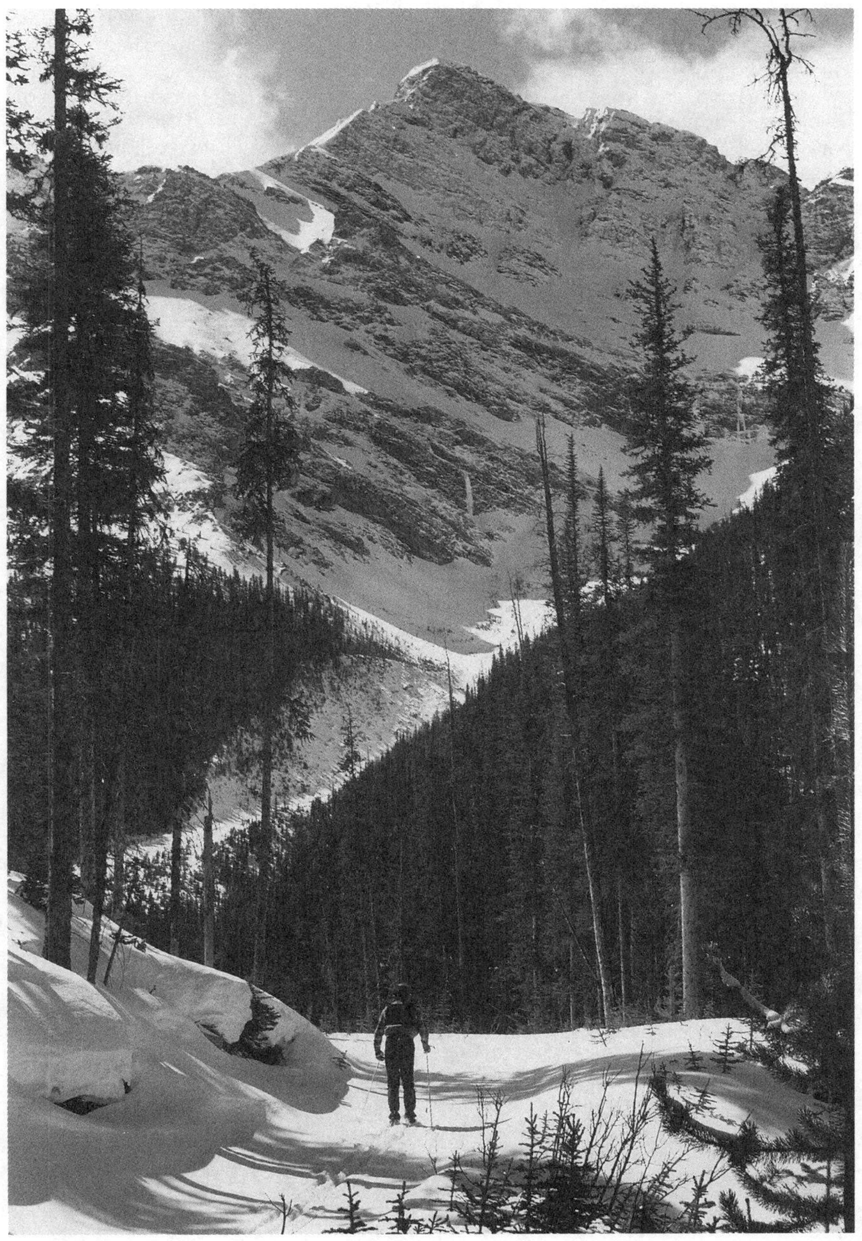

Yellow/Green Connector. Cegnfs overlooks the trail from across the highway.

Photo opposite:
Yellow/ Green at the fen.

More about the trails We owe not only the trails but also the highway to Spray Lakes Sawmills. Five years after setting up Sawmill No. 1 at Mud Lake in 1953, they moved down the valley to Sawmill parking lot, building the road as they went and there erected Sawmill No. 2. The connecting link to Kananaskis Trail was still a few years down the road and even then it was virtually impassable with wall to wall mud puddles (we never did make Mud Lake from this direction), so it was only when the road was rebuilt in K-Country's time that people started taking note of the recreational possibilities down this end of the valley. I'm sure every cross-country skier driving the road in summer must have noticed the amazing web of ready-made ski trails criss-crossing the hillsides between James Walker Creek and Chester Creek. In the winter of 1981 people actually mounted ski expeditions up the road from Lower Kananaskis Lake to the sawmill site just to look at the future parking lot for ten minutes.

It was some time around 1982 that serious rumbling began from all quarters to plow the road in winter. A decade of lean snow years everywhere else except up the Smith-Dorrien was making peace-loving touring folk unusually grouchy. For racers and race organisers the situation was desperate going on frantic because on January 14/15 Alberta was supposed to be hosting the Western Canadian Championships and though Bragg Creek was being groomed for stardom, odds of holding races there on any given day in 1984 were 7-2 against.

The skier's dream came true in the winter of 1983, the first year the road was being plowed on a regular basis, and while everyone else was making haste to Burstall Pass, Tony and myself with Albert Mazzucchi scoured the logging roads from one end to the other looking for connections across Headwall Creek. Then we tried the frontal approach up what is now Green to the fen and discovered that wonderful run down to James Walker Creek with its connection to Red/Yellow/Green. Of course the skiing then was not so wonderful since the snow was heavily booby-trapped. But that could be fixed and that fall saw work parties from the Foothills Nordic Ski Club (including such future Olympic heavyweights as the Chairman of Alpine, and the Secretary, the Chief of Course and the Volunteers Co-ordinator for cross-country) hefting chainsaws around the 5 and 10 km courses. A month later we tested out the fledgling loops and declared them a go, forgetting that touring along the roads with numerous stops, ostensibly to pull on or off jackets or to point out some spectacular bit of scenery was totally different to racing the trails. We were pretty ignorant of racers' needs at this time.

After the Western Canadian Championships on trails which were forerunners of the trails at the Canmore Nordic Centre and exhausted everyone, the Provincial Parks took over and began clearing more roads and making the odd connection to provide tourers with less extreme hills and second, to make a nice little network for Sunday tourers between the two parking lots at Sawmill and Chester Lake. Although out of favour for races (too high in altitude), the trails are still used by racers, by World Cup racers no less who are not adverse to a whirl or two for acclimatization purposes.

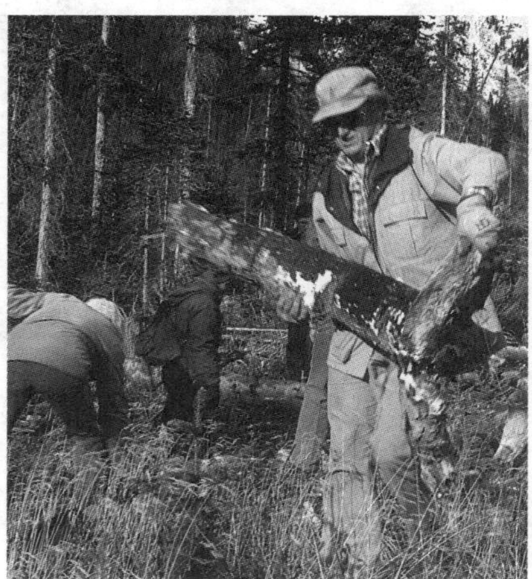

The Volunteers Co-ordinator clearing Green trail.

WARSPITE LAKE

Backcountry & Route

Intermediate
4.3 km circuit
Height gain 130 m, telemarking slopes about 510 m
Maximum elevation 1823 m, telemarking slopes about 2200 m
Map 82 J/11 Kananaskis Lakes

Access Smith-Dorrien/Spray Trail at Black Prince day-use area.

Facilities Washrooms, picnic tables at parking lot. Bench along trail.

Overview A short, sweet half-day trip which follows the well-signed summer interpretive trail. Most often used to get to the celebrated Black Prince telemarking slopes.

From the garbage disposal unit head down to the Smith-Dorrien River. (Should the river not be completely frozen, there's a bridge about 100 m upstream.) Now on the west bank, you follow a logging road up a moderately steep hill into a cutblock and there turn right onto the interpretive trail. Just past a bench (scenic view of Mt. Kent) the trail dips into the dark forest of Warspite Creek and arrives at a junction low down. Go either way. Both forks converge on Warspite Lake, a white meadow contained within a jumble of boulders.

See the gap between the spruce on the west side of the lake? It's worth pushing the extra 100 m into the meadow beyond for the awe-inspiring view of Mt. Black Prince, its east face a frozen confection of cliffs and icefalls.

Black Prince telemarking slopes!

Photo: Alf Skrastins

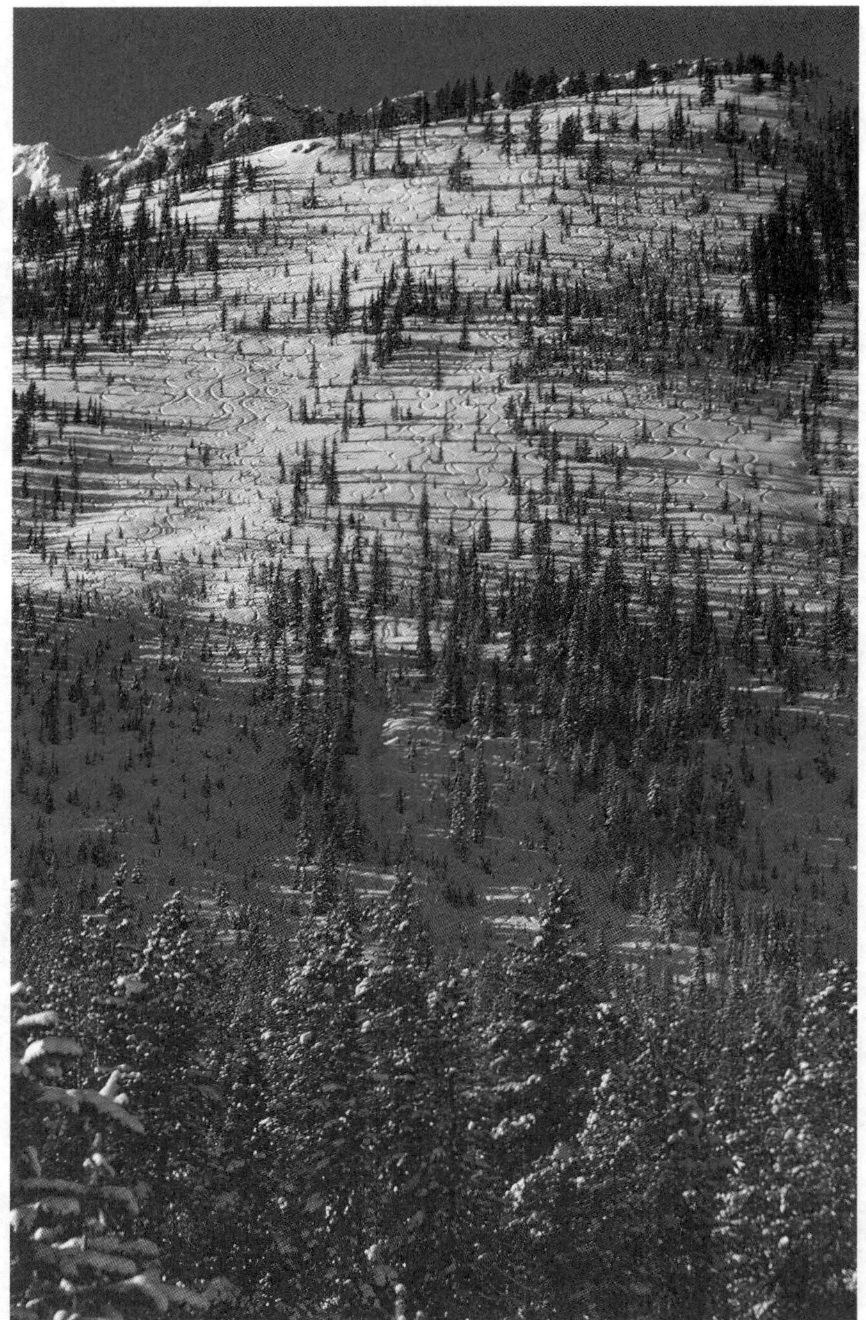

Black Prince telemarking slopes on a busy day. Photo: Alf Skrastins

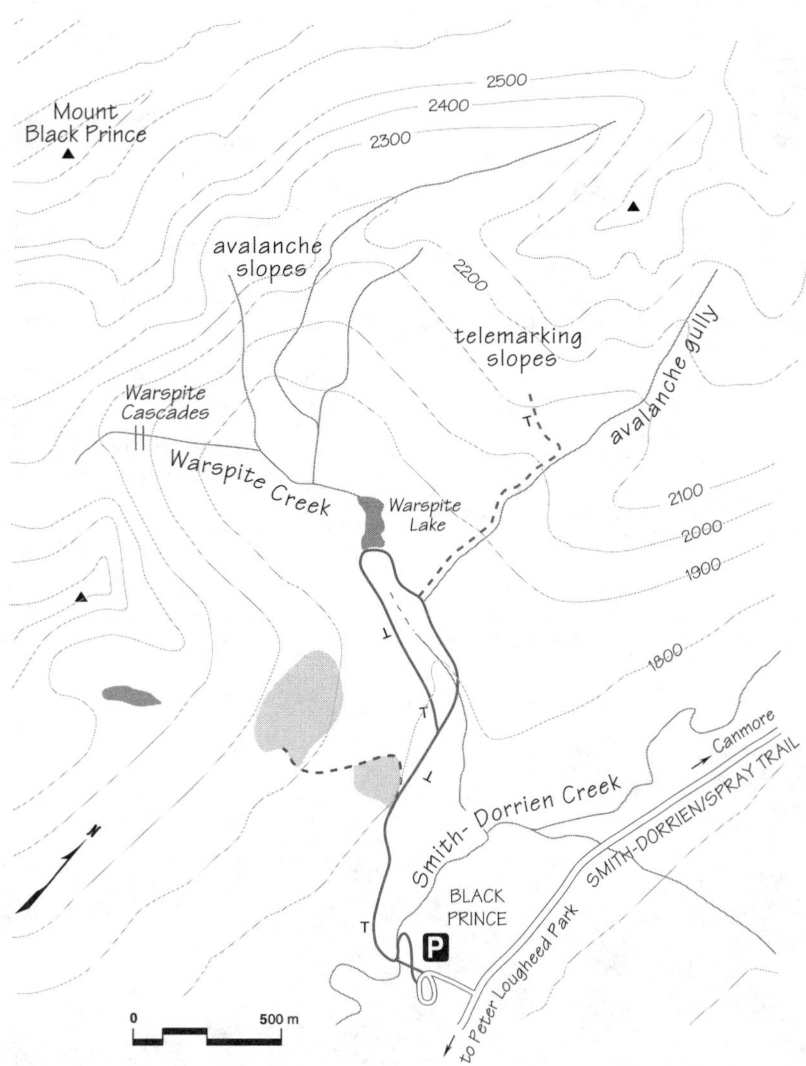

Option: Black Prince Telemarking Slopes

The lightly treed ridge north of the lake is one of K-Country's premier telemarking slopes. Getting there is actually quite easy and in fact most of the skiers using the trail are headed that way. At the forks go right and cross Warspite Creek. About half-way to the lake turn right up the obvious draw (tributary) which is followed only to where you can start heading left up the ridge in a thinning forest. (Out of the trees the tributary is a dangerous V-shaped avalanche collector.)

GYPSUM MINE

Backcountry

Easy intermediate
15 km return
Height gain 470 m
Maximum elevation 2130 m
Map 82 J/11 Kananaskis Lakes

Access Smith-Dorrien/Spray Trail at Peninsula parking lot. Only the first parking area is plowed.

Facilities Washrooms at the parking lot, picnic tables.

Overview The objective — a gypsum quarry site — is reached by a reclaimed road winding up the north ridge of Mt. Invincible. There is, however, more to this trail than just a simple plod up a road. Namely six avalanche chutes. Of all the routes in this book, this is potentially the most deadly so you've got to be pretty darn sure that conditions are safe before leaving the parking lot. On the plus side, this is one of the best trails for panoramic views.

Ski along the access road to the second parking lot where you transfer onto the old highway. When it turns right, you go left down the old Gypsum Mine road, crossing Smith-Dorrien Creek close to Lower Kananaskis Lake (bridge out) and continuing in a southerly direction to the right-angled bend leading into the hara-kiri traverse. The "road" to left was the first attempt to reach the gypsum deposit and is hopelessly overgrown.

So you turn right and traverse the gable end of the north ridge which requires crossing six avalanche chutes separated one from another by thin ribbons of trees. In the best tradition of avalanche safety, spread out the party and don't stop to look at Kent Ridge.

Taken from the highway, this photo shows the trail and the potentially dangerous traverse across avalanche chutes.

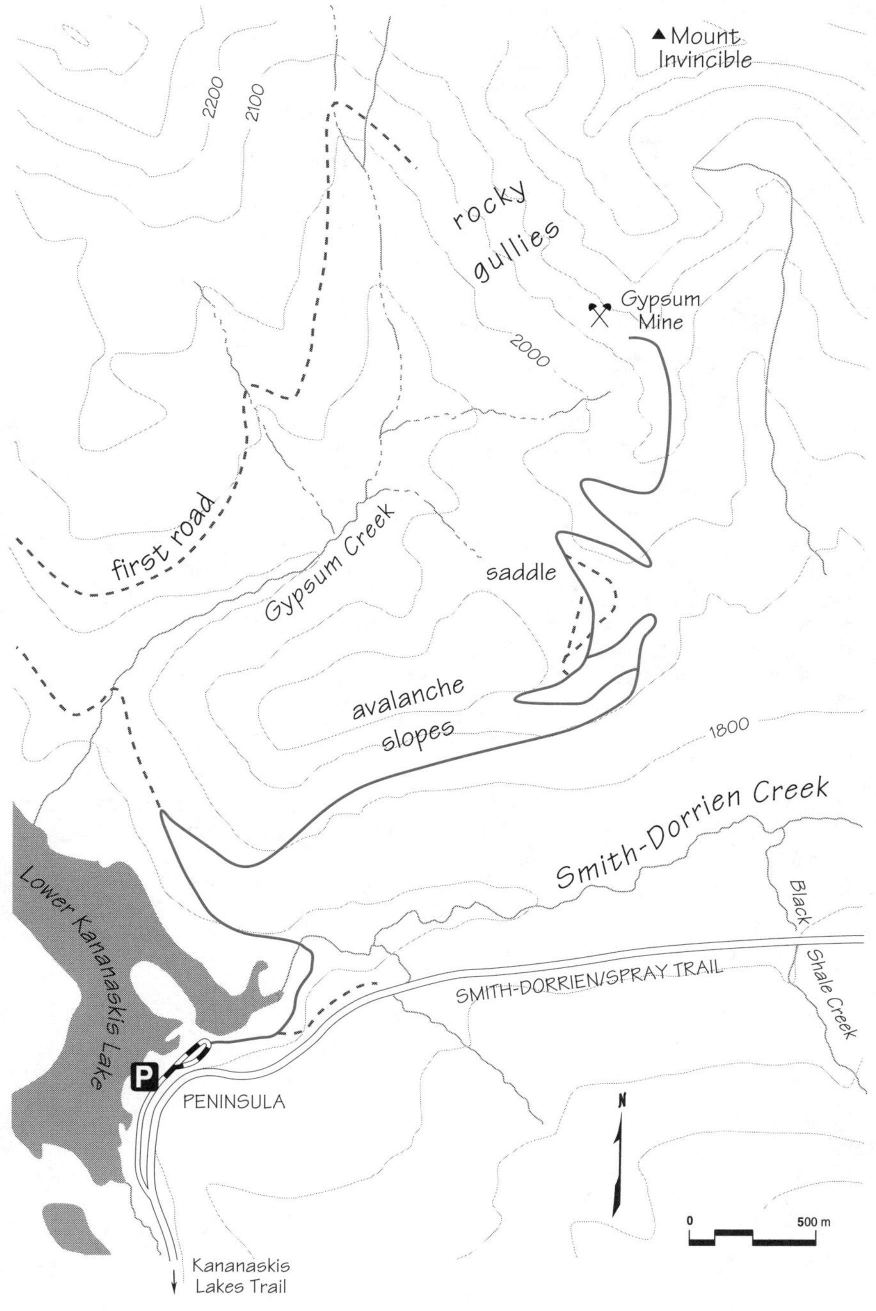
Mount Invincible
2200
2100
rocky gullies
Gypsum Mine
2000
first road
Gypsum Creek
saddle
avalanche slopes
1800
Smith-Dorrien Creek
Black Shale Creek
Lower Kananaskis Lake
SMITH-DORRIEN/SPRAY TRAIL
P
PENINSULA
N
0
500 m
Kananaskis Lakes Trail

Safety tactics done with, you arrive at a left-hand bend signalling the start of the middle section with its choice of zigs (see map). Here the country is remarkably open and as you climb out of the saddle some wonderful views open up of the Opal Range and the Smith-Dorrien Valley.

Finally, the road straightens and runs along the right side of the ridge towards the cliffs of Invincible. A more satisfying end to the trip can hardly be imagined when the road dekes through an unsuspected gap below the cliffs and enters the quarry overlooking the headwaters of Gypsum Creek. Obviously, winter is the worst time for poking around such places and there's probably avalanche danger from above, but you can't complain about the view: an Opal panorama, and further to the right Mt. Rae and the Elk Range.

Return A nice easy run if you stick to the road. But why not take short-cuts between zigs? Lower down, some people really go out on a limb by climbing onto the gable end from the saddle and making a 100 snappy turns down potential avalanche slopes just west of the chutes.

More about the trail Gypsum (hydrous calcium sulphate). Used in the manufacture of cement, plaster, asbestos, rubber, insecticides, drugs, paint, glass, ceramics, crayons and chalks; used in the filtering and refining of oils and in the purification of water. This incredibly versatile mineral was first reported as available on the slopes of Invincible in the 1964 Report (65-1) of the Geological Survey of Canada and resulted in instant interest by CP Oil & Gas. In 1966 a 21 year lease was transferred several times removed to the Alberta Gypsum Company who wasted no time in building an access road up Gypsum Creek, an undertaking doomed to failure on the lip of a rocky gully, separated from the deposits by several more rocky gullies. So they then built your ski trail up the easy north ridge which, when you think about it, was an incredibly costly undertaking for only a few years of operation, because in August of 1970 the lease was cancelled. The company had failed to make a cash deposit to cover land restoration costs. I laughed out loud when I read this because, although the government eventually sowed grass seed on number two road, number one road was left to its own devices and is doing very nicely thank you. So good in fact it harbours the thickest jungle this side of the west coast.

KANANASKIS LAKES SKI TRAILS

Groomed

97.2 km of trails
Maximum elevation 2125 m
Map 82 J/11 Kananaskis Lakes

Access Kananaskis Lakes Trail, accessible from both the Smith-Dorrien/Spray Trail and Kananaskis Trail (Hwy. 40).

Facilities and Services Ten parking lots: Pocaterra, Canyon, Visitor Information Centre, Elkwood, William Watson Lodge, Boulton Creek, Boulton Bridge, Lower Lake, Elk Pass, Upper Lake. Four have something other to offer than washrooms at air temperature.

Pocaterra Hut usually opens the first week in December through to the end of the ski season. Hours are 9 am to 5 pm, 7 days a week. It's a spartan staging area with indoor picnic tables, indoor washrooms, and current information on trails, weather and avalanche conditions. A public telephone is located behind the building near the parking lot.

Next up the road is the infinitely more luxurious Visitor Information Centre which is open 9 am to 5 pm, 7 days a week all year round (excepting April). Its pleasures include an information desk, interpretive films and displays, public telephones, indoor washrooms and a deluxe lounge with fireplace, soft carpet, soft couches, and entertainment through the picture windows of beginner skiers and Jackrabbit groups.

William Watson Lodge has RV sites and incredibly low-cost accommodation for handicapped persons and senior citizens in eight cottages sleeping a total of 80 persons (tubs or showers, kitchens). The main lodge has a fireplace, library, laundry, kitchen and dining area. Equipment available for guests includes 2 pulks and 2 cross-country racing sledges. For reservations (accepted up to four months in advance), phone 591-7227/7229 Monday-Friday, 8.30 am to 4 pm, or write William Watson Lodge, Peter Lougheed Provincial Park, Box 130, Kananaskis Village, Alberta T0L 2H0.

Moving on to Boulton Creek, Boulton Creek Campground loop B is plowed for campers who should know that the grocery store at Boulton Creek Trading Post is closed in winter.

Day visitors to Boulton Creek parking lot have a choice of either eating packed lunches huddled in the car with the heater turned full on, or of patronising the Trading Post cafe where a first rate cook (formerly of Canmore Nordic Centre) dishes up full breakfasts and such popular lunch items as soups, sandwiches, burgers and muffins at very reasonable prices. Trail guides and related literature is sold from the front counter. The cafe opens December 25th through to January 1st, then weekends only 10 am to 4 pm until about the end of March.

Other facilities include Lower Lake group camp, accessible by vehicle or by ski. For reservations contact the park office at 591-7222 or write Peter Lougheed Provincial Park Office, Box 130, Kananaskis Village, Alberta T0L 2H0.

Interpretive ski tours are offered to groups. Contact the Visitor Services Supervisor 591-7222.

Three training grids are presently available for instructors: William Watson Lodge, Baseball Diamond Meadow near Boulton Creek Trading Post and the meadow near Pocaterra Hut.

Regulations No dogs allowed.

Annual Events Kananaskis 45 Loppet "The Great Cookie Race" takes place the second or third weekend of February.

Overview If you're into groomed trails with a backcountry feel to them, then this is your ultimate playground in the Canadian Rockies. Unless you go on a weekday, though, or when the temperature drops below -20°, this is not the place to be alone — just you and the trail. Skiing here is a social occasion, with stops at every junction, picnic table and parking lot to chat. "Well, well, fancy bumping into you here!" (you're not really surprised), is followed by intense discussions on the relative merits of doing such and such a trail this way round or that way round. Sometimes I get the impression I'm in some kind of silently acknowledged race to see who can get to Elk Pass first, or the Lookout first, or down Fox Creek to the parking lot first.

Because the area lies on the Great Divide, the snow flies thick and fast from late November to the end of March. Having said that, higher elevation trails at the south end of the park are often ready by the beginning of November and are still going strong at the end of April. In 1990 fanatics were still flogging up to Elk Pass in June! Conditions can vary from high to low points, and from north to south, particularly in late winter-early spring time. So unless you can hack a few hours of skating carry a variety of wax to cover both klister conditions and powder.

Within the parameter of rolling hills covered in forest, the terrain is remarkably varied with trails following creeks, benches, occasionally powerline right-of-ways, climbing ridges to viewpoints, crossing meadows and lakes and winding through close-knit spruce forest where your sole illumination is the snow on the ground. But wherever you go, one of the thrills of skiing Kananaskis is the sight of high mountains rising up on every side.

Another of the attractions, for me at any rate, is the fact that trails are not all regulation 4-m width which gets very boring. What you have here is an eclectic assortment of grizzly trails, pack trails, bike paths, specially constructed ski trails, old roads, powerline access roads, even Highway 40 has been conscripted. Trails are packed, trackset, two-way and well-sign posted at junctions. 4 m-wide trails are prepared with both classical and free technique skiers in mind. Grooming usually takes place on Thursdays, so if it dumps a metre of snow on Friday night make sure you get a late start and head for Lookout trail.

Up-to-date brochures are available at all parking lots and information centres.

Canadian Ski Patrollers (yellow and blue jackets) patrol the most popular trails on weekends between the hours of 10 am and 4.30 pm.

Finally, unless familiar with country *au natural*, stick to the signed trails. They're more fun anyway. This is not just cautionary claptrap: a few years back two skiers got lost taking a short-cut and spent a harrowing night out in the depths of a gully, writing help messages with spruce boughs. It was over a day before they were found by a search party. And *they* were less than half a kilometre from a heavily-travelled trail!

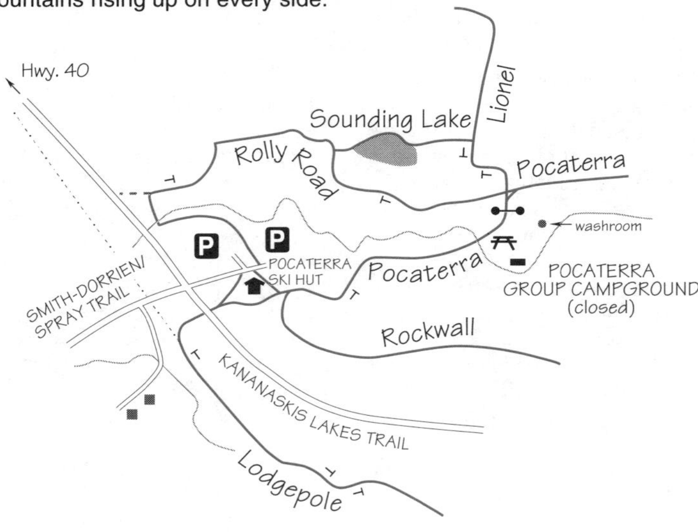

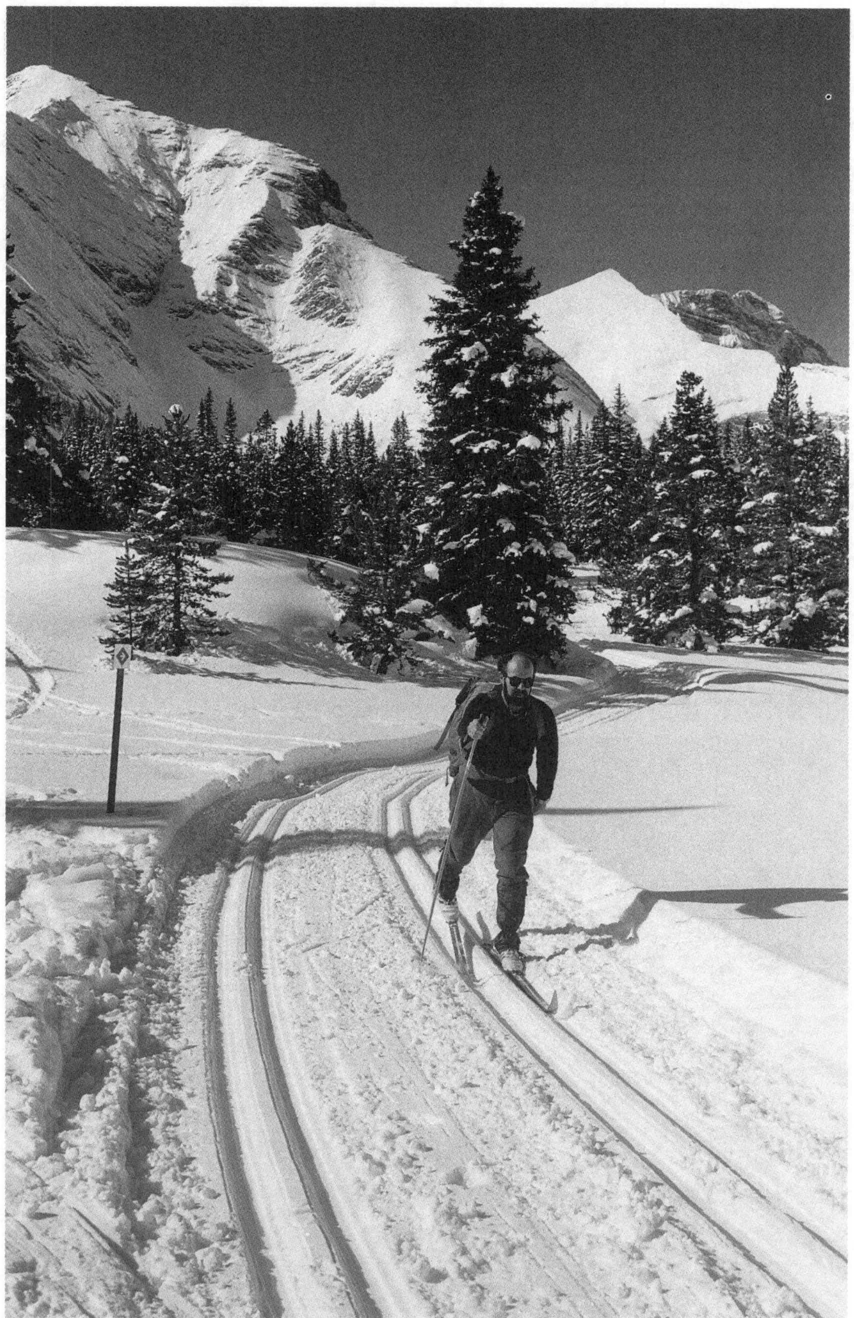

Elk Pass trail in upper Fox Creek. Superb weather, superb snow, superb tracks.

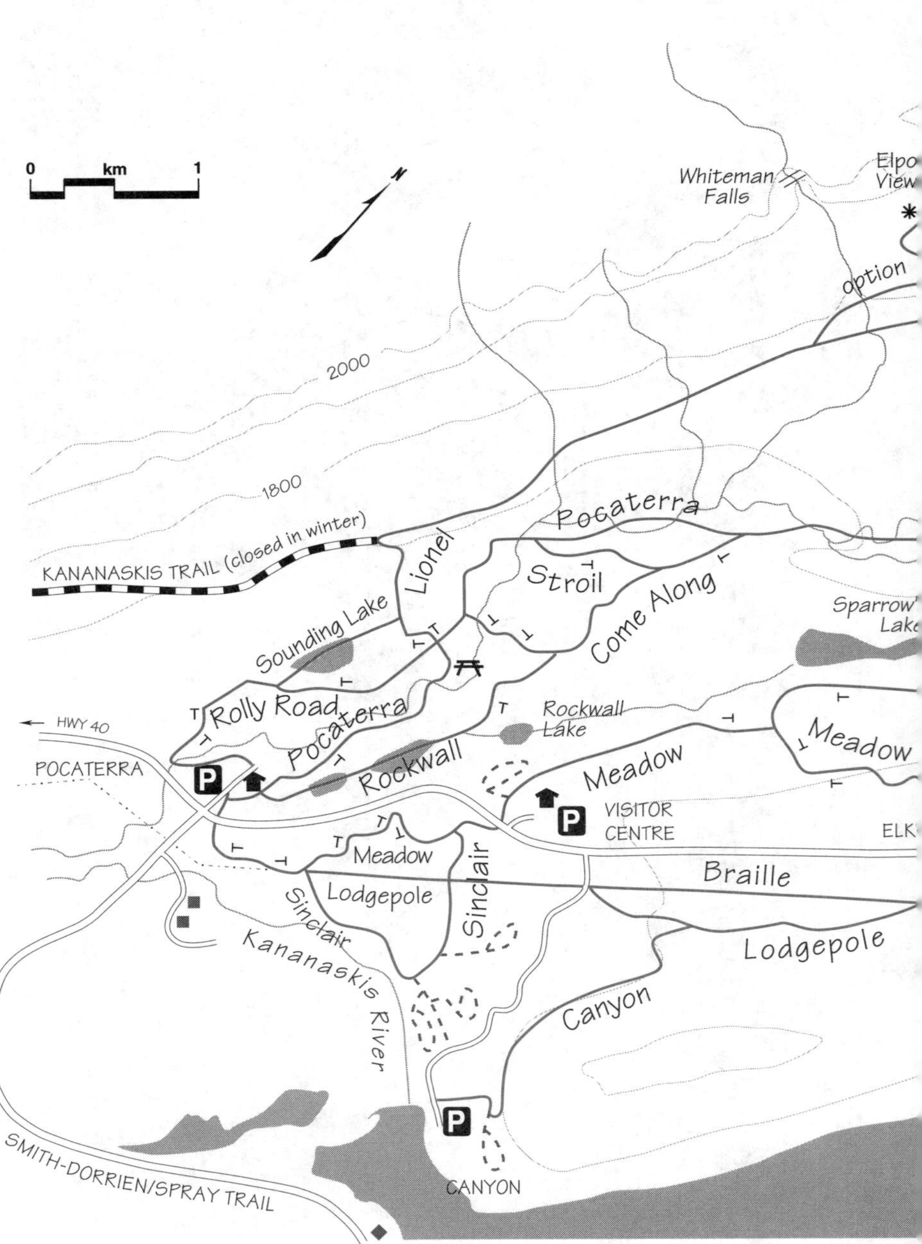
0
km
1
N
Whiteman Falls
Elpo View
option
2000
1800
Pocaterra
KANANASKIS TRAIL (closed in winter)
Lionel
Stroil
Come Along
Sparrow' Lake
Sounding Lake
Rolly Road
Pocaterra
Rockwall Lake
Meadow
HWY 40
POCATERRA
Rockwall
Meadow
VISITOR CENTRE
ELK
Meadow
Sinclair
Braille
Lodgepole
Sinclair
Kananaskis River
Lodgepole
Canyon
SMITH-DORRIEN/SPRAY TRAIL
CANYON

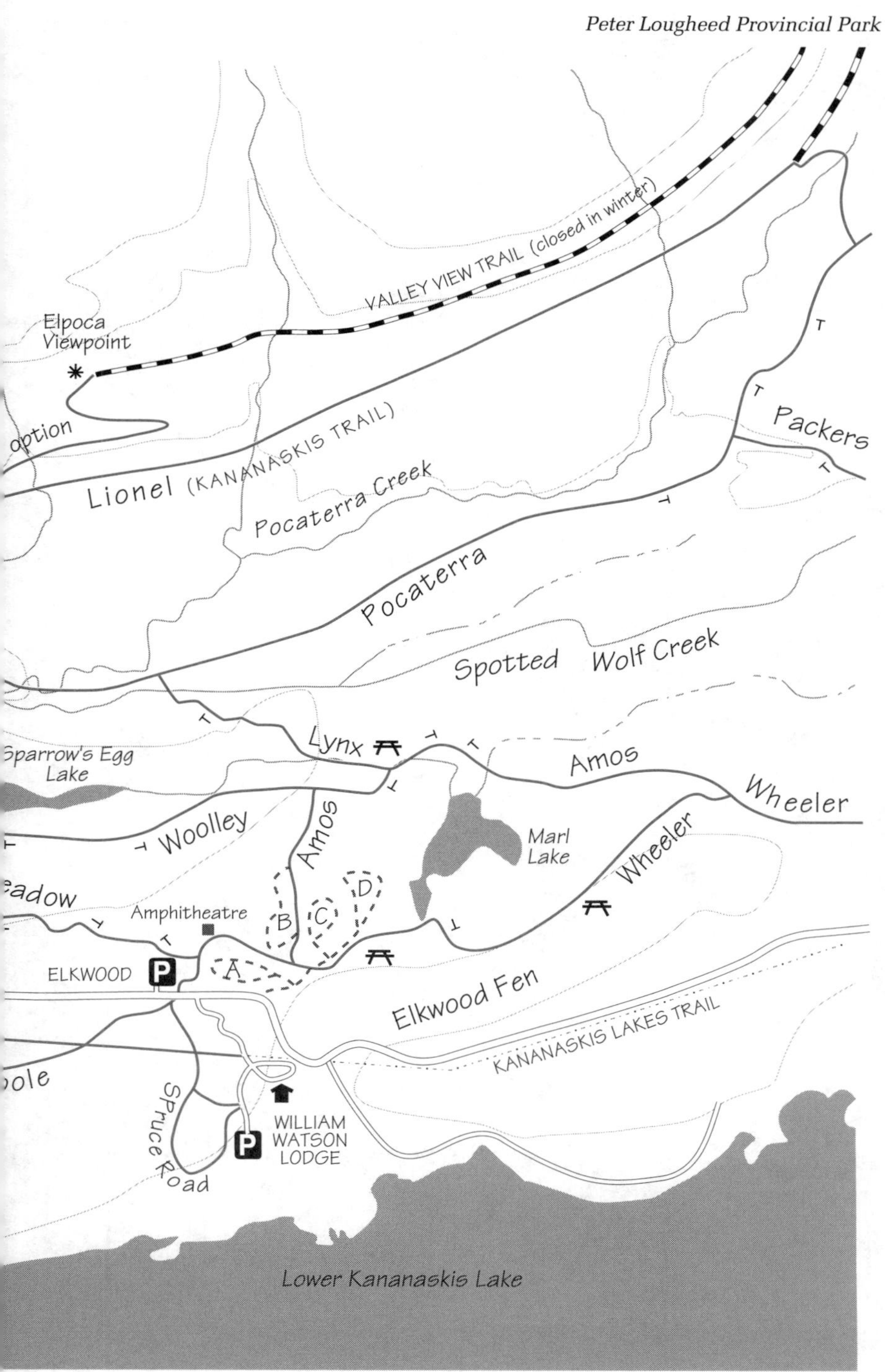
VALLEY VIEW TRAIL (closed in winter)
Elpoca Viewpoint
option
Lionel (KANANASKIS TRAIL)
Pocaterra Creek
Packers
Pocaterra
Spotted Wolf Creek
Lynx
Amos
Wheeler
Sparrow's Egg Lake
Woolley
Amos
Marl Lake
Wheeler
eadow
Amphitheatre
A
B
C
D
ELKWOOD
Elkwood Fen
KANANASKIS LAKES TRAIL
oole
Spruce Road
WILLIAM WATSON LODGE
Lower Kananaskis Lake

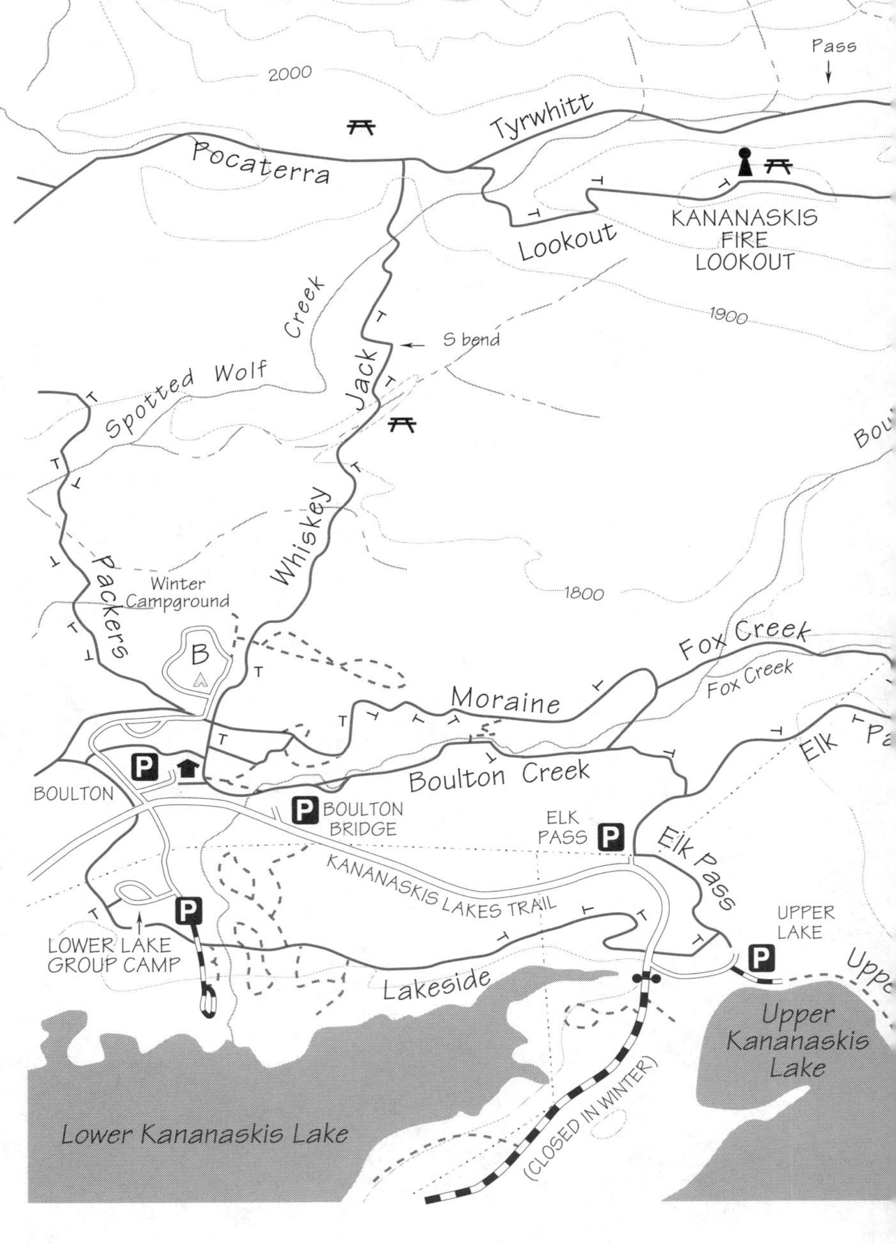
2300
2000
Pass
Tyrwhitt
Pocaterra
KANANASKIS
FIRE
LOOKOUT
Lookout
1900
Creek
S bend
Spotted Wolf
Jack
Whiskey
Packers
Winter
Campground
B
1800
Fox Creek
Fox Creek
Moraine
Elk
Boulton Creek
BOULTON
BOULTON
BRIDGE
ELK
PASS
Elk Pass
KANANASKIS LAKES TRAIL
UPPER
LAKE
LOWER LAKE
GROUP CAMP
Lakeside
Upper
Kananaskis
Lake
Lower Kananaskis Lake
(CLOSED IN WINTER)

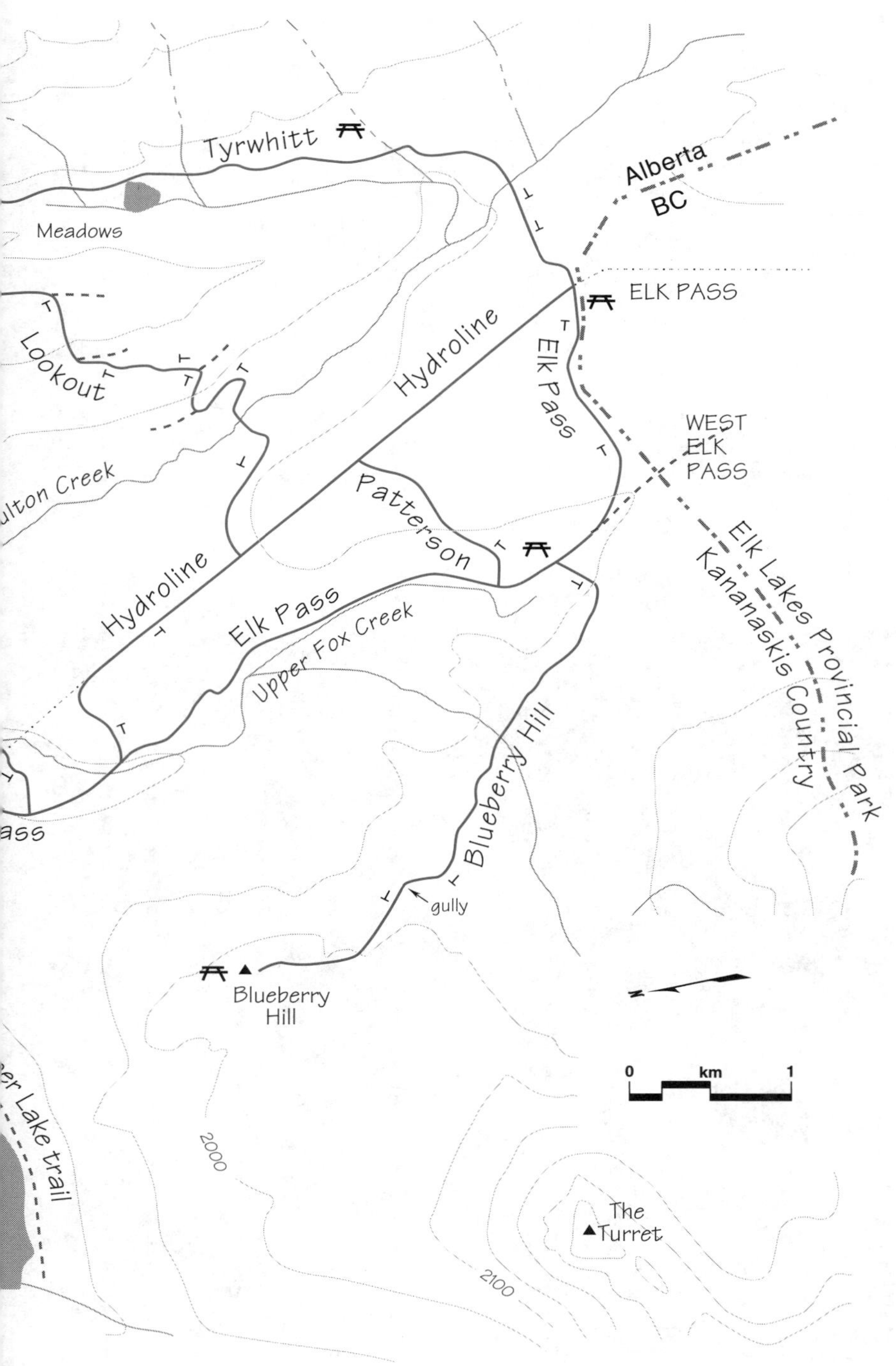
Tyrwhitt
Alberta
BC
Meadows
ELK PASS
Lookout
Hydroline
Elk Pass
WEST ELK PASS
ulton Creek
Patterson
Elk Lakes Provincial Park
Kananaskis Country
Hydroline
Elk Pass
Upper Fox Creek
Blueberry Hill
ass
gully
Blueberry Hill
0 km 1
er Lake trail
2000
The Turret
2100

POCATERRA

Easy intermediate
10.3 km
Height gain north to south 293 m

This long thoroughfare stretches from Pocaterra Ski Hut to Whisky Jack and connects with ten other trails, six of which branch off in the first 3.4 km.

The relatively flat lower third follows winding Pocaterra Creek through willowy muskeg, crossing and re-crossing the stream on wide bridges and is generally patrolled by ski patrollers and on occasion by a Great Horned owl defending its territory. Kananaskis group campground located near the junction with Rolly Road offers picnic tables and a washroom for people who haven't got very far.

The middle section beyond Lynx junction is a steady climb up a treed ridge, with Pocaterra Creek in an astoundingly deep rift on your left. Most people don't bother, but if you can spare time out from trying to pass the 20-kid school group, go and have a peek over the edge.

The top stretch after the junction with Lionel (in reality the Kananaskis Fire Lookout access road) zips along the base of Tyrwhitt Ridge and qualifies as the coldest, windiest section of any trail in the park. Unfortunately, the picnic table at Whisky Jack junction is usually full of skiers recovering from the climb up Whiskey Jack.

In reverse, this is just a super run with a couple of easy intermediate downhills sandwiched between Lionel and Packers followed by a long runout which requires using every means at your disposal to keep the momentum going to Lynx junction. I don't know about you but I always forget about the dip near the finish at Pocaterra Hut.

Waxing up in front of Pocaterra Hut

ROLLY ROAD
Intermediate
1.5 km

Starting from behind Pocaterra parking lot, this trail crosses Pocaterra Creek close to Kananaskis Lakes Trail, then turns sharp right onto the old Pocaterra Creek tote road, alias Rolly Road, alias the Kananaskis group campground summer access road for vehicles. Basically, the trail climbs to Sounding Lake junction, then descends to Pocaterra trail at the campground. Taken in reverse, the sharp left-hand bend near Kananaskis Lakes Trail and the steep hill preceding it are definitely something to be aware of (the runout's not very good). I've seen beginners unashamedly hoofing it back down this hill to the parking lot.

SOUNDING LAKE
Easy
0.7 km

A narrow trail which is very scenic, especially at Sounding Lake where mountains rim every horizon. In the 1992/3 season the trail is due for rerouting *around* the lake (probably the east side) after a piston bully broke through the ice, forcing K-Country's star tracksetter, Clarke Smith, to wade waist deep through water to affix a tow chain.

ROCKWALL
Intermediate
1 km

Most of the trail follows a long flat meadow (marsh, beaver ponds) below the Rockwall. A brief hill between the meadows and Come Along trail on the ridge top gives it the intermediate rating. Early and late in the season be wary of a long runout across the "meadow" else you may find yourself coming to a standstill in water up to the ankles. It has happened.

COME ALONG
Intermediate
1.5 km

A thoroughly enjoyable trail winding along a timbered ridge top. Best skied south to north for the superb two-tiered descent to Pocaterra.

STROIL
Intermediate
0.6 km

Stroil links Come Along on the ridge top to Pocaterra in the valley bottom. Honestly, the "difficult" hill at the north end is merely an intermediate hill that would be trackset at the Canmore Nordic Centre. It's incredibly wide and has a good runout. The S-bend on Whiskey Jack is far worse.

Don Gardner named Stroil after an ethereal being, ultimately evil, who makes a habit of carrying kettles around with him. Don't ask me why. Ask Don next time you see him.

LIONEL
Easy, with one easy intermediate hill above Pocaterra
7.2 km

This trail opens at 1 am on December 1st every year and without doubt is the easiest and most boring of all the trails in the park because of a 5.5 km stint along the closed portion of Highway 40. Best skied in reverse direction in fast icy conditions. The scenery is great though, especially if you take the optional detour up also-closed Valleyview Trail to the viewpoint. Rank beginners should park at the winter gate across Highway 40 if you want to avoid the trail's north end which is narrow and sports an intermediate hill between Pocaterra and Sounding Lake trails. The south end utilizes the fire road to Kananaskis Fire Lookout and is easy.

SINCLAIR

Easy intermediate
2 km

Sinclair undulates nicely along the bank of the Kananaskis River canyon, though since it was widened it is not the interesting intermediate trail it once was. At the half-way point you're very close to Canyon parking lot in case you want a transfer to Canyon trail. Then it's away again into the trees to rejoin Lodgepole and climb up to Meadow. Not groomed in the 1991/2 season.

CANYON

Easy
1.4 km

A very pleasant wide trail, usually deserted, which joins Canyon parking lot to Lodgepole. It too was not groomed in the 1991/2 season. Half a kilometre from the parking lot, a clay pit site allows a spectacular view of the Opal Range. Just once, aim to be there in late afternoon when the mountains catch fire from the westering sun.

LODGEPOLE

Intermediate
4.7 km

Running south of the road, Lodgepole connects Pocaterra Ski Hut to Elkwood parking lot with a connection to William Watson Lodge. It crosses Kananaskis Lakes Trail twice, Canyon parking lot access road once and does a stint along a powerline right-of-way, so it's not exactly an attractive trail to ski in its entirety. Having said that, it has a lovely undulating stretch between Canyon access road and William Watson Lodge where it retreats into the forest. Were it all like that! You should also know that the trail is easy except for one exciting intermediate hill at the north end under the powerline. If you want to keep on the easy stuff plan a loop from Elkwood or Canyon.

WILLIAM WATSON LODGE ACCESS TRAIL

Easy
0.6 km

A flat trail connecting William Watson Lodge with Spruce Road, Braille, Lodgepole and finally the Elkwood parking lot.

SPRUCE ROAD
Easy
0.8 km

The short flat loop accessed from the parking lot and cabin access road at William Watson Lodge is superbly suited to handicapped skiers and raw beginners. Pick up a headset from the lodge and listen to tapes recounting the history of the Kananaskis.

BRAILLE
Easy
2 km

Braille connects Canyon parking lot access road at Lodgepole to William Watson Lodge access trail via the powerline right-of-way. Slightly up, then slightly down, it is of little interest to sighted skiers who don't have to dodge power poles.

AMOS
Easy
2.4 km

An enjoyable trail named for Paul Amos (Stoney Indian and blood brother to George Pocaterra) whose Stoney name was Spotted Wolf. Often combined with Wheeler, its narrower width and undulating nature require a little more expertise from beginners. North of the junction with Lynx in the meadow, the trail has now taken over what was once part of Woolley before moving away across a fen to join loop B access road of Elkwood Campground.

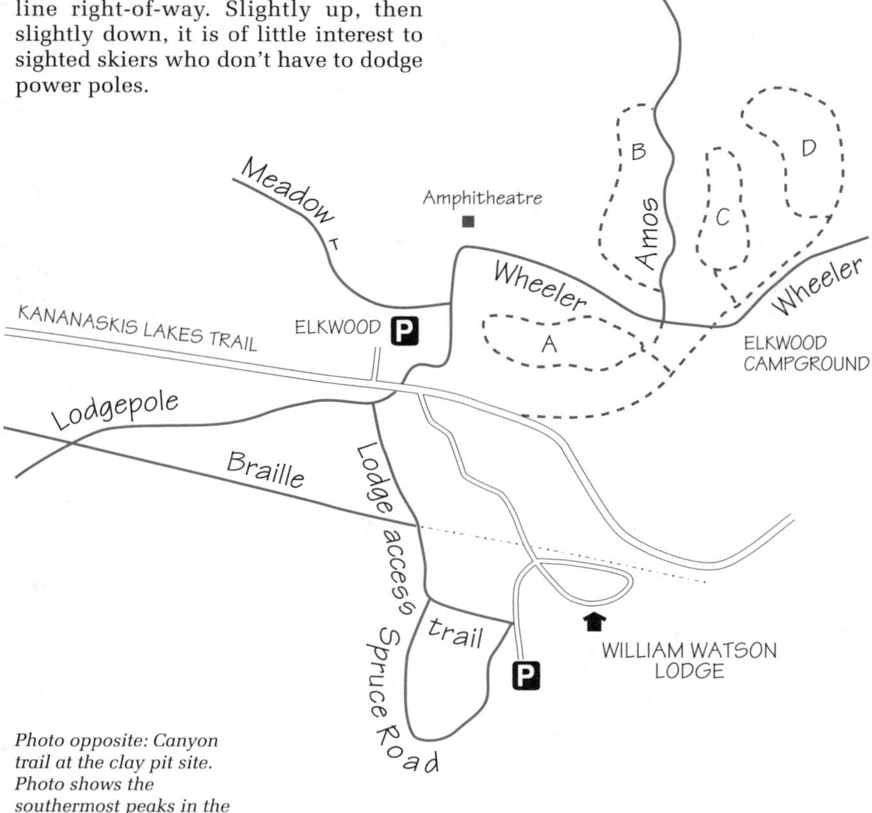

Photo opposite: Canyon trail at the clay pit site. Photo shows the southermost peaks in the Opal Range, Mt. Elpoca and Gap Mountain.

MEADOW

Intermediate, with easy middle section
5.3 km

Connecting Elkwood parking lot with the north end of Lodgepole via the Visitor Information Centre is a useful trail which divides naturally into three very different sections.

Between Elkwood parking lot and Woolley junction is a twisting forest trail recently widened to take the fun out of cornering and dodging oncoming skiers at the same time. I have to admit it's a lot safer, though.

In the middle is the meadow. Because of its close proximity to the Visitor Information Centre, this meadow is noisy with family groups and beginners, kitted out in the latest clashing psychedelic colours, swarming all over its barely perceptible incline which for absolute novices is about as challenging as Mount Everest. At its busiest, the snow looks like the Bonnybrook train yards and if you're not concentrating it's easy to get switched onto the wrong line and find yourself joining a Jackrabbit class.

After crossing Kananaskis Lakes Trail you're liable to be alone on a superb 4 m-wide trail which roller-coasters its way down some huge hills to Lodgepole.

WOOLLEY

Intermediate
2.2 km

This narrow trail connects Meadow to Amos without going through Elkwood parking lot. Exciting hills at the north end contrast with a flat section winding about the edge of ponds and meadows near Sparrow's Egg Lake. With unrestricted views across to the Opal Range you should be able to spot frozen Whiteman Falls.

The "e" in Woolley is not an error on someone's part. Though the trail could be construed as being wild and woolly, my guess is that it's named after surveyor William Woolley-Dod who was in the area in 1932 with a survey crew. Right Don?

WHEELER

Easy with one easy intermediate hill
4.7 km

The summer bike path connects Elkwood parking lot to Whiskey Jack, giving access to Lakeside, Amos, Packers, Boulton winter campground, Boulton Creek parking lot and the Boulton Creek Trading Post.

I can't imagine why the official park brochure rates this trail as intermediate. It's wide, has a mildly undulating south end and a flat middle section running along a bank top where you can divert to tastefully placed picnic tables looking across Sidathka ze pteraogo ze "long dried-up marshland flats" to Mt. Indefatigable. It's true there's a hill at the north end but an intermediate hill? I'm totally mystified since it's certainly ten times easier than any hill on Pocaterra. Beginners may choose to snowplow if they wish.

The only possible problem with the trail is the Elkwood campground road system. After a heavy snowfall it only needs the first skier to get off track, either deliberately or by accident and the pack following along behind will be doing a tour of campground loops A, B, C and D.

A tip: near Elkwood parking lot the trail passes the amphitheatre which offers seats and a roof for skiers with packed lunches. I've often used it on days when the snow is hissing down.

LYNX

Intermediate
1.7 km

A roller coaster of a trail which climbs over a succession of timbered ridges between Amos and Pocaterra. Nothing desperate. The small creek running downhill from the junction with Amos widens into a succession of beaver ponds and a lake called Sparrow's Egg below the Rockwall.

Opposite: Packers, the top end.

PACKERS

Intermediate
3.1 km
Height gain west to east 103 m

Nowadays, the old pack trail connecting Lower Kananaskis Lake ranger station (site under water) to the Pocaterra Tote Road in the direction of Highwood Pass is used as a link between Boulton Creek parking lot and Pocaterra trail over 100 m higher up the slope.

What with hills meriting caution signs and bends superelevated the wrong way, it gained quite a reputation for awkwardness in either direction. I mean, the steepest downhills occurred in the uphill direction for heaven's sake. Well, if you haven't skied this trail recently, you're in for a treat. It still surprises with steep uphills and downhills in both directions and the flat meadows near the Pocaterra end are still totally uncharacteristic of the rest of it, but now the trail has been widened and the awkward bends ironed out. It's actually enjoyable!. Upgrades to difficult when icy.

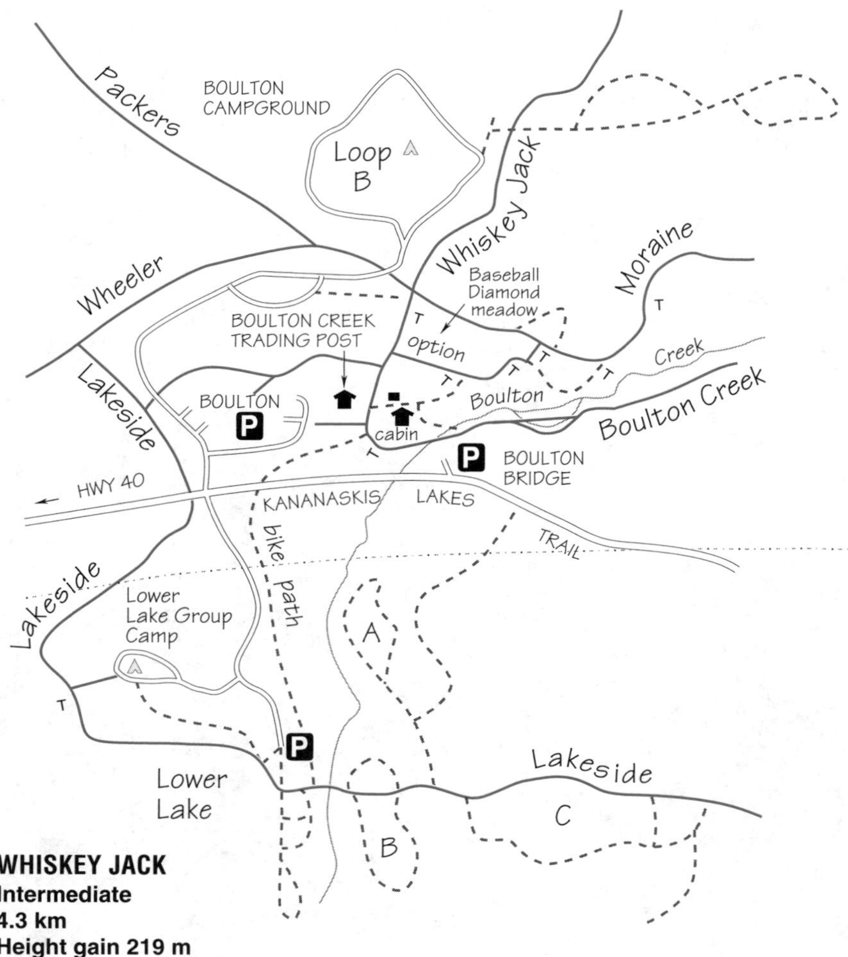

WHISKEY JACK

Intermediate
4.3 km
Height gain 219 m

Whiskey Jack is the quickest route to Kananaskis Fire lookout. Or it can be successfully combined with Packers and Pocaterra but more usually with Tyrwhitt, Elk Pass, Fox Creek and Moraine to make the most popular (18 km) loop in the network.

Basically, it crosses all the headwaters of Spotted Wolf Creek, so you can expect short flat sections interspersed with long uphills, typical of which is the first hill at the junction with Wheeler/Moraine. Since becoming an access to both these other trails, this first hill has become a bottleneck of skiers queuing at the bottom for herringbone privileges and skiers queuing at the top waiting for take off. By far the steepest hill on Whiskey Jack, though, is the celebrated S-bend, scraped and shaped by desperate snowplowers out of control. When the going gets icy, this one upgrades to difficult.

In reverse, Whiskey Jack's a fast fun descent from Pocaterra/Tyrwhitt junction to the cafe door and on down to Boulton Bridge parking lot past the old ranger station on the bank top. Incidentally, 90% of skiers pick up the trail from Boulton Creek parking lot.

BOULTON CREEK
Easy
2.5 km

From Boulton Bridge parking lot the single-width trail follows the west bank of Boulton Creek (open water with dippers) and though generally believed to be flat, has the odd dip and bend — usually in combination — which keep you on your toes when conditions get at all icy. The steepest hill lies between Moraine and Elk Pass trail. I'm not mad about this trail, but beginners seem to flock there in droves.

MORAINE
Intermediate
2.4 km

A delightful trail of the narrower variety with hills at both ends. The middle section undulates past numbered posts (I refer you to the summer interpretive trail brochure) and offers up fine views of Mt. Indefatigable from the bench top.

I'm not keen on the latest ending, though, which merges with a campground access road at site #9 and delivers you to the top of the first hill on Whiskey Jack where you join the queue. I much prefer the original trail which cuts left at site #3 and, in keeping with the rest of the trail, twists its way down the hill into Baseball Diamond Meadow opposite the Trading Post. Some folks even appear to follow the interpretive trail all the way down to Boulton Cabin (three short steep hills).

FOX CREEK
Easy intermediate
1.6 km

A thoroughly engrossing forest trail when skied in the downhill Elk Pass/ Moraine direction. Because of its narrow width you are constantly adjusting to changes in direction lest you run smack into a lodgepole pine. That schuss across the single-track bridge over Boulton Creek still catches me unawares. One of my favourite trails when tracks are fast.

LAKESIDE
Intermediate
6.4 km

Lakeside connects Wheeler near Boulton Creek parking lot to Elk Pass trail near Upper Lake parking lot. A lot of people, including me, like this trail a lot despite the fact it's a bike path, crosses Kananaskis Lakes Trail twice and intersects a half dozen campground roads. It's reminiscent of Wheeler only the hills are steeper, though definitely *not* difficult as little red dots indicate on the trail brochure. The views are good too. From near Lower Lake parking lot (another starting point) you can see clear across Lower Kananaskis Lake to Mt. Indefatigable, Mt. Sarrail and Waka Nambé, while salt lick meadow further south allows a unique view of Blueberry Hill and The Turret. The steepest hill is the one between the salt lick and Elk Pass trail. In the season of 1991/2, only the section between Wheeler and the cutoff to Lower Lake group campground was trackset.

Lakeside. The Turret from the salt lick.

ELK PASS

Intermediate
7 km
Height gain 274 m
Maximum elevation 1975 m

There is no doubt that Elk Pass on the Great Divide is the most popular destination in the park. It isn't the environs of the pass or the views which attract, but rather the character of the trail itself coupled with consistently excellent snow conditions which draws skiers back to Elk Pass long after the snow has melted from low down the trail.

The trail really starts from Upper Lake parking lot, but most people join in at Elk Pass parking lot — 900 m of easy skiing from Upper Lake. Because the ongoing route follows the Elk Pass powerline access road all the way, you do some weird things in the next 1.5 km like plod, gasping, up a long steepening hill to join the powerline on the always windy ridge top, then, having gained height won most laboriously, loose it all in one headlong rush to Fox Creek.

A little further on, Hydroline junction seems to be a natural gathering spot for people trying to make up their minds which way to go. No question but the steady climb up upper Fox Creek is the best route to Elk Pass. The creek is incredibly scenic, especially the upper part where the trees thin out and you're into sunbathing meadows with picnic tables and waiting whiskeyjacks. Past the junctions for Blueberry Hill and West Elk Pass, the trail re-enters closed forest, and in three waves climbs between very tall spruce to Elk Pass at the powerline right-of-way. Just to the right, a padlocked gate on the access road marks the Great Divide proper. What, no picnic table?

The **return** is *memorable*, an almost unbroken schuss all the way down to Hydroline junction. Your skis rooted in the deep tracks of upper Fox Creek, you wave and shout rude names at all upcomers to move over onto the uphill track because you don't want the glorious run to stop. Ever. In actual truth, though, the uphill grind to the powerline is a welcome break from being a downhill fixture threatening to turn into an icicle. Long downhills have their drawbacks. Strangely, I find the final downhill the hardest of all, meaning I'm usually out of control and hell-bent on making the parking lot without stopping.

HYDROLINE

Hard intermediate
3.9 km
Height gain 178 m
Maximum elevation 1975 m

This is the kamikaze alternative from Elk Pass to Fox Creek. Also the route onto Lookout south. For most of its length it utilizes the powerline right -of-way and is pretty dull as trails go with a pet wind which makes things uncomfortable and fills in the tracks. The sudden drop into Fox Creek is the fun part.

PATTERSON

Intermediate
0.9 km
Height gain 58 m

Named after Raymond "The Buffalo Head" Patterson, this powerline access road provides a far less crowded descent to upper Fox Creek from Hydroline, or, alternatively, a far less crowded ascent to Elk Pass, although I must admit I've only ever skied it in the downhill direction because the hills are so enjoyable. The greatest danger occurs on the bottom runout where you are in imminent danger of being run over by Elk Pass skiers during late afternoon rush hour.

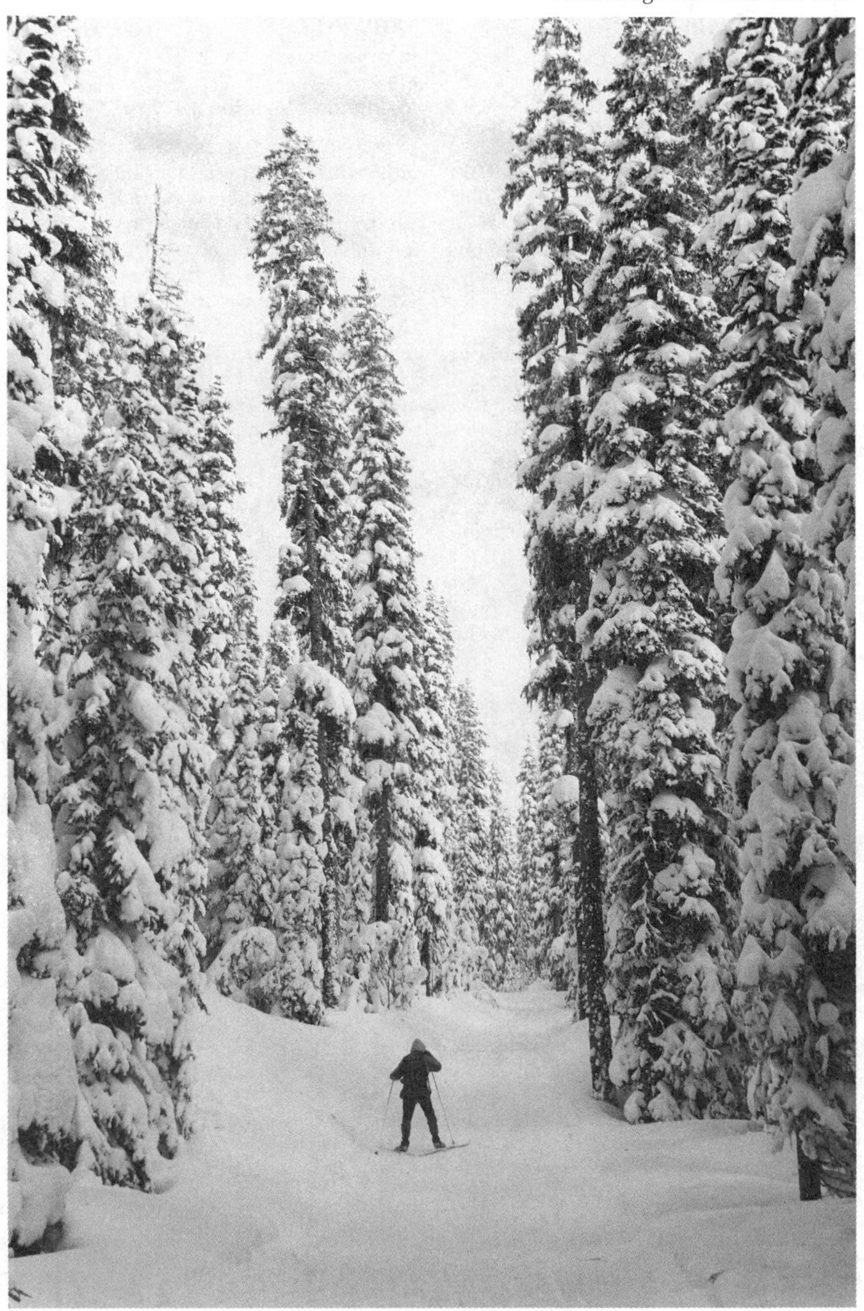

Tall spruce. The final climb to Elk Pass from Fox Creek.

BLUEBERRY HILL

Intermediate
3.2 km
Height gain 158 m
Maximum elevation 2057 m

This once challenging spur from Elk Pass trail takes you to a superlative viewpoint overlooking Kananaskis Lakes. A fine day is mandatory as is a pair of binoculars, wineskin and lawn chair. A picnic table is provided.

After that first hill up the bank, the trail winds innocuously enough through open forest and you'll be wondering why this easy trail has an intermediate rating? But imperceptibly the angle is steepening and it is only on the descent, when gathering speed at an alarming rate while dodging upcoming skiers does the answer become clear. Actually, the very worst part, a tight twisting gully, has been reworked and widened as has that steep little uphill beyond. Even the final approach to the high point has been "improved".

TYRWHITT

Intermediate
4.5 km
Maximum elevation 1975 m

Everybody's favourite. Just a great ski in either direction (I won't go into the relative merits of which way round is best). The trail connects Pocaterra to Elk Pass via a notch about ten metres higher than Elk Pass sandwiched between Kananaskis Lookout hill and Mt. Tyrwhitt's north ridge. Of course, the best part of the trail is the meadows, the highest continuous section of trail in the park with superb snow, superb views of the Elk River Mountains and if you're lucky lots of sunshine. It's also a favourite spot with grizzlies so don't come back in the summer. The steepest climb is the one from Boulton Creek to Elk Pass. This used to be very tricky to descend, but since being widened in 1982 has become just another intermediate hill. Assured of no-one coming up, even I can schuss the whole thing with something approaching nonchalance.

Blueberry Hill. A tremendous view across Upper Kananaskis Lake to Mt. Putnik.

Approaching Kananaskis Lookout from the south leg of Lookout.

LOOKOUT

Difficult
6.8 km
Height gain from Tyrwhitt 204 m
Height gain from Hydroline 274 m
Maximum elevation 2125 m

Lookout traverses Kananaskis fire lookout hill which is the highest point in the trail system. The usual route of ascent (and descent) is from Tyrwhitt, and is chiefly remembered for the steep, straight hill sandwiched between two reasonable sections where it is your job to keep to the side of the trail. A final climb brings you to the lookout, or rather to picnic tables in the meadows for general collapse. You can usually spot people who've come up the south side by signs of even greater collapse and the fact that they're wearing a T-shirt at -20°.

Before returning the same way, it would be remiss of you not to stagger over to the lookout platform for the view of Kananaskis Lakes. Then, an exercise or two to get the quads working fit and you're off, remembering two nasty corners preceding the straight where opportunity exists to bowl down the uphillers like ninepins.

Despite this hill, any sensible person would return the same way, for the trail between the summit and Boulton Creek is unquestionably the most difficult in the park. By that I mean its steepness is sustained. Going down you have my permission to be a chicken and wait for a dump of powder the night before like I do. Actually, the two steepest parts of the trail have been widened to such an extent you can now make some pretty telemark turns. No need for crash and burn technique.

Going up the south leg tests your herringboning skills to the limit; even racers can't skate all the way up this one without a break! But don't let the climb deter you. You can see some pretty amazing sights during temperature inversions when clouds of warmer air lolling about in depths of Elk Valley spill over the Great Divide and frost the spruce trees along the ridge-line, leaving the summit in sunlight above the clouds.

More about the trails When George Pocaterra went on his famous trapping trip with the Stoneys in 1906 he was not the first white man into the Kananaskis Lakes area by any means. But for some reason there's a multitude of features named after him. It seems to have begun when the Stoneys called the creek they travelled along Wasiju Wachi tusin ta Waptan Ze "Crazy mischievous white man creek", meaning where this Wasiju Wachi was taking a leak. That's how Pocaterra Creek got its name. And Elpoca Mountain, Pocaterra Dam, Pocaterra tote road, Pocaterra trail, Pocaterra cabin etc. etc.

Seven years later the Alberta/BC Boundary Commission under A.O. Wheeler was building monuments and cairns from one side of Elk Pass to the other. At this time there was a hunter's trail from Lower Kananaskis Lake up Fox Creek and over West Elk Pass to the Elk River. There were also secret ways over the Divide which only the Stoneys and George Pocaterra knew about. Perhaps you remember chuckling over the passage from "The Buffalo Head" where Pocaterra, Raymond Patterson and Adolf Baumgart, who had ridden over Highwood Pass and were about to depart on one such trail to Elk Pass to hunt — likely following the line of the fire lookout road — got caught by a greenhorn forest ranger from Australia near Pocaterra's cache, and rather than disclose the secret trail to a stranger intent on upholding the area as a game preserve, rode at a great rate in a "gust of fury" all the way down Packers to the ranger cabin at Lower Kananaskis Lake. The ranger had had enough by this time and while he was recuperating, the party was able to slip away up the regular trail. (I sympathize, I have the same feelings about greenhorn rangers from Toronto).

Anyway, the regular trail must have fallen into disuse because by 1940 district ranger Joe Kovach is working hard to keep the Elk Pass trail open. Only 10 years later he's making more notations in his diary about inspecting road work by Calgary Power for a tram line along the powerline access road, the route of today's Elk Pass trail!

But going back to the 1930's which was the heyday of forest rangers and trainee tourists. 1930 was the year the Kananaskis Lakes were taken out of the National Park, thus paving the way for roads and water power projects. The road started in 1934 from the Seebe end of the Kananaskis Valley and eventually succeeded in reaching Lower Kananaskis Lake ranger cabin where the main attraction was the life-size figure of a nude woman carved into the trunk of a nearby tree by Jack Fuller. Though the actual site lies under water close to Lakeside trail below Lower Lake group campground, the cabin and garage were moved up one terrace and can still be seen today across Whiskey Jack trail from Boulton Creek Trading Post. I'm sorry to say the carving was whisked away and is probably residing in somebody's basement.

You can take a peek at that first road by cutting across Kananaskis Lakes Trail and the powerline from Pocaterra Hut via a trail on *the east bank* of Pocaterra Creek. That log ruin between the road and a bend in the creek was formerly christened Scott Cache but was later known as Johnny Musko's cabin after a poacher who kept today's retired rangers hopping on their toes during the latter years of the game preserve era of 1930-56. Of more significance to skiers, in the fall of 1947 Pocaterra was superintending a tote road up Pocaterra Creek to one of his coal claims, putting in seven large bridges and three small ones. In case you haven't twigged, Pocaterra's road is Pocaterra trail and — here's a surprise — Rolly Road!

The greatest changes occurred in the late 1940's , early 50's. Notwithstanding the Pocaterra tote road, the Eastern Rockies Forest Conservation Board in 1948 directed construction of the Forestry Trunk Road from Coleman to Nordegg following a line similar to today's highway apart from one deviation now called Valleyview Trail which skiers like to wander up from Lionel for the view. The same year that slash for the new road was burning in Highwood Pass, Kovach walked up Pocaterra's tote road and blazed a route across to the proposed site of Kananaskis Lookout to be built in 1952. Essentially you follow his same route today when you ski Pocaterra trail to the lookout.

By 1955 the water in both Lower and Upper Kananaskis Lakes had been bottled in behind dams, and powerlines and powerline right-of-way access roads went winging north down the Kananaskis Valley to Barrier Lake and south over Elk Pass into B.C. For a Kowalski tour of damage done to the environment may I suggest Lodgepole, Sinclair, Lakeside and Elk Pass trails with visits to Canyon Dam parking lot and the parking lot at Upper Lake.

Out of all the mishmash of old tote roads, packtrails and powerline right-of-way access roads came recreational ski trails in the 1970's. The first blue brochure (surely a collector's item, so hold on to it) shows three loops none of which exist today: King Creek Fan Loop which followed the original road north of Kananaskis Lakes Trail, Rockwall Loop which went up the Pocaterra tote road and back down under the Rockwall, and Boulton Creek trail which tagged along the east shore of Lower Kananaskis Lake. You were asked to report skiers who were going too fast or cutting down trees and admonished never to touch an injured skier on the trail. I really have trouble with the first one, given that in the early days before grooming it took us half a day with a party of ten to break trail to somewhere around Lynx on Pocaterra.

In 1976, the year before Kananaskis Country was inaugurated, consultant Don Gardner was brought in to figure out a huge new system of interconnecting trails which meant building some new ones like Tyrwhitt and Blueberry Hill and upgrading others like the challenging trail up the south side of Lookout hill which led to one of George Pocaterra's coal prospects on the shoulder. Clearly Don suffered during those three months of trail clearing in the late fall of 1977, reporting -50° temperatures and 24 inch overnight snowfalls. Since then, some trails like Marl Lake have been dropped, others upgraded, new trails added, and a slew of parking lots, campgrounds and facilities built to make it the ultimate playground in the Canadian Rockies.

Side by side with the tourers were the racers, what few there were at that time. I should specifically mention Valerie and Rudi Setz who initiated the Kananaskis 45 Loppet or "The Great Cookie Race" in 1977 and which has been run ever since by the Foothills Nordic Ski Club as part of the Calgary Winter Festival. Who will ever forget the very first race, certainly not those of us who smothered our bases with red klister for the ice low down, then were wobbling around with six inch heels in the fresh powder up at Elk Pass. From what I recall most competitors wore knee-length wool knickers and carried packs stuffed with spare clothing, spare cables, bales and baskets, electrical tape and fruitcake. I wouldn't surprise me to hear that someone carried a snow shovel. Nowadays, what you wear reflects not only your slimness but also your skiing status and I'm afraid I haven't quite graduated to a lycra racing suit.

WEST ELK PASS AND ON?

Backcountry

Easy to pass
Intermediate to Lower Elk Lake
0.5 km to West Elk Pass from Elk Pass trail
4 km to Lower Elk Lake from pass
Height gain to pass 10 m
Height loss to lake 177 m
Maximum elevation 1905 m
Map 82 J/11 Kananaskis Lakes

Access Kananaskis Lakes Ski Trails, Peter Lougheed Provincial Park. Via Elk Pass trail described on page 192.

Overview Here you are on the Elk Pass trail, just past the Blueberry Hill turn-off, and not feeling up to the final hill. Well, have I got the perfect alternative: West Elk Pass. Skiers with energy can get to Lower Elk Lake via the summer trail alongside Elkan Creek but route-finding can be downright puzzling in the winter, so I'd only recommend it as a downhill option and suggest you return via the more infallible route up the powerline.

Just before Elk Pass trail leaves upper Fox Creek to make the final climb, step right (summer signpost under snow) and continue to follow the open draw to West Elk Pass which turns out to be a very longitudinal meadow. The actual pass is marked by a 3 metre-high information board completely buried under snow by winter's end and only identifiable by an enormous mushroom cap of snow. Isn't this beautiful bright meadow so much more pleasant than summer's green swamp? And you don't have to stick to the gooey trail in the trees but can glide down the centre of the meadow, marvelling at the changing facets of Mt. Fox and the rising up of the gothic mountains of the Elk River. If you're into Sony Walkmans, now is the time to pop in a tape of Ravel's Daphnes and Chloe Suite, the Sunrise bit.

Going on? This fine form of progress ends at the meadow's south end where the infant Elkan Creek suddenly drops into a deep canyon. It's time to take to the trail on

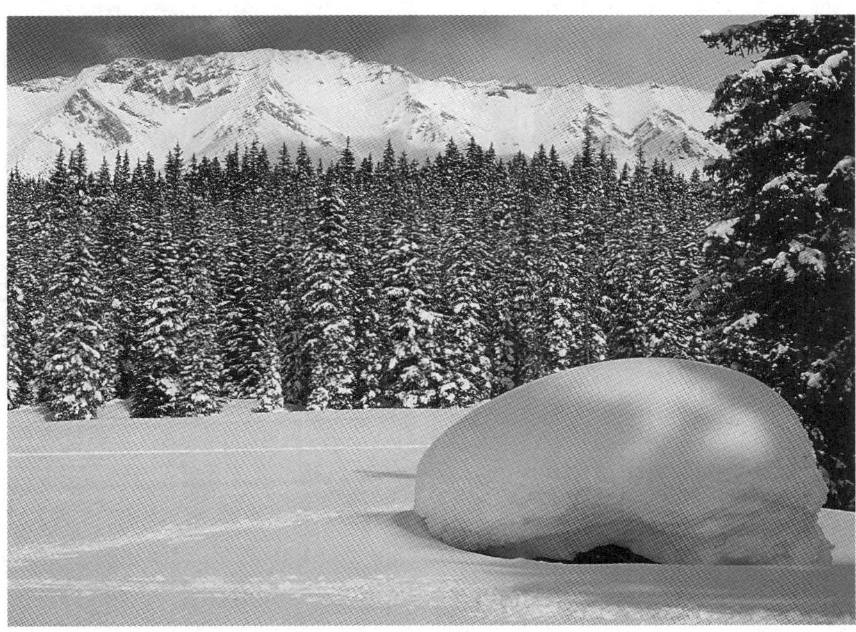

West Elk Pass. Below the mushroom is the 3 m-high information board.

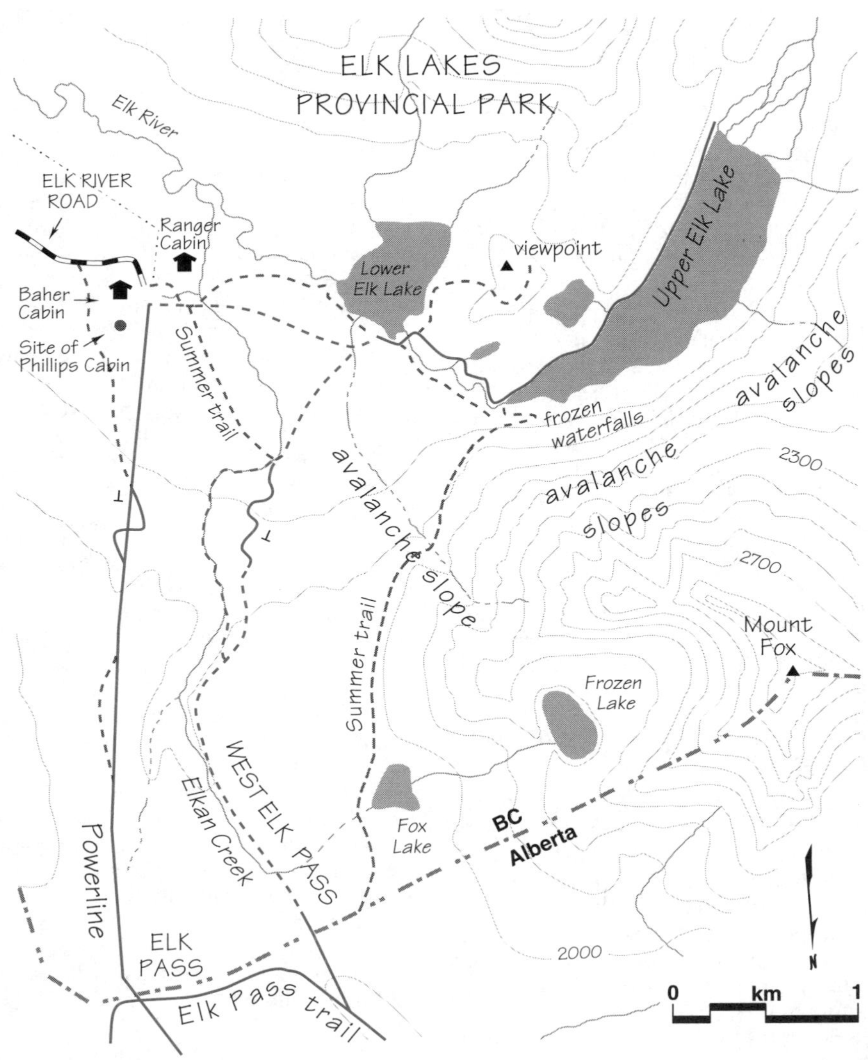

the right bank. But just a moment! If the snow is 9 feet deep, the summer trail is also 9 feet below your skis and you are 9 feet up in the spruce branches. So just do the best you can, joining up bits of openings and when the ground steepens, pushing through branches on your way down the right side of the canyon. Some skiers give up and elect to drop into the canyon at some point where they won't kill themselves. Whatever, the trail crosses the creek at the bottom of the hill and with less snow this is where you should be able to pick it up in the forest. From here, it's simpler just to head straight across to Lower Lake — who cares if the meadow is a huge summer bog.

ELK LAKES FROM ELK PASS

Backcountry

Intermediate
4 km to park boundary from Elk Pass,
7 km to Upper Elk Lake
Height loss 238 m
Maximum elevation Elk Pass 1975 m
Map 82 J/11 Kananaskis Lakes

Access
1. Kananaskis Lakes Ski Trails in Peter Lougheed Provincial Park. Via Elk Pass trail at Elk Pass described on page 192.
2. The alternative is 87 km of unplowed Elk River Road north of Elkford, British Columbia for which you need a snowmobile. Sometimes the road is plowed up to the 23 or 49 km mark if logging or exploration is going on. Contact Elkford Chamber of Commerce Tel: 604-865-4362 or Fax: 604-865-2442 for the latest road conditions.

Facilities Primitive shelter at park entrance. Five km down the unplowed Elk Valley Road is Tobermory cabin which is open to anyone courtesy of the BC Forest Service. Inside are 3 bunks with mattresses, wood stove, table and chairs, cooking utensils.

Overview If you want to escape the rat race of the groomed trails then Elk Lakes is the popular place to go. The usual way in and back out is along the powerline from Elk Pass, a total distance from Elk Pass parking lot to Upper Elk Lake of about 28 km return trip. Be aware of one tedious drawback: a 238 m climb on the return trip.

Some people like to make it a weekend trip and this was fine before the Phillips cabin was burned down by three drunken dingbats a couple of years ago. The neighbouring Baher cabin is a wee bit drafty while the luxurious Tobermory cabin is another 5 km down the road and liable to be packed by snowmobilers exhausted after a hard day of intense snowmobiling.

From Elk Pass set off down the powerline right-of-way. Apart from one steep section two thirds down, the gradient is moderate throughout and with the usual responsive snow you can have a fine time making telemark turns around giant-sized slalom poles. At the bottom of the hill you flog across flat meadows and arrive at the end of the access road from Elkford — the Elk River Road. To your left is Baher's cabin, while on your right is the park entrance and a little way along the summer trail, a spanking new ranger's cabin with space for fifty, which is, unfortunately, closed to the likes of you and I.

You need to know nothing about the summer trail to Lower Elk Lake. In winter, it's all much simpler. Starting from the warning sign at road's end "No motorized vehicles", you simply push west along a band of meadow, aiming to reach Lower Elk Lake just beyond the backcountry campground which is also closed. Amazing stuff snow, the way it covers up bogs and head-high willow bush.

From Lower Elk Lake to Upper Lake you can either force a route up the connecting river, bearing in mind that the Elk is quite often open so there is some squeezing to do between trees and obligatory falling into tree holes. Or you can locate the summer trail on the west bank. On balance this is probably better since it deposits you directly on Upper Elk Lake opposite impressive avalanche slopes and frozen waterfalls.

Return the same way. A point to remember, the steep bit up the powerline right-of-way can be avoided by using the access road at this point.

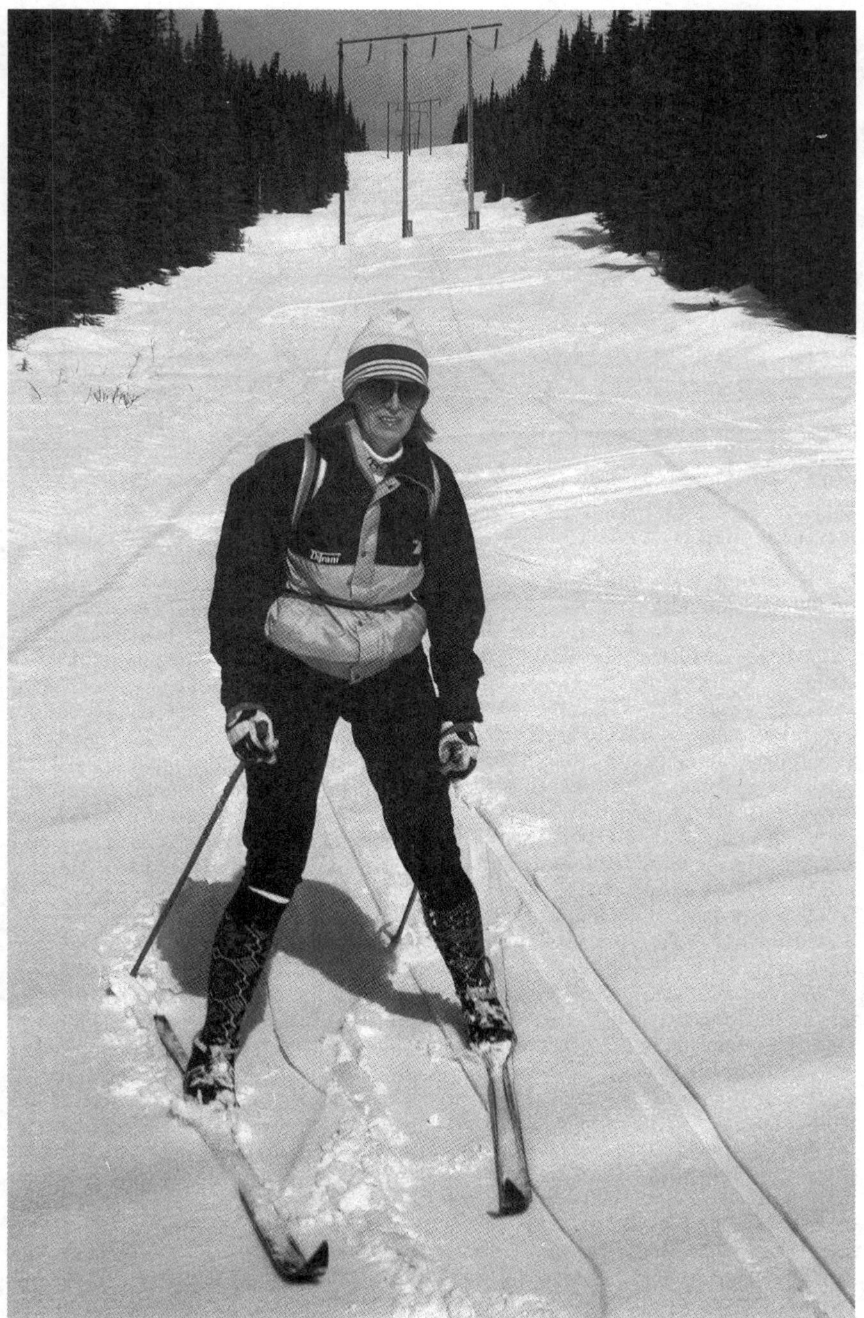

The run down the powerline right-of-way.

Phillip's cabin (left) and the Baher cabin at the entrance to Elk Lakes Provincial Park.

More about the trails The upper Elk Valley is synonymous with hunting and trapping and with guides like "Old Man" Phillips and Mike Baher who built a string of cabins up and down the valley and into Cadorna Creek. Phillips' clients generally came in via West Elk Pass trail with the packhorse grocery delivery service of George Bearns. That's because Phillip's cabin was located right where the entrance to the provincial park is now, at the edge of a meadow with that wonderful view of the mountains to the west. He must have been miffed when in 1949 the powerline over Elk Pass passed right in front of his front door.

For some reason I haven't yet fathomed, the disastrous conflagration of 1936 which started in Forsyth Creek and spread up the Elk Valley and across to the Highwood Valley and the upper Sheep is named after Phillips — the Phillips Fire. Ironically, though the fire spared the cabin, another 50 years of use by ski tourers and snowmobilers was to pass before the cabin burned down to the ground in 1989 at the hands of three snowmobilers from Alberta who'd had too much to drink. It's unclear whether they had sneaked in under cover of darkness along the ski trails.

So in 1949/50 the Gowganda Timber company was constructing the powerline access road starting from Elkford, while at the north end, Calgary Power was doing its road work for a tramline. In fact, if you had been skiing Elk Pass before 1979 you would have seen a caboose sitting at the edge of the powerline near the summit and would probably have made use of it for shelter like we did.

The powerline access road is now the 87 km-long Elk River Road from Elkford and it must be in pretty good shape if we can drive our clapped-out van along it without a disaster happening. So you get lots of hunters driving up the road in summer and snowmobilers in winter. Reading through the log book at Tobermory Cabin, you get the impression the hunters hereabouts are a responsible lot, though personally I can't imagine what perks people get out of killing animals. So therefore I am glad the authorities are resisting Highway 43 Association's plans for a highway over Elk Pass which would only encourage those city pinheads who think indiscriminate shooting from a moving pick-up is macho. However, none of this should bother you. The headwaters of the Elk was made a provincial park on May 18th 1973, and everything is banned except travel on your own two feet.

THE FORKS

Backcountry

Easy
11.3 km
Height gain 70 m
Maximum elevation 1792 m
Map 82 J/11 Kananaskis Lakes

Access Kananaskis Lakes Trail. Upper Lake parking lot at the end of the plowed road.

Facilities Washrooms at parking lot. Backcountry campground at The Forks.

Overview The Forks means the forks of the Upper Kananaskis River where the trail also forks, the north fork going to Lawson Lake and the west fork to Three Isle Lake. I can't in all conscience recommend either lake as an optional destination. Yes, I know people ski to both places but you take chances with some formidable avalanche slopes crossed at mid height.

The other thing about this trip is that while the grade is easy, the distance is long. But not as long as plodding further up the closed section of road to Interlakes parking lot, then skiing along the fire road which, incidentally, is partial to avalanches from Mt. Indefatigable. If you go this way, add on 2 km.

You're going to start with a boring ski across Upper Kananaskis Lake, so follow the ice angler's trail out onto the ice. As you pass out of the bay, steering between lawn chairs, you pass a rocky promontory on the right where the stone chimney of Gaherty's cabin stands tall like a lighthouse. Apparently the president of Calgary Power had the cabin built in 1933 as his own private honeymoon suite.

At the risk of sounding like a park employee, use your judgement before crossing the lake to the promontory at the north-west corner. I don't want to be sued. And don't do anything stupid like veering towards the north shore where warm springs bubble up creating thin spots in the ice. There was horrible accident at this spot during tree clearing when a cat went through the ice and the driver drowned. If, like me, you always feel vulnerable out in the middle of a big lake which is more than a metre deep and not an incipient fen, you can always ski around the south shoreline.

Crossing Upper Kananaskis Lake. Behind is Mt. Tyrwhitt.

Photo: Alf Skrastins

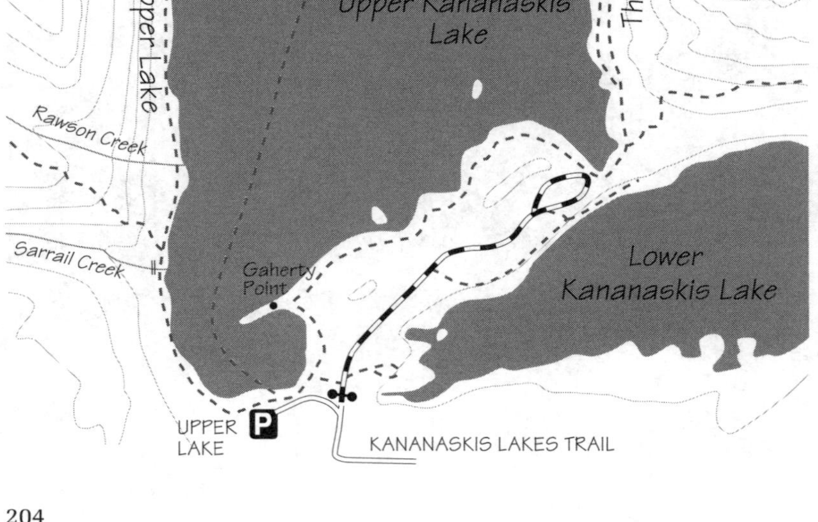
Three Isle Lake
Lawson Lake
0 km 1
FORKS
Kananaskis River
2300
2400
Mount Lyautey
Lyautey Glacier
rock pile
upper falls
Lyautey
Foch Creek
1800
Kananaskis Falls
Hidden Lake
Three Isle Lake trail
Hawke Island
Upper Kananaskis Lake
Upper Lake
Rawson Creek
Sarrail Creek
Gaherty Point
Lower Kananaskis Lake
UPPER LAKE
P
KANANASKIS LAKES TRAIL

The scenery for the next hour is magnificent: the cliffs of Mt. Sarrail and Mt. Lyautey sweeping down to the lake, and round the corner and through the gap of the Kananaskis River the dramatic shape of a mountain which was chosen to commemorate Field Marshall Radomir Putnik, a Serbian Army officer, later the war minister during the First World War.

Reaching the peninsula tip you have a choice of either following the campground trail up the peninsula, then turning left onto Upper Lake trail, or skiing up the bay on the port side, navigating between stumps, to the Upper Kananaskis River which can be followed to below Kananaskis Falls where you must take to the bank on the right. I recommend the latter option. But either route brings you to a bridge over the river where Upper Lake trail meets Lyautey.

The next stretch follows Lyautey trail or adjacent sandbars and willow flats. Again, you have a choice of either sticking with the trail which involves a diagonal climb across the bottom of an avalanche slope, or of following the river which appears the easier route until you hit the upper falls. This time the detour up the right bank is much steeper. From the junction of trails as shown on the map it's more interesting to stay with the trail which winds along the mostly flat south bank for the last lap to Forks backcountry campground right under Mt. Putnik. Not that you can see much from there.

More about the area From archaeological finds near Moraine trail it's known that Neolithic Indians were hunting game around the lakes in 5,500 BC. In modern times it was the Kootenai in canoes chasing elk around the islands followed by the Stoneys who came on the scene in about the late 1700's and chased the Kootenai back over the Divide into BC. By the mid 1800's parties of white men, women and children were either on their way through to Oregon or looking for a pass suitable for a road or a railroad over the Great Divide by the most difficult route they could find — North Kananaskis Pass.

In 1883 the directors of Eau Claire Lumber Company of Eau Claire, Wisconsin (later to be the directors of the Canadian Anthracite Coal Company at Canmore) wandered around the area assessing lumbering possibilities and in the process renamed the lakes Thorpe and Ingram after themselves. As an afterthought they suggested dams be built at the outflow of each lake. In 1914 W.C Hendry of the Federal Government's Water Power Branch made the same recommendation in an official report. Mind you, he also lusted after Bow Lake, Hector Lake, Baker Lake, Ptarmigan Lake and Redoubt Lake which were also inside the National Park boundary at the time.

In 1974 when plans were announced to make the area into a provincial park you didn't know whether to laugh or cry "too late!". As CNPA executive president Norman Smith feared, the egg of the cobra was allowed to hatch and as soon as Kananaskis Lakes had been booted out of the National Park for good in 1930 by provincial government persuasion, Calgary Power moved in, raising water levels in the upper lake by means of a primitive log dam, the forerunner to the earth dams of the early 1950's. Unfortunately, all this happened in the days before Vivien Pharis was willing to throw herself in front of a bulldozer.

As you will have gathered from reading this book, I am not only anti-golf courses but also anti-dams if they involve such gorgeous lakes like this one. I'll leave the last word to Raymond Patterson who wrote in a letter to George Pocaterra dated September 17, 1963. "If you haven't seen it, don't go. I imagine some people must get some pleasure out of the place — there certainly were enough people there, trying...Do you remember some bird writing in the Albertan & signing himself "Artist"? His letter was to the effect that the proposed dam would make the lake more beautiful than ever! The whole thing is a forcible reminder that we do indeed live in a country where the dollar comes first".

ELBOW LAKE WITH OPTIONS

Backcountry & Route

Intermediate
1.3 km to lake, 3.8 km to glacier, 4.3 km to Desolation Flat
13 km to lake from Boulton Creek
Height gain 150 m to lake, 500 m to base of glacier
Maximum elevation 2105 m at lake, 2743 m at top of glacier
Map 82 J/11 Kananaskis Lakes

Access
1. Before midnight on November 30th Kananaskis Trail (Hwy. 40) at Elbow Pass trailhead. Note: Highway closed between December 1st and June 15th.
2. After December 1st start from Boulton Creek parking lot on Kananaskis Lakes Trail.

Facilities Washrooms at the parking lot, picnic tables and backcountry campground at Elbow Lake.

Overview A popular trail (official and signposted) to be squeezed in before the highway closes. Even in the short days of November you should have lots of time for going further down the Elbow Valley to Desolation Flat or for climbing up to the source of the Elbow River at Rae Glacier which, like the Robertson, draws hordes of summer skiers.

Of course, the lake is still accessible after December 1st via Packers, Pocaterra, Lionel and Highway 40 to the Elbow Pass parking lot, all of which adds up to a grand total of 26 km to the lake and back.

When avalanche hazard is high or extreme, don't stop to play on the avalanche slope.

From the parking lot, the old road heads diagonally right up the slope. To foil 4-wheel drive vehicles, small boulders have been positioned along the side of the first and steepest hill which is now a good 60 cm narrower than skis in a regular herringbone or snowplow position. Remember this for the return. At the halfway point, the road levels across the runout zone of a large avalanche slope, then divides and re-enters forest. Right is official and best for uphill work. Turn right when you join the direct way and with increasing ease climb to the watershed at Elbow Pass. From the top, Elbow Lake is reached in two ticks.

There's something anticlimactic about lakes in winter, but the mountains on either side are suitably impressive with Tombstone towering up on the left and the Mt. Rae massif, the highest peak east of Highway 40, arrayed all round the right side of the lake and all down the valley as well. Not so pretty are huge signs, warning, explaining, congratulating, to which I have taken a loathing and which are appearing at every mountain lake in K-Country. If we have to have signs, let's keep them down at the trailhead and not at the lakes where, quite apart from detracting from the spirit of the place, they ruin a good photograph.

Picnic tables and campsites are around the corner to the right.

Option: Desolation Flat
Start this easy option by skiing down the length of the lake. At a sign advising you of the Provincial Park boundary, rejoin the road and bowl down the upper Elbow Valley until your tips run aground on frozen shale and grass. You just about capsize with surprise. Ahead is a new brown landscape. From one side of the valley to the other and as far downstream as you can see is grass with a permanent bent to the east. George Edworthy called it Desolation Flat. This is one of those places where Chinook winds concentrate, the spruce trees of five minutes ago turned to krummholz sheltering behind little rocks. There may be snow everywhere else, but here winter is a non-starter. You may even feel like going for a little walk.

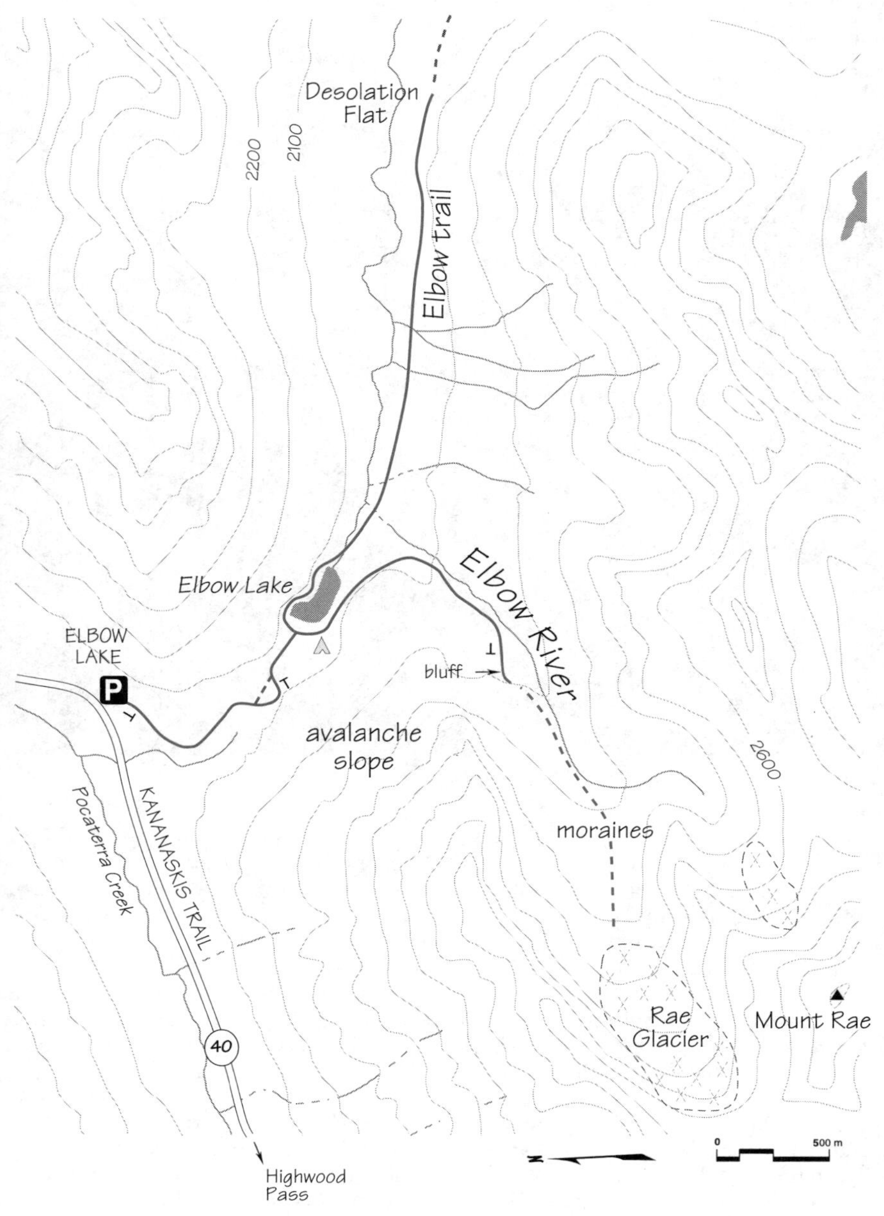
Desolation Flat
2200
2100
Elbow trail
Elbow Lake
ELBOW LAKE
P
Elbow River
bluff
avalanche slope
2600
moraines
KANANASKIS TRAIL
Pocaterra Creek
40
Rae Glacier
Mount Rae
0
500 m
Highwood Pass

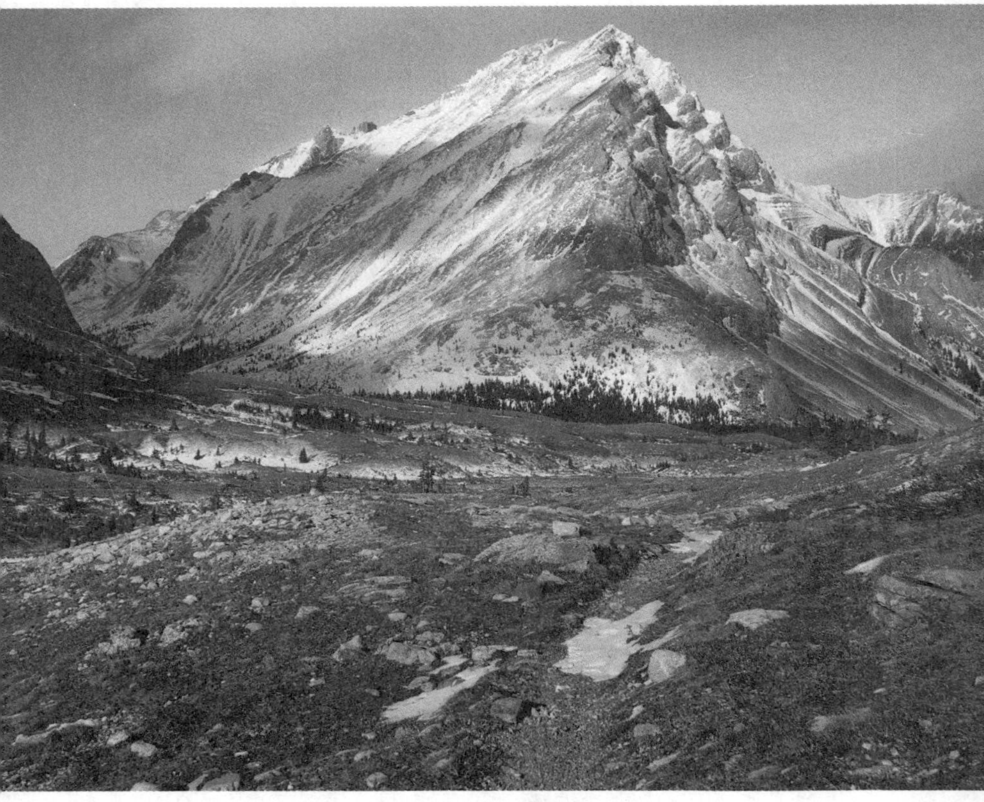

From a metre of snow to nothing. Desolation Flat in mid-winter.

Option: Rae Glacier

Judging by the ski tracks, everyone picks a different route up to the ice. I believe the summer trail to be the most foolproof approach but please yourself on the descent. It starts from two thirds down the east side of the lake, cuts across to the infant Elbow River, then follows along the right bank of the river and when that shows signs of being canyonised, moves up onto the right bank which is followed to the top of a knoll (view). Or you can track through more sheltered snow to the right of the bank in a shallow bowl and creep up behind the knoll.

A short distance beyond the knoll you return to the creek bottom which is easily done on skis lower down, or minus skis higher up by a descending traverse. The wind does a bit of sweeping at this spot and in November this is definitely the worst bit of the whole trip, being neither rocks nor snow, but rocks with snow in the cracks. Real pole breaker terrain. Follow the valley up and where it turns left, strike up the moraines by joining together ribbons of snow. Again, in November the moraines are unlikely to be completely snow-covered.

The Rae is a steep little glacier, but free of crevasses apart from the bergschrund high up on the right. If you can make the col you can look down into Ptarmigan Cirque.

LITTLE HIGHWOOD PASS

Route

Intermediate
4 km to pass
Height gain 466 m
Maximum elevation 2554 m
Map 82 J/11 Kananaskis Lakes

Access Before midnight on November 30th, park on the south-bound shoulder of Kananaskis Trail (Hwy. 40) 5.4 km south of Elbow Lake parking lot or 1.9 km north of Highwood Pass. On your right is a cut off loop of the old road. Note: Highway 40 at this point is closed between December 1st and June 15th.

Overview A short, deep route to a high pass above treeline with plenty of opportunity for telemarking. Don't go when avalanche danger is high or extreme. Nasty surprises are also waiting if you deviate from the route. Unfortunately, at the time when avalanche conditions are more predictable, the highway is closed.

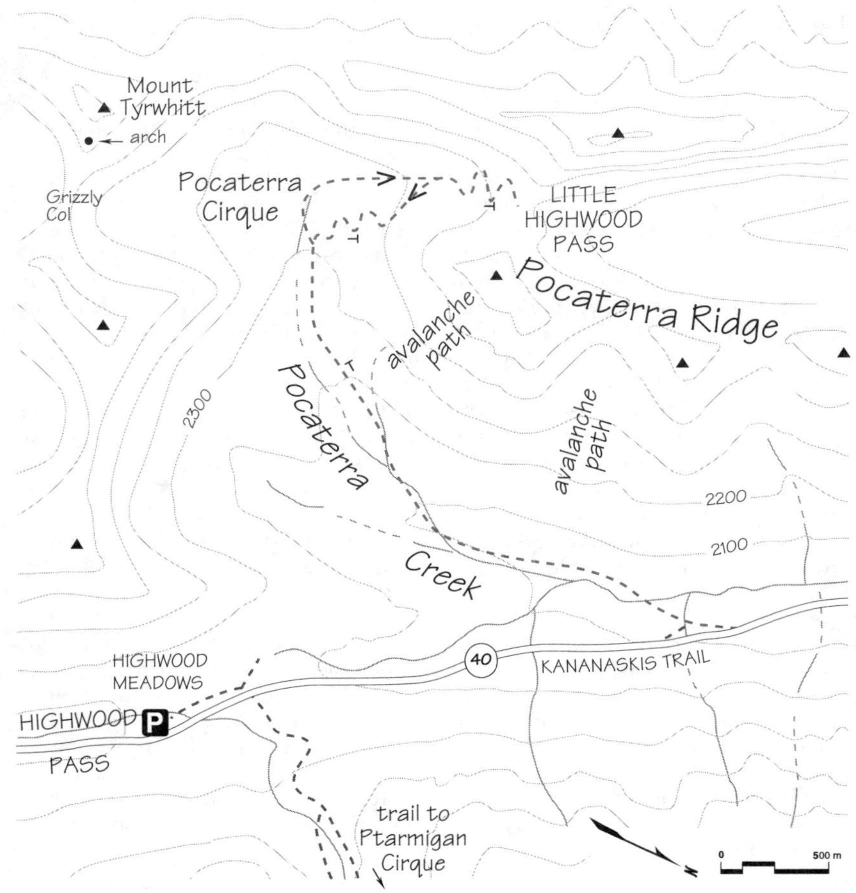

Start off along the old road on the west side of highway for a few minutes, then head off right into the forest, slanting left and joining up openings as you descend to Pocaterra Creek. You should bottom out opposite a large avalanche bowl.

Cross the creek, turn left and follow Pocaterra Creek around the end of Pocaterra Ridge. The going is flat and easy, mostly in the open. But round the bend a big step looms right across the valley floor with the main creek rising in waterfall steps. No need to panic. To your right is a convenient tributary. Hurry up the first hundred metres of tributary, then switch to the open slopes on the left, climbing up at any place you fancy to the bench top. The further right you go the closer you are to the avalanche danger zone. Reserve the right side for a quick descent if you must.

Continue easily up valley, rejoining the creek at a flat. This is your first view of Grizzly Col and the hole in Mt. Tyrwhitt's east ridge. Amazing things, arches. Have you seen the matching one on the *east* side of Highwood Pass just south of the parking lot? But back to skiing up the creek. Follow one side or the other under the steep telemarking slopes of Pocaterra Ridge to a point where your tips are literally touching the east face of the Great Divide. Here the little creek turns a right-angle to the north and makes a beeline for Little Highwood Pass. There should be "No Loitering" signs at the entrance. The initial trench is positively claustrophobic and fills in with snow dribbling down from the slope on the left. In mid trench, the floor widens but now you have something else to worry about — the slope on the right. On the final approach, it's safer to switchback up the centre. Arriving on the narrow pass, you pull on a wind jacket and from a place of perfect safety watch fascinated as the prevailing north winds rearrange the loose snow, blowing it over cornices for deposition on that slope to the right.

Return Despite the overwhelming attraction of the lee slope, make your fancy moves down the centre of the draw. At mid trench, traverse off left via a bench onto a steep ridge, then wiggle, or in my case wobble, down steep powder slopes with tree islands to Pocaterra Creek near the flat. From here, return the same way you came in.

Option: Going farther

In case you are thinking of it, moving on over the pass down the unnamed valley to Highway 40 opposite Valleyview Trail has quite a few problems quite apart from the fact that you'll need 2 cars. It would probably be a really nice trip in February-March time, but *not* in November when much of the upper valley is bare and unconsolidated snow lying loosely on the willow bush low down is a torment.

Feeling perverse, we tried it once from the valley bottom up and it took us over half the day to get half-way to treeline. We found a much better way out by keeping high on the west and north slopes of Pocaterra Ridge which avoided most of the willows but by then the snow squalls had increased to a mega-blizzard and the snow was piling up to our thighs. It was with great difficulty that we could move at all down a 30° slope. When we finally reached the road we found the snowplow had gone by and raised a formidable barrier between the road and the parked car, necessitating a prolonged dig with skis. Yes, as usual at the beginning of the season we were so well organized the shovels and chains were still in the basement of the house. The other thing that can happen to you, as it did on this occasion, is that an avalanche falls across the road mid-way between the two parking lots which means that everybody parked on the "wrong" side has to return to Calgary via Longview. Tough luck if you're stuck at Valleyview turn-off. On November 24th 1990, the highway closed a week early and you would have had a seven month wait to pick up your second car.

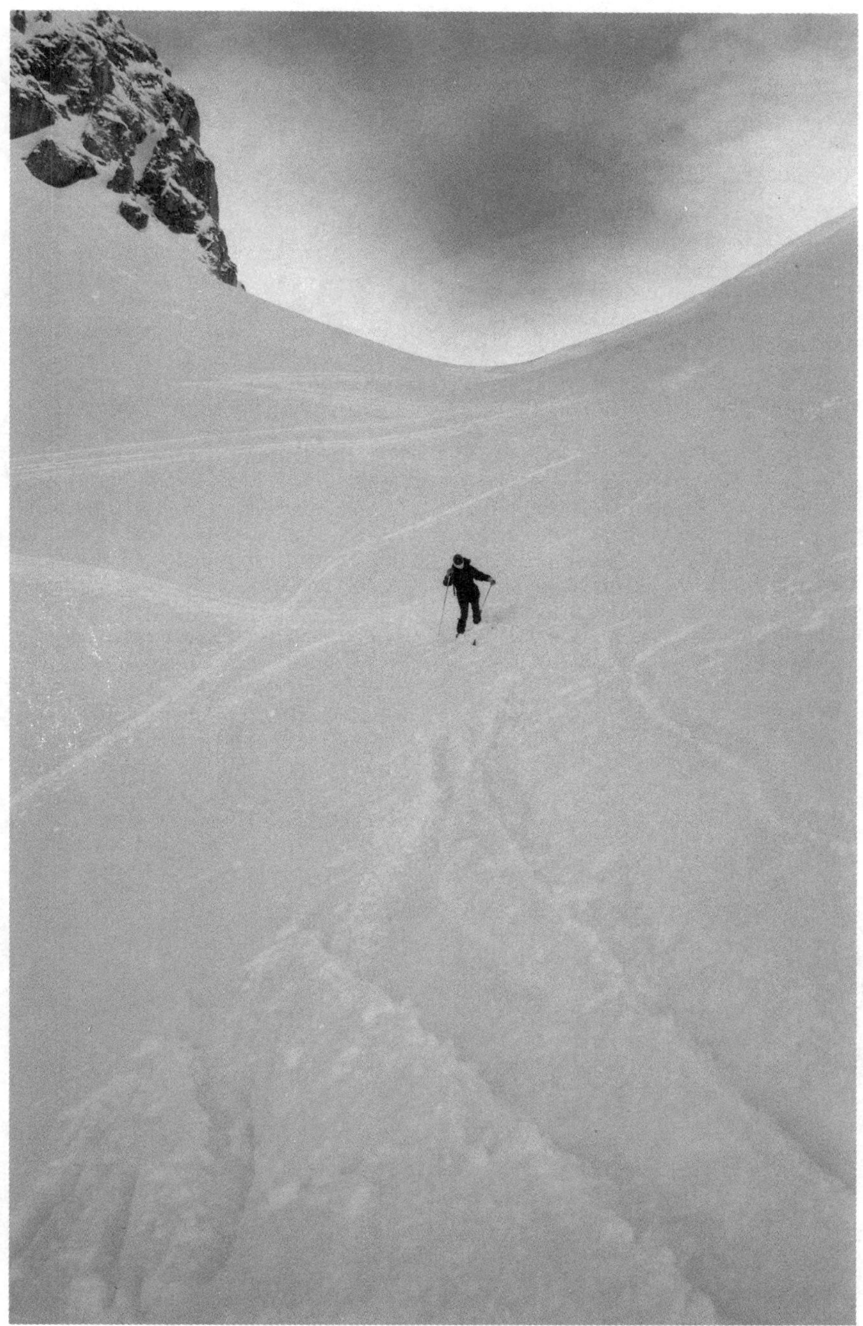

November powder! Descending Little Highwood Pass in the shadow of Mt. Tyrwhitt.

MOUNT LIPSETT TRAIL

Backcountry

Intermediate
5 km to end of road
Height gain 512 m
Maximum elevation 2377 m
Map 82 J/10 Mount Rae

Access Kananaskis Trail (Hwy. 40). Park on the highway about 13.2 km south of Highwood Pass, or 3.7 km north of Mist Creek crossing. Note: this section of highway is closed between December 1st and June 15th.

Overview This must be a superb trip in good weather. Unfortunately, the few times I've skied the old coal exploration road onto the south-east ridge of Mt. Lipsett the views have been obscured by mist, falling snow, or both (see photo). The period of mid-November to December 1st is not renowned for sunshine, but barring a weekend expedition, two weeks is all the time you have to sneak in this gem of a trail.

Climb up the bank onto the Mt. Lipsett coal exploration road starting in the bush. Keep left at the first junction, and cross the old highway three times removed, which means scaling a massive berm built to deter all terrain vehicles. The road continues, climbing by the side of a creek, then winding about a great deal, gaining height exceedingly slowly on its way to the south-east ridge.

Now heading along the ridge, you traverse on the west side through small windy openings into the whitebark pine zone. At the next division keep right, climbing ever higher to treeline which is where the skiing generally ends. In misty November some of the things you can't see from the open slopes include Mist Mountain, Odlum Ridge and Storelk Mountain.

Option: Mt. Lipsett South (2575 m)
Can you go on? It depends on your soles. If wearing death-defying plastic smoothies with heel and toe protuberances which are definitely not good for ridge walking, you'd be mad to try. But with vibram soles and two ski poles you may just make the south summit. Bear in mind the cliffs on the right and the consequences of a slip.

Return It's great run. In November there's the odd outbreak of the shales, but generally the reclaimed road has an excellent base for the minimum amount of snowfall — clover.

Traverse along the west side of the ridge. Mt. Lipsett south summit showing through the typical grey murk of a November day.

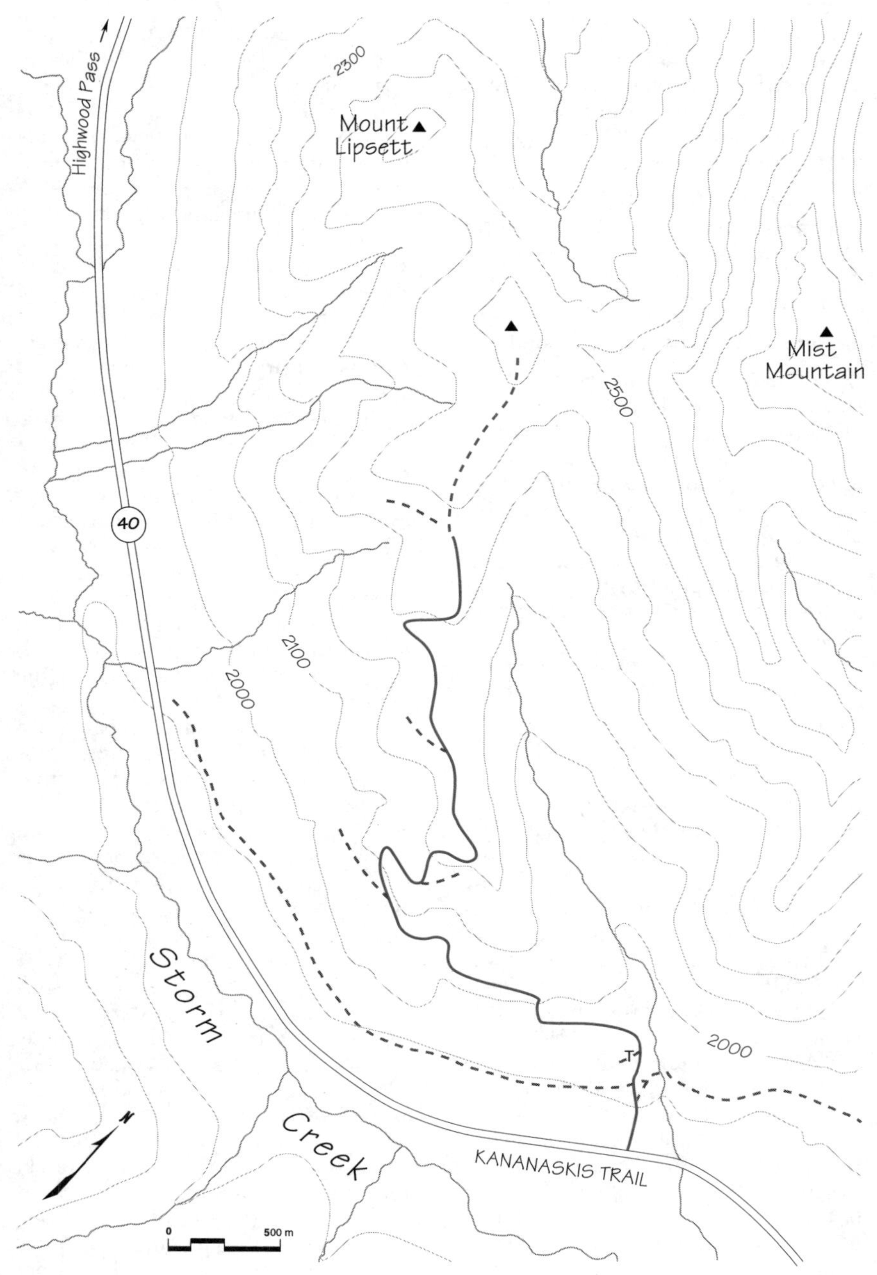
Highwood Pass
2300
Mount Lipsett
Mist Mountain
2500
40
2100
2000
2000
Storm
Creek
KANANASKIS TRAIL
0
500 m

MIST RIDGE

Backcountry & Route

Intermediate
7.5 km to ridge top
15 km circuit only via Picklejar Creek
Height gain 747 m to ridge top
Maximum elevation 2423 m ridge, 2240 m Cliff-Picklejar pass
Map 82 J/10 Mount Rae

Access Kananaskis Trail (Hwy. 40) at Mist Creek day-use area. Note: Highway 40 is closed between December 1st and June 15th.

Facilities Washrooms at parking lot.

Overview Another must-do trip to be squeezed in before Highway 40 closes at midnight on November 30th. The winter route is exactly the same as the summer route onto the south end of Mist Ridge i.e. via the coal exploration road which peters out on exposed ridges where a blizzard can whip up in no time, so pack a fleecy jacket and windproof pants. Headlamps are deemed essential for a return down Picklejar Creek.

The first 2 km follows Mist Creek trail with signposts and red markers on trees.

Following red markers, head north towards Mist Mountain and cross Highway 40 in just a few minutes. The red triangles resume from the other side of the road and in another few minutes bring you to the highway before this one. Turn right, then left at the signpost onto a coal exploration road rising along the east slope of Mist Creek valley. Higher up, the road develops a bad case of berms. Now the danger of vehicles clanking up the road has passed, I wish Parks and Rec would have a go at ironing out the bumps which I loathe even more on a bicycle. At 2 km, the angle eases and you arrive at a signed junction where the official route up Mist Creek carries on as a narrow trail in much the same line as before, only downhill. I must admit I have never skied up Mist Creek and I think it's because of this huge dip into a side creek. Psychologically, the climb up out of it is just too unpalatable for the end of the day when you're whacked.

Your exploration road, however, turns right. The trend is uphill between alders on the south-east slopes of an unnamed tributary, the road winding in and out of the folds of a nameless ridge. At viewpoints you look a long way down into the nameless creek and across to nameless ridges between nameless cols. Even the peaks of the Highwood Range, starting to poke up behind the lower ridges, are nameless. Nearing a road junction, the slope tilts alarmingly and the trees thin out. It's only November and already the road is filling in. Another month and the road will be a 40° slope in keeping with the rest of the hillside. Keep left at this junction. (The right-hand road leads to a high col and would be an excellent way into Picklejar Creek if it didn't cross a dangerous avalanche slope at mid height. Don't go.) Meanwhile, your road seems in no hurry to ascend. It is, in fact, descending very quickly into the head of the nameless tributary.

On the rise again, it enters meadows at a clump of whitebark pines and switchbacks easily to a col between another nameless ridge and the south end of Mist Ridge proper. Not much shelter here on windy days unless you hop over the ridge into the trees. To the north, rising above Cliff Creek, is a most unusual view of Gibraltar Mountain looking very unlike its usual picture postcard self.

The road carries on, first on the east side, then across the billowy shoulder of Mist Ridge to a tiny col on the west slope. Through the V appears a picturesque hillock with a crown of trees and the long east face of Mist and Storm Mountains, their wavy rock bands accentuated by snow. From here you either hike or ski depending on conditions another 76 vertical metres to the top of South Peak, springboard for the splendid Mist Ridge arrayed in front of you but definitely not a trip for today. Wait 8 months.

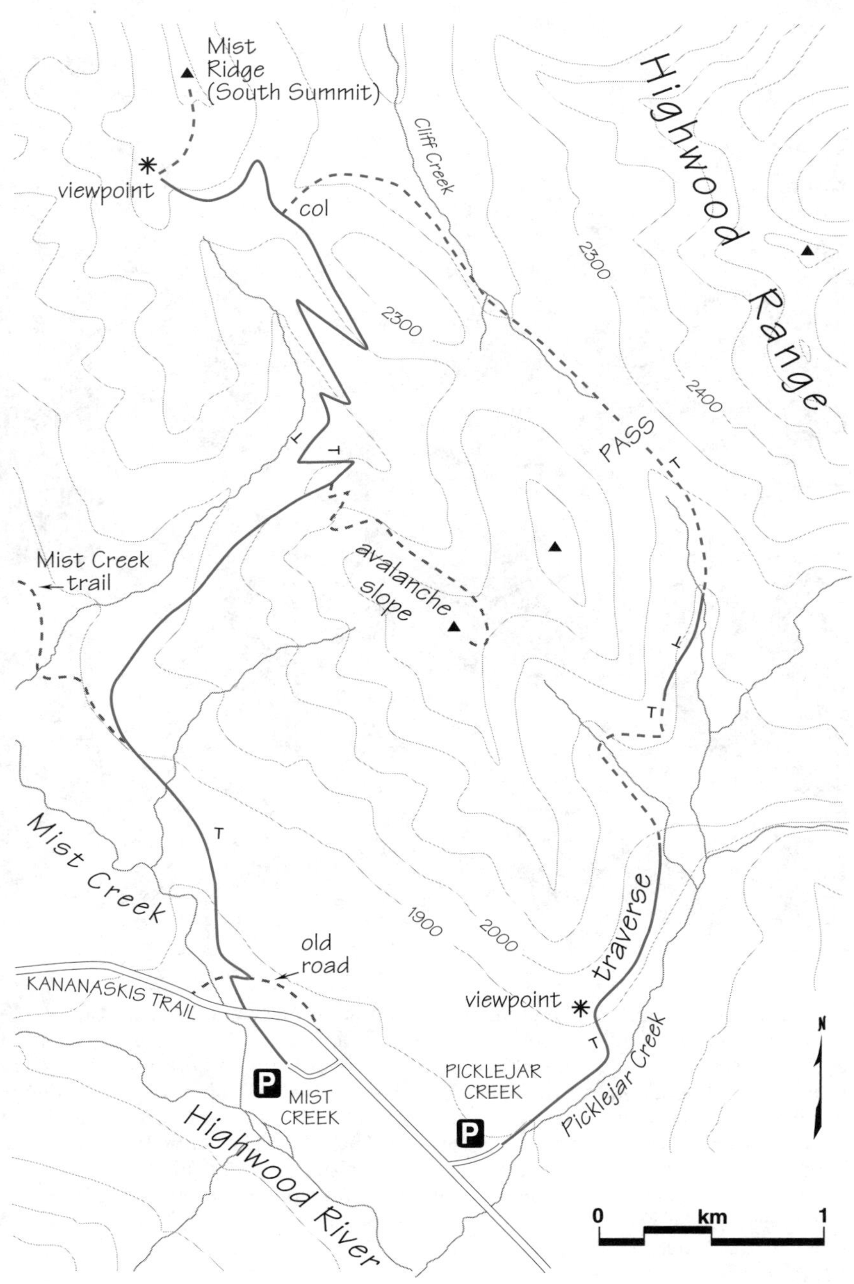
Mist
Ridge
(South Summit)
viewpoint
col
Cliff Creek
Highwood Range
2300
2300
2400
PASS
Mist Creek
trail
avalanche
slope
Mist Creek
1900
2000
traverse
old
road
KANANASKIS TRAIL
viewpoint
MIST
CREEK
PICKLEJAR
CREEK
Picklejar Creek
Highwood River
N
0
km
1

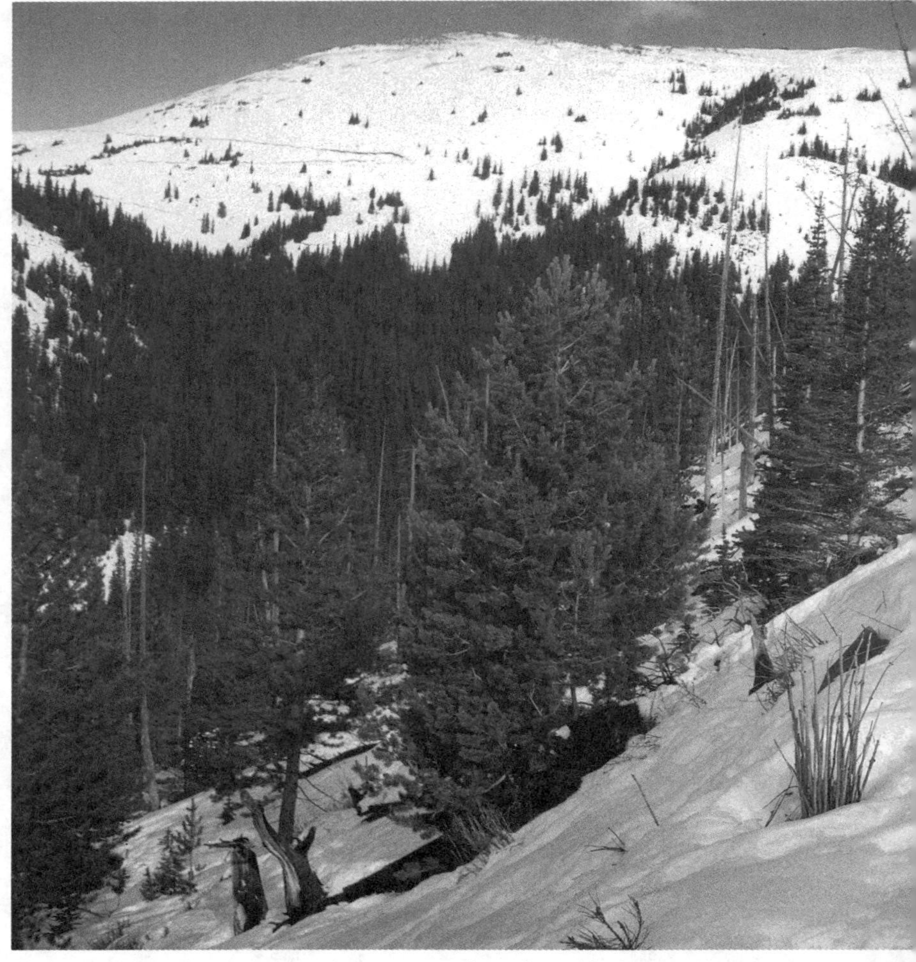

The traverse above the unnamed creek. You can see the trail switchbacking up the open ridge to the col (far left) below the south end of Mist Ridge's south summit.

Return From the final col, depending on how much the elk have messed up the snow, you can ski down to the whitebark pines without going all the way around the boonies. The uphill after the creek crossing is a bit of a bummer, but after that it's a fast run and quite technical, requiring quick weight changes on the traverse to avoid lurching over the edge. Lower down, the berms can be used to good effect to jump start gentle runouts.

Option Return: Via Picklejar Creek
A different return route with a good chance of being caught out in the 4 pm dark of late November. What's needed is a start earlier than 11 am, and a fleet of trail breakers. The temptation can be easily resisted if there's only two in the party and the sun's gone down behind Mist Mountain.

Start from the windy col below the south end of Mist Ridge. Slip down and right into Cliff Creek, a broad shallow valley by this point, busy accumulating all the snow that blows off the ridges. Much heavy duty trail breaking is needed before you reach Cliff-Picklejar pass in gorgeous meadow and larch country. Accompanying you during your trek is the most desolate looking bunch of mountains you've ever seen, their sides swept clean by wind, disclosing miles and miles of frozen talus. These are the unnamed peaks of the Highwood Range.

It's a carefree run down the Picklejar side, for beneath the snow is award-winning bunch grass. Initially, aim for the left side of the infant creek which is becoming progressively entrenched below the right bank which rises from stream to ridgetop in one fell swoop. Just before a little bend where the trench threatens to become a canyon, cross to the right bank and find the summer trail which slants right to left onto the ridge and requires only a few herringbone steps.

On the ridge is where you lose the trail, presuming you ever found it in the first place. Just ski down the steeper bit into trees, then head right and cross a tiny creek between this ridge and the bigger ridge to the west *before* this creek also becomes entrenched. Head a fair way down the creek's west bank to a bench above the final drop-off to Picklejar Creek where you should rediscover the trail. It pays to find this trail since it takes you, and all the valley's animals, apparently, out to Highway 40. If we could find it in the dark, then so can you (we had forgotten our headlamps).

The trail meanders along the top of cliffs on a bench which lapses temporarily at the point where rocky ridges on both sides of the valley meet in a V. It looks a bit like a goat trail at this point. Shortly after this comes proof that the end of the trail is close at hand: an open shoulder and a view all round of Highwood Valley and of most interest, naturally, Highway 40. A few downhill turns and you're into the last lap, a wider trail between more cliffs on the left and a bog which oozes water all over the trail between May and November. Finally, there's a horse rail to lean against and Picklejar day-use area where all washrooms are closed for the season. Just when you need one.

All that remains is to follow the access road out to the highway, turn right and ski north for just over one kilometre to Mist Creek day-use area.

ODLUM CREEK

Backcountry & Route

Intermediate
9 km to pond
9 km to meteorological station
Height gain 334 m to pond, 440 m to meteorological station
Maximum elevation 1966 m at pond, 2073 m at meteorological Station
Map 82 J/7 Mount Head

Access Kananaskis Trail (Hwy. 40) at Lantern Creek day-use area. Note: this section of Highway 40 is closed between December 1st and June 15th.

Facilities Washrooms at the parking lot.

Overview After biking, skiing is the next best way into the head of Odlum Creek. Can a cutline make a good ski trail? The answer is a resounding "yes" in the case of Odlum Creek, especially when the normal route in up the logging road is twice as long and entails two river crossings with the water still running at one degree above freezing point.

From the parking lot, walk north along the highway to a cutline access road whose entrance is partially blocked by a huge boulder painted with the red letter "M" for masochist. Put on the skis and keeping left, zip down the access road to the Highwood River which in late November is usually so depleted at this point you can hop across on rocks. The road continues on the other side, swinging round to the right where it joins a major east-west cutline. (You can spot it winging up the hill on the east side of the highway).

Turn left. The following climb up a two-tier hill is the steepest en route and lumpy with round rocks garnered from the riverbed. In early season you pick your way up and just as carefully pick your way down again on the return. This gets you onto a slightly undulating bench

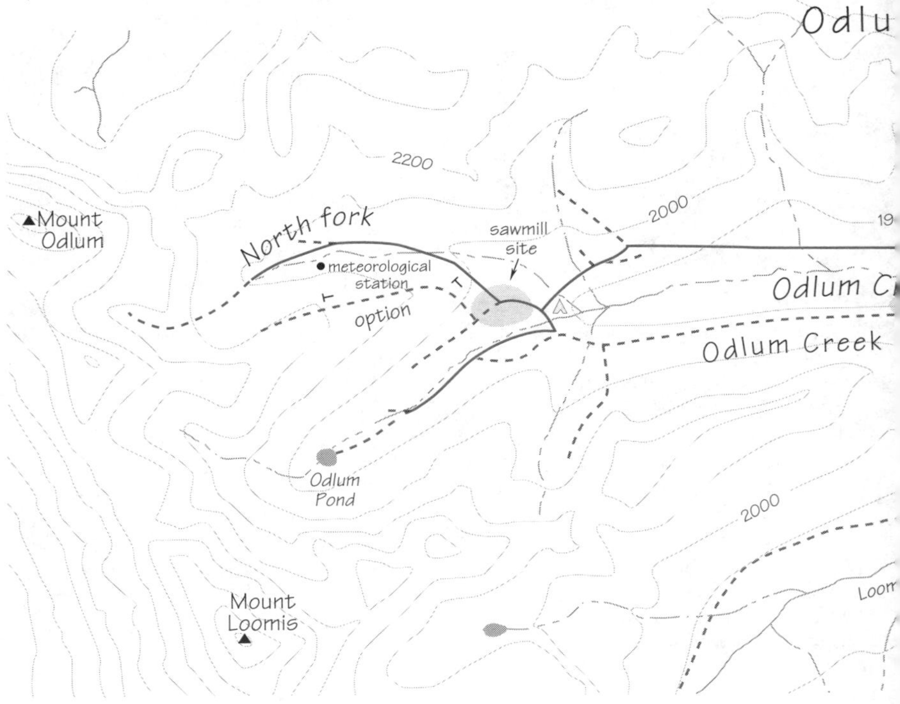

below the steep south slopes of Odlum Ridge, a very pleasant section which ends with a downhill run to Odlum Creek. Although the cutline crosses and re-crosses the creek at this point, you may just as well follow up the creek bed.

You can really make good time up the next 3.5 km of cutline, a slightly-rising straight with no turning or turn-offs until you get to the high point. Keep left here. Similarly, ignore other side roads on your way down across the north fork to the main Odlum Creek logging road, reached at Pete Schweindt's sawmill site. Just before the junction, closeted within an island of spruce trees, is an emergency campsite with rustic chairs and a table which threatens to collapse as soon as you set your thermos down. In case you've brought hot dogs, a cast iron frypan is hanging from a nail off a tree. And I believe I also saw a kettle and assorted pots big enough to cook up a batch of spaghetti for six people.

Option: Odlum Pond

Turn left at the junction onto the main Odlum Creek logging road. Cross the bridge over Odlum Creek, then find the logging road nearest to the creek and follow it to within half a kilometre of your objective where the road crosses the creek. Continue up the south side of the valley through meadows (bogs and summer sloughs) to Odlum Pond, enclosed on three sides by steep slopes. While a pleasant spot in summer with water, grass, and waterfalls falling artistically from the backdrop, in winter everything is white, or rather blue since the sun never gets a look in for five months after September. Probably, you won't want to linger overlong in the chill and besides, you are standing in line of fire from a huge avalanche gully. In summer, amputated branches litter the grass, while trees across the lake, note, have all had their crowns lopped off.

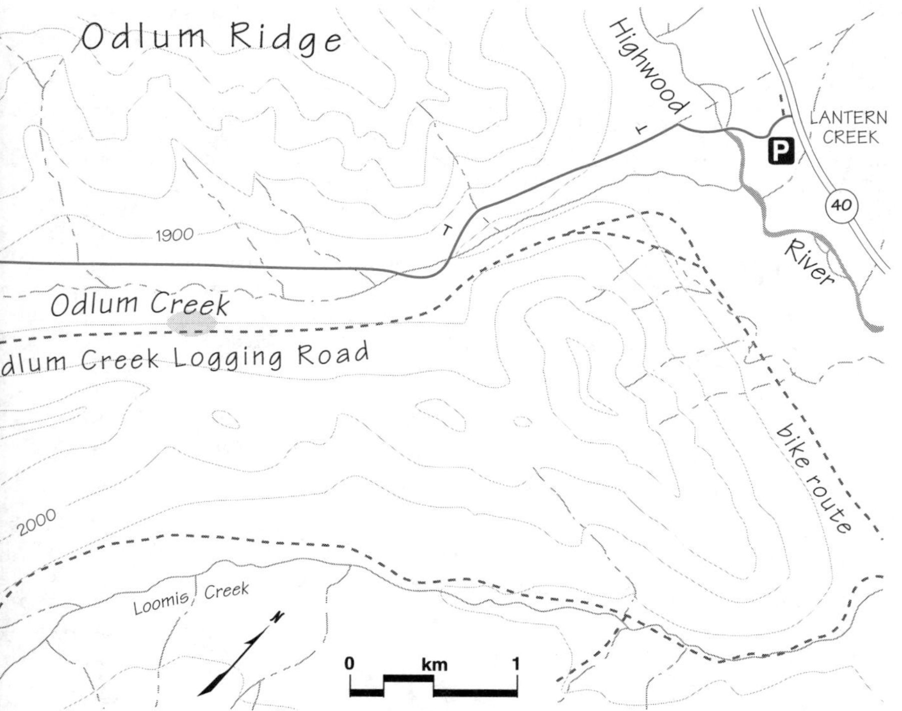

Odlum Creek explorations. The main logging road beyond the sawmill site.

Option: North Fork

At the junction with the main Odlum Creek logging road turn right but don't go too far. You want to turn right up the next side road. Since it's completely obliterated in the area of the sawmill site, aim for a tall dead tree standing between the twinned first section. Once you're in the trees, it's obvious. (Incidentally, the *next* side road on the right from the junction climbs part-way up the ridge between the two forks and is well worth investigation by downhill devotees.)

But back to the north fork road. After the first hill, the angle slackens off as does the pace (the snow is definitely deeper). Cross the north fork, keep left everywhere and ultimately, guided by 3 m-high metal rods for the benefit of meteorologists travelling by snowmobile, arrive at the meteorological station. If you're expecting someone to welcome you with cup of hot coffee you're in for a disappointment. Beyond the station, the road soon ends but that's OK, it has delivered you to meadows at the head of the valley where opportunities exist everywhere for telemarking under the larches.

MCPHAIL CREEK

Backcountry

Easy to camp site
Intermediate to headwall
Intermediate Muir Creek option
8.5 km to camp site
13 km to base of headwall
6.5 km Muir Creek option return
Height gain 356 m, Muir Creek 320 m
Maximum elevation 1890 m
Maximum elevation Muir Creek 1859 m
Map 82 J/7 Mount Head

Access Kananaskis Trail (Hwy. 40) at Cat Creek day-use area. Note: Highway 40 is closed between December 1st and June 15th.

Facilities Washrooms, picnic tables and shelter at parking lot.

Overview A long route but an easy one, using logging roads to reach the bottom of the headwall below Weary Creek Gap. When Highway 40 is closed after November 30th it's not realistic to start from Highwood Junction and expect to be back before dark. If starting from Cat Creek before November 30th pack a towel, oversized runners and neoprene bootees, or waders, or yellow K-Country garbage bags.

The old road leaves the far end parking lot and heads up the meadows of the Highwood River valley. Keep left on the flats and climb over a ridge to a crossing of the Highwood River at 2.5 km. The word "crossing" takes on a whole new meaning in winter, or to be exact, before the water freezes over. Hopping about in deep snow, squeezing neoprene bootees into size 14 runners is no mean feat and there's never a bench when you need one. Prairie chicken dance over, cross the river (anticlimactic) and repeat dance on the other bank, with additional steps to towel the feet dry before they contract permanent frostbite. This dance can be very entertaining to rich skiers with waders.

A warm-up hill brings you to two junctions. Go either first right (steeper shortcut) or right at the junction with Carnarvon Creek trail. As you settle into a long spell of easy skiing above McPhail Creek, you feel you're really on your way at last. Some time later you make your first acquaintance with the E-W cutline by crossing it, then reach the big bend and realize you are hardly any further into the valley than you were an hour ago. The mountains at the valley head seem a million miles away.

But finally, after a short downhill, you get to turn your tips to the west. The going is fast and easy along an open bank with views. Note that a dip precedes the junction at the 6.5 km mark with the Muir Creek exploration road which crosses the creek.

In the meadow following keep right and climb a small hill back into the trees. At the split in the road it's better to keep left. A left-hand bend signals the approach glide to an old sawmill site down by the river which is the 8.5 km turnaround point, summer camp site and snacking spot. Unfortunately, the rusty van has been airlifted out and all you can expect is another stand-up lunch.

To reach the headwall requires another 4.5 km of intermediate skiing and a closer acquaintance with the cutline. If you think you can hack both, continue along the road which climbs back into the forest to a T-junction with the cutline. Turn left. Taking on its alter ego personality, the road-cutline roller coasters for the next 2.5 km between pincer-like ridges guarding the inner valley. With speed slackening due to prolonged bouts of herringboning, there is plenty of time to peruse Mt. McPhail, alias Pyramid, which lies dead ahead in line with the road. Undeniably, the scenery is becoming very impressive in every direction. The third, last uphill can be avoided by a road around the bottom to the left, a good thing to know about.

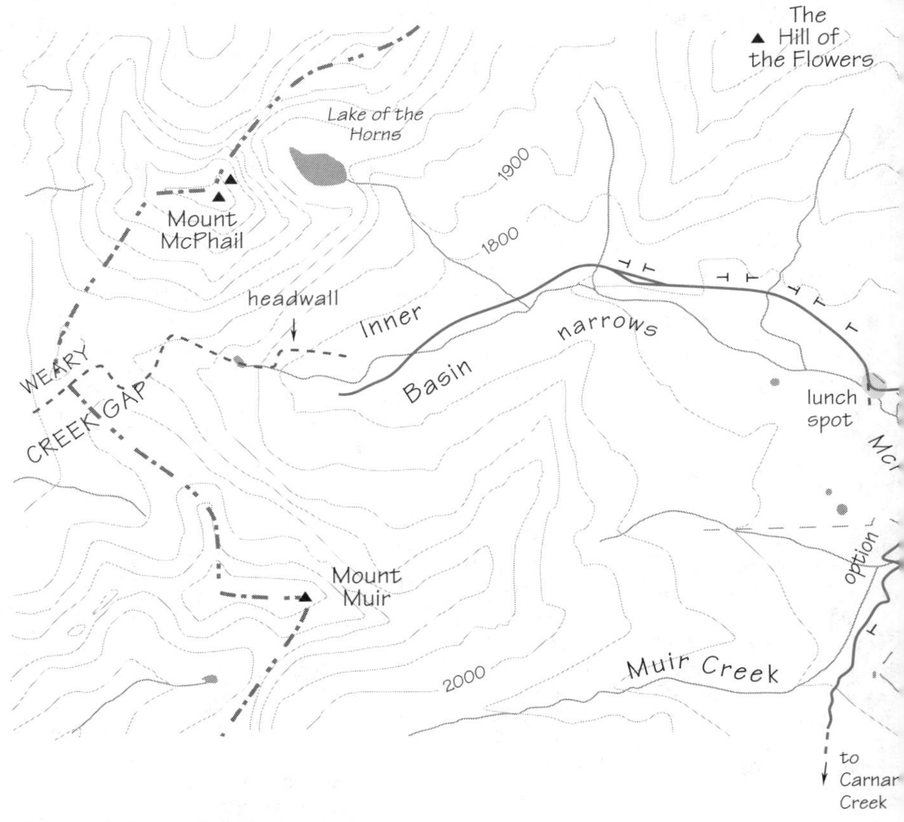

The Inner basin is a bit of a shock, more so in winter. Logging has been supplemented by the 1936 holocaust and the only bits of coniferous forest left is a patch below the Lake of the Horns and another on The Hill of the Flowers. An empty land except for hibernating grizzlies and the stray skier. The road crosses the flats and three creeks including McPhail Creek and ends below the headwall in bumpy meadows. Ice smears the cliffs and snow obliterates the old elk trail up the ledges to Weary Creek Gap.

Option: Muir Creek and over?

At the 6.5 km mark turn left on to the Muir Creek road which crosses McPhail Creek. You're going to be joining the cutline which rises in front of you like the 60 m jump at Canada Olympic Park. Fortunately this bit's circumvented by the road doing a spot of winding around to the right, but you haven't totally escaped some hard work, for as soon as you gain the cutline you're into a three-wave uphill. Keep alert for where the road leaves the cutline and descends slightly to cross Muir Creek. For the next 2 km it wiggles above the east bank gaining height rather slowly, then ends abruptly some 100 m below the ridge.

Experts at finding needles in haystacks should consider joining this trail to the Carnarvon Creek option described on page 227. Rated difficult, it has some killer hills on the Carnarvon side.

More about the trail McPhail Creek has always been easy of access, starting with the thousand-year old "Elk trail" by which elk commuted from BC over Weary Creek Gap to wintering grounds on the west slopes of the Highwood Range and which was later used by generations of Kootenai Indians chasing after the elk. The elk is one reason why this section of Highway 40 is closed after November 30th when elk hunting closes on November 28th, though I can't imagine why the odd skier down in the valley bottom minding his own business should be considered as great a threat as the hunter taking pot shots. Of course the real issue is hunting *out of season*. And we all know what happened in 1988 when the highway was open all winter.

Mind you, even animals in the adjoining provincial park aren't safe and I shall always remember the killing of a moose at Highwood Pass one late November by some idiots shooting from a vehicle. I often wonder if it was the same young bull that we and carloads of other telemarkers were admiring just a few days earlier. The thought of such a beautiful animal, legs folding and eyes dulling as it sinks into the snow makes me so angry I want to banish the perpetrators to life imprisonment in Backcountry Winter to live off willow brush. Some of the rangers have even better suggestions.

But back to McPhail Creek. For a period in its history it was known as Bunk Creek after bunks of logging sleighs were found stacked up against the forge of Mr. Wilson's abandoned winter camp. Rancher-author Raymond Patterson describes zig-zagging back and forth across McPhail Creek (the bridges had all rotted) as he followed the old logging road to the camp which was sited "on a little flat on the right bank of the creek, tucked up against a low cliff". Even in 1936 the buildings were in bad shape — the logs rotting, the roofs falling in — so it's doubtful whether there's anything left to find today. In Patterson's time this road was the way in to the inner sanctum and when you reached the camp you found a

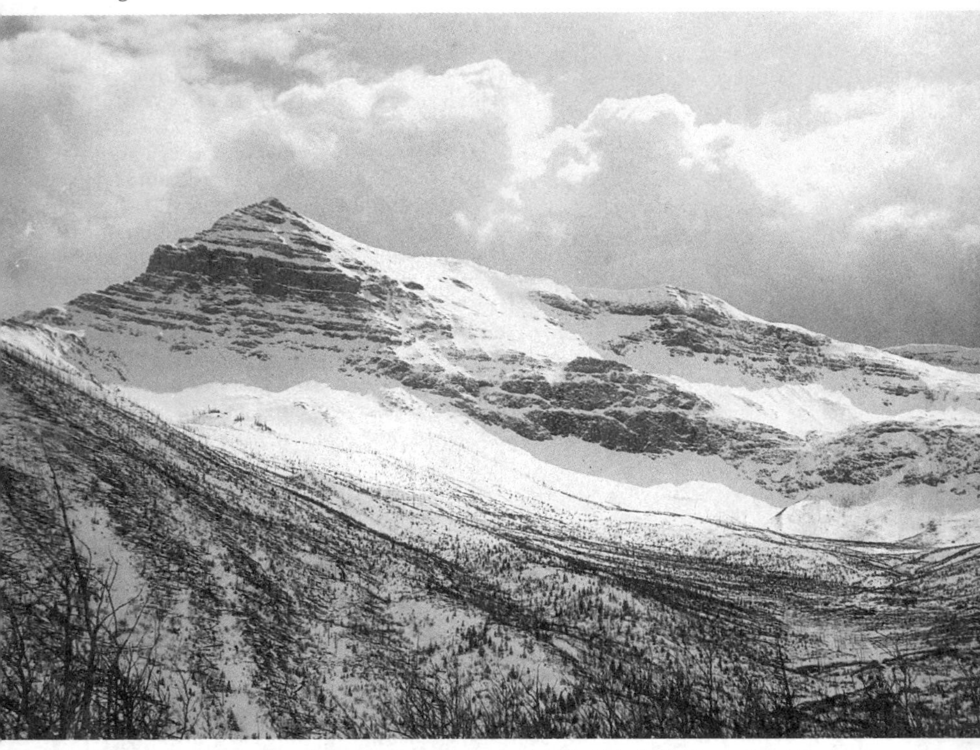

View from the narrows of the devastated inner basin. Mt. Muir (left), Weary Creek Gap and headwall (centre), Mt. McPhail (right).

way up the bank to the elk trail on the bench. Since then the bulldozing of a major logging road most likely by the Stan McLeod Timber Company gathering mine props after the 1936 fire has changed the line of approach and made things easy for skiers.

1936. It was the last day of September and Patterson was on his way to Weary Creek Gap to climb Pyramid, a wonderful viewpoint to survey damage caused by the Phillips fire of three months earlier and which was still smoking in spots. He was mortified to find that Bunk Creek was cleaned "as clean as a whistle" and that between the old burn of 1910 and the headwall "there was not literally a living thing — not even a willow". Although we have willows 55 years later on, there is not much else apart from stunted aspens and pine seedlings hidden by snow cover.

What many people don't realize is that the conflagration, which showered ash on Calgary and is the reason why lodgepole pines cover most of the Eastern Slopes, actually entered Alberta via Weary Creek Gap from the Elk Valley. Though deliberately watered down in "The Buffalo Head" lest the author be sued, the background story makes a wonderful addition to the Bumper Book of Bumbling Bureaucrats (or, as Patterson called them "a poor, cheap, shoddy lot") with a story which can be pieced together from various sources including Patterson's wrathful letters to George Pocaterra. It seems that forest rangers Harry Wileman and "Freddy Nash and his merry men" could have very well stopped the fire at the gap where it "pinched out to as narrow as 15-20 ft." and "in places only burned through grass". But when Nash phoned head office with the suggestion

of digging a fire break he was overruled and rebuked for wasting good government money on a long distance phone call. Sure enough, the fire jumped the headwall into Bunk Creek, fanned out and had a "month's freedom" in the Highwood River Valley and most of the tributaries, and though Nash managed to stop the spread up Mist Creek, there were other ways for the fire to get to the Sheep River than Rickert's Pass and erase a good portion of the forest to the boundary. By the time fire fighters — men on the dole, this was the hungry 30's — were sent to the scene it was far too late and in any case Patterson accused the fire crews of not the slightest interest in seeing the fires brought under control as long as they got another day's fire-pay.

And then there's the story of the axes. Ordered to return axes to head office, Nash refused since they might still be needed to control hot spots and sent back the broken ones for repair. With amazing alacrity out came a government official and dumped the broken axes at Nash's feet and drove away with all the good ones. An incensed Nash charged the Forestry Department and was fired, though later reinstated at the insistence of local ranchers who knew a good man when they saw one. Patterson, who is good at such things, summed it all up for Pocaterra, "throughout the summer the BC Forestry paid no attention and sent not a man, while our own outfit waited until the thing had become unmanageable before acting. Between the two, in the interests of economy, they have burnt off the watershed of a continent — however the money will be available for paying the weed inspector, or straightening out the corners on the Cochrane Hill. We must look on the bright side of things."

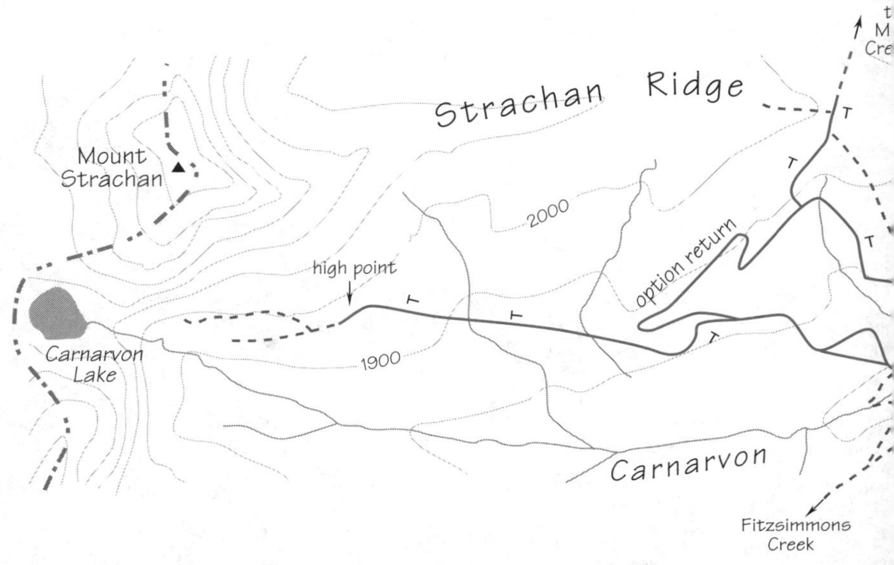

CARNARVON CREEK

Backcountry

Intermediate
Difficult to Strachan Ridge
9 km
15 km from Highwood House
Height gain 472 m
Height gain Strachan Ridge from bench 305 m
Maximum elevation 1966 m, ridge 1951 m
Map 82 J/7 Mount Head

Access Kananaskis Trail (Hwy. 40) at Cat Creek day-use area. Note: the highway is closed between December 1st and June 15.

Facilities Washrooms, picnic tables and shelter at parking lot.

Overview On balance, this is a much more interesting trip than McPhail Creek. It's shorter — accessible in one day from Highwood House if needs be, and has much more interesting hills. Again, you're on logging roads leading to a viewpoint of Carnarvon Lake headwall which looks even more terrifying under snow.

For the first 2.5 km, follow the McPhail Creek trail and procedures as described on page 221. At the second junction after the Highwood River crossing, turn left for Carnarvon Creek.

The new logging road crosses McPhail Creek and rises like a corkscrew to a nice flat bench above Carnarvon Creek. Progress is very pleasant with occasional views of the Strawberry Hills across the creek. Discounting an intermittent cutline going in the same direction as the road, count secondary roads to the right and remember the third one at a bend. It's followed by a slight downhill to an important junction at the 5.5 km mark. Should you go left here and cross Carnarvon Creek, you'll be on the Strawberry Hills Loop described on page 233.

Your road heads right *uphill* and divides almost immediately. Choose the left-hand road if you wish to short-cut. After the roads rejoin, keep left and *descend* to cross a side creek. (You're reserving that uphill road on the right for the descent.)

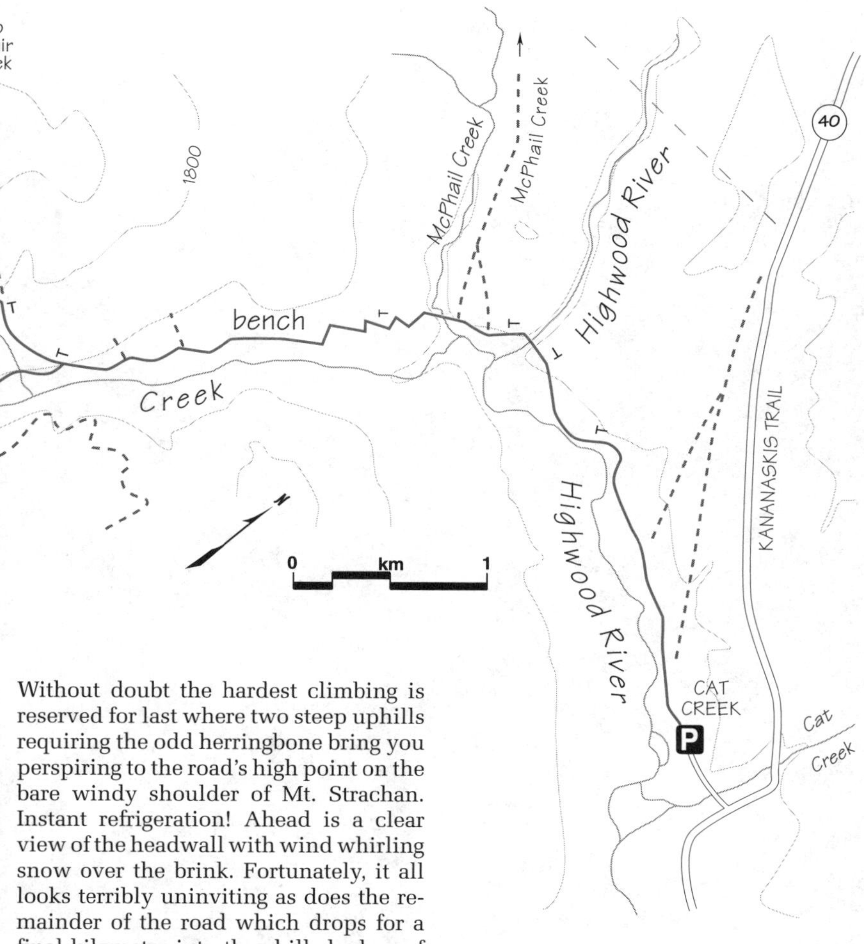

Without doubt the hardest climbing is reserved for last where two steep uphills requiring the odd herringbone bring you perspiring to the road's high point on the bare windy shoulder of Mt. Strachan. Instant refrigeration! Ahead is a clear view of the headwall with wind whirling snow over the brink. Fortunately, it all looks terribly uninviting as does the remainder of the road which drops for a final kilometre into the chill shadow of the cliff wall.

Option Return A decision has to be made. Do you want to deviate? If you do, then turn up the first road to the left (the one after the slight uphill) which winds uphill to the west, then makes a long traverse east to a T-junction with the ruins of two cabins. A right turn assures you of a screaming downhill back to the road on the bench east of the Strawberry Hills turn-off.

Option: to Muir Creek A note for the curious: if you turn left at the T-junction with the two ruined cabins you're on a muscle-aching course for Strachan Ridge. In summer, menziesia bushes between trees discourage random ridge wandering but in winter this is not a problem, neither is the run down the bushy north slope to the Muir Creek road, though locating the road is a bit like finding the proverbial needle in the haystack. See page 222 for a description and map of the route down Muir Creek to McPhail Creek.

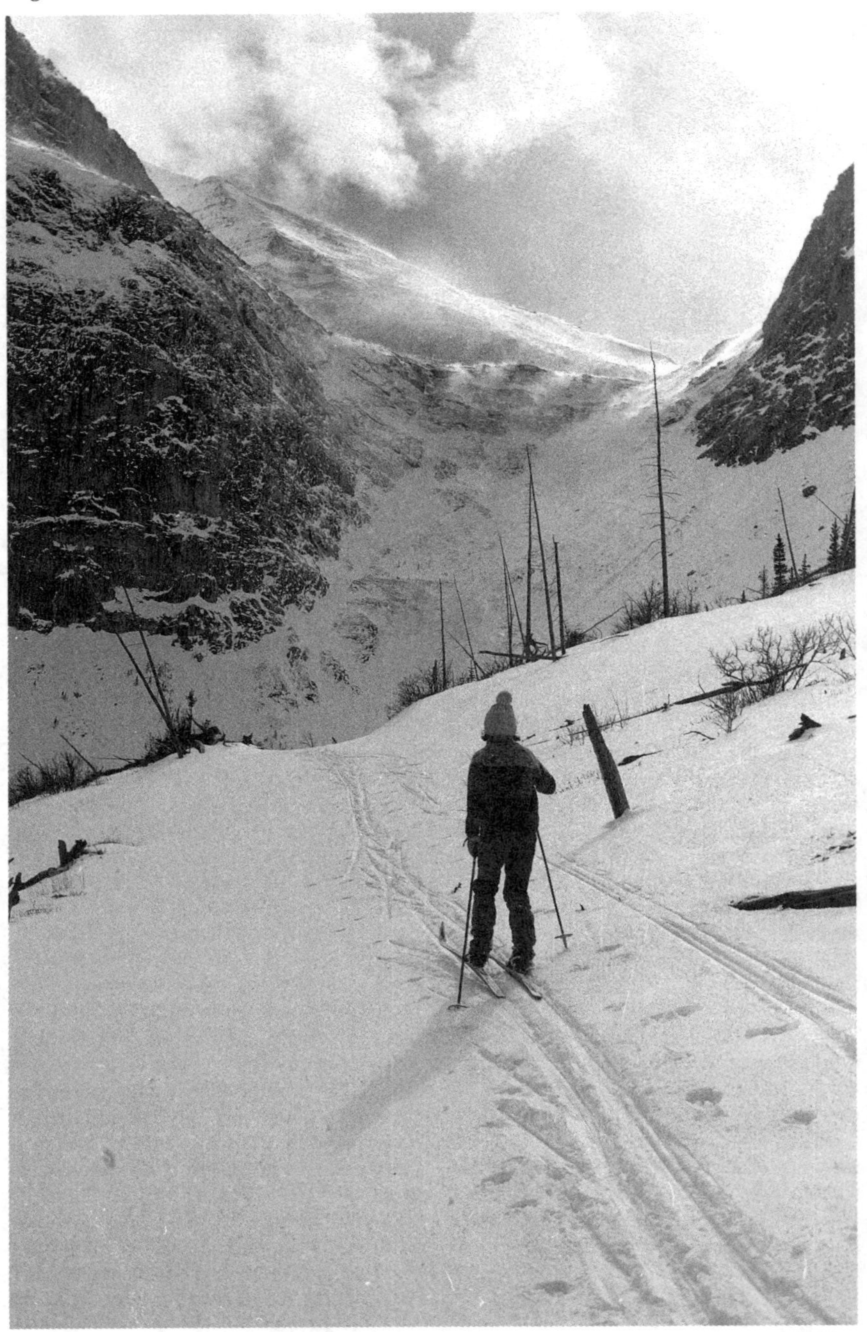

Carnarvon Creek. View from the trail's high point of the headwall guarding Carnarvon Lake.

FITZSIMMONS CREEK

Backcountry

Intermediate
9.3 km from access #1 to pass
10.5 km from access #1 to Baril Creek
11.7 km to Coyote Hills
Add on 2.5 km if starting from access #2 or #3
Height gain to pass 330 m, 427 m to Coyote Hills
Maximum elevation 1845 m at pass
Maximum elevation Coyote Hills 1911 m
Map 82 J/7 Mount Head

Access

1. Kananaskis Trail (Hwy. 40) at Fitzsimmons Creek day-use area. Note: this section of Highway 40 is closed between December 1st and June 15th.
2. Highway 940 about 1.5 km south of Highwood House.
3. Highway 940 at Highwood House.

Facilities Washrooms and picnic tables at Fitzsimmons Creek. If you don't mind sharing the overflow with snowmobilers, Etherington Creek campground up the road from Access #2 is open all winter.

Overview I really enjoy this logging road which makes an attractive route to the Fitzsimmons-Baril watershed. Apart from the obvious trip to the pass and back, there are other options such as making a loop with Baril Creek trail (17.5 km round trip), incorporating the Strawberry Hills Loop (29.2 km round trip), heading off up the Coyote Hills road (23.4 km round trip), or exploring the maze of secondary roads with map, compass and air photo. Let's face it, if Highway 40 was open all winter to Cat Creek from Highwood House, and Highwood House was available for soup and crackers, this end of the Highwood would be buzzing with cross country skiers. Another Mud Lake.

But it's not, and the best shortest access from Fitzsimmons Creek day use area lacks a bridge over the Highwood River. When the river is guaranteed frozen, Highway 40 is closed and unless there's been two weeks of the sub zero you can expect some open water before December 1st when the road closes. Access #2 is a much longer trail, available all winter long, starting from Highway 940 south of Highwood House. A third alternative is to ski up the flats of the Highwood River from behind Highwood House. Clearly, you are faced with Hobson's Choice until December 1st after which all distances become equal.

Start 1. From access #1 cross the Highwood River, then head south-west across open flats (there is a track), aiming for the mouth of Fitzsimmons Creek and a 4-way junction in the trees. Turn right uphill.
Start 2. For 3.5 km ski the trail near the demarcation of forest and beaver ponds. You cross Fitzsimmons Creek, then turn left at a 4-way junction.
Start 3. Ski up flats of the Highwood River to the north bank of Fitzsimmons Creek where you can pick up an old road leading to the 4-way junction in the trees. Carry on up the hill.

From the 4-way junction, four effortless switchbacks bring you to the level of a bench, the start of a scenic traverse between the river in a mini-gorge on the left and the open slopes of the Strawberry Hills on the right. In the spring you may not get any further than this; I know I would be up those grassy slopes like a shot. At 5 km the road dips to cross the north fork, then rises to a junction. In fact, in the space of a kilometre there are three junctions and you keep left at all of them. (Conversely, for Strawberry Hills Loop and Carnarvon Creek turn right every time).

After the last junction you are on a clear course for the pass between Mt. Armstrong and the Coyote Hills. A clearing signals the start of secondary logging roads and skid trails leading off every which way to left and right. Excuse me if I can't fit them all onto one small-scale map. The main road though is obvious, being wide enough to take covered wag-

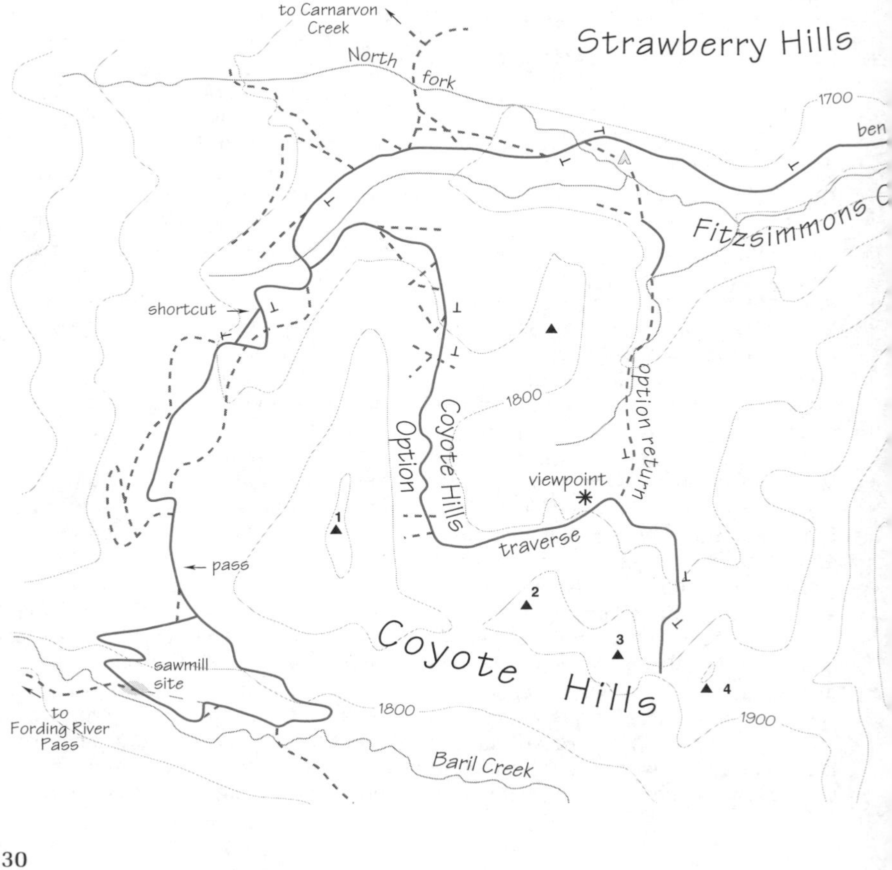

to Carnarvon Creek
Strawberry Hills
North fork
1700
ben
Fitzsimmons C
shortcut
1800
Coyote Hills Option
option return
viewpoint
traverse
1
pass
2
3
4
Coyote Hills
sawmill site
to Fording River Pass
1800
1900
Baril Creek

ons, and kicks off from the clearing with an uphill climb. From the top it's important you curve left, dropping down through some meadows to cross the bridge over Fitzsimmons Creek. After this comes two uphill semicircles, the second of which can be bypassed by a straight short-cut too steep to bother with from this direction. At the high end of the second semicircle a road on the left (the one before the extension to the short-cut) tempts you along the east side of the valley. The main road runs along the west side and in between the two is a longitudinal meadow now hidden from view by a zillion fire succession lodgepoles grown to adolescence. Shortly before the east side trail joins in (difficult to spot),

Opposite: The gentle climb to the Fitzsimmons-Baril watershed. In the background are the Strawberry Hills.

the road kinks left, then resumes its southward direction down the middle of a really wide right-of-way signifying the watershed. For a "boring flat pass in the trees", there's a thrilling view of Mt. Armstrong's eastern escarpment.

Keep left and come to a division of useful roads. Both lead down to Baril Creek; the left-hand to the second creek crossing east of the sawmill site; the right-hand and choice of covered wagons to the third creek crossing west of the sawmill site. Clearly, a finishing loop is possible on the Baril Creek side by combining the two roads and a little bit of Baril Creek trail, and equally clearly, it involves another 80 m height gain to get back up to the pass. If you find yourself hesitating, call it a day by not going and return the same way.

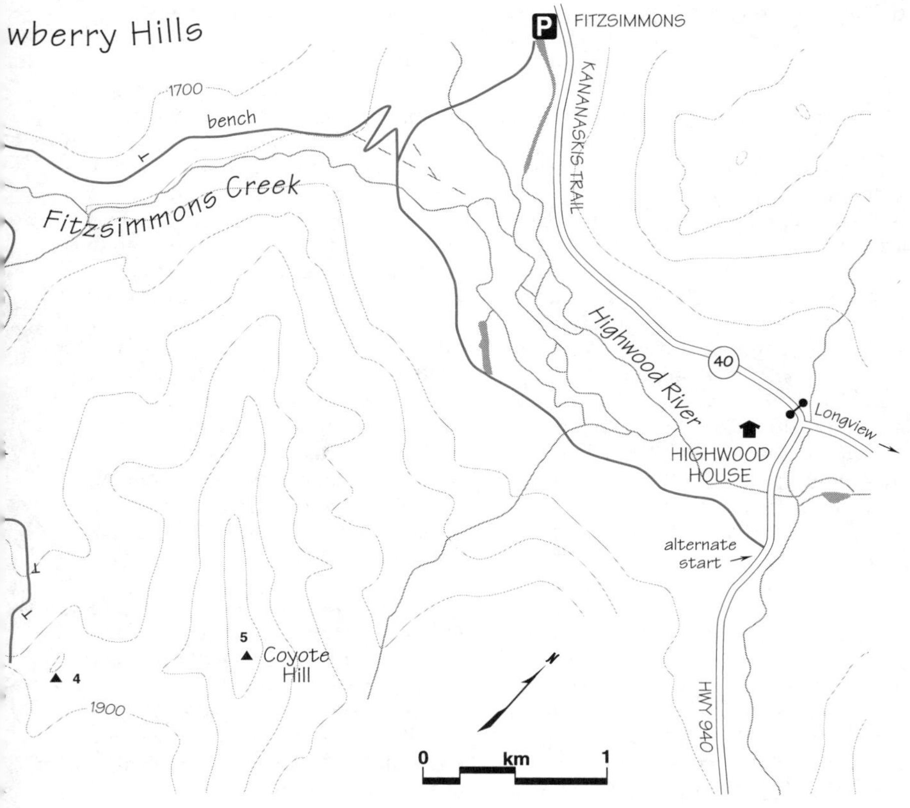

Return You'll be elated by the return run which has a lot more downhills than you might think. Don't forget the short-cut on the first of the semi circles.

Option: Coyote Hills

The Coyote Hills logging road has all the required elements of a great ski trail: hills and flats in the right proportion, a grassy base clear of deadfall and rocks, plentiful snow, a north-facing slope which keeps the snow and one fabulous viewpoint. It just doesn't go anywhere useful. The 1905 m col along the main ridge is totally enclosed in trees though you could, I suppose, flog up one of the little hills on either side for a 360° degree view. No, the real beauty of this trail lies in the getting there, or rather, in the getting back!

Your logging road leaves the left side of Fitzsimmons Creek logging road just after the bridge crossing at the 7 km mark. Initially it heads *wrong-way downstream* then flattens and starts turning right, all around the north end of hill #1 to the start of the long uphill. For the next kilometre the road is obvious, rising majestically through the middle of a mish-mash of secondary roads turning off to right and left. At this point you're in the process of crossing over a low col between hill #1 and an outlier to the north-east.

A gentle downhill and you're into the traverse below hills #2 and #3. It's at the end of this section that you're treated to a grand view of Mts. Armstrong, Strachan, a bit of Muir, the Strawberry Hills (hiding all but the tip of Mist Mountain) and the Highwood Range. Then it's back into the ubiquitous pines for the finale — the steeper climb up to the col between hills # 3 and #4. The way it ends in forest is disappointing, but never mind there is the run back down to look forward to.

Descent short-cut I don't know why I mention this since it robs you of an assured downhill run, but maybe you need to be home early to get changed for the Opera.

On your way back down, turn right at the viewpoint onto a dead-end road heading out along a side ridge. The ridge and road ends soon enough, leaving you with a steep drop down a 50 m-high hillside into a valley, wide, flat and open and no longer holding the Fitzsimmons Creek beaver ponds which, cartographers note, have moved across Fitzsimmons Creek to the north bank. If you follow the left edge of the meadow you automatically hit the narrows where the stream escapes and a few minutes later an old road on the left side of the creek. Follow this road for about half a kilometre before turning off to Fitzsimmons Creek. Hidden under the snow are all kinds of summer trails made by anglers making their way to the mythical beaver ponds, and which converge on the creek just downstream of the confluence with the north fork. Gain Fitzsimmons Creek logging road by plowing up the right side of the north fork for five minutes.

More about the trail It's so refreshing to find a geographical feature named after a person who knew the area and was not a defeated French general or a seaman from a sunken battleship. Charlie Fitzsimmons was actually on the spot as foreman of John Lineham's logging Camp No. 1 on the banks of Fitzsimmons Creek. Known as the "Bible quoting logger", he was born to Irish immigrants at Oak Lake, Manitoba, gave up training in the priesthood and came to Alberta as a woodsman. Don't waste your time looking for remnants of the logging camp; it all disappeared in the 1936 inferno, but basically what happened was that trees felled in winter were stacked up on the river banks ready to be floated down the Highwood in the spring runoff. This is where Charlie gained his reputation, by going out onto dangerous log jams and placing dynamite at exactly the right spot to get things moving again.

Of course, the logging roads you are skiing on date from a much later period. Fifteen years after the Phillips Fire came roaring over Weary Creek Gap, the Stan McLeod Timber Company moved into the area and for 17 years worked systematically down McPhail, Fitzsimmons, Baril and Etherington Creeks, cutting mine props from the burnt timber.

STRAWBERRY HILLS LOOP **Backcountry**

Intermediate
15 km loop only
29.2 km return loop via Fitzsimmons Creek trail from parking lot
28 km return loop via Carnarvon Creek trail from parking lot
8.5 km west leg between Fitzsimmons and Carnarvon Creeks
21.1 km loop via Fitzsimmons Creek, West leg and Carnarvon Creek trails
Height gain loop clockwise 372 m, anti-clockwise 378 m
Height gain west leg 177 m south-north
Maximum elevation 1905 m west pass
Map 82 J/7 Mount Head

Access
1. Kananaskis Trail (Hwy. 40) at Cat Creek day-use area. Via Carnarvon Creek trail (page 226).
2. Kananaskis Trail (Hwy. 40) at Fitzsimmons Creek day-use area. Via Fitzsimmons Creek trail (page 229).
Note that this section of highway is closed between December 1st and June 15th.

Facilities Washrooms and picnic tables at both parking lots.

Overview Popular with mountain bikers and covered wagon drivers, the logging road system around the Strawberry Hills is the Jack of all Trails. And that goes for skiers too. I mean, you can start from either the Carnarvon Creek or the Fitzsimmons Creek end and make the recommended loop around the Strawberry Hills, or use the west leg to make a shorter loop (believe it or not) with Fitzsimmons and Carnarvon Creek trails. South to north is recommended. Or, why not use the loop to access the Strawberry Hills? By late winter when the warming sun and westerly winds uncover the grass, it makes a nice change to combine skiing with a spot of early hiking to the ridge tops.

Accessing the loop
From Carnarvon Creek (1 km)
At the 5.5 km point on the bench you turn left and ski down to Carnarvon Creek. A short curving hill up the south bank brings you to a 4-way junction. The loop is to left and right.

From Fitzsimmons Creek (1.8 km)
After you've passed the 5 km mark on the Fitzsimmons Creek trail where it dips to cross the north fork, turn next right up a long hill. Keep right, then turn right onto a good flat road which re-crosses the north fork higher up. At the following junction you join the loop.

The loop Going anti-clockwise from the Fitzsimmons end, you glide up an easy hill with a terrific view behind of Mt. Armstrong and the headwaters of Fitzsimmons Creek. The left-hand bend is where the energetically inclined can most easily make the recommended hike up the south-east quadrant of the hills. Or, resisting temptation, continue along the road to South pass at a 4-way junction in the trees. The road to left, besides offering an alternate route as shown on the map, goes by way of the col between the two westerly summits. Possibilities here for bagging the two tops en ski. And should you turn left about a third of the way along this road you end up below the south ridge, in a good position to pick off the south summit and schuss down the east face, choosing from *over a dozen* parallel skid trails. Trouble is, all this messing about can occupy the allotted number of daylight hours.

If inclined to wait until the invention of the portable ski lift, continue on the regular road which means turning right at South pass junction and traversing the head of Strawberry Creek, delving in and out of every nook and cranny. You can't see anything of the zebra-striped hillside above or catch even a glimpse of Strawberry Creek until you're about two thirds along. Here the road dips to the creek

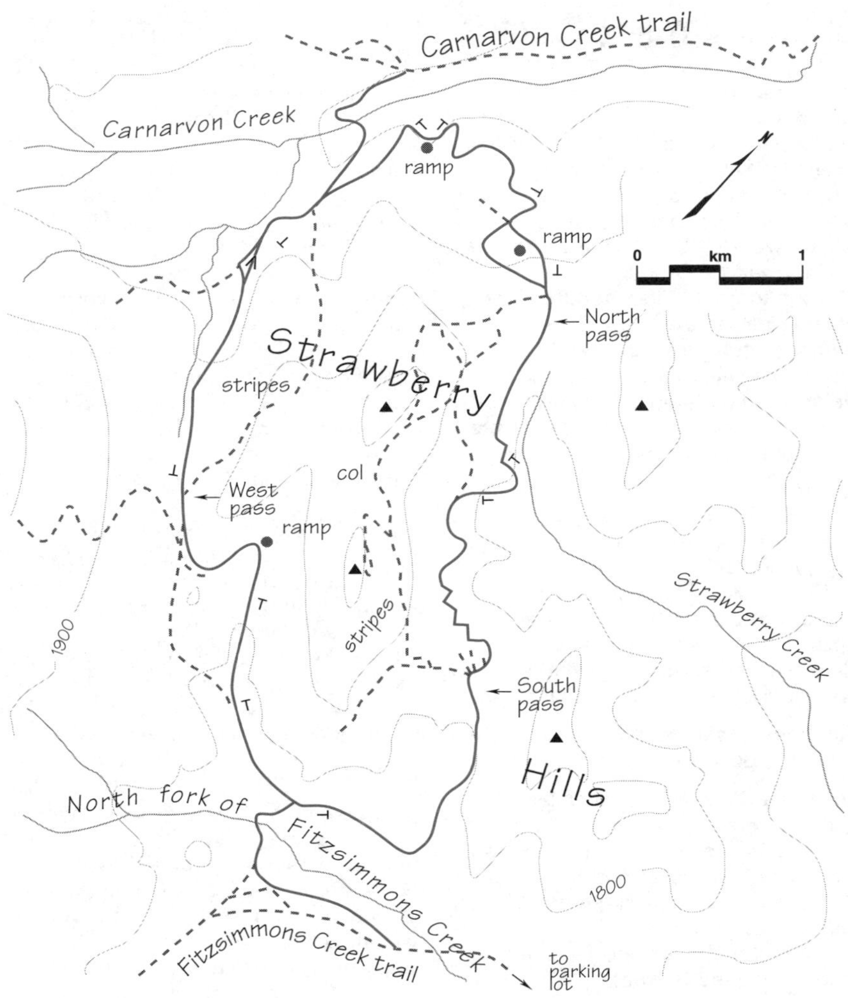

(view of the north-east quadrant of hills), then makes a gradual climb past valley meadows to the North pass.

The descent to Carnarvon Creek is good fun and surprises for the number of meadows allowing views of Mist Mountain and the Highwood Range, and later on Mts. Strachan and Muir. Two confusing spots: the first right off the bat where the "obvious" road to left takes you back to where you started from at South pass. So either head down the second road on the left (gentler) or point your skis straight down the open hillside. The second opportunity for straying occurs at a 4-way junction just after the straight-down skiers have passed the first log loading ramp. Here you turn right. A second ramp marks the road's lowest point and also the place where you turn west and begin a gradual climb to Carnarvon Creek access; another 4-way junction. Ski straight across.

The more-travelled west leg kicks off with bends. At a division go right (short-cut straight on for clockwise skiers only), then, lest you want to explore the upper reaches of Carnarvon Creek, cut back left and settle into a long uphill straight,

View from the south-east hills to the west hills and their maze of logging roads leading to the col. The lowest road is the loop's east leg.

boring unless you're one of the lucky ones travelling in the opposite direction. I believe I counted something in the region of 20 plus skid trails on the uphill slope but unlike their counterparts on the other side of the ridge they don't go anywhere interesting. A steeper than usual incline leads to West pass.

Just the other side of the pass, short-cut left on a road which omits a downhill-uphill combination. However, should you wish to explore the lower slopes of Mt. Armstrong keep straight, then turn right in the dip.

At the rejoining of short-cut and road, you start the second big downhill of the day, following the road as it sweeps to the left — ruins of loading ramp at the inner bend — and on down by the side of Fitzsimmon's north fork. En route, open slopes invite further sorties onto the hills. Should you go, a fabulous view unfolds of the Great Divide sweeping north and south. More than likely BC clouds will be riding up on the backs of the mighty peaks of the High Rock Range, keeping the sun shining on the Strawberry Hills in Alberta. Back on the road, you're only a short distance away from the junction with east leg. Here turn right to cross the north fork and so return the usual way.

BARIL CREEK TO FORDING RIVER PASS

Backcountry & Route

Easy to junction with Fitzsimmons Creek logging roads
Hard intermediate to pass
6 km to first Fitzsimmons Creek logging road, 13 km to Pass,
5.5 km to Aldridge Creek end from pass
Height gain to pass 870 m
Maximum elevation at pass 2368 m
Map 82 J/7 Mount Head

Access

1. Highway 940. Official south bank start. 3.3 km south of Highwood House, park at the side of the highway below an open area. With no trail sign for help, you'll have to search the trees along the right-hand edge of the clearing for the start of the trail.

2. Highway 940. North bank start. About 3 km south of Highwood House park at the side of the highway.

Overview Tedious in summer in its lower part, the Baril Creek trail is a much more interesting trip under snow which hangs around past Easter usually. For a day trip, ski to the sawmill site or better still, make a loop with two roads climbing up to the Baril-Fitzsimmons watershed. If you're set on flogging all the way into Fording River Pass, do yourself a favour and make it a weekend trip *at least*. Three days allows one day thrashing Aldridge Creek headwaters.

To a large extent the route follows a Great Divide Trail access route (logging road) and is marked with pale blue rectangles painted on trees which are winter invisible. Higher up, the winter route (exploration road) crosses sections of the Great Divide Trail itself which is marked with red rectangles meaning "don't follow in winter".

In winter, there is a choice of starts:

Start 1. If you don't mind one extra uphill, then the official summer trail along the south bank is for you. The narrow trail leads in a few moments to a logging road where you turn left, winding up over a ridge and back down to valley bottom where another road — start #2 — comes in from the right across the river.
Start 2. My own preference is for start #2 where you ski along the flat meadows of the north bank to a bend in the creek and pick up the road which crosses the creek and joins the south bank road at its lowest point. Turn right.

One kilometre from the junction of starts you embark upon a long relatively flat stretch where you can really knuckle down, but just make sure you're not making good time down the wrong road. There's more than is shown on the map! When covered by snow, disused roads filling in with miniature pines are indistinguishable from any other road as is the cutline which the road twines about. Well, it gives you something to think about for the next little while because the scenery on either side of forested ridges is not exactly eye-catching.

What happens next is that your road joins a more major logging road come in over the ridge from Etherington Creek. Now you feel you're getting somewhere because in no time at all you're accelerating into Baril Creek and herringboning up the other bank to a junction where the road ahead becomes the east route to Fitzsimmons Creek. You turn left, intersect one road and at the next intersection (ahead is a serpentine cutline) scoot off left down the road which leads alongside the creek to the sawmill site. Just beyond the clearing, the west road to Fitzsimmons Creek turns off to the right.

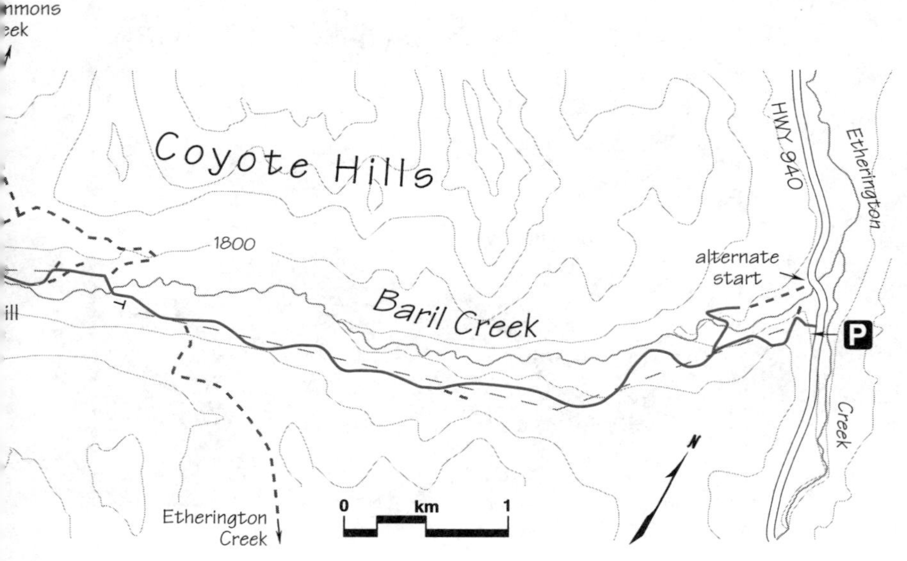

To Fording River Pass

Keep left on the road which crosses Baril Creek. That's the easy part done. Coming up is the first serious climb of the day, an up-down combination with steeper short-cuts to climb over a ridge. Arriving at creek level once again, disregard all the red markers urging you to turn left. Instead, cross the creek on the road which settles into a tedious uphill grind, though I have to admit there's a pleasant section somewhere in the middle where the road winds very prettily through a shallow draw. But then you round a corner and after noting red squares on both sides of the road where the summer trail chickens out on a traverse, find yourself face to face with the crux — a section of grade 7 exploration road requiring heavy duty herringboning and even sidestepping. I defy racers to skate up this one. The wonder is how 4-wheel drive trucks ever managed to get up this hill in the first place. But ultimately you reach the shoulder of Mt. Armstrong where the problem *now* is the sheer abundance of stones combined with a windy corner. The pass is in sight off to the west across a deep shadowy gulf which is the head of the valley and as you jolt your way down to valley bottom take comfort in the fact that down there in the trees await good sheltered camping spots. If you forgot the tent, a log establishment with headroom for two 5 year-olds is available just round the bend and up to the right.

You get no idea from looking at the topo map that the valley head is ringed with cliffs and climbing out of it means another horribly steep hill with the option of an impossibly steep short-cut best reserved for the descent. But with the next zig right you enter open country, a wasteland of wind-crusted snow and bedrock littered with boulders dropped by melting glaciers. Not surprisingly, the marker system breaks down since there are no trees. The road is also lost. Just keep fairly high tucked under Mt. Bolton and keep watch for a wooden triangle marking the top of the pass. Into sight comes a superb view of unnamed BC mountains, while to the south, across the backbone of the pass, is Cornwell Cirque, famed among geologists for its perfect symmetry.

Bedrock and boulders at Fording River Pass.

Boulton-Armstrong Col. Can you spot five skiers? You are looking into the headwaters of Aldridge Creek under Mt. MacLaren, enticingly close but more safely reached by the long route.

Option: Bolton-Armstrong Col
From near Fording River Pass above treeline you simply skirt around the base of Mt. Bolton. It's amazing how much easier this route is in winter when snow covers acres of tiresome scree and levels out the little rockbands.

An ascent of Mt. Bolton via its broad, relatively easy-angled north-east ridge is not out of the question for aficionados. I have never tried it myself, preferring to play about on the gladed slopes of Mt. Armstrong instead.

If camped in the valley head return by following the drainage down to the drop-off, then circle left down to the road.

Option: Aldridge Creek Headwaters
In summer, the cross country skier's Shangri-La is most readily reached from Bolton-Armstrong Col via a steep trail. In winter a problem blows in. To be precise, the wind blowing all the loose snow off the bedrock and dumping it down the north slope from the notch, turning it into one of those dreaded lee slopes you've been warned about by avalanche experts. By the time you've dug a snowpit to assess avalanche conditions and argued the pros and cons, you may as well have skied in the long way round.

This means continuing down the road from the pass into British Columbia (300 m height loss), then turning right onto the Aldridge Creek road which brings you easily and safely into the upper valley (height gain as much as 350 m).

ZEPHYR CREEK PICTOGRAPHS — Backcountry

Easy
4.5 km
Height gain 195 m
Maximum elevation 1643 m
Map 82 J/7 Mount Head

Access Highwood Trail (SR 541) at Sentinel day-use area. If the gate is not locked, turn into the left-hand parking lot. Otherwise, park on the shoulder of the highway.

Facilities Washrooms at parking lot.

Overview An easy, educational trip for the whole family with a destination: the Indian rock paintings in Painted Canyon no less.

From the parking lot head for the Highwood River and turn left. Just upstream of Zephyr Creek effluence you intersect a logging road, follow it up the right bank to a T-junction, then turn right onto a new road which apparently ends in the large meadow below the north ridge of Mt. Burke. Which way?

For Zephyr you wind around the left-hand perimeter of the meadow into the left-hand valley where the road becomes perfectly obvious once you're in the trees. From here on, everything is straightforward; a flat road plod by the side of the creek.

When opposite the first side creek to the left, leave the road (a cairn may be visible) and ski along Painted Creek into the canyon which is heavily into white rock. At the second narrowing, just before the valley opens up, look for rock paintings about one metre up from the ground on the overhanging yellow wall to your left. In 1975 part of this wall collapsed, destroying six of the eight paintings which lie in fragments under the snow, a jigsaw which can never be put together again. All that remains is a stick figure of a man closely pursued by an unidentifiable large animal with erect ears and a long tail, half a bird trailing feathers which lies about half a metre to the right and higher up the wall some tally marks, long vertical finger-width lines which presumably have some significance though to me they look as if the artist, work done, was merely wiping his fingers on the rock to get rid of the last of the red ochre.

Higher up the ridge are more pictographs and petroglyphs only viewable by means of a steep scramble and best left for a fall trip.

Return A gentle downhill glide.

More about the trail The art work is relatively recent. Archeologists believe the artists were neither Stoneys nor supernatural beings but were probably Kootenai Indians who lived near here on the fringe of the prairies some 300 years ago before the Stoneys arrived and that the paintings were the successful conclusion of a Vision Quest Ceremony which would explain the isolated location of the site well away from known camp sites and the major trail along the Highwood River. The abstracts are apparently characteristic of Columbia Plateau art.

Let's get this right. Petroglyphs are carvings in rock, while pictographs are drawings or paintings on rock. Painted Canyon has both, in two different places, hence the awful confusion by visitors, even by Stoneys whohave visited the site and left offerings of cloth and tobacco. Daniel Wildman Jr. in a letter written in 1923 explains, "in the Spring you see on the rock pictures of Tipis, pictures of people hunting the buffalo, with their war bonnets on. The next time you will visit the spot the pictures are all changed, all different. It is a house with a ball on top, or a man walking followed by many dogs, or again the full moon. Next time, all the paint is changed, somebody is shown going up the mountains to hunt animals, to hunt bear, goat, sheep and jumping deer. Next time it will be a picture of a moose. At other times it is a moon with seven horizontal lines under the moon". I'm sure the recipient of the letter, ethnographer Marius Barbeau, said "thank you very much!". But wait. There was a new development. Councillor of the Bears Paw Band James Rider added, "a year last summer (I) went to the rock. The pictures I had seen there before had moved up higher. That is the third time they had moved up to my knowledge." He claimed that "a great number of people have seen the paintings. Some have made fun of them; that is why they have moved up on the stone wall".

So when you visit, please go in a respectful frame of mind.

Lower pictographs. Stick figure of a man pursued by a large unidentifiable animal.

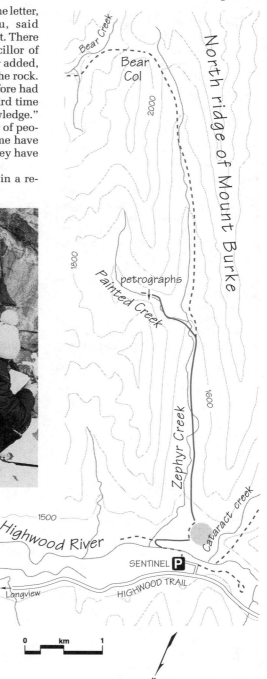

Bear Creek
Bear Col
North ridge of Mount Burke
2000
1800
petrographs
Painted Creek
1600
Zephyr Creek
Cataract creek
1500
Highwood River
SENTINEL P
HIGHWOOD TRAIL
Longview
0 km 1
N

SANDY MCNABB SKI TRAILS — Groomed

37.2 km of trails
Maximum elevation 1640 m
Map 82 J/10 Mount Rae

Access Sheep River Trail (SR 546). Two starting points:
1. Sandy McNabb winter campground parking lot.
2. Sheep River Visitor Information Centre at Long Prairie Creek.

Facilities
1. Washrooms at parking lot. Sandy McNabb equestrian campground doubles as a winter campground. The group campground, located half-way down the access road on the left, is opened on request by writing Joe Burritt, c/o Elbow Ranger Station, Bag #1, Bragg Creek, T0L 0K0. Winter picnickers should head for summer's group campground at the end of the plowed access road.
2. The Information Centre is open on weekends for information and advice when conditions are favourable for skiing.

Overview Perhaps you are one of those people who have a preconceived idea about these trails beings boring. OK, so they don't have as many hills as West Bragg. But when conditions are optimum, skiing at Sandy McNabb is an absolute delight, the way the trails wind about aspen woodlands, along valley bottoms and up to viewpoints on the ridge tops. It's an excellent beginner's area, the best there is, and because most of the trails are old logging and exploration roads you can expect the regulation 4 m-width for side by side chatting. Junctions are signposted and sections graded easy, intermediate or difficult.

Loops can be combined in various ways to make trips lasting anything from half an hour to all day if you take the perimeter trail of 21 km and stop at all the viewpoints for a sunbathe. This touches on the problem with Sandy McNabb — sun *and* Chinook winds. It's rather like West Bragg in this respect only worse because the prevailing aspens don't make very good sun breaks or wind breaks. And since it also lies in a naturally low snowfall area you have to pick your days carefully. Why not check trail conditions before you go by phoning the Visitor Information Centre at 933-7172.

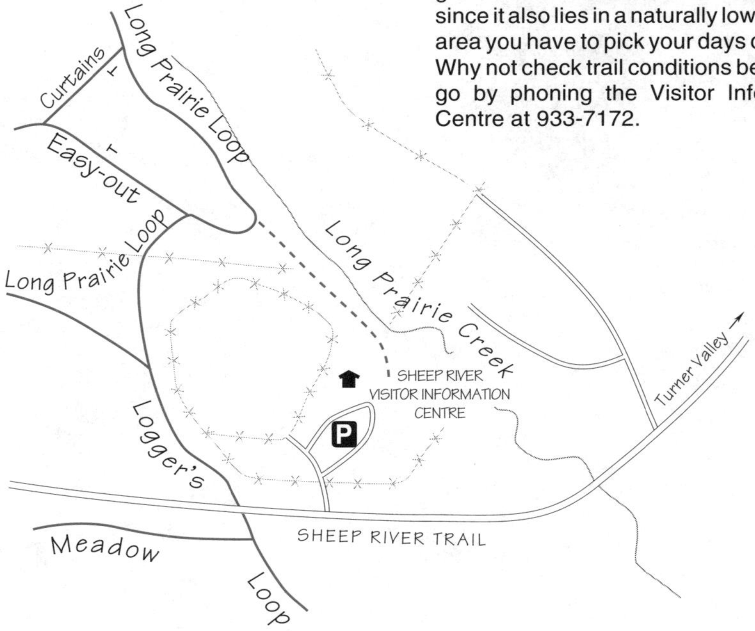

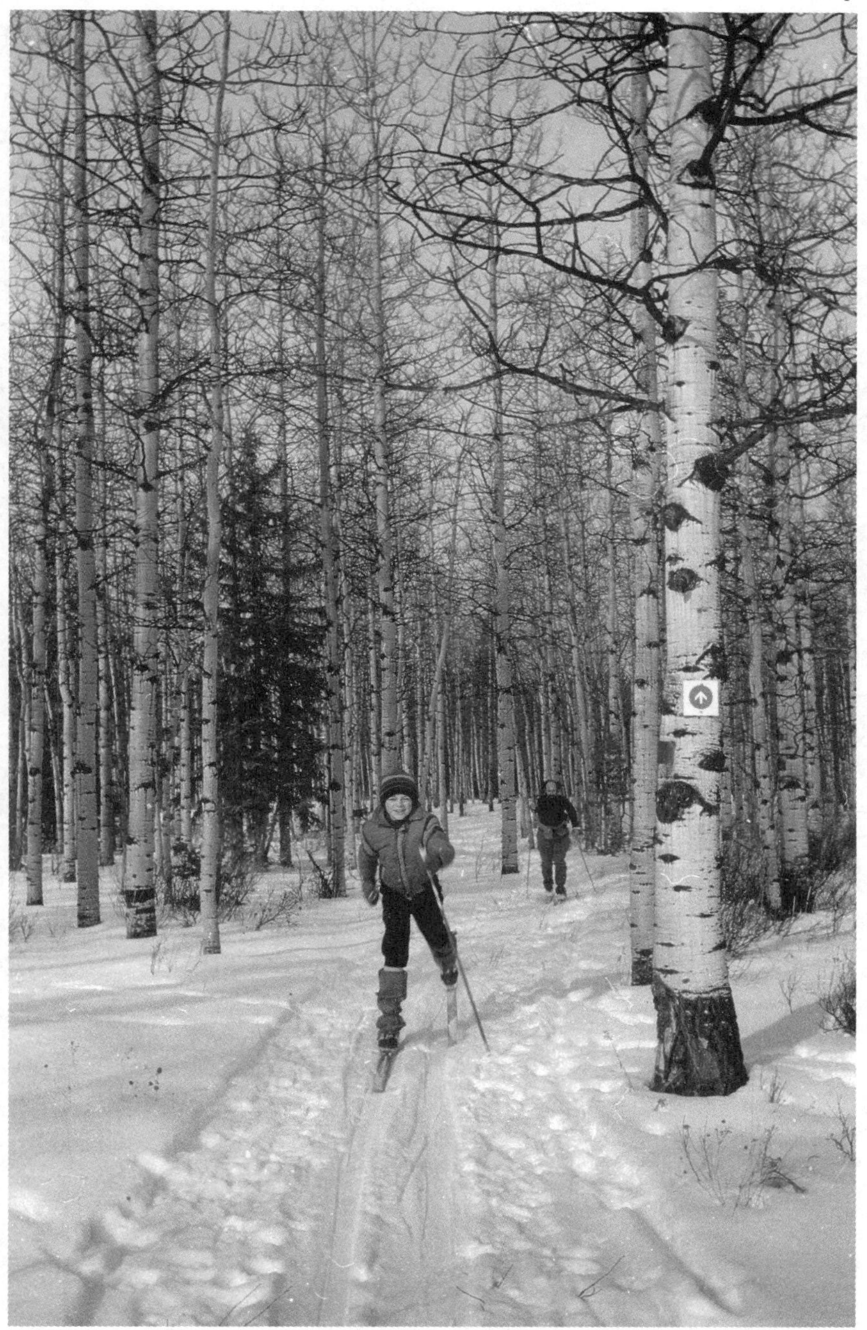

Skiing between the aspens on Sandy McNabb loop.

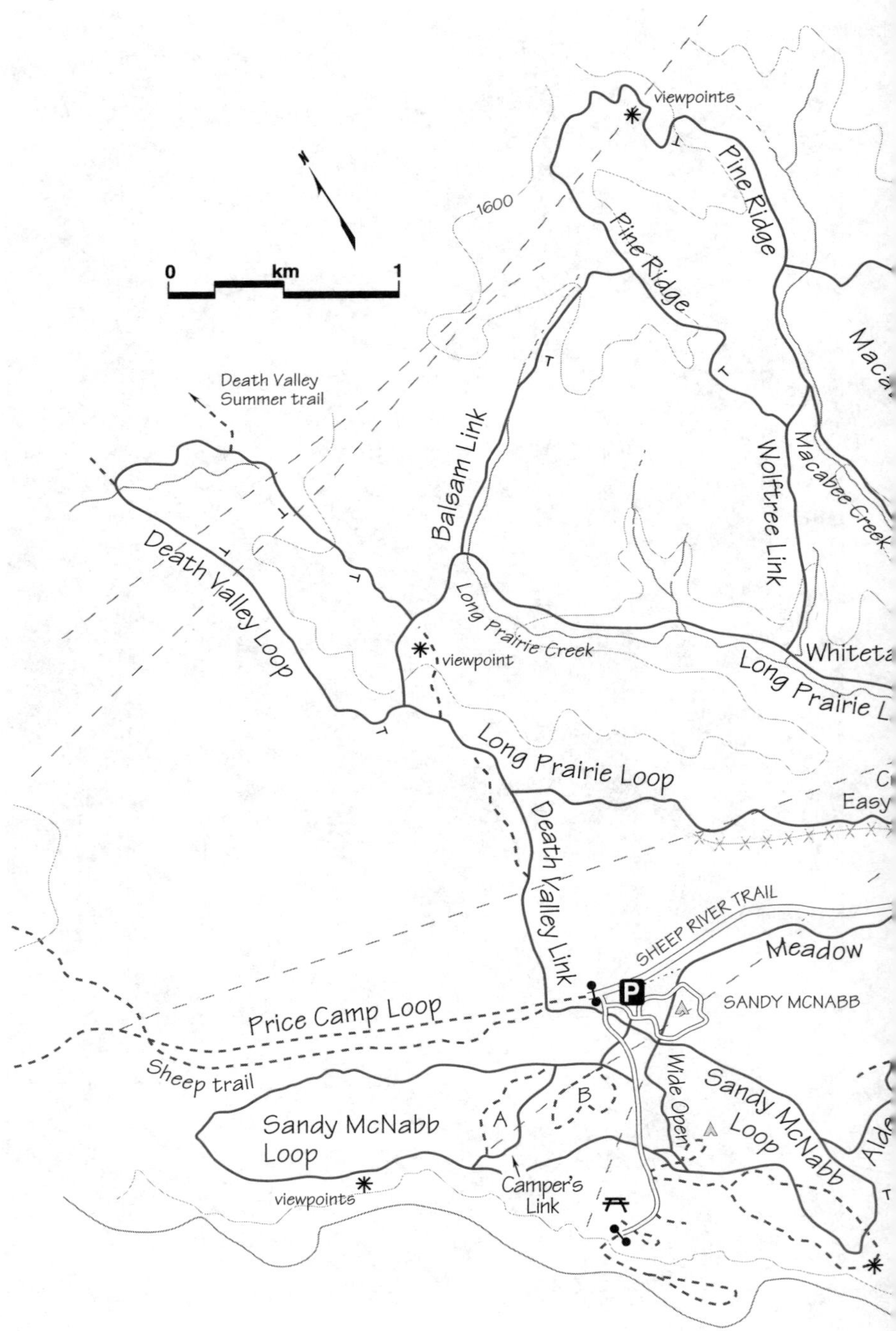
viewpoints
Pine Ridge
1600
0
km
1
Pine Ridge
Maca
Death Valley
Summer trail
Balsam Link
Wolftree Link
Macabee Creek
Death Valley Loop
Long Prairie Creek
viewpoint
Whiteta
Long Prairie L
Long Prairie Loop
Easy
Death Valley Link
SHEEP RIVER TRAIL
Meadow
SANDY MCNABB
Price Camp Loop
Sheep trail
Wide Open
Sandy McNabb Loop
B
A
Sandy McNabb
Loop
Alde
Camper's
Link
viewpoints

Pine Ridge
Macabee Loop
Wolftree Link
Macabee Creek
1500
Turner Valley
5
Macabee Loop
Whitetail
Long Prairie Loop
Arctic Hill
view
Arctic Hill
1500
Curtains
Easy-out
SHEEP RIVER VISITOR INFORMATION CENTRE
Long Prairie Creek
P
Meadow
Sink Hole
SANDY MCNABB
Loop
Chain-up
Logger's
Sandy McNabb Loop
Alder
1500
1400
viewpoint & seats
Sheep River

LONG PRAIRIE LOOP

Easy intermediate
5.5 km

Technically, this trail starts at the signpost in the ditch almost opposite the access road to Sheep River Visitor Information Centre. However, the ranger won't ball your head off if you slip behind the building and cut up Long Prairie Creek to hit the trail near Easy Out. Going clockwise, you follow the flat west leg below aspen hillsides past the junction with Death Valley Link to an open hillside on your right. This is where the red-triangled summer trail to Death Valley takes off, but because it's likely to be denuded of snow, being south-west facing, turn right at the following junction and climb through trees to a crossroads on a ridge top. As advertised in the brochure, a view of sorts is available — if you focus carefully between the branches. I recommend backtracking on the summer trail for a few metres to the top of the meadow for a superb uncluttered view of Junction Mountain Lookout, and all the unnamed summits of the Highwood Range.

Going east now, descend the far side of the ridge into Long Prairie Creek which returns you to the Visitor Centre. As you glide down pastoral meadows between occasional aspen clumps look for one tree in particular carved with the words "Nov 1919, fine day, lots of grass, R.L Carry" (I have to admit I've not found it yet.) Another interesting aspect of this valley, given it's a nice sunny day, are the number of deer mice running around, diving into and out of snow tunnels.

CURTAINS

Hard intermediate
0.3 km

An even steeper short-cut between the west and east legs of Long Prairie Creek which may not be groomed. Who cares; it's all over in 20 seconds.

EASY-OUT

Intermediate
0.3 km

Easy-out offers a more hilly link between the two legs of Long Prairie Loop.

DEATH VALLEY LOOP

Intermediate
3.5 km
Height gain 91 m

This is the only trail which takes you over the watershed into Death Valley — albeit briefly. If not too sure of your proficiency, ski the trail in a clockwise direction so as to take advantage of the 4 m-wide exploration road north of the reclaimed meadow on the west leg where one of two steep downhills is located. The other hill occurs at the south end of east leg which is tight, twisting, rooty and ultimately rocky, following in part the summer hiking trail into Death Valley. Taken in the downhill counterclockwise direction, this hill is technically the most difficult in all the trail system.

Of course it's up to you, but rangers ask you not to extend the trip further into Death Valley but to let the valley's considerable population of ungulates and feral horses do their annual survival course unimpeded by human beings rushing around on boards.

DEATH VALLEY LINK

Easy
1 km

A flat trail winding through mixed forest which connects Sandy McNabb parking lot and all trails south of the highway to trails north of the highway. That K-Country brochure writers are worried sick about skiers ending up under a car for failing to look both ways when crossing roads is well-known, but it would now seem to include roads *closed* to traffic. Whoops!

ARCTIC HILL
Intermediate
1.2 km
Height gain 76 m

Named after a section of the original highway below the hill which still tends to slipperiness when the rest of the asphalt is dry, Arctic Hill should only be skied in the west to east direction. This way, after admiring the view of the Front Ranges from the ridge, you get to enjoy the long run down the cold north slope which holds the snow well and has a little surprise in store — a sharp left-hand bend near the bottom of the hill. Don't say I didn't warn you!

WHITETAIL
Easy
0.3 km

Whitetail offers the shortest and easiest access from Long Prairie Loop into Macabee Loop.

WOLFTREE LINK
Easy
0.9 km

Named after "large full-branched spruce trees", Wolftree follows an aspen draw to a junction with Pine Ridge west leg in 0.8 km, then continues for another 100 m (one short downhill) into Macabee Creek drainage where it arrives at a second junction with Pine Ridge and Macabee Loop trails.

BALSAM LINK
Intermediate
1.6 km
Height gain 91 m

Initially, the trail follows the west bank of Long Prairie Creek through open woods of aspens and balsam poplars well-gnawed by elk and moose, then crosses the creek and climbs a good deal more steeply onto the ridge top where it joins Pine Ridge in lodgepole pine forest.

MACABEE LOOP
Easy
3.9 km

A very pleasant circuit which I like to ski in clockwise direction in order to reserve east-facing snow for the downhills. Actually, the whole of the east fork of Macabee Creek holds the snow pretty well. Conversely, the western leg which travels along the bottom of open slopes and aspen forests in Macabee Creek tends to suffer from Chinooks. Though officially named after the McAbee family of four brothers and two sisters who came to the area in 1887, the creek has also been known as Yeskey or Teskey Creek.

PINE RIDGE
Intermediate
3.5 km
Height gain 113 m anti-clockwise
Maximum elevation 1640 m

The loop climbs to two fine viewpoints looking north-east towards Calgary on a ridge top which at 1640 m is the highest point in the trail system. Steep hills are encountered between Wolftree and Balsam Link, and between Macabee Loop and the summit. Again, you're better off to ski the loop in a clockwise direction so to keep better snow conditions for the downhills.

LOGGER'S LOOP
Easy
6 km

An excellent trail for beginners, following flat logging roads past two clearings logged in the late 1960's and early 1970's to make fence posts. The two arms of the logging road are connected in the middle by a narrower trail winding about the base of two densely-wooded hills and this is where you'll find the best snow. The only hill of any consequence occurs at the east end of the south leg with a run down to Alder junction.

MEADOW TRAIL

Easy
1.4 km

When not following powerlines, Meadow runs along the south side of SR 546 in the ditch (meadow). Connects the Visitor Centre to Sandy McNabb parking lot.

WIDE OPEN

Easy intermediate
0.4 km

This trail bisects Sandy McNabb Loop just to the east of the day use area access road. A good downhill run when skied in the north-south direction.

CAMPERS LINK

Easy
0.4 km

A short-cut which utilizes the east leg of loop A campground road

CHAIN-UP

Easy
0.5 km

A wide flat trail which bisects Logger's Loop. Boggy ground underfoot made chains a necessity for logging trucks.

SINK HOLE

Easy
0.2 km

At the south end and half-way along the trail are large holes in the ground called kettles which were likely formed by melting glacial ice blocks. In summer all you see are two perfectly round black ponds.

ALDER

Easy
0.6 km

This useful little connector joins Logger's Loop with Sandy McNabb Loop via Tussock Pond.

SANDY MCNABB LOOP

Easy with one intermediate hill
5.7 km

A complicated trail which starts behind the trail sign in the Sandy McNabb parking lot, then immediately divides. If you head left (recommended direction) you follow an old river terrace to Alder, then gradually increase speed down a hill with two short intermediate pitches to a lower terrace where you intersect the summer interpretive trail. Unlike what most people think, the interpretive trail is never followed, so to reach the viewpoint with seats and interpretive signs # 7, 8 and 9 you must detour a little to the edge of the former river bank. It's an interesting view across the Sheep River to Coal Creek and Mt. McNabb.

The trail now doubles back through the heart of a bog (summer paddling trail), intersects the interpretive trail at sign #4, then splits to cross the group campground access road on either side of the gate before arriving at the bottom of Wide Open. Go left to cross the day-use access road.

What follows is more bank top meandering past more viewpoints before you circle around to the campground access road opposite loop A. Opposite loop B the trail takes off uphill to the parking lot, recrossing the day-use access road en route. If you're one of those people who finds it irritating to have to take your skis off and put them on again only ten seconds later *twice* in one ski trail, then consider combining the east leg with Wide Open. Personally, I am not above tiptoeing across the asphalt as long as the road is narrow enough, but then I don't have skis worth 500 dollars. Also I wouldn't advocate this method for a wide strip like Highway 40.

Photo opposite: Pine Ridge viewpoint looking north-east over the prairies.

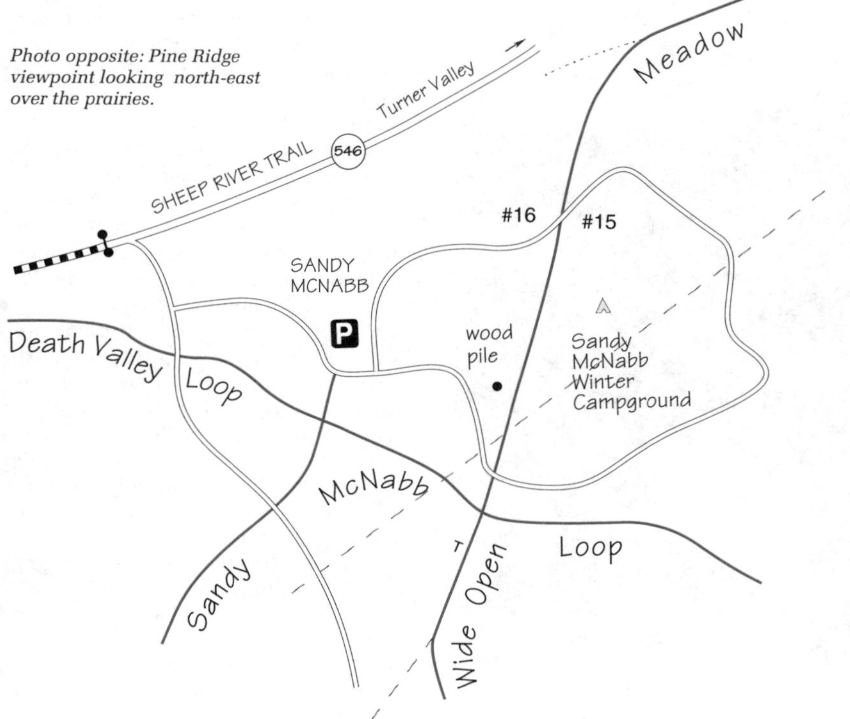

More about the trails You won't win a free copy of the guidebook by deducing that Alexander "Sandy" McNabb was a Scottish immigrant. He and his brothers settled in the Turner Valley area during the oil boom years of 1913-14 to work for Royalite Oil Company and it was on his days off that Sandy would go fishing at his favourite spot on the Sheep River below the day-use area. This is not the reason why the recreation area, campground, ski trail network, ski trail, hiking trail and a mountain are all named after him otherwise we'd have every picnic spot in the area named after Joe Bloggs. No, you have to earn the right and in Sandy's case, since he was largely instrumental in founding Turner Valley's Fish and Game Association, association members called the old fishing spot Sandy McNabb's Camp and the name just mushroomed from there.

Like West Bragg, oil rigs moved into the area not long after the road was built. For instance, Long Prairie Creek near the Visitor Information Centre was the site of Paramount Oil Company's No. 1 well in the late 1920's. So far I haven't been able to locate the cellar built into the creek bank, perhaps because it's been demolished. And there was also a rig near the top of Arctic Hill which was definitely removed in 1933.

Unlike West Bragg, none of the trails result from heavy duty logging. Logger's and Chain-up for instance date from thinning operations during the late 1950's, 1960's and early 1970's which make a lot of sense to anyone who's ever had to bushwhack through a matchstick forest without a suit of armour. In this case, I believe the fledgling pines were turned into fence posts. The rest of the trails are either improved rangerider-cow trails (grazing leases originated in 1914), campground roads or exploration roads which is not to say they haven't had a logging truck running along them now and then and here I'm thinking specifically of recent cutblocks along the west leg of Death Valley Loop.

Gone are the days when logging was logging. Now there are such things as computer simulations, sensitivity ratings and visual impact assessments examining angle of view or screening of view, though in my experience some logging companies need a slap on the wrist for not keeping to guidelines set out by Alberta Forestry, Lands and Wildlife and for doing things like logging down to creekbeds. In the case of Death Valley Loop cutblocks I didn't notice whether the edges were feathered or undulating, and I forgot to ask Leonard whether this was thinning logging (definitely not), sanitation logging (probably not) or landscape logging (possibly). I will hazard a guess at wildlife enhancement logging for all that wildlife in Death Valley.

Sandy McNabb. One of the many fine views across the Sheep River valley.

PRICE CAMP LOOP

Backcountry

Intermediate
11 km loop
14.7 km Foran Ridge return
Height gain 229 m, Foran Ridge return 442 m
Maximum elevation 1509 m, Foran Ridge 1676 m
Map 82 J/10 Mount Rae

Access Sheep River Trail (SR 546) at Sandy McNabb Recreation Area.

Facilities Washrooms at parking lot. Sandy McNabb equestrian campground doubles as a winter campground. The group campground, located half-way down the access road on the left, is opened on request by writing Joe Burritt, c/o Elbow Ranger Station, Bag #1, Bragg Creek, T0L 0K0. Winter picnickers should head for summer's group campground at the end of the plowed access road.

Overview Though I prefer summer — I miss flowers, the colour of lakes, the flow of water, the infinite variety of vegetation, I have to concede that winter brings one or two advantages. For instance, river crossings are a doddle. And this loop, though it follows official equestrian trails with signs at junctions and red triangles on trees and posts, is not easily available to the hiker because of two crossings of the Sheep River.

An important tidbit comes from Leonard Kennedy of Turner Valley Ranger Station who tells me the Sheep River is susceptible to ice jams upstream in the gorge which means that sudden releases of water could conceivably leave you stranded on the south bank.

From the parking lot you have to get down the hill to the Sheep River. The quickest route is via Wide Open to Sandy McNabb at the group campground access road, then alongside the access road (equestrian trail under snow) to the winter gate. Transfer to the access road and just after the bend drop down to the river at the red markers. Unlike Wolf Creek, you cross the Sheep upstream (right of) Coal Creek effluent where you'll pick up an old road. Keep right.

You are now following the Mount McNabb equestrian trail which soon narrows to trail width, and parallelling the river, climbs gradually onto a higher terrace with aspens. After 3 km of pleasant skiing with occasional views of the gorge below, you arrive at the junction with Price Camp trail. Here, Mount McNabb trail turns left up a hill, an option I can't recommend unless 50 centimetres of snow has fallen the night before.

So at the trail junction you go straight on a new trail which moves away from the river into pine forest, crosses a NE-SW cutline, then crosses March Creek which is followed upstream to a very large meadow with the ruins of two buildings — all that's left of Mr. Price's logging camp. Outcropping planks are a great incentive to fish out the sandwiches.

Carrying on, you make a right-angled turn to the right (north) and hurtle down a steep hill past an intersection with another NE-SW cutline to a T-junction with Sheep trail at a signpost. Turning right, you parallel the cutline, then join it for short downhill stint before wandering off rightwards and recrossing the original cutline. From the site of John Lineham's lower logging camp the trail descends to the one spot where the black shale walls of the canyon collapse into trees, enabling you to cross the river and wind up the opposite bank to Highway 546 without scaring yourself silly. Ironically, the best view of the day is from the roadside viewpoint at Windy Point.

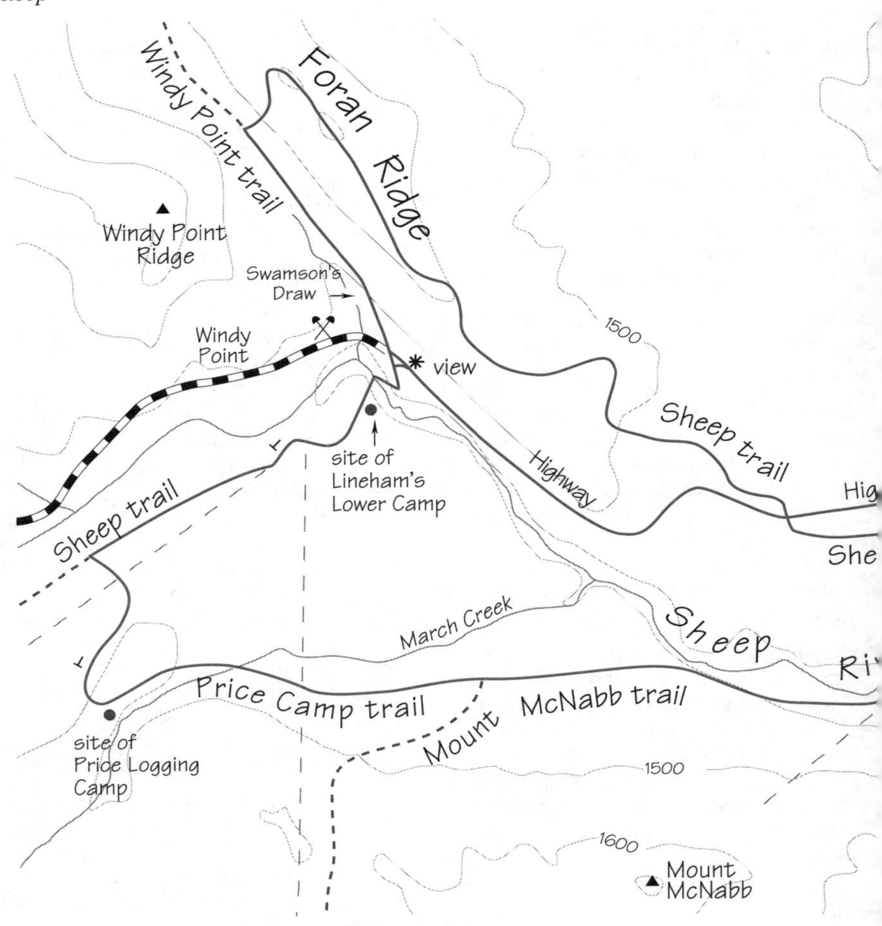

There's a choice of routes for the last leg to Sandy McNabb Recreation Area. Obviously it's faster, easier and more boring to ski along the unplowed highway for 4 km. After 2.3 km you have the option of transferring onto the more aesthetic Sheep trail.

Another suggestion, snow willing, is to turn up Windy Point/Sheep trail which climbs Swamson's draw between Foran Ridge on the right and Windy Point Ridge on the left. When you reach the pass between the two at a signpost, turn right onto Sheep trail. Of course you can't spot the trail since every little aspen clone has been yanked out and the slope kept spotlessly open for the benefit of wildlife, but just aim up and left for the top of Foran Ridge. (En route, don't be surprised to find your priority shifting from rushing home to watch the hockey game on TV to playing about in the snow.) Once on top you should be able to pick up the trail again in the pines and follow it down the SSE rib — good views lower down — to the highway where you can either transfer onto the road or continue along Sheep trail which runs parallel. Whatever, the last stretch into the parking lot is via Death Valley Link.

More about the trails I wish I could tell you something about Mr. Price's logging camp but my information is limited to the fact that it operated in 1936 when there was a resurgence in logging in the area. I can only conclude, therefore, that the photo I have in my possession taken in 1911 showing two bunkhouses with pole roofs dates back to John Lineham's time and could be a photo of Lineham's Lower Camp near the Sheep River. The pole roofs are interesting. Apparently, roof lumber was so scarce it was moved around with the logging camps which of course explains why you keep coming across so many roofless old cabins. But I digress. Going back to John Lineham, he opened up a sawmill at Okotoks in 1891 (Okotoks' main industry for the next 25 years) and started logging up and down the Sheep River. Like today, logging took place in winter when the river was frozen, the logs piled up on the banks of the Sheep waiting for spring runoff when they could be floated down river to Okotoks. An imposing figure of a man, Lineham was 6 ft. 9 inches tall, weighed 325 lbs, and was so superstitious he would never start a new job on a Friday. You can read all about him during a summer walk around Junction Creek interpretive trail.

Unfortunately, no such interpretive signs are available to go with the viewpoint at Windy Point on Highway 546. In the trail guide I made an incredibly stupid error by spelling the section of road to the east and the ridge above FOREIGN. They are of course named after Bill FORAN who was not only a foreman of lumber camps but also a foreman of road building since most of the roads in those days were built by the logging companies. To the west is Windy Point proper where logger and former miner Bill Iceton blasted a single file road out of the hillside — the bane of Model T Fords when Chinook winds spread layers of ice all over the road in winter. Even with precut ruts many passengers elected to get out and walk.

In between the Foran and Iceton sections of road is Windy Point Creek or Swamson's Draw utilised by Windy Point/Sheep trails and which lies smack on a thin ribbon of coal running south to the mouth of Coal Creek where Dave Blacklock had a small mine going in 1916. Pre the 1920's this spot was known as Franks' Cabin, Frank being Frank Swamson who held a coal lease on 1280 acres hereabouts. It's worth examining the rock face left of the draw where a few wooden stakes protruding from the rubble pinpoint a 30 m-long shaft. Apparently, the coal was a slack brown lignite which burned well enough but gave out no heat so nothing ever came of it. It's interesting to learn that the infamous Julius Rickert took up the lease in 1920.

WOLF CREEK

Backcountry

Intermediate
8.6 km to viewpoint
Height gain 335 m
Maximum elevation 1661 m
Map 82 J/10 Mount Rae

Access Sheep River Trail (SR 546) at Sandy McNabb Recreation Area. Drive down the day-use area access road which is usually plowed to the winter picnic site, two terraces up from the Sheep River. Park on the road at the winter gate.

Facilities Washrooms at Sandy McNabb parking lot. Sandy McNabb equestrian campground doubles as a winter campground. The group campground, located half-way down the access road on the left, is opened on request by writing Joe Burritt, c/o Elbow Ranger Station, Bag #1, Bragg Creek, T0L 0K0. Winter picnickers should head for summer's group campground at the end of the plowed access road.

Overview Expect a day of conflicting emotions; elation at the plentiful snow, frustration at the lack of it, complacency at the easy trail, shock at several steep hills misplaced from the Canmore Nordic Centre. One thing you *can* say with certainty; this trail has an extraordinary viewpoint at the end of it.

The exploration road makes a good getaway for people fed up with crowds on groomed trails, though you may run into the local trapper on his way over to upper Coal Creek on a snowmobile. Since the route is an official hiking and equestrian trail, red triangles mark the way as well as occasional snowmobile tracks.

From the gate, ski down the last zig of the access road to the lowest terrace above the Sheep River, but just before the road completely flattens, cut down right to the Sheep River. Now in summer the Wolf Creek trail on the other bank starts from the mouth of Coal Creek, but in winter there are no such constraints like finding the easiest fording place and you can slip across the Sheep River anywhere and pick up Wolf Creek trail further to the east.

Straight off there's a steep little climb to the second terrace, but after this the road settles down and winds easily uphill for 2 km, passing through a gate into a huge meadow which has had the snow removed as well as the aspens. A fallen tree tempts a rest stop or turnaround point for half-day trippers who could consider climbing up the bare hill to the left. Up ahead, Blue Ridge gives you some idea of how far you have to go to a destination located 2 km *beyond* the ridge.

Continue around the left side of the meadow and back into the trees above Wolf Creek. Choose from either the road or the red-triangled summer trail nearer to the creek bank. Suddenly the friendly profiles of ridges are no longer off to the west; you are coming in amongst them and with them comes increasing potential for straying. You won't be the first or the last person to ski merrily up the west fork which is as deep and as wide as the main creek. Just remember when standing dithering on the bank top to keep left on the road which *drops* to the creek bottom, then climbs up a nasty steep hill. This hiatus is followed by a pleasant stretch along a bench to trouble spot number two — a T-junction where you join a cutline. Go right.

Zip along the cutline into the inner fastness of the creek between Mt. Dyson and Blue Ridge, noticing how the snow is rapidly improving in quality and quantity with every glide, thanks to a high forest dam blocking not only the end of the valley, but also the sun and the wind.

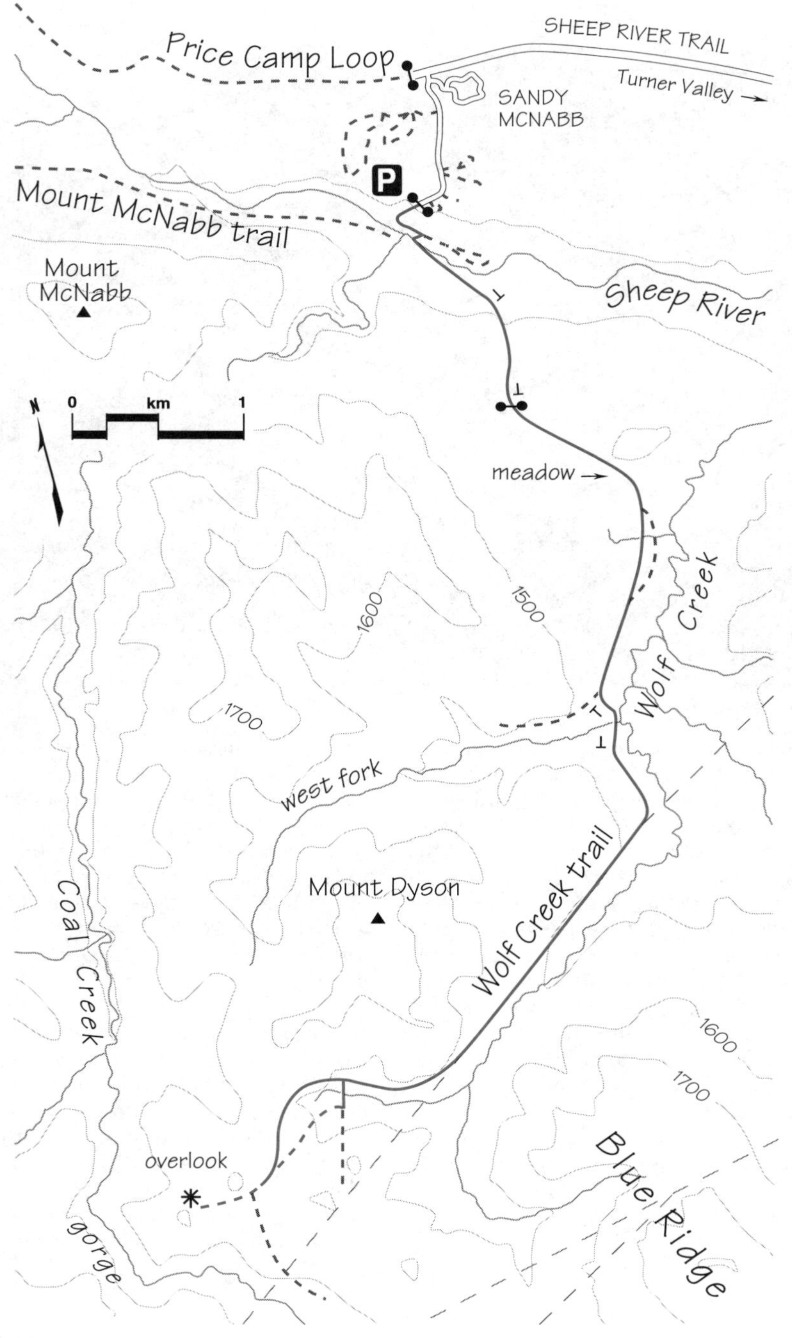
SHEEP RIVER TRAIL
Price Camp Loop
Turner Valley
SANDY MCNABB
P
Mount McNabb trail
Mount McNabb
Sheep River
N
0 km 1
meadow
1600
1500
Wolf Creek
1700
west fork
Wolf Creek trail
Mount Dyson
Coal Creek
1600
1700
overlook
Blue Ridge
gorge

Coal Creek gorge at trail's end. Photo: Tony Daffern

When up against the dam, turn right onto the cutline access road, leaving the cutline to climb to the pass the "hard way". After a kilometre the road, too, crosses the creek and goes winging up to the watershed ridge. If you enjoy sidestepping and getting tangled up in alder bushes that's up to you. Much better to follow the wonderfully graduated incline of the valley, either via the west bank summer trail (red triangles) or alternatively, via the initial hill of the access road and the east bank, gradually swinging left in both cases to the low point in the watershed ridge.

Emerging from the forest is a bit like removing your sunglasses in the middle of the Icefields. Blinking away in the bright light of the snowy meadows on the west side of the ridge, you're treated to a sweeping panorama of the Front Ranges and can have fun picking out the various peaks. "Surely that's Junction Mountain lookout that we went to last weekend". But you really need to go just that little bit further, following red triangles to a lookout knoll, where, with a feeling of intense astonishment, you can look down into Coal Creek Gorge — the greatest moment of the day.

Return The descent between ridge and cutline is superb: easy powder skiing through open forest with no chance of hitting a tree. The only other spot worthy of comment is trouble spot number two where you turn left off the cutline. Should you miss this junction, the penalty is two days lost on the cutlines of the K-Country boundary. It has happened!

JUNCTION MOUNTAIN FIRE LOOKOUT

Backcountry

Intermediate
27 km return
Height gain 789 m
Maximum elevation 2240 m
Map 82 J/10 Mount Rae

Access Sheep River Trail (SR 546) at Indian Oils parking lot. Note: the section of road west of Sandy McNabb Recreation Area is closed from December 1st to May 15th.

Facilities Washrooms and picnic tables at parking lot.

Overview Although the route to Junction Fire Lookout follows a fire road all the way, it demands you be a competent backcountry skier simply because you'll be going a long way back into the backcountry and the lookout is unavailable for B & B, although the neighbouring stone wall offers possibilities for those of you with aluminized polyester emergency space blankets. Unless there's a broken trail, you're into several hours of intense trail breaking on east-facing slopes, while higher up above treeline, where the wind sends all the snow to Calgary, there's a good chance of contacting hypothermia. The alternative to all this misery is a short 10 km day trip to Dyson Creek and back.

Unfortunately, this interesting trail is accessible only before midnight on November 30th which means you've also got to be fast moving to avoid an impromptu bivy at four in the afternoon.

The fire road, called Sheep trail at this point, has a minor problem right at the outset where you cross the Sheep River at Tiger Jaw Falls. The bridge supports are unsupported. The gravel all washed away after the incredible runoff of 1990, so if you find the bridge dismantled or hung with warning signs, you'll have to head upstream a bit to the horse crossing where the river is more likely to be frozen.

Straight off you're got this long pull up and over the open shoulder of Mt. Hoffman. On the other side, part way down a hill, you part company with Sheep trail and zip down a steeper hill to the meadows of Dyson Creek. The name "Dyson" is relatively new. To be exact, the document was approved, signed and stamped by the minister on September 6th, 1951, despite the fact the name had been in general use for Coal Creek under Mt. Dyson.

The fire road carrying on across the creek is now called Green Mountain trail as per the signpost. At the following junction keep right on the fire road which finally comes into its own. For the first little while you cruise along a low ridge between Dyson and North Coal Creeks, then turn a left-hander and are confronted by a long and steep hill. "Oh no!" After the initial bombshell, the angle slackens somewhat, the road winding in and out of every headwaters of North Coal Creek, touching briefly on a col of bare shale — howling wind — then resuming the traverse with further sections of herringboning. Above and below are very steep slopes covered in spruce trees hung with lichen.

Shortly after the lookout comes into view, you turn another corner and climb to treeline at another windy col. Strangely, the snowy vertical world has turned into a rolling desolation of browngrass and stones glued together by ice under the eastern escarpment of Junction Mountain. Since the lookout is located on the gable end of meadows a kilometre away, it pays to stow your skis under a pile of rocks and walk up either the road or the broad ridge to its left which is lined by a battered assortment of flagged trees trained by the wind to grow branches only on the lee side.

What a view! The big spread of Junction Mountain to the east, then north to south: Mt. Rae, Gibraltar Mountain, Shunga-la-She, Junction, Bluerock and Moose Mountains, Calgary, Plateau Mountain and Mt. Head. A quick snack in the lee of the lookout, and it's time to be heading back down. Now this is something to look forward to.

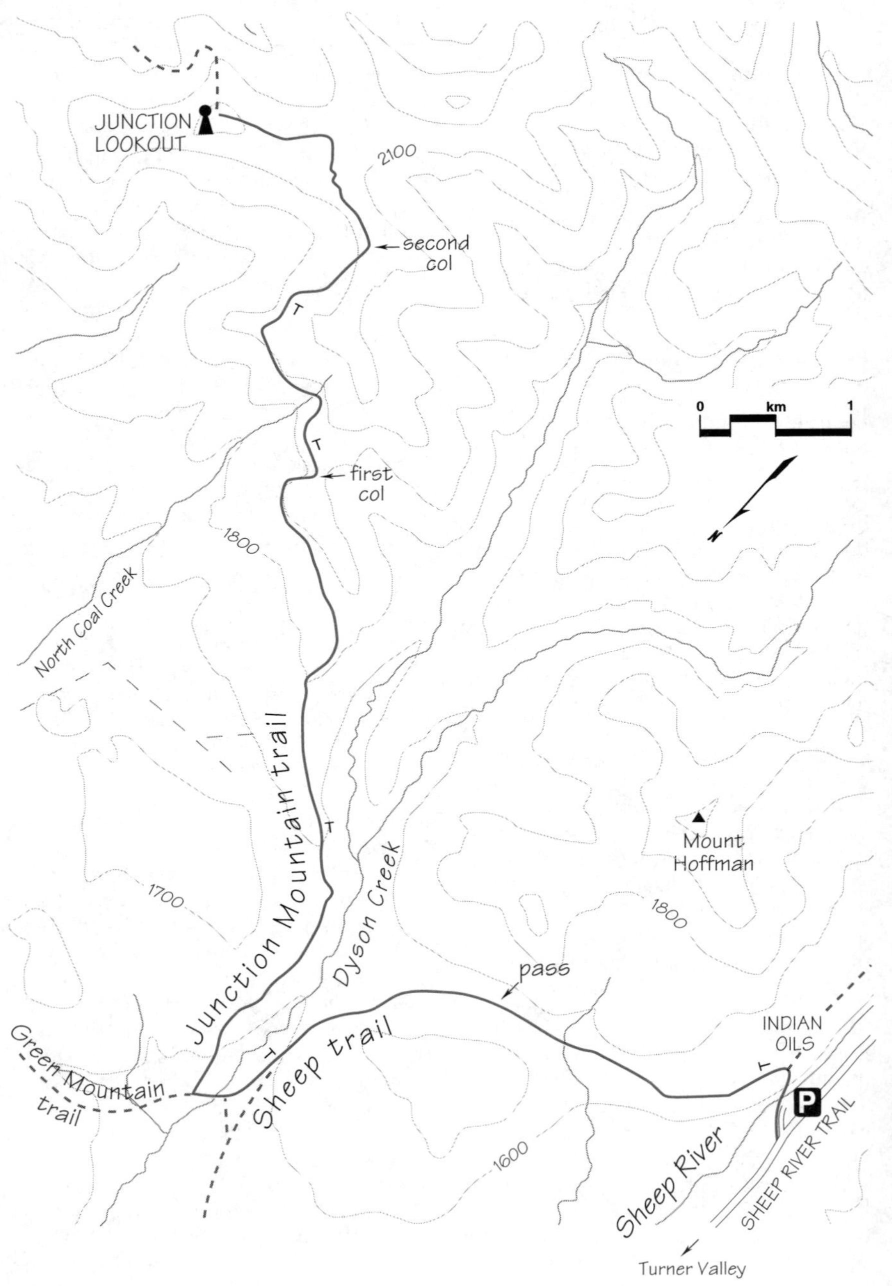
JUNCTION
LOOKOUT
2100
second
col
first
col
1800
North Coal Creek
Junction Mountain trail
Dyson Creek
0
km
1
N
Mount
Hoffman
1700
1800
pass
Green Mountain
trail
Sheep trail
INDIAN
OILS
P
1600
Sheep River
SHEEP RIVER TRAIL
Turner Valley

More about the trail When we first skied to Junction Lookout we took the Teskey road to Dyson Creek. As you drove past Gorge Creek on the way to the parking lot you may have spotted it on the opposite bank, rising from left to right. What you can't see from SR 546 is the bend near the top which even then was offering a thrilling goat's eye view into one of the Sheep's many celebrated gorges, which is why I am not recommending it for general use today, quite apart from the fact that there's no bridge over the river at this point. And also I wish to remain friends with K-Country. It's amazing to think that for eight years, trucks from Bighorn Lumber Company (which was logging in Dyson at the time) rumbled up and down this road without even one incident of brakes failing at Hell's Fire Pass as the loggers used to call it.

Prior to all this activity, Teskey road was the treeline telephone trail between ranger stations, and after crossing Dyson Creek it took off to North Coal Creek along what is now called Green Mountain trail. 1929 saw the building of a new trail, forerunner of the fire road, branching off the telephone trail and climbing up to deserted meadows below Junction Mountain. If you've got an imagination like mine, you can picture forest rangers "wearing chaps and ten gallon hats" squinting through binoculars and saying something like, "Yes Jack, I think this would be a good place to build a lookout. Up north you can just see the lookout we put up on Moose Mountain last year and Mt. Burke to the south looks like another good location". In the years before radio, all lookouts down the eastern slopes had to be built within sight of one another, though how they communicated is a mystery. By flashing mirrors or by smoke signals, perhaps. Anyway, Junction and Cameron Lookouts were both built in 1929, Junction towards the tail end of the year in September when the snow lay thick on the ground and packhorses laden down with building materials plodded up a trail as yet unstumped. The present lookout is the third on the site, a far cry from the first little wooden box held down with cables to stop it from blowing away.

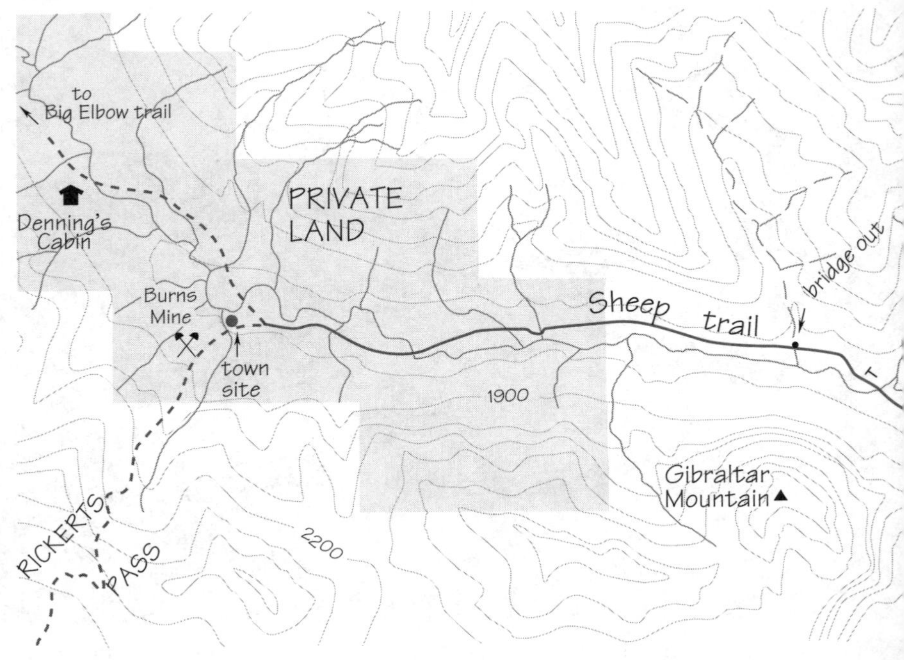

SHEEP TRAIL TO BURNS MINE

Backcountry

Intermediate
10 km to Burns Mine
12.75 km to Denning's Cabin
Height gain 250 m
Maximum elevation 1826 m at corral
Map 82 J/10 Mount Rae

Access The end of Sheep River Trail (SR 546) at Junction Creek day-use area. Note: the section of highway west of Sandy McNabb Recreation area is closed between December 1st and May 15th.

Facilities Washrooms and picnic tables at parking lot.

Overview After November 30th you can only ski this trail by mounting a week-long expedition from Sandy McNabb which is a great pity since the old road to the corral at Burns Mine makes just a super day trip. Technically, it's a shade more difficult than the fire road up the Little Elbow, the hills being longer and steeper and the bridge more exciting. Route finding is a breeze, you just stay on the road all the way and ignore red triangles where the summer trail makes forays into the forest.

Burns Mine town site meadow is the logical turnaround point when breaking trail. Denning's cabin is perhaps too far. By that I mean it takes a good half hour to get a good fug going from the stove and in November the dark descends by four thirty. Far better to reserve the cabin for a weekend when you can make a leisurely trip in weighed down with bottles of Beaujolais.

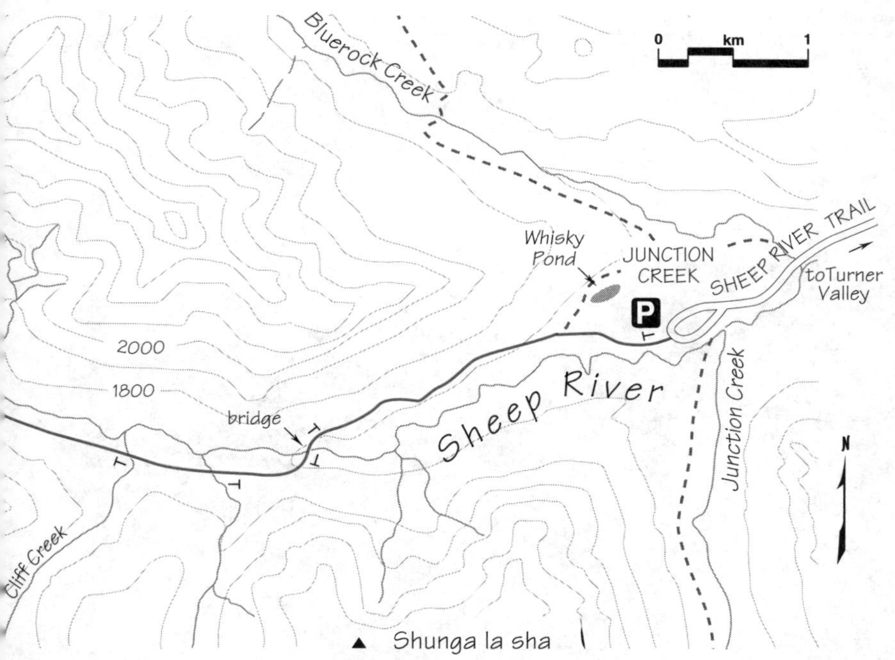

Duck under the gate and get onto the old Sheep River road which straightaway rises to a viewpoint on the bench. As you undulate along the bench for the next 3.5 km, Gibraltar Mountain fills the V ahead, its menacing presence felt all the way along the trail to the corral which lies 3 km beyond the mountain. Hmmm...

The next point of interest is the bridge crossing. There used to be a bridge nearer the water called Brown's Bridge which was superseded by this later edition which, though structurally sound, grows more skeletal with each passing season. A few years back, when the bridge was auditioning for an Indiana Jones movie, you did a balancing act on the stringers at either end, then tiptoed across the middle section, being careful not to get your baskets wedged in the holes or worse, skis lined up with the gaps between slats. It's all right now, though, ever since K-Country nailed down a few extra planks. The stint along the south bank has lain in the shadow of Shunga-la-she and Gibraltar since October and the cold of the tomb settles in the valley bottom. Here you'll find the best hills with the best snow, especially the one up from the bridge.

Recross the river on snow and climb up the second steepest uphill to another bench. At a narrow side creek you'll discover soon enough the need to detour below a spectacularly collapsed bridge. From a little beyond this point enjoy an unobstructed view of Gibraltar's overhanging east face glowing an eerie yellow from reflected sunlight and the scenario of a 9-day climb in 1971 which had the distinction of being the very first extended aid climb in the Canadian Rockies. Not surprisingly, the early travellers called the mountain Sheer Cliff.

Near the bridge crossing (bottom left) you get this awesome view of Gibraltar Mountain.

Past Gibraltar the character of the valley changes, becoming flatter, wider and sunnier. Moose wander the valley floor munching willow brush. After one last uphill at a stony side creek, the road levels and crosses the Sheep River. One straight kilometre more and you're leaning, but not *too* hard, on the corral fence in the meadow where the buildings once stood. A signpost points to Rickert's Pass and the coal mines but there's absolutely nothing to see under snow so don't bother going. There is, however, looking back, a delicious view of Gibraltar showing off its overhanging profile.

Return Two downhills are outstanding: the winding downhill to the second river crossing (good runout), and downhill number two to the bridge where it's advisable to come to a screeching halt at the "danger" sign.

Option: Denning's Cabin
The cabin lies another 2.75 km up the road on the left-hand side after the second creek crossing. Primitive facilities include: a wood stove, table, benches, bunk beds with sagging springs (some covered by plywood), a limited number of pots and plates, three can openers and a privy so tucked away behind the large barn it requires a major orienteering expedition in the middle of the night. At the risk of sounding like a park brochure, please tidy up before you leave and take your empties with you.

More about the trail When I think of the name "Burns" I always think of our local deli. "Three hundred grams of Burns Black Forest ham please". So do most people associate the name with supermarket meats or with the Burns Building in downtown Calgary which was saved from the wrecker's ball, but over the years the Burns empire has had its finger in an incredible number of pies. Incredibly, one man started it all: Pat Burns, who came up with the idea of supplying meat to railway, construction and lumber camps while the CPR line was progressing westwards in the 1880's. When he reached Calgary he established slaughter houses, bought a string of retail shops, branched out into hogs, sheep, dairy cattle, poultry, and eggs, and bought up so many ranches it was said he "could ride from the US border to Calgary without leaving his land." And of course, the "Meat King of the Northwest" was one of the Big Four who financed the very first Calgary Exhibition and Stampede.

And then there was his coal mining venture up the Sheep River. I'm not surprised you've never heard of it because it never really got rolling and much of the coal is still stockpiled, growing grass, waiting for the railroad which never came. It's a difficult story to unravel but it apparently all started in 1896 when ten men put in $100 each and sent the French-born Duc de Braban (alias mining engineer Julius Rickert sporting a magnificent handle-bar moustache) and ex-policeman Arthur Brown up the Sheep River on a prospecting trip for coal. It was during this trip that Rickert discovered his little bit of immortality in Rickert's Pass. Anyway, the upshot was that in 1909, 1911 and 1912 Pat Burns bought the surface and mining rights off Rickert and Brown and set about obtaining land grants including 1920 acres to be set aside for a townsite. Subsequently, the cookhouse, bunkhouse, hospital and bath house were built not on level ground near the corral but much higher up the sloping meadow near to Rickert's Creek.

After incorporation on June 13, 1913, the Pat Burns Coal Company dug a half-mile long adit and ran a narrow-gauge railroad from prospective mines in Rickert's Creek and Sharp's Creek to the meadow where the coal was stockpiled across the trail from the corral. That's the hillock. Some of the coal was actually sent out by horse and buggy along the trail. But unfortunately, when the huge problem of transportation seemed likely to be solved, the post war slump closed the mines in 1921 while the Calgary and South-Western Railway was still in the railbed or tree clearing stage, its ultimate destiny to become a roadbed for SR 546 and today's trail which is certainly fortuitous from the recreationist's point of view. Not so good is the fact that one of the work camps is credited with igniting the 1919 flagration which burned through to the Bow/Crow forest boundary

So that was the extent of Burn's involvement with the coal mines apart from an incident in 1932 when Rickert sued Burns over alleged non-payments dating back to 1911. As it happened the plaintiff never turned up for his day in court, perhaps intimidated by the lawyer for the defence, the irrepressible Paddy Nolan who had meanwhile uncovered some startling facts about Rickert. He was not French. Some say he came from the eastern US. He was not a registered mining engineer in Alberta, and he was not the Conte du Braban. There was in fact no de Braban or de Barbant listed in the French nobility guide. Then by some strange chance, the 1932 edition of L'Illustration Journal contained a photograph of a glamorous young couple, neither of whom sported a handle-bar moustache, but who were indubitably the Duc and Duchess de Brabant, a hereditary title reserved for the crown prince of Belgium!

Both mines were reopened briefly during 1945-51 by promoter Mervin Brown of Allied Industries who sent a few promotional truckloads off to Midnapore to be put on the train for Ontario. With the resurgence in exploration around this time, you could reasonably expect the continuation of the road up and over Tombstone Pass to the Little Elbow River to be an exploration road. You would be wrong. It is actually a fire road built by the Alberta Forest Service.

With the coming of K-Country, the powers that were arbitrarily decided that Junction Creek was to be the terminus of the new Sheep River equestrian trail and hung a "Closed to Motor vehicles" sign on the gate which gave a completely erroneous impression of the road beyond which was more akin to the road out of Baghdad after the Desert Storm offensive and would have been better travelled by tank. You've only got to see Don King's photos of cars bogged down in creek beds and the Blayney brothers hacking their way through the bush with machetes to realize a trip over to the Elbow was not an expedition to be taken lightly. Nevertheless, ever since the closure I've been kicking myself for not making more effort to climb all those hills and explore all those side valleys in the days when you could do your hiking by car.

So though it requires a little more effort these days to reach Burns Mine you can still browse the historical trash of the mines themselves, but will be out of luck if you're looking for the townsite which was razed to the ground in 1960 by the Alberta Forest Service, not withstanding that the buildings were located on private ground. In fact you'll be astonished to learn that 67% of the land is *still* owned today by the Burns family and the other 33% by the Royal Trust Company in trust for five charities, an island of private land in the midst of K-Country.

There just remains the mystery of Brown's Bridge. Was it named after Arthur Brown, a John Brown who worked for Burns, or Mervin Brown the promoter?

Inspecting the old corral at Burns Mine town site. Gibraltar Mountain shows off its eastern profile.

WEST BRAGG CREEK SKI TRAILS

Groomed

50.8 km of trails
Maximum elevation
Map 82 J/15 Bragg Creek

Access

1. Main Access. From the village of Bragg Creek, take the road signed Wintergreen Ski Area. Cross the Elbow River bridge, turn left and follow West Bragg Creek Road to its end at a parking lot 1.3 km into Kananaskis Country. Although West Bragg Creek Road continues, a gate prohibits public vehicle access.
2. Elbow Falls Trail (SR 66) at Allen Bill Pond parking lot.

Facilities

1. West Bragg Creek parking lot: washrooms and picnic tables. On weekends a patroller is available for advice from 9:30 am to 4:30 pm at the trailer in the parking lot. If you want, you can register your trip. I am still expecting a coffee and hot dog van to turn up on busy weekends, but so far no luck.
2. Allen Bill Pond parking lot: washrooms, picnic tables, fire pits, skating and hockey rinks. Note that Elbow Ranger Station across the road is manned on weekends for *emergency purposes only*. Trail information is available from Elbow Valley Visitor Information Centre back down the highway near the K-Country boundary.

Overview This is a justly popular ski area. I love it. On sunny weekends, cars overflow the parking lots and are backed up the road almost to the K-Country boundary. That's because West Bragg has something to offer everybody, from rank beginners to families with kiddies and dogs to madcap senior citizen groups to racers-in-training.

The mesh of official trails, comprised of old and new logging roads, exploration roads, cutlines and new trails, range far and wide over a rolling countryside of open valley bottoms and pine-forested hillsides, and are signed at junctions with "you are here" signposts or with arrows.

Nor should the unofficial trails be forgotten just because they're not groomed. For instance, if you're travelling east along the westernmost part of the Crystal Line and wish to turn up the west leg of Sundog, you're not going to turn off left onto the "now" Crystal Line because it's official and go all around the boonies, up and down dale, when a nice little schuss down the "old" Crystal Line will get you to your junction in one minute flat. The same goes for the unofficial connector to Elbow trail off Sundog which I will continue to use when heading south rather than risk being flattened by downhillers on the official trail which is best reserved for south to north traffic anyway. So though the unofficial trails may not be in pristine shape you can be sure they will be skier-set.

When there is snow West Bragg is very very good and when there is none it is awful, says I who has just returned from a truly terrible trip around Telephone. At West Bragg, snowfall usually occurs when the wind is blowing out of the north or east and the temperature is hovering around a chilly -20°. Periodically, the area is swept by Chinook winds, which, having deposited all the snow on the mountains to the west, roar through the treetops under blue skies and denude snow from open areas in a matter of hours, which is what happened to me on Telephone. A blissful 13.8 degrees is too much of a good thing in mid January! This does not mean that the season is necessarily a short one. I have skied Telephone successfully in October and encountered powder on the Crystal Line at the end of March.

All trails are patrolled on weekends and holidays between the hours of 8.30 am and 4.30 pm by Canadian Ski Patrol volunteers who are identified by yellow and blue jackets with maple leaf and cross, and by huge packs stuffed with all the paraphernalia needed to lend first aid to humans and equipment.

Skates and hockey sticks for Elbow trail are optional.

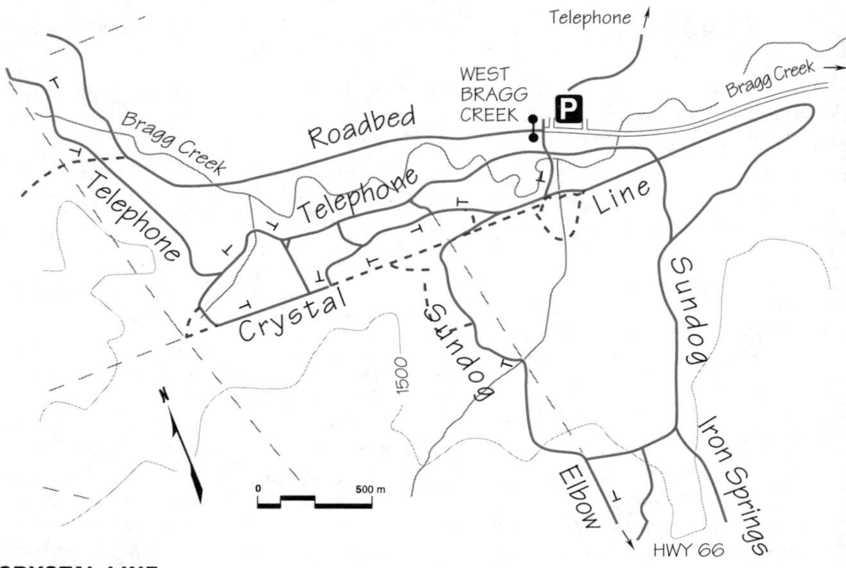

CRYSTAL LINE
Easy intermediate
3.4 km

This cutline used to be the Yonge Street among trails south of the road and was so straight (though undulating) you could see skiers from the distance of a kilometre or two away. A cautionary tale is told by a friend, a rather gregarious type, who was trying to catch up with the bulkily dressed figure in front of him to exchange a few pleasantries, only to find the "skier" was wearing a fur coat with teeth and claws as accessories. Yes, early and late in the season, bears are still roaming around. Binoculars are advised. My friend always carries them in his pack.

As of 1992 the trail improvers elected to fill in a few of the dips and turn people off the mid portion of the cutline onto the winding trail to the north, thereby eliminating the crunch at Sundog junction and, by a lot of dirt pushing, the wee side creek with the half-moon detour. (You can still go that way if you want.)

Overall, it's a pretty good trail for beginners who can snowplow and herringbone.

SUNDOG
Intermediate
4.7 km

At one time Sundog had innumerable variations including one rated difficult which was built for a race which never happened, and which is now sprouting tiny lodgepoles. It's all much simpler now. There is an east leg which is easy and scenic (view of Moose Mountain), travelling alongside cutblocks in various states of reclamation with explanatory signs. And then there is the west leg, a genteel bobsleigh run in the south to north direction. Actually, it's not *all* downhill, I always forget about that horrid little uphill after the creek crossing.

Where both legs meet in the middle, three trails take off to the south, Iron Springs, the easier start to Elbow trail which has recently been demoted to unofficial and the official Elbow trail which involves much uphill and dodging of downhillers yelling "get out of the way!".

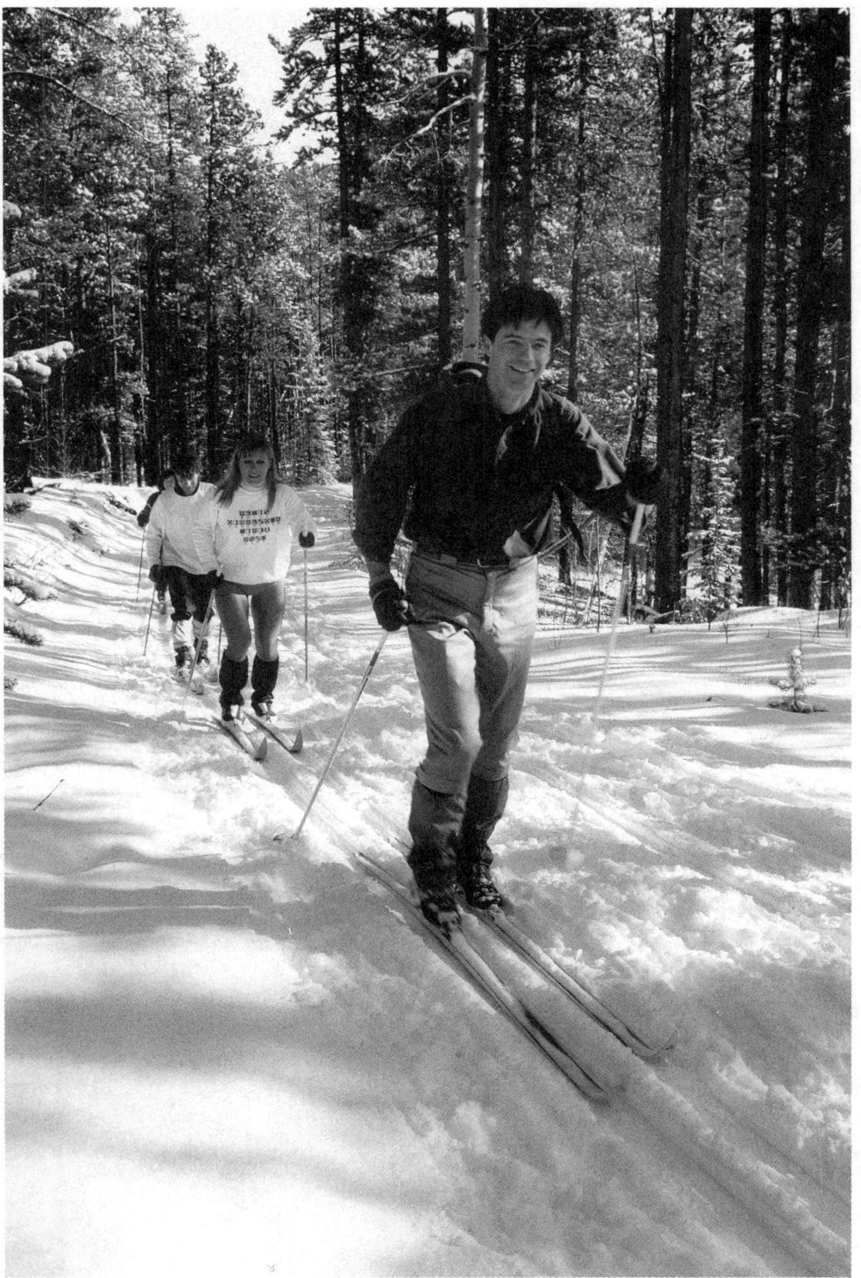

Elbow trail just north of Iron Springs Cutoff.

ELBOW TRAIL

Intermediate
6 km from Sundog
Height gain south-north 126 m, north-south 105 m
Maximum elevation 1525 m

Snaking south from Sundog, this is the only trail connecting the two parking lots, West Bragg Creek and Allen Bill Pond recreation area on SR 66. There are advantages to skiing it in both directions: for instance, south to north has the steepest downhills. Probably the best idea is to make it a two-way trip, or utilize Iron Springs trail to make a loop. I prefer starting from the West Bragg Creek end and lunching at Allen Bill Pond which has a wood pile, picnic tables with fire pits, lots of Sunday tourists for psychoanalysis and a skating rink available for a twirl or two which makes for a change from skiing. Besides skates, I would strongly advise packing matches and a foil-wrapped culinary masterpiece since crunching frozen tuna sandwiches is a totally unnecessary torture when everyone else around you is cooking burgers. Someone's mother took pity on me once and offered me a piece of birthday cake. Strange place for a birthday party given it was about -20° and the party goers were huddled, shivering, around a campfire. However, having said all of the above, most skiers — especially family units — tend to start from the Allen Bill Pond end, and so too will this description.

From Allen Bill Pond far end parking lot, the trail goes *under* the highway bridge, then over tiny Ranger Creek footbridge and follows a long flat straight alongside the Elbow River. Keep left and after passing the voluntary registration box and passing through a gap in the fence (in winter you are not required to wrestle with the gate), you turn left and climb, curving right, onto the bench top. Taken in reverse direction, this hill is signed "Steep Hill" which it isn't, but there *is* a very sharp left-hand bend with a net strung across to catch errant skiers. The next kilometre is a delight, an undulating stretch along a sunny bench top between aspens. Keep left at a junction with a cutline access road, then turn left onto the cutline itself which you will follow with diversions all the way to Sundog.

Beyond Iron Springs turn-off, comes the long haul to the Elbow River/Iron Creek watershed. On the far side a half circle diversion to right leads past Iron Springs Cutoff, then back to the cutline for more climbing past intersecting cutlines to a high point, a flat 100-metre stretch on top of a pine ridge. What, no view? Who cares. There's a jewel of a downhill coming up. Taken in the opposite direction it's a bit of a grunt. Inevitably, just as you start feeling pleased with yourself for getting into fast herringbone mode with breath control, racers come skating nonchalantly past, chatting brightly to one another. But back to the downhill. Through a teary blur, keep to the middle road at the bottom and remember the ice, like the sign says.

This is followed by a long stretch alongside willowy Iron Creek to the Iron Creek/Bragg Creek watershed at a small meadow. At the split en route, the "High Road" to left is best reserved for skiers coming in the opposite direction who are treated to a downhill. We'll take the easy "Low Road" to the right.

Now there are two ways to Sundog. The official left-hand trail requires climbing further up the cutline to the trail's high point. You pivot a moment, then hurtle down the straight to the junction where you execute a stop christie and look back to see how many uphillers you've mown down. The unofficial right-hand trail, on the other hand, though no longer trackset, dekes neatly through the gap.

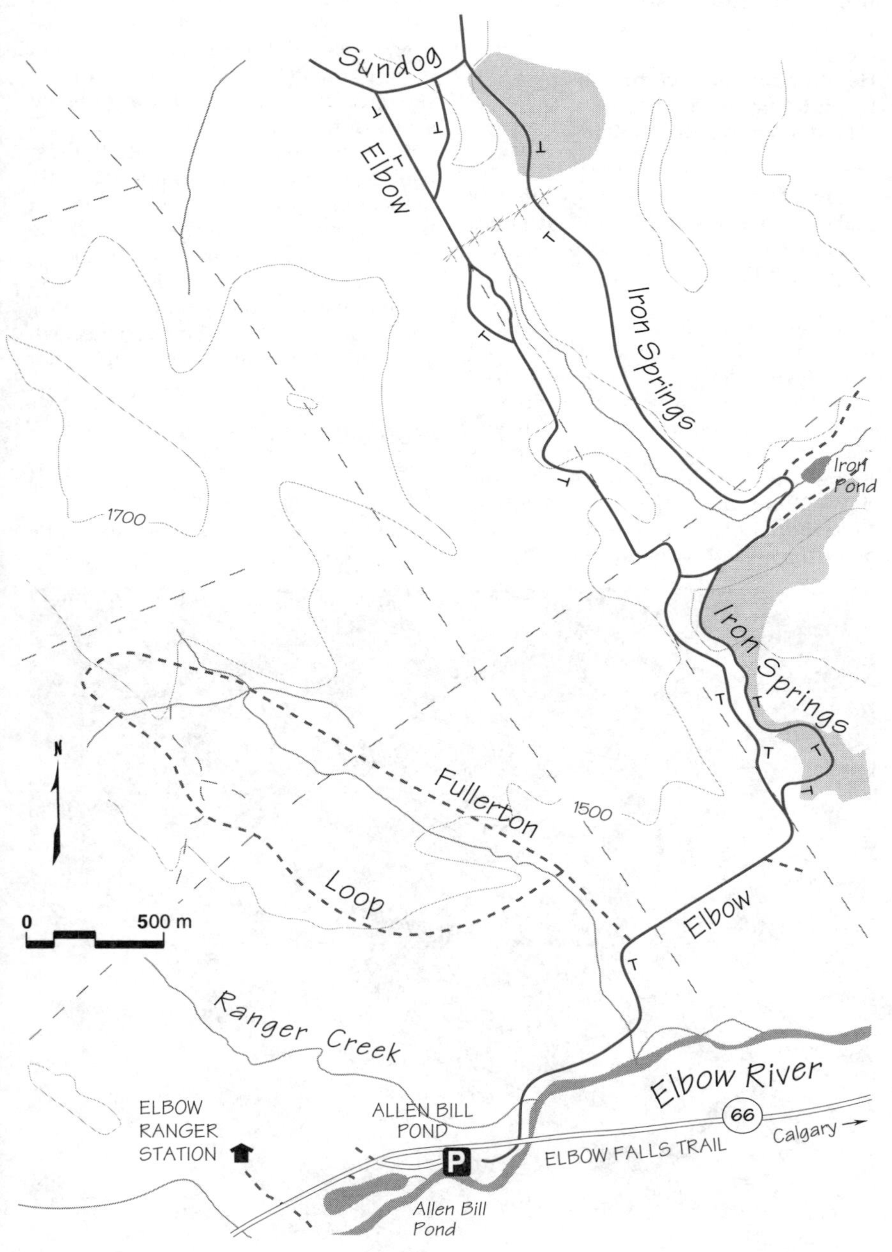
Sundog
Elbow
Iron Springs
Iron Pond
1700
Iron Springs
N
Fullerton
1500
Loop
0
500 m
Elbow
Ranger Creek
Elbow River
ELBOW
RANGER
STATION
ALLEN BILL
POND
P
66
ELBOW FALLS TRAIL
Calgary
Allen Bill
Pond

IRON SPRINGS TRAIL

Easy intermediate
4.6 km
Height gain south-north 120 m, north-south 86 m
Maximum elevation 1550 m

Exposed to the debilitating effects of sun and wind, the cutblock trail nevertheless makes a welcome addition to West Bragg since it enables you to make two new loops with Elbow.

Like a few other souls who like to get off the beaten track I've been skiing the old logging road for years despite the trail closed signs but have always entered from the north. Now there's a brand new connector from the south which leaves Elbow shortly after you turn left onto the S-N cutline and climbs to the Elbow River/Iron Creek watershed. You edge along the left side of cutblocks, then slip through a fringe of trees into Iron Creek valley at the pond which has migrated from the last edition of the topo map and is now found further to the east. It's a sheltered sunny spot with lots of fallen aspens for seats.

Here the route transfers onto the east bank logging road and climbs gradually to the Iron Creek/Bragg Creek watershed half-way up a ridge. You pass through the drift fence and are greeted by this fabulous, albeit long distance view of Moose Mountain and by the wind which comes gusting up the open cutblock unchecked. The run down to Sundog should be a lot better now the trail is packed.

IRON SPRINGS CUTOFF

Easy
0.2 km

A useful connector if you want to make a shorter loop.

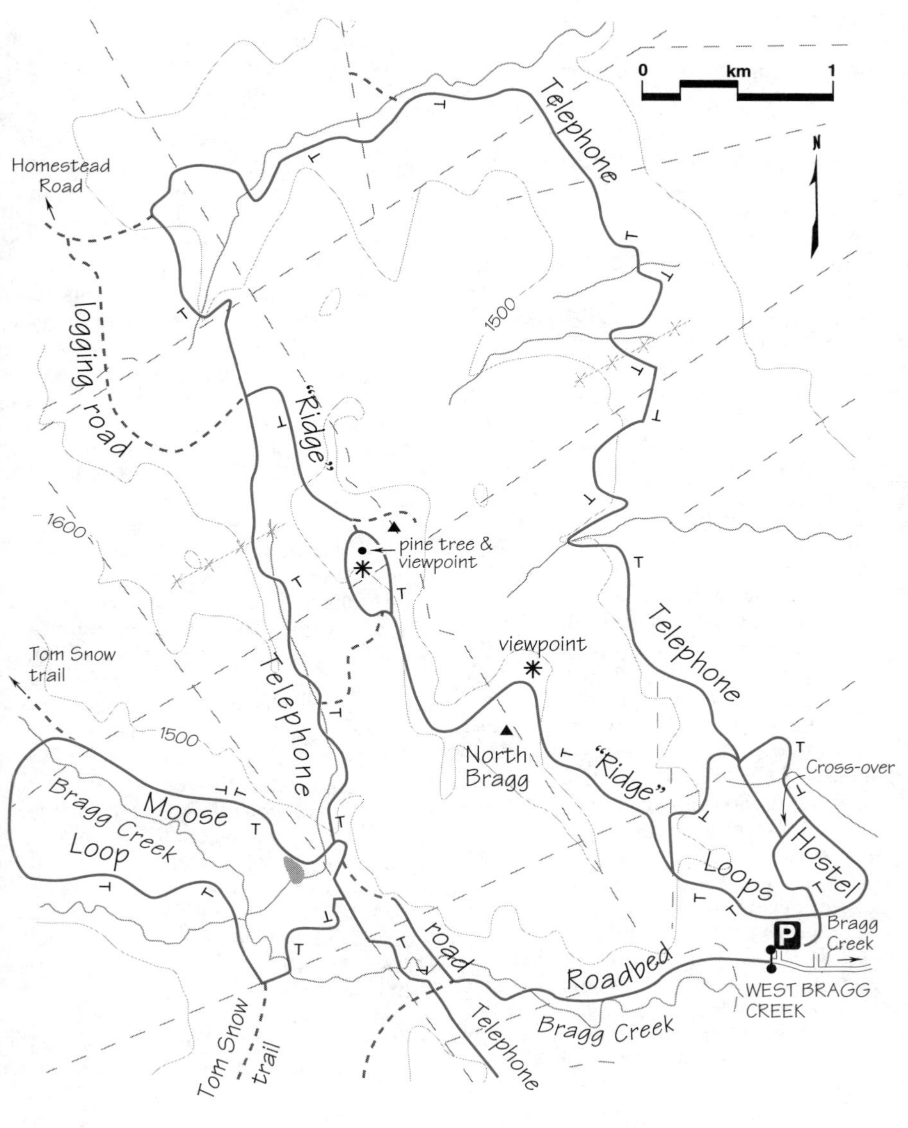

Photo opposite: Senior Citizen group enjoying a day out on the south leg of Telephone.

TELEPHONE LOOP

Intermediate
16.5 km
Height gain 230 m

Something awful has happened to Telephone. Lovers of the loop — and there are many of you out there who seem to ski nothing else at West Bragg — will be sickened to learn that the whole of the north end, that delightful stretch along a remote valley where the spruce trees grew tall and the snow lay deep, is irretrievably lost. A major logging road has been dozed over the top of the trail. As I skied slowly down the road the first time in a state of shock I found myself apologizing to all those once lovely trees now cut up and trashed by the side of the road and cut down to the creek in some places. The ambience of the place had completely vanished. Worse, I discovered that the road stops abruptly part way down the east leg which suggests the whole of the east leg is next due for improvement. Although K-Country assures me this isn't so and are as mad as everyone else about the road which was supposed to have taken a higher line out of sight of the trail, I am keeping my fingers crossed. In the winter of 1992/3 another 12 cutblocks are scheduled!

Not everyone gets as emotional as me about such things and I dare say some people will enjoy whipping around the loop on a regulation 4 m-wide road when all the logging is done. But you know, one of the joys of Telephone is the narrow width of the trail, assuming that encroaching willow brush is cut back each season. So *at the moment* it is still the reserve of strong skiers who can handle its intermediate hills combined with this narrowness and remoteness, though it appears that nowadays if you do something stupid in the remote, you need only wait for the next logging truck to whisk you off to the Homestead Shooting Range.

It's a matter of much debate which way round the trail should be skied. It's almost getting to point where the ski patrol could take a poll in the parking lot. Advocates of counterclockwise laud the long but tricky downhills of the east leg, plus the opportunity to cheat on the last lap by taking to Roadbed. Clockwise fans, including purveyors of the official viewpoint, extol the easier downhills (true) but forget to mention the uphill grind at the three-quarter mark which is disheartening if you're already on your last pair of legs.

Going clockwise From the parking lot cross the road, then take the right-hand bridge over Bragg Creek onto an undulating stretch with three connectors to Crystal Line, where, being "Telephone Men", it is your duty to overtake crocodiles of struggling beginners. The crowds thin out when you turn right and zip along to Roadbed which is crossed at its highest trackset point. A short steep step takes you down to Bragg Creek valley bottom.

The old trail used to wind along the flat valley bottom, but now crosses the creek and climbs steeply, wending left to join a NW-SE cutline which typically climbs up and over a ridge back to valley bottom — surely a bit of overkill to avoid a few patches of river ice I would have thought. (In reverse direction, the hill above Bragg Creek is a fast hard-packed downhill needing caution on the runout.) Ski past the west leg of Moose Loop to left and the unofficial short-cut to Roadbed to right in the meadow. A short stint through trees brings you to the junction with Moose Loop's east leg at a signpost where Telephone, much the narrower trail, strikes off to the right.

In a few minutes you are confronted with a dire warning about entering deepest Telephone and are you prepared?, a K-Country attempt at humour given that you're feeling shattered after an initial bit of steep herringboning and are already almost 4 km into the trip. But after the sign the angle eases off and what follows is a joyful, effortless sprint up a little valley to a pass slung between two low ridges. Beyond the drift fence an equally gentle descent is rudely interrupted in less than a kilometre by traffic signs and a brand new logging road cutting across the trail at right-angles. Depending on traffic and the day of the week this is "Ridge trail". It's another half kilometre from here to the T-junction where you turn left and shortly join forces with another logging road which starts you off along the new north leg. With hardly any trees between you and the Homestead Shooting Range to muffle the sound, the constant pop pops is positively jarring.

The north leg alongside the unnamed creek used to be such fun, but now you have this boring road, especially wide and boring at the big hill, a good hill ruined and which unaccountably reminds me of the 14th Street hill in Calgary below the Jubilee Auditorium, only this road is sprinkled with rocks churned up by logging trucks. I believe I walked it the first time. One supposes that After Logging the telemarkers will have a field day with this hill. But most people will be glad to climb out of the valley and onto the east leg where the logging road comes to an end. The east leg has character. The trail is once again narrow and constantly dipping in and out of side creeks with hills in both directions, the first dip you come to being the worst (best?) example with the added worry of ice flows in the creekbed. Mostly, though, the trail is definitely uphill to the last side creek where it makes a bigger indent than usual, then straightens out with a few short downhills to raise a flagging morale to the north intersection with Hostel Loop at a signpost.

Continue on in the same direction, generally downhill past Cross Over (left, a seat too late) to the south intersection with Hostel Loop on a flat bench. Slow down, then gathering speed, make the final descent to the parking lot.

The west leg of Telephone. Starting down the hill to Bragg Creek.

HOSTEL

Intermediate
3.6 km
Height gain 45 m

It probably makes sense to ski this little loop circling about Telephone in a clockwise direction so as to reserve the better snow for the downhills. This means that straight off the bat you're faced with the long climb up the south-facing hill to the NE-SW cutline . Then comes the reward. Not the view (discounting cutblocks, this loop is absolutely viewless), but a long winding descent with a gem of a left-hander down to Telephone north junction — slow, there's always knots of people hanging about — then on down the cutline and around a corner into the low point of the east leg at a creek crossing. There's a remarkably stiff climb up other side after which the trail calms down, passing Cross Over to the right and slowly climbing back the bench from where you started. On the right are some enticing telemark slopes.

ROADBED

Easy
1.8 km

The continuation of the West Bragg Creek Road beyond the gate is not only the very best trail for beginners, it's also a useful cheater's short-cut to and from Telephone and Moose Loop which I've used many a time. Expect gentle hills and lots of sunshine. Now if only hikers and locals taking their dogs for walkies could be trained to walk at the side of the road....The trackset stretch ends where Telephone crosses the road.

CROSS OVER

0.2 km
Easy

Midway along the east leg of Hostel Loop, Cross Over connects with Telephone trail, thus enlarging the possibilities from simple loops to more complicated figures of 8 and letters "p" and "b".

Near the parking lot are some flat easy trails for beginners and their dog.

The east leg of Moose loop. A view of Moose Mountain across the flats of upper Bragg Creek.

MOOSE LOOP

Intermediate
5.5 km
Height gain 60 m
Maximum elevation 1490 m

In everybody's opinion, this trail's better skied in the counterclockwise direction, so follow Telephone (or Roadbed and Telephone) to the east leg junction. Round the next corner you have a treat in store, a colourful view of Moose Mountain across the valley of Bragg Creek where wall to wall willow bushes glow a gorgeous wine-red colour in the low sun of winter. The trail used to continue up the valley in the open and was susceptible to sun and wind, but now climbs into the pines and joins forces with the wide swath of the reclaimed Shell Oil exploration road which is well sheltered from Chinooks and not half as boring as you might expect.

At the turnaround point the reclaimed road crosses the creek, then climbs fairly steeply at first to the loop's high point where it turns right, becoming Moose Mountain Loop described on page 280. You, however, keep left on an older narrower road, a thoroughly enjoyable winding road with one or two fast downhills near the valley bottom. A short stint downstream and you recross Bragg Creek into the trees and head across to Telephone at the cutline, finishing with a steep downhill step.

Optional access Now it will have occurred to you that the east leg makes a rather good novice trail. Trouble is it's sandwiched between two sections of intermediate trail. There is a way around this problem though, and since plenty of people go this way, it's usually skier trackset. What you do is ski along Roadbed from the parking lot, cross the bridge, then turn first right onto the Shell Oil exploration road which recrosses the creek and climbs a reasonable hill to boulders. Deadend. A narrow trail continues across meadows, dropping slightly onto Telephone at a point halfway between the two junctions with Moose Loop. Now you're set.

"RIDGE TRAIL"

Backcountry
Intermediate
4.3 km
Height gain 183 m
Maximum elevation 1631 m

From the ski trails signs of logging in the area, meaning cutblocks, are tastefully hidden from view. So I thought I'd give you a tour of the cutblocks between Hostel and Telephone, which, incidentally, offer some remarkable views over the foothills. Don will probably have my head for including this unofficial route in with the groomed trails. But there's a chance, says Don, of the road along the ridge becoming a member of the official trails club one day when the seedlings grow up, since it makes available a shorter loop for people who don't want to ski all the way around Telephone. Although it skis equally well in either direction, this description runs north-south.

North-south You're on the west leg of Telephone and have obeyed the traffic sign to stop. Now turn east and follow the new logging road up the hill into a large cutblock folded over both sides of the ridge. When the road levels, transfer across a few metres of open ground to another road on your right which is circling the west-facing slope around a very tall tree left standing in a fit of whimsy by the loggers. Unless there's a metre of snow I recommend skiing the road in counterclockwise direction. So turn right down a long easy hill remarkable for the panorama it reveals to the south.

At the bottom of the hill keep left, then right at the bend, still following the major road as it heads south, climbing through a belt of reprieved trees to the ridge again — shorn on both sides — then rising some more to North Bragg, a triangulation point dating back to 1895 when Arthur Oliver Wheeler produced his phototopographic map of the area. I have this vision of him tramping all over the ridge looking for a clearing, but nearly a hundred years on there's no problem and you now have this fabulous view of Moose Mountain north to Logan Ridge which I got to know intimately during the search for Orval Pall and Ken Wolff.

Payoff time. Just a super run down the shady east slope where the powder parts like waves from the bow of a ship. The movement slows as you cut across the top of a lower cutblock and cross a cutline, then accelerates for a final glide onto Hostel Loop at the NE-SW cutline where all good things do not end.

The quickest way home is to turn right and schuss back to the parking lot.

More about the trails It's hard to imagine what West Bragg looked like in its pristine state. You have only to look at an air photo to see how chopped up it is with roads, cutlines and cutblocks and can only be thankful there is not a row of holiday cottages along Roadbed or a subdivision called Sundog advertising Moose Mountain views.

The first serious inroads appears to have been made by the horse and buggy trail to Thorn (or Thorne) coal mine, worked briefly around the late 1880's or early 1890's. Sorry about the "ors"; my excuse is that it's not listed in the comprehensive Mine Atlas of Alberta. But I'll wager that Thorn or Thorne was the same John Thorne who, after a brief stint of digging up mostly iron pyrites, decided to call it a day and move down to Coal Coulee near Longview where he operated the John Thorne coal mine between 1907 and 1909. Anyway, his trail could be considered the forerunner of not only Roadbed, the west leg of Moose Loop and Shell Oil's original exploration road, but also some if not all of the West Bragg Creek Road, an amazing accomplishment when you consider that A.W. Bragg was not yet squatting on a piece of land next to an unnamed creek. I was less surprised to learn that the treeline telephone system and pack trail between Jumping Pound and Elbow Ranger Stations came down the west leg of Telephone Loop in around 1913 and carried on down Ranger Creek to the Elbow River.

Skipping 60 years and several post and pole logging operations in the early 1960's, we come to the mid 1970's when Spray Lakes Sawmills moved into the area south of the parking lot and cut ski trails. Seismic crews had also been busy in the area *par example* Crystal Line, but the only rig of interest to us skiers was the one on the ridge between the west leg of Telephone and the east leg of Moose Loop which made available the cheater's short-cut up Shell Oil's exploration road. Until it revegetated, the steep bit up the ridge to the rig was an extremely popular piste. My memory of it is sitting beside a white-faced young woman with a badly gashed knee and muttering inanities like "it doesn't look too bad" (you could see the bone) while fervently wishing the rescue party on snowmobiles would reach us before we both contacted frost-bite of the gluteus maximus.

Of course, none of the above would have affected you and I if there hadn't been two momentous happenings in the late 1970's. The creation of a provincial recreation area (K-Country) in 1977 and the building of a Youth Hostel on the east end of the bench above the present West Bragg parking lot. The initial proposal for a hostel near the ranger station had been shot down. Unfortunately, the hostel came to a sad end in the early Spring of 1984 when a fire jumped the fireplace and fanned by great winds blowing out of the west spread quickly throughout the rest of the building. According to various sources who were there at the time, it's fate was sealed by bureaucratic bumbling which caused a 40 minute delay while official permission was obtained for sending a fire truck from Cochrane.

The Bragg Creek Hostel burning down.

Photo: Geoff Williams

But despite its short life, that hostel served a purpose. Being miles away from the fleshpots of Calgary — Bragg Creek didn't count at that time — hostellers got fed up with sweeping out the dorms and regularly skied the cutlines, exploration and logging roads, though how they managed it without a trail brochure remains a mystery. I distinctly remember ambling along the west leg of Telephone with houseparent Avril Derbyshire and her two red setters and when it got too overgrown having to short-cut over the ridge via a cutline. And then there was the trail which left the front door of the hostel and went down the meadow to a small pond just east of Hostel's east leg.

The west leg of Moose Loop was part of a long distance snowmobile trail in 1979 when hosteller Don Gardner recommended the area for ski trails and promptly got the job, with advice from Rudi Setz and Lars Fossum, of making sense of existing roads and supervising construction of new trails like "Telegraph" (alias Telephone) which proved to be a nightmare because of heavy bush at the north-east end. Still, as Don says, "it's worked out better than I told the client".

West Bragg has always been a training place for Calgary's nordic ski racers. For a while it seemed a great place to hold races as well and in the 1982/3 season the trails underwent a further refinement with widening here and there and little connectors pushed through to make loops of 2.5, 5, 7.5 and 10 km which Geoff Williams, in the days before portable satellite survey systems, measured down to the last millimetre before producing the one and only accurate map. The rank and file of Foothills Nordic Ski Club got involved as well and I remember several exciting weekends spent picking up rocks. Unfortunately, we never held a bona-fide race at West Bragg as it proved impossible to pick a date ahead of time in case the dreaded Chinook came roaring through the night before.

But undeterred, the Calgary 1988 Olympic Winter Games Organising Committee produced some truly impressive maps and statistics in 1984 and for a while it seemed that West Bragg was bound for glory after all, to be seen on television sets all around the World. But eventually, the possibility of being embarrassed by Chinooks, the prohibitive cost of laying snow-making equipment along every trail plus grumbling from some Bragg Creek residents who couldn't put up with two weeks of shuttle buses despite assurances of a new access road to be built from the south up Ranger Creek; all of this killed the idea. And the Olympics went to Canmore instead.

To everyone's surprise, trail improvements went on quietly. For instance, Shell Oil's 1982 exploration road to a rig on the east slope of Moose Mountain became Moose Loop's new east leg. And a renewed spate of logging by Spray Lakes Sawmills starting in 1985 resulted in a better alignment for Hostel Loop and new trails like Iron Springs and "Ridge Trail", all of which elicited no comment from the public until they had a go at Telephone in 1991.

That same year K-Country did a major reshuffle and in so doing demolished a landmark, or to be scrupulously correct, filled it in. I am referring of course to the dip in the Crystal Line which several refinements ago was bypassed by the half- moon traverse but was still there for reckless young kids and old timers reliving the thrills of yesteryear though it was never as good as the original's badly canted right-hand bend which regularly pitched skiers off into the bush, while those who made the bend went slithering all over the ice on their backsides. Oh yes! It was definitely more fun playing around at West Bragg before the trails were groomed and everyone wore Lycra and fleecy jackets.

UPPER BRAGG CREEK

Backcountry

Easy
5 km to meadow from Moose Loop
Height gain 61 m
Maximum elevation 1743 m
Map 82 J/15 Bragg Creek

Access Via West Bragg Creek Ski Trails as described on page 265.

The trail leaves the north end of Moose Loop's east leg just before it crosses Bragg Creek. To the right of the directional arrow is a red triangle nailed to an aspen with the words "Tom Snow".

Overview If you're tiring of groomed trails, then a nice, easy trip up upper Bragg Creek to the watershed meadow is just the thing. You'll be skiing the Tom Snow hiking and equestrian trail, so navigation boils down to searching for red triangles on trees.

Cross the meadow, searching for the first red triangle to set you off along a trail alternating between aspen/pine hillsides and creek bottom meadows. Across Bragg Creek, the east slope of Moose Mountain is sporting its new chequerboard look for the 1990's, but you leave all this behind you when you enter a narrow passage between high banks twisting right, then left. A gate in the drift fence across the narrows precedes a dark stint under the spruce trees, after which the valley unfolds into a sizeable meadow at the watershed.

Understandably, the Tom Snow trail continues along the edge of the trees into Moose Creek but why follow it? The meadow may be a bog in summer growing dwarf raspberries, but in winter it's a gorgeous snow meadow, a serene sun trap with treed ridges rimming every horizon. But quiet it very often is not. Anyone wandering over the ridge to the east is likely to be shot, notwithstanding notices (riddled with bullet holes) all round the perimeter of the Homestead Shooting Range. Of course, most people who go there are law-abiding, but then there's the lunatic fringe who shoot bullets through the regulation K-Country washroom door without checking first to see if anyone is sitting on the loo. I say you can't be too careful.

Option Return Via Moose Mountain loop as described on page 280. Read thoroughly before embarking on something you may regret.

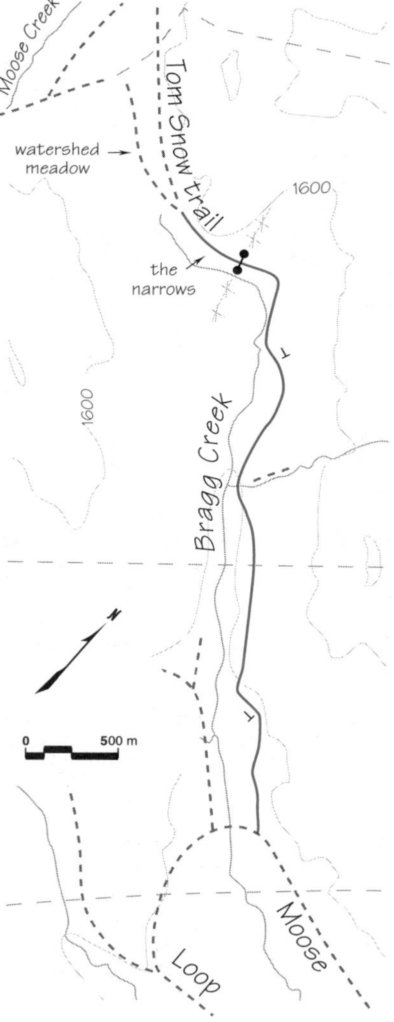

MOOSE MOUNTAIN LOOP

Backcountry

Intermediate
10.4 km to Moose Loop via cutblocks
13.9 km to Moose Loop via Upper Bragg Creek
Height gain 340 m main loop
Maximum elevation 1737 m
Map 82 J/15 Bragg Creek

Access Via West Bragg Creek Ski Trails. See pages 265.
1. The highest point of Moose Loop's west leg.
2. Moose loop west leg just west of the northernmost crossing of Bragg Creek.
3. The terminus of Upper Bragg Creek trail in the watershed meadow.

Overview One half of the route follows reclaimed exploration roads and the other half cutblocks and logging roads. The reluctant cutblock skier has the option of staying on cutlines and trails throughout but must do penance in the shape of 3.5 extra kilometres. Because of the loop's exposure to sun and wind, it avails you to ring up the weather office beforehand to find out when a good dump of snow and minus temperatures are forecast. Mind you, I've skied this trail in late March and had a really good time, but then I was lucky.

The original race round "Moose Mountain Course" was scheduled for anti-clockwise direction which doesn't mean that you have to follow suit; in fact, it would be daft to climb *up* the most delectable downhill this side of the Kananaskis Valley.

Going clockwise From the high point on Moose Loop turn up Shell Oil's reclaimed exploration road which, like the yellow brick road, seems to go on for ever. You can't lose it, a white slanted swath with room for 20 abreast which winds ponderously up the ridge, first on one side, then on the other, and finally along the ridge top to the high point. Here, the original exploration road comes in from the left and in the angle there's a nice spot in the trees for R & R.

For the next 2.5 km the route cuts across the grain of the country, falling and rising, falling and rising. This was OK when there was a road but now, for the first kilometre, the angle of slant becomes untenable and the wind picks away at one rocky corner (remnants of road are discernable just above the trees). With feelings of relief you reach the well site on the next open ridge.

Aim north-east towards the continuation of the old road — it's the one to the left — and drop down into the next tributary. You're in for a treat, a quite magnificent hill with first class powder and a vertical height loss of 116 metres! The creek at the bottom has a lovely secluded feel to it, probably because the loggers haven't shown up yet. I have a message for them: please don't touch this hill. Or this valley with its sandstone outcroppings.

Note the antiquated snowmobile sign as you wind up the other 20% of usable road to a col on a third ridge. The huge cutblock in front is a shocker, though admittedly giving a fine view of Ole Buck Mountain. Here there are two options to argue over:

Return via cutblocks Turn right and ski carefully down to the lowest part of the col, where, like magic, an opening appears on the south side and you slip through into another cutblock, the first of a string down the unnamed tributary whose two heads you crossed earlier. Surprisingly, the first two cutblocks appear free of booby traps, a summer inspection verifying that the grass does indeed grow waist high, so you can actually enjoy the glide down #1, through the narrows and *up* into cutblock # 2 without worrying overmuch about running your tips into a stump. Here, you join a road and follow it down and across the creek and up into cutblock #3 from the opposite end of which another road links with cutblock # 4 which is heavily mined with slash. By keeping to the left edge (road?) you can avoid the worst of it and

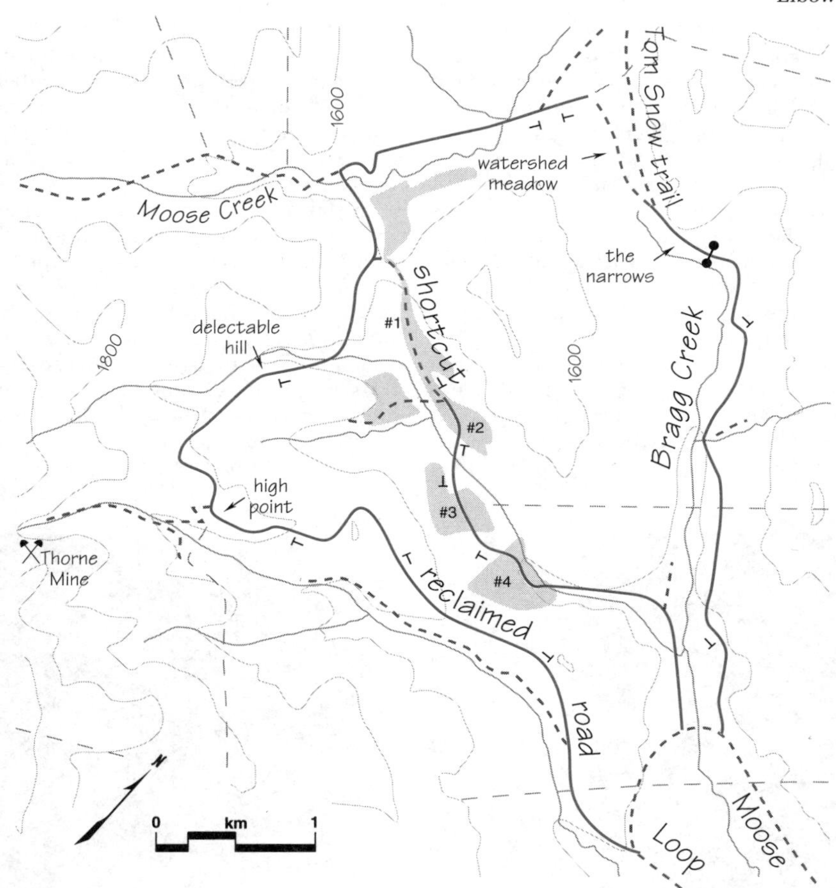

are in a position to pick up the obvious road on the north side of the creek. Turn right at the T-junction, cross the creek for the third time and arrive back on Moose Loop just west of the northernmost crossing of Bragg Creek.

Return via Upper Bragg Creek Whatever you do, don't stray into the huge cutblock; the road is still available at the left edge, winding downhill into Moose Creek. Cross the creek and turn right onto a cutline. What's this? Snowmobile tracks! Say what you like about snowmobiles, there are times, when exhaustion is setting in for example, when you'd give your last Mars Bar for a corrugated snowmobile trail. (Personally, I would not be averse to a tow.) Unfortunately, the straying snowmobile from Sibbald Flats Snowmobile Recreation Area turns left at the next junction after the creek crossing and unless you feel like going north to Jumpingpound Creek — I thought not — continue along the cutline to the Bragg Creek/Moose Creek watershed at the meadow. There, pick up Upper Bragg Creek trail as described on page 279.

More about the trail It's hardly surprising that so few people remember the Moose Mountain Ski Marathon of March 5th, 1979 since it never came off. But briefly it was the brainchild of such unlikely collaborators as the Calgary Ski Club, the Calgary Snowmobile Club, the Youth

Hostels Association, Shell Canada and the Foothills Nordic Ski Club under Larry Gabert, Rudi Setz, Karen Peterson and Duchane Richard who at the time wore woolly climbing knickers and smoked a pipe but now sports a mohawk haircut and races for the Yukon in a figure-hugging pink lycra suit. How times change. As another example, the word "loppet" was not yet in vogue; instead we talked about Moose Mountain Marathon or Moose Mountain Course. On February 3rd of that year we tested it out, leisurely skiing the east leg of Moose Loop, continuing north on upper Bragg Creek, west along Moose Creek cutline, then — the best bit — south on Shell Oil's challenging exploration road which crossed the cold east slopes of Moose Mountain against the grain of the country, a section whose race profile confirmed that the hills would have qualified the road for a 10 km Olympic sprint. Unfortunately, the night before race day a Chinook whittled all the snow away from the flats and the race was cancelled.

In 1982 Shell Oil pushed a new wider road up from the south end to a well at the mid point, overriding some 2 km of old road and in the process making a new east leg for Moose Loop Then, during the intense logging of 1988, more old road went under the plough and bits between missing portions went unvisited and grew alder bushes. The net result is that of the usable road, I estimate only 30% still exists. But it's the best part.

The delectable hill on the old road.

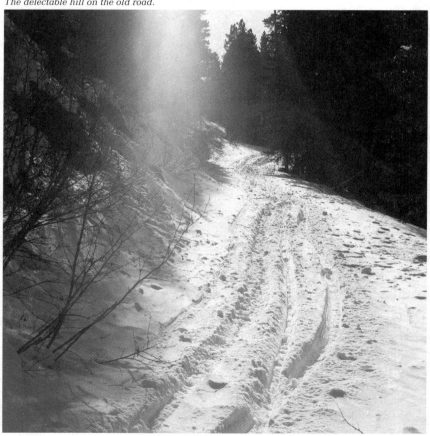

THORNE CREEK

Backcountry

Easy
Intermediate loop
4.7 km from Moose Loop to mine
7.6 km loop from Moose Loop
Height gain mine 326 m
Height gain loop 387 m
Maximum elevation mine 1828 m
Maximum elevation loop 1737 m
Map 82 J/15 Bragg Creek

Access Via West Bragg Creek Ski Trails as described on page 265.

Ski the west leg of Moose Loop to the high point (page 275).

Overview Yet another Daffern special as our friends would say with resignation. You follow various logging and exploration roads into a valley you would probably never think of going up normally, and which leads to Thorne coal mine where there is absolutely nothing to see above the snow. However, it makes a good excuse for visiting a scenic valley head where a little telemarking isn't out of the question before returning home.

From the high point of Moose Loop's west leg set off up the Shell Oil reclaimed exploration road. At the intersecting cutline, zip left down a hill and cross Thorne Creek into the lower cutblock on the south bank. Turn right and find the logging road which leads up-creek, ultimately crossing the creek into a middle cutblock and petering out. Continue through a few token trees into the upper cutblock. If you like your forests intact, this journey into the heart of Thorne Creek is a depressing one.

At the narrows, you cross a cutline at the bottom of the U and carry on up valley. After a few minutes of historic travelling along the hundred year old access track you pick up Shell Oil's original exploration road (now cutline access road) on the left bank and keep on heading up valley, taking special note if you're thinking of doing the loop of the first open hillside on the right where the road loops back to the cutline.

The final stretch is the best. An offshoot of road, then you're back on the historic track, climbing a little more steeply through spruce forest with instantly improved snow. Suddenly, you emerge into a meadow surprising for its huge size given it's natural and made all the more secluded by the valley ending suddenly below the bulwark of Moose Mountain.

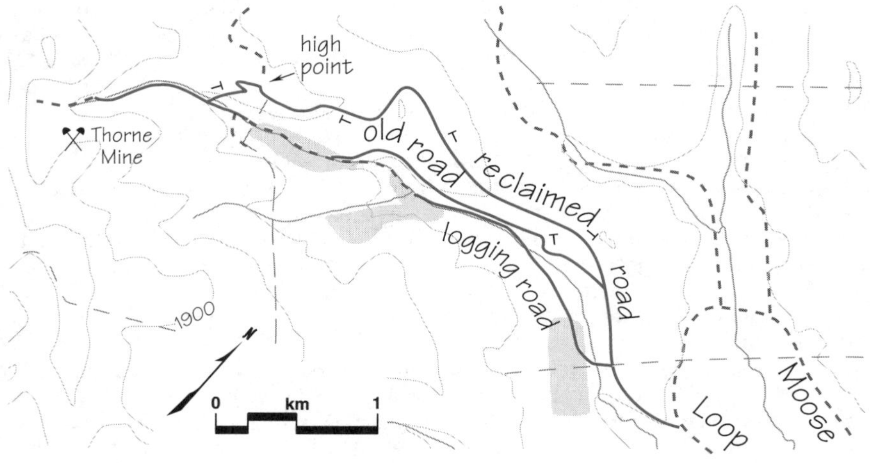

The great white way. Shell Oil's newest reclaimed road used to make the loop. This is also the route of ascent for Moose Mountain loop.

Return An intermediate variation is available as follows:

After the narrows and two thirds down the upper cutblock, Shell Oil's original exploration road resurfaces on the left side and runs alongside the middle cutblock a way before making a gradual climb under sandstone outcrops to a high point, then dropping equally gradually to a low point just above the logging road between middle and lower cutblocks. If you've been having problems with wrap-around alder on the last downhill, drop back onto the logging road at Last Chance. If not, snow being sufficiently deep, carry on along the exploration road which features a short ferocious downhill, then a straight with an up-down-up combination ending with a push through jungly alders onto Shell Oil's reclaimed road. (In five years time this last section may become submerged altogether.) Turn right and return down the slanted cut to the west leg of Moose Loop.

Return option: To make a loop
When level with the open hillside on the left bank, turn left across the creek (road indiscernible at this point) and climb diagonally right up open slopes. Once into the trees the road is obvious, winding lazily to the ridge top gained at the high point of Shell Oil's newest reclaimed road. Simply turn right and follow it all the way out to Moose loop. After revamping, it banks either left or right depending which side of the ridge you are on.

POWDERFACE CREEK TO PASS — Backcountry

Intermediate
9 km to pass
Height gain 509 m
Maximum elevation 2027
Map 82 J/15 Bragg Creek

Access Elbow Falls Trail (SR 66) at Powderface Creek parking lot. Note: At this point the highway is closed between December 1st and May 15th. Luckily, the winter gate is just down the road at Elbow Falls, so between these dates, park at the gate and ski about 500 m up the highway to the trailhead.

Facilities Seasonal washrooms at Powderface Creek parking lot, year-round washrooms at Elbow Falls parking lot which also has picnic tables.

Overview Most valleys north of Elbow Falls Trail are experimental wind tunnels for Chinooks much like the avenues in downtown Calgary. This one is different though, being blocked off at the west end by a high ridge, the low point of which is commonly called Powderface Pass, a name in keeping with the subdivision nomenclature common to most K-Country names. Windy Pass would be more appropriate, but I suppose you would have to start numbering them Windy Pass #1, Windy Pass #2, and so on. The net result is that Powderface is the only valley hereabouts which keeps sufficient snow for skiing. The route follows an old exploration road with a bit of modern trail tacked on to the end, and is well-marked with red markers and signposts at junctions.

I'm not overly fond of the start to this trail. Straight off you're into the hardest work of the day, waves of steep, stony uphills, and when you get to the top all you do is go down again to cross Powderface Creek. Wondering why the road couldn't have made a nice little traverse, you set off along the north bank, climbing almost imperceptibly between side slopes of lodgepole pines. In lieu of flowers, most interesting things to do are identify animal tracks and count gaps in the forested ridge to the right. Even Powderface Ridge up ahead is just another treed ridge from this direction. At 3 km you reach a meadow with a signpost where Prairie Link trail turns off to the right through gap #3.

It was here where an Edmonton skier took a wrong turn in the darkest days of mid winter. Mind you, he started for the pass at 3 pm from the parking lot and on the way back went left instead of right (it was dark and snowing heavily), and was forced to shiver a long night out under the

Powderface trail between the first creek crossing and Prairie Link junction. Up ahead is the forested east face of Powderface Ridge.

pine boughs before being rescued at sun-up by a ranger on snowmobile. Now there's nothing wrong with skiing in the dark and as you'll have gathered I do quite a bit of it myself, but it pays to know the area first. Also the signpost system breaks down if you don't have a flashlight. No, what amazed me was his foresight in packing a complete change of clothes for this very contingency.

In another kilometre the road re-crosses to the south bank, signalling a drop in temperature, deeper snow and a trudge up the switchbacks into spruce forest festooned with black bryoria. The road ends at the top of the V-shaped bit of valley, and a trail carries on. With trees wide apart the trail is easily lost (it keeps higher to the right than you think), but however you get there, the pass is easily identified at the demarcation of trees and grass. Apparently, driving west winds have driven all the trees and snow over to the east slope. There's also a large cairn. A walk on the grass to look at Nihahi Ridge is traditional before returning home.

Return A terrific downhill run. Beware of the final descent into the parking lot; loose stones can make for a jarring experience .

Return via Prairie Creek? It's a strange thing that while Powderface Creek has snow, neighbouring Prairie Creek has none.

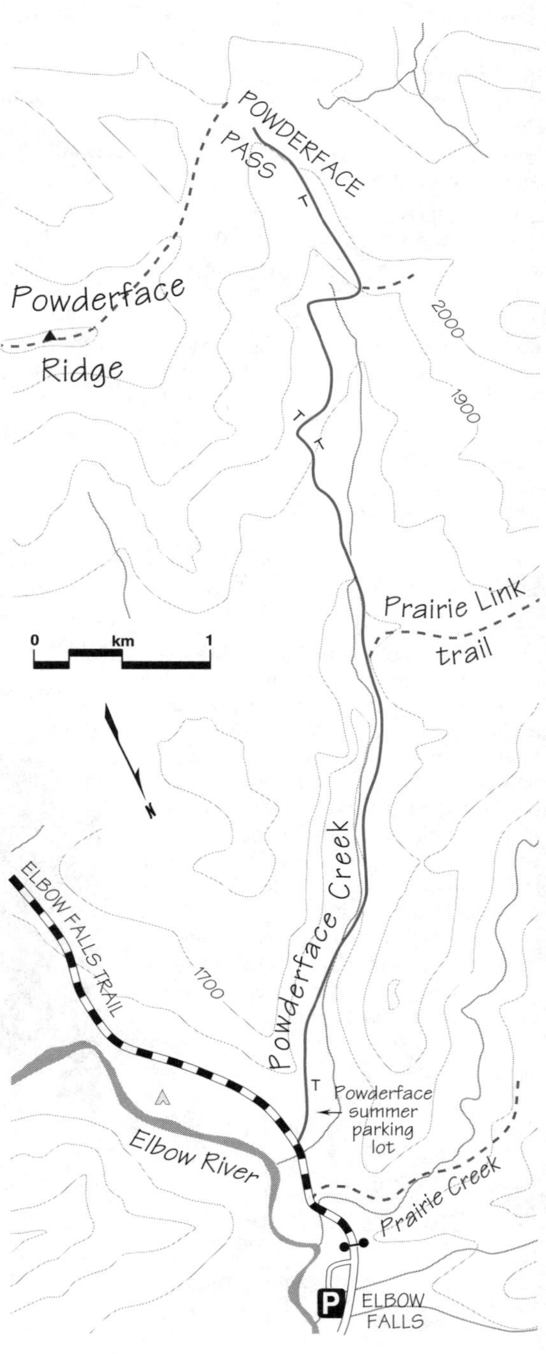

LITTLE ELBOW TRAIL TO THE FORKS — Backcountry

Intermediate
10 km
Height gain 228 m
Maximum elevation 1812 m
Map 82 J/15 Bragg Creek, 82 J/10 Mount Rae

Access Elbow Falls Trail (SR 66) at the far end of Little Elbow Recreation Area campground access road. Unlike in summer when disgruntled hikers are forced to walk another kilometre (two, return), the gate at the start of Little Elbow trail is opened in fall to let hunters and early season snowmobilers into a small, select parking lot. Note: SR 66 is closed between December 1st and May 15th at Elbow Falls.

Facilities Campsites, washrooms and picnic tables in Little Elbow Recreation Area campground. Picnic tables at Mount Romulus backcountry campground.

Overview Little Elbow trail, an official summer trail signed at all junctions, has two big problems for skiers. First, SR 66 closes beyond Elbow Falls at midnight on November 30th so you have to get this trip in before the snow is at its optimum. And second, this is a designated snowmobile trail, though as a rule snowmobilers don't even think twice about this trail until after the highway closes. Still, if we're lucky enough to get a big dump of the white fluffy stuff in November, then rush out pronto to the trailhead. This trail's nicely undulating, has spectacular scenery, picnic tables for recuperation at the turnaround point, and ongoing options.

Mt. Romulus comes into view at the 7 km mark. Note the summit cornice which hangs around until early summer and is visible from Calgary.

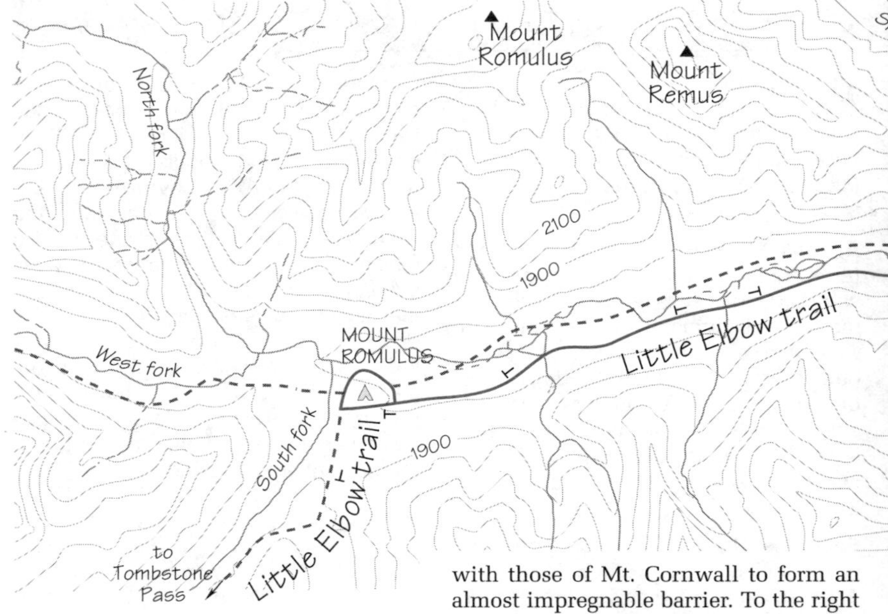

For the first 3.5 km the old fire road runs along the north bank of the Little Elbow River and is mostly flat apart from a few short sharp hills in the downward direction which is annoying since the route is supposedly heading upstream. Shortly after Nihahi Ridge trail turns right at a signpost, the road goes between, which is not, I hasten to add, Pern *non*space, although I sometimes think it would be a useful skill for skiers late for dinner dates to learn , but *between ridges* into the inner fastness of the Front Range where the mountains are made of limestone and sport cliffs. Around Nihahi Creek trailhead in the narrows, spruce trees harbour great horned owls which, unlike the Pocaterra Creek militia, don't as yet have a taste for skier's toques. And so you come to the blue bridge over the river, a good turnaround place for half-day trips.

Between the bridge and your destination you can expect flat straights alternating with steeper longer hills, mostly in the uphill direction. I believe the worst is the first one above the bridge. Accompanying you on the left throughout is a long line of cliffs, those of Glasgow merging with those of Mt. Cornwall to form an almost impregnable barrier. To the right across a flat valley floor are more cliffs rearranged vertically to form Mts. Remus and Romulus, the latter a black square monster topped by the thin white line of a cornice visible from Calgary.

At the forks turn right onto the Mount Romulus campground access trail which eventually loops back to the road at the big bend. Picnic tables near the registration box make a strong case for ending the trip right there.

Options
If you reach the picnic tables for elevenses and feel like a little light climbing, by all means carry on along the road towards Tombstone Pass at the head of the south fork (8.3 km). I can guarantee a superb return run. Another option is to head further west on a roller coaster road leading into the "Back O' the Opals" (7 km to the forks).

Return Much faster than you might think. In November take care not to come to grief on the downhill before the blue bridge where a bit of bedrock lurks below a layer of unconsolidated snow. Sidestepping is judicious.

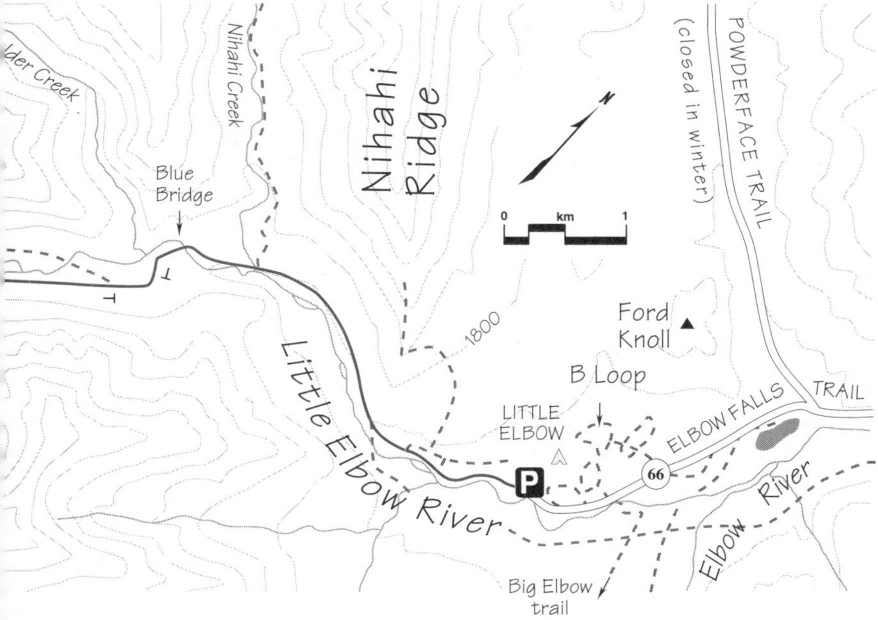

Coffee break before tackling the final uphills. Behind the skier is the long east ridge of Mt. Remus.

COX HILL! Backcountry & Hike

Intermediate
7 km to summit
21.4 km loop
Height gain 735 m to summit
Height gain 917 m loop
Maximum elevation 2210 m
Map 82 O/2 Jumpingpound Creek, 82 J/15 Bragg Creek

Access Powderface Trail (the highway) at Dawson Day Use Area. The road south to Elbow Falls Trail is closed December 1st to May 15th.

Facilities Washrooms and picnic tables at parking lot which doubles as a winter campground.

Overview I wonder if anyone else has been stupid enough to do this trip? But so many people expressed interest after hearing about our own epic, they actually want to have a go themselves, which just confirms to me that backcountry skiers are all masochists at heart (though the view from the top *is* superb). So long as you know you're going to be doing some walking and don't go equipped with Gortex racing boots with toe and heel protuberances, you should be all right. For more skiing, go after a good snowfall and before a Chinook. Knowing the route in summer is also a prerequisite.

Returning the same way is less interesting than the alternatives. They include completing the route down Jumpingpound Mountain's north ridge, then skating along Powderface Trail in the wake of snowmobiles back to the parking lot (definitely easiest, especially if you can arrange a tow), dropping down to Powderface Trail from Cox Hill (shortest, most adventurous), or — definitely longest in terms of time — returning like we did over Lusk Pass to Stony Creek trailhead on Sibbald Creek Trail (Hwy. 68). You need two cars for last trip and more than five hours of daylight.

From the trail sign, follow snowmobile tracks out along Tom Snow trail which crosses Jumpingpound Creek on a good bridge, and climbs up to a junction. Turn right. At the cutline, turn left. Cox Hill trail starts on the right about 100 m up the cutline at a red equestrian sign.

The trail's narrow width and steep angle takes a bit of getting used to as it corkscrews up the north ridge. Alternately herringboning and walking, you are probably calling me all sorts of names, but it gets better — honestly. In fact, after the steep, rocky bit, you're striding along in some great snow all the way to the bottom of the summit knobbin. This is the crux. It's strange how an innocent grass slope can be transformed by winter into something perilous. In this case the summer trail disappears in another half zig under a coating of iron-hard windcrust which covers the slope from top to bottom and where the penalty for not setting your edges with assiduousness is a 60 metre slide to the bottom. Alternatively, you can hike up grassy ledges before you get to the *mauvais pas*. Arrive one way or the other onto the lower summit which is connected to the main summit by a ribbon of snow curling over into a cornice. The view from Cox Hill is, as always, spectacular.

The skis must now be removed as you move on, hiking along the south ridge with that gorgeous view of the Fisher Range off to the west. All this is no great hardship unless the west wind happens to be blowing a gale. Unfortunately, the ground underfoot is not plain sailing and with skis acting like a spinnaker you tack from side to side, lurching across frost-shattered rocks and bits of frozen grass, looking for cairns to guide you down to treeline. A few minutes after spotting the red marker — on with the skis — you've probably lost the trail in forest glades. It's important to remember that the Cox Hill-Jumpingpound Mountain col lies *diagonally* left and not get carried away by the excellent powder, unless of course you're taking the short-cut to Powderface Trail.

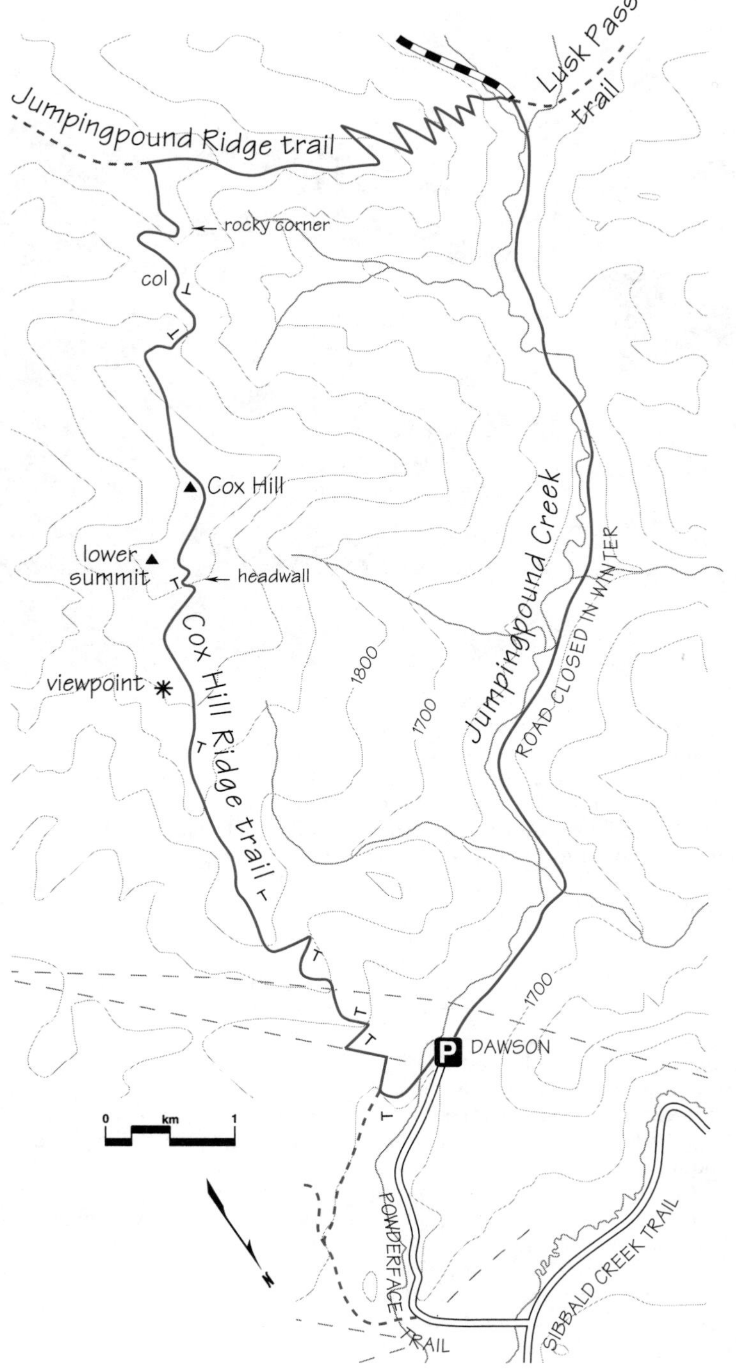
Jumpingpound Ridge trail
Lusk Pass trail
rocky corner
col
Cox Hill
lower summit
headwall
viewpoint
Cox Hill Ridge trail
1800
1700
Jumpingpound Creek
ROAD CLOSED IN WINTER
1700
DAWSON
0 km 1
POWDERFACE TRAIL
SIBBALD CREEK TRAIL
N

The ribbon of snow rising to the main summit of Cox Hill (right).

From the col the ridge up Jumpingpound Mountain looks higher and steeper than one would wish for at this stage in the trip. Thankfully, the trail is obvious as it makes two zigs onto the rocky upper section where all the snow gets blown off. It's only short and if you're as obstinate as Pete you'll insist on skiing up the shale and sidestepping little rock steps.

It's shortly after the trees and snow recommence that you come to the ridge top and civilisation in the form of a signpost marking the meeting of two trails. To the south another windblown grassy ridge marches off towards the summit of Jumpingpound Mountain. Normally such a sight is enough to make your mouth water but now all you want to do is go home and preferably via a downward dash through the powder. So turn right into the trees and enjoy yourself. Just so you know you're not going wildly off course, know that the initial 1.8 km of north ridge trail has one or two minor *uphills* before you reach umpteen easy-angled zigzags winding down to the road.

Your sigh of relief to be off the ridges is short-lived. It comes as a profound shock to realize you're 8.4 km away from any road which has cars. As roads go, Powderface Trail isn't that bad, being snowmobile packed and undulating. But still tedious. Sometimes it pays to be friends with a snowmobiler.

More about the trail Did you know the west slopes of Cox Hill were once touted for an alpine ski area and an Olympic one at that! For slalom and giant slalom events, anyway. As you will discover, once you're off the windswept ridges the snow is great in the trees. It must be, because partners in the proposal for "Jumpingpound Creek Ski Area" included such heavyweights as Rodney Touche, John Gow, Jim Buckingham and Charlie Locke who already owns three ski areas.

INDEX

ACKNOWLEDGMENTS

I thoroughly enjoyed chatting to Don Gardner, Harry Connolly, R.J. Burns, Ruthie Oltmann, Ron Henderson, Bill Brooks, Chester Mjolness, Leonard Kennedy, Len Wilton, Dean Marshall, Joe Burritt, Jim Clow, Jan Simonson, and the staff at BC Parks, Wasa.

As always, Don Cockerton from the Kananaskis Country Office in Calgary was most helpful in answering hundreds of questions as was Don Morberg who is now off running his own business.

Thanks also to Ken McKay and the helpful staff at Elbow Ranger Station.

Alf Skrastins contributed some terrific photos as usual. I also want to thank Clive Cordery, Peter Haase, Alan Kane and Bruce Jamieson for taking time to look through their slide collections.

A not unusual sight at Burstall Pass parking lot.